After the
HARKNESS
GIFT

After the

HARKNESS

GIFT

A History of PHILLIPS EXETER ACADEMY *since 1930*

JULIA HESKEL *and* DAVIS DYER

PHILLIPS EXETER ACADEMY

Exeter, New Hampshire

Published by

University Press of New England

Hanover and London

Phillips Exeter Academy
Published by University Press of New England,
One Court Street, Lebanon, NH 03766
www.upne.com
© 2008 by Phillips Exeter Academy
Printed in the United States of America
5 4 3 2 1

Library of Congress Cataloging-in-Publication Data
Heskel, Julia.
After the Harkness gift : a history of Phillips Exeter Academy since 1930 /
Julia Heskel and Davis Dyer.
    p.   cm.
Includes bibliographical references and index.
ISBN-13: 978-0-9769787-1-8 (cloth : alk. paper)
ISBN-10: 0-9769787-1-7 (cloth : alk. paper)
1. Phillips Exeter Academy—History. I. Dyer, Davis. II. Title.
LD7501.E936H47   2008
373.742'6—dc22   2007048505

Contents

Authors' Preface

This book provides a historical perspective on Phillips Exeter Academy, particularly since a major bequest by Edward S. Harkness in 1930. The Harkness Gift enabled the Academy to make extraordinary changes in its pedagogy, architecture, and daily life. Exeter made a near-total commitment to "the tutorial or conference method" of instruction, abandoning large classes featuring lectures and recitations in favor of discussion-based learning in small groups. It doubled the size of its faculty and renovated existing classrooms and built new ones. It also constructed four new dormitories and renovated eight others, enabling it to become a self-contained residential community.

One of the most enduring symbols of the changes at Exeter is the Harkness Table prominently displayed in every classroom. Adapted from a design by Corning Benton, the school's treasurer and an amateur cabinetmaker, a typical table is oval and intended to seat thirteen — a teacher and a dozen students. Everyone faces everyone else. Everyone participates. "Harkness teaching and learning," writes Principal Tyler C. Tingley, "encourages students to question assumptions, make independent judgments, and test hypotheses. It asks students to think for themselves and to become adept at expressing original ideas. Most of all, students in the Harkness classroom learn to listen to each other and to value differing points of view."[1]

The Harkness Table has become a central metaphor at the Academy, describing not only what occurs in the classroom but also what transpires in the larger Exeter community, in official meetings of faculty, administrators, trustees, and student organizations, as well as in informal gatherings of teachers, coaches, dorm faculty, and students. Grafted onto the New England colonial traditions of the school — traditions of congregational governance, religious toleration, and democratic town meetings — the Harkness spirit of inquiry and discussion has informed how Exeter has adapted over the years and how it is evolving now.

The Harkness Table is thus also a central metaphor in this book. The book does not strive to be an authoritative narrative history in the manner of some earlier histories of Exeter, or of, say, Frederick Allis's comprehensive account of Phillips Academy in Andover.[2] Rather it is designed as a series of related historical essays that focus on key topics and themes in Exeter's history, especially the impact of the Harkness Gift, as a way of penetrating the school's operations and providing (we hope) a clearer and more widespread understanding of its development, functioning, and achievements.

————

The origins of this book trace back more than a decade, when the Academy's board of trustees retained The Winthrop Group, Inc., to conduct a series of oral history interviews with members of the Exeter community in preparation for the eventual task of writing a new history of the Academy. The board had several motives in authorizing this work: a generation of faculty hired when the Academy expanded in the 1930s had retired in recent decades, and the trustees wished to honor their achievements and capture their experiences while memories were as fresh as possible. In addition, the previous history of the Academy had been published in 1957 and had tapered down its narrative with the retirement of Principal Lewis Perry soon after the end of World War II.[3] Obviously, much had happened at the Academy since the mid-1940s that had not yet been the subject of serious historical inquiry.

But perhaps the most important reason to undertake the project was that it seemed necessary and timely, in keeping with Exeter's modern tradition of reflection and self-assessment — what Principal Kendra Stearns O'Donnell (1987–1997) called a "bias for informed decision making." She recognized that the pace of change at the Academy and in the world around it was accelerating and sought to establish a record of the school's history as a baseline for understanding and managing its ongoing evolution. Principal Tingley (1997–) likewise embraced the project, viewing it as an opportunity for Exeter to learn from its past and for others to learn from Exeter's experience.

During the 1990s, Davis Dyer and Jeffrey F. Rayport of Winthrop Group carried out several dozen oral history interviews with faculty and *emeriti*, faculty spouses, staff, and trustees and former trustees of the Academy. Dyer and Rayport also outlined an approach to a new history of the Academy that served as the genesis of this book. It would cover the Academy's evolution since 1781 but emphasize the period since the Harkness Gift in 1930. It would feature a topical and thematic, as opposed to a chronological, approach to Exeter's history, focusing on how the Academy sought in changing circumstances to fulfill its core mission to teach knowledge and impart goodness, to serve an increasingly diverse and heterogeneous population of students, and to govern and support itself. Finally, it would seek to understand the impact of an Exeter education on students and how it prepared them for college, careers, and success in later life.

The trustees accepted the book proposal and willingly allowed the Academy's past to be examined by professional historians. This decision is a tribute to the healthy self-confidence of a leading institution of its type. Most histories of independent schools fall into one of two camps: affectionate portraits by faculty or alumni that dwell on the good parts of the story, often with fundraising objectives in mind; and, from an opposite perspective, muckraking exposés, often by disillusioned graduates, that portray these schools as bastions of elitism and privilege in cold and harsh overtones. (In the movies, this polarity is represented on the one hand by *Goodbye, Mr. Chips* and on the other by *Class*.) It seemed to decision makers at the Academy, as well as to the Winthrop Group historians, that these conventional views of independent schools missed the much larger story of how these institutions evolve over time, especially against the backdrop of fundamental changes in American society, in the demographics of the population, the career prospects for young women, and the shift into a "post-industrial" or "knowledge-based" economy. It seemed important to understand how Exeter accommodated and adapted to these trends and to identify the continuities and changes in the way it carried out its mission to deliver a consistently superior secondary school education.

Finally, the book became a portrait of the school that includes the blemishes. It does not gloss over difficult moments in the school's past. Nor does it elevate these moments into something more than they were: occasional difficulties and missteps in an institution with an overwhelmingly positive story to tell.

————

Following the initial round of interviews, this project endured a hiatus of several years while Exeter raised funds to support it, and the Winthrop team underwent changes of its own. By the time the project resumed, Julia Heskel, a historian and classicist, had joined Winthrop and quickly assumed a leading role on the project. Although the basic conception of the work was already in place, she brought a fresh perspective to the project and changed the tenor and tone of the work in countless positive ways. The chapters that follow were written by Heskel and Dyer, with the latter responsible for the final revision.

The Prologue sets the stage by describing the circumstances of the Harkness Gift in 1930. Chapter 1 puts the gift in context by flashing backward in time to describe the evolution of the Academy from its founding in 1781 through its first 150 years. Chapters 2 through 8 then examine the impact of the Harkness Gift on the Academy by examining particular topics in detail. Chapter 2 deals with governance and provides a basic chronological frame for the remainder of the book. Chapter 3 focuses on the impact of the Harkness Gift on teaching and learning in the classroom, while chapter 4 considers the Academy's charge from founder John Phillips to unite goodness with knowledge in the cultivation of young minds. Chapter 5 describes the Academy's adjustments and accommodations as it came to serve an increasingly diverse population of students, faculty, and staff. Chapter 6 covers the coming and completion of coeducation over a 25-year period. Chapter 7 looks at Exeter's finances and describes how the Academy funded its growth and change since 1930. Chapter 8 examines the effect of an Exeter education on its graduates as they moved on to colleges and careers. The book concludes with an epilogue that reflects on the long-term impact of the Harkness Gift at Exeter from the vantage point of the early twenty-first century.

———

Many people contributed to making this project happen. At the Academy, an advisory committee of faculty and trustees oversaw the project from its beginning through the completion of the initial draft manuscript. We are indebted to members of the committee for their patience and commentary on the work, from outline, through draft chapters, to revised manuscript. The members included Frank Gutmann, mathematics instructor *emeritus*; Chauncey C. Loomis '48, Dartmouth professor *emeritus* and former Exeter trustee; Christine Robinson, English instructor; Robert N. Shapiro '68, lawyer and former trustee; Stephen C. Smith, history instructor; Jacquelyn H. Thomas, Academy Librarian; and Rev. Robert H. Thompson '72, Academy minister. Although not formally a member of the committee, Lynda Beck, former vice principal, also offered many helpful comments and suggestions.

Once the committee signed off on the manuscript, selected faculty and staff gave a careful review to individual chapters. We are grateful to Donald Cole, Susan Herney, Polly MacMullen, Charles Pratt, Charles Terry, and David Thomas for their comments and suggestions.

We wish also to thank the several score of Exonians past and present who participated in this project through interviews and/or provided documents, advice, and suggestions. Principal O'Donnell was a strong supporter of the project in its earliest incarnation and submitted to several long interviews about her tenure. Principal Tingley gave generously of his time for several interviews while subjecting drafts of the manuscript to close reading. Julie Quinn, director of communications, also read several drafts of the manuscript carefully and suggested many significant improvements. Many trustees and former trustees were interviewed for the project, including Principal Steven G. Kurtz (1974–1987) and six former presidents (the late F. William Andres '25, John R. Chase '46, Ricardo A. Mestres '51, James A. Newman '33, Dudley W. Orr '25, and Calvin H. Plimpton '35). Many other trustees, faculty, staff, students, and alumni participated in the interviews and every one of them helped us not out of duty but out of a sincere conviction that the story is important and deserves to be rendered in its complexity. The list of names is too long to be included here, but readers will find them spelled out in the notes to the book.

Many others gave extraordinary support to the project, including Jacquelyn Thomas and Julie Quinn as our principal contacts at the Academy and Robert N. Shapiro as our liaison with the trustees. Academy archivist Edouard Desrochers proved a marvelous resource. He possesses an encyclopedic knowledge of Exeter's history and knows where everything is. We never asked him a question that he could not find a way to answer. Many current and former administrators also helped out: Harold Brown, Mark Davis, James A. DelBuono, Joseph E. Fellows, Mary B. Gorman, Susan J. Herney, Moya Joosten, and James Theisen contributed valuable information and insights and helped us to make sense of the evolution of a complex institution. Jane Durnan and Susan Goraczkowski provided excellent administrative assistance.

At Winthrop Group, many past and present colleagues helped to make this book possible by providing advice, helpful criticism, research assistance, and transcriptions of interviews. Our gratitude for this help extends particularly to Paul Barnhill, Pamela Bracken, Lincoln Caplan '68, Deb Conry, Susan Doctoroff, Linda Edgerly, Margaret Graham, Elizabeth McIver Neiva, Bettye Pruitt, Jeffrey Rayport, Marta Rodriguez, Abe Rosner, George Smith, Suzanne Spellman, and Susan McWade Surapine.

After the
HARKNESS GIFT

Prologue: Something Revolutionary

W̶e do not know exactly when or where the meeting occurred that changed everything at Phillips Exeter Academy, except that it was late in March 1930 in New York City, possibly at 654 Madison Avenue, where philanthropist Edward S. Harkness maintained a suite of offices. Present were four men: Harkness, his associate Malcolm Aldrich, Lewis Perry, the Academy's principal, and Jeremiah Smith, Jr., president of its board of trustees. They shared "a delightful luncheon conversation" that centered on some proposals to revamp the Academy's approach to teaching its students.[1]

Harkness '56 and his good friend Perry '53 played the leading roles in the conversation. The previous September—a few weeks before the great stock market crash that foreshadowed gloomy years to come—Harkness had indicated to Perry his willingness to make a major donation to the Academy. He had recently funded the "House Plan" at Harvard, enabling the college to reorganize around residential communities modeled on the Oxford and Cambridge colleges, and he suggested he might do something similar for Exeter. "If you will get up a scheme," he invited Perry, "I'll give you all the money you need to put it into operation. I'd like to have you go abroad, take someone with you, be gone a couple of months, and see what you can find out."[2]

The lone surviving heir of one of the original partners in John D. Rockefeller's Standard Oil Company, Harkness possessed at the time "one of the largest fortunes in American history." Childless himself, he spent his adult life quietly but methodically liquidating his great wealth, pursuing "its complete redistribution back to the people of the country from whose natural resources it came."[3] Although he had helped to endow a perpetual foundation—The Commonwealth Fund, established with his mother in 1918 to support medical research and education—and was soon to underwrite another—The Pilgrim Trust, to fund a variety of educational and cultural projects in the United Kingdom—Harkness preferred to dispense his fortune himself and expected to witness its impact during his lifetime. Accordingly, he took a lively personal interest in each gift. From the early 1920s to his death in 1940, according to one tally, he made 1,332 separate donations of amounts of $5,000 or more, totaling more than $129 million, to medical, educational, and cultural institutions in the United States and United Kingdom.[4] He provided the principal funding to establish the Columbia-Presbyterian Medical Center in New York. He followed up his major gift to Harvard with a comparable donation to Yale to underwrite the "College System." He gave generously to St. Paul's School (his alma mater), Exeter, Andover, Lawrenceville, Taft, Mt. Holyoke College, Wellesley College, and St. Andrews University in Scotland, among other institutitions. His motive for supporting education partly reflected Harkness's unhappy experience as an indifferent student who had slipped through St. Paul's and Yale. In later life, he devoted hard thinking to the question of how schools and universities could provide a richer, more personal educational experience for students.[5]

In the spring of 1930, Perry was completing his sixteenth year as Exeter's principal. His tenure had begun inauspiciously when, soon after his appointment was announced, a fire destroyed the third Academy Building. Perry rallied the community from that disaster, however, and through the years proved not only a popular and able leader on campus but also an exceptional fundraiser. In 1918, he established an annual giving fund and announced a capital drive to build the endowment to $2 million. Although the drive fell short of this goal, the Academy recorded noteworthy gifts during the 1920s that enabled the construction of the Lamont Infirmary, the Thompson Science Building, Jeremiah Smith Hall (a classroom building), Amen Hall (a dormitory), a new gymnasium and field house, and the Exeter Inn, as well as the purchase of Phillips Church. Several gifts loomed with the Academy's 150th anniversary in 1931 in prospect.

During the 1920s, Perry collected three separate gifts from Harkness totaling $445,000, which were used to improve faculty salaries and increase the endowment. A deepening friendship between the two men undoubtedly affected Harkness's generosity. They had met at a wedding in St. Paul, Minnesota, in 1902 and had subsequently stayed in touch.[6] They saw each other periodically in New York after Harkness nominated Perry as a trustee of The Commonwealth Fund. Occasionally they vacationed together. According to Perry's biographer (and successor as Exeter's principal), William Saltonstall, Perry paid no heed to Harkness's great wealth and treated him as he would any other friend. When they went out for the evening, Perry would insist on splitting the tab. On one such occasion, Harkness apparently exploded: "Dammit, Lewis, don't you know I have money? Everyone else asks for it; why don't you? Do you want to know why I love you more than any man I have ever known? You were such a damn fool, you didn't know that I had money!"[7]

In the fall of 1929, when Harkness proposed to make a major gift to Exeter, Perry at once realized the magnitude of the opportunity "not only for Exeter, but for secondary education in general. . . . I doubt whether any school in the world has had the chance that seems now to have come to us."[8] He appointed a "Harkness Committee" of senior faculty and administrators to consider proposals. In January 1930, with Harkness footing the bill, Perry set sail with his closest friend at the school, George B. Rogers, for the United Kingdom. During the next two months, they visited seventeen schools, including Winchester, Eton, Harrow, Rugby, St. Paul's, and Westminster, as well as two universities, Oxford and St. Andrews.[9] They found much to admire but certain features particularly impressed them: the house system with a house-master or house-tutor acting as adviser to each boy, sections of students of similar ability (an arrangement that Exeter Latin classes had found advantageous), new methods of instruction in science and mathematics, advanced work done by boys in the sixth form (twelfth grade), and courses of study tailored to the individual student.[10]

Soon after their return, Perry, Rogers, and other members of the Harkness Committee readied some informal proposals for Perry and trustee president Smith to discuss with Harkness. Drawing heavily on learning from the trip to the United Kingdom, they suggested providing a tutorial program to supplement formal instruction, an advisory system to support individual students, an honors program for the strongest students, and a program of visiting lecturers. Class size would be reduced somewhat and additional faculty would be hired. Toting up the expenses, Perry estimated that it might cost more than $1 million, a nearly unimaginable sum at the time, for the Academy to put these changes into effect.[11]

Harkness, however, was unimpressed. In a letter to Perry following the luncheon conversation in New York, he pointed out the plan "lacks definiteness." He asked for clearer statements of "the outstanding benefits you expect to derive" and "to what extent and in what way is Secondary School education in this country going to be benefited?" Harkness further wanted specifics on the optimum size of classes, the way the tutorial system would function, and the amount of money needed. "When you went abroad," he wrote,

> I had hopes that you would come home with several suggestions of a fundamental nature that were so sweeping and so different from methods prevailing here that one could see at a glance that were they adopted, the whole educational system in our Secondary Schools would be changed, but

changed enormously for the better. Such, of course, may be the case but, frankly, your plan does not make these things clear to me and I have yet been unable to get my teeth into anything that promises great fundamental benefits to our educational system.[12]

According to Aldrich's a memorandum of the meeting, Harkness clearly had expected a much bolder proposal from the Academy. "It is quite evident our minds didn't meet," Harkness is quoted as saying:

> We are not thinking of the same thing. . . . You are thinking of improving an existing institution by building on what you have got now. I am thinking of something much more radical than that; something that is revolutionary in Secondary School education; what I am thinking of would mean probably scrapping everything and starting on an entirely new principle. I want to see somebody try teaching — not by recitations in a formal recitation room where the teacher is on a platform raised above the pupils and there is a class of 20 or more boys who recite lessons. That is what I am trying to get rid of. I think the bright boys get along all right by that method, but I am thinking of a boy who isn't a bright boy — not necessarily a dull boy, but diffident, and not being equal to the bright boys doesn't like to speak up in class and admit his difficulties, so doesn't get much out of the class, and has nobody to sit down with him and explain things carefully and patiently with him. What I have in mind is teaching boys in sections of perhaps 8 boys in a section, not in a formal recitation room, where there would be a desk and a raised platform with an instructor behind the desk, but where 8 boys could sit around a table with a teacher who would talk with them and instruct them by a sort of tutorial, or conference method, where the average, or below the average, boy, would feel encouraged to speak up, present his difficulties, and the teacher would know and realize what his difficulties were. This would be a real revolution in methods.[13]

The meeting concluded politely with Harkness inviting Perry and his colleagues to think things over and get back to him if they wished him to consider something more ambitious. In his handwritten notes of the exchanges, Perry reported that "Harkness felt that we did not have anything new enough or fundamental enough. . . . Any scheme which we have at present he might aid, but would not go into *deeply*." Rather, Harkness "has his mind fixed on smaller classes — eight or ten — and on the Conference method of instruction. . . . His whole idea is the dull boy, like himself who was in a large class in mathematics and did not know what was going on." "Remember the *Conference* system of teaching. That is the big idea! . . . Not recitations, *conferences*."[14]

Perry partly bristled at the notion that Exeter's proposals had not gone far enough, portraying the conversation as between, "on one side a stubborn man with an idea," and "on the other an eminent schoolman who feels he (Harkness) may be wrong." Subsequently, he recalled Harkness as saying,

> if we didn't agree with him that we would not have much chance of convincing him that our ideas were the right ones, and while the matter was left rather vaguely in the end, my impression was quite clear that what he wanted to know was whether his ideas appealed to us and we were willing to try them with enthusiasm; that if we weren't, he would not be interested much, if at all, in any other method; that he probably didn't want us to argue with him in an attempt to convince him that he was wrong and we were right, and that after thinking it over he would like to know whether we were prepared to adopt his plan or not.[15]

Still aware that they faced an extraordinary opportunity, however, Perry and his advisers went back to the drawing board. During the summer and early fall they thought bigger and developed a plan more to Harkness's liking. It combined Harkness's insistence on the "conference method" of instruction and features Perry and Rogers had admired in the English public school system.

Perry outlined the main points of the new plan (which soon came to be known as the "Harkness Plan") in a letter to Harkness dated October 30. Exeter would shrink the size of average classes from twenty-five students to ten, and classes would contain boys of similar ability and would proceed at the pace best suited to them. The doubling of the number of sections would necessitate hiring twenty-five new teachers, including two instructors from England who would offer advice on how to improve the science program. The expanded faculty would provide the basis for a house system. Each teacher would act as adviser to about a dozen students, and every boy would reside in the same dormitory for the last three years of his stay at the Academy.

Tellingly, Perry also declared that "All Instruction Will Be Carried on by the Conference or Tutorial Method of Instruction." He explained: "What we have in mind . . . is the substitution of 'serious consultation or discussion' for 'the delivery of something memorized.'" Perry added:

> The situation we picture would be (1) a conference room, equipped with books, pictures, and whatever else would be appropriate to the subject;

(2) small groups of students as nearly homogeneous as such a large school would make possible, sitting around a table meeting with a teacher with discernment, sympathy, background, and a live and full knowledge of his subject, who would guide and direct the discussion of the lesson. With the smaller groups and the conferences the teacher would see more completely the content and the processes of the student's mind. The greater class discussion inherent in the conference plan would train each boy gradually to learn to talk and to think while he is talking. The net result would be that the boy would become more grown-up, would think of his studies as something more real, and would have an interest, a compelling motive which he would carry to college. The successful teacher in the conference plan would be, not a drill master, but a partner in a human enterprise. We plan to supplement this by frequent conferences of the boys individually with their instructors, preferably in the instructor's study. Such conferences would be anything but formal instruction; rather talk about work and the boy's attitude to it and the direction or method of study.[16]

Together with the house system, the conference method would provide an individual boy with more attention while preparing him for study in college.

The total estimate of the plan came to $5,840,000, including $2,140,000 for the construction of classroom and dormitory buildings and $3,700,000 for endowment for faculty salaries, board, and sabbaticals, plus building maintenance. The construction estimates covered the conversion of the Academy Building recitation rooms into seminar rooms; the construction of a new classroom building, Phillips Hall; the construction of four new dormitories, each with a dining hall, and the renovation of eight existing ones. Exeter, Perry predicted, would become "a center for experimentation and guidance in American secondary education that would always continue."[17]

Satisfied with the committee's proposal, Harkness wrote to Perry on November 6, "The plan discussed therein for changing the method of teaching and housing at Exeter coincides with my ideas," and he committed the sum of $5,840,000 to support it. Perry wrote back at once extolling the gift, which was announced on November 16 and mentioned the following day in an editorial in the *New York Times*. Respectful of Harkness's wishes, the Academy did not disclose the size of the gift.[18] As it turned out, it was the largest donation the philanthropist would make to any secondary school.[19]

The magnitude of the gift was as astounding then as it is now, but it was not Harkness's intention to impress. He typically avoided publicity and, unlike many philanthropists, refused to allow any buildings he funded to bear his name. On the Exeter campus, however, the name has survived in a more pervasive form, attached to the teaching plan he advocated, a symbol of an enduring pedagogical revolution he made possible. What neither he nor Perry foresaw, however, was the far-reaching impact of the gift, and especially of the conference method, on the everyday life of the Academy through seven decades and counting.

1 Before the Harkness Gift

During its beginnings, in the 1780s, Phillips Exeter Academy was a tiny institution with large and lofty goals: a "public free school," it sought to instruct youth "not only in the English and Latin grammar, writing, arithmetic, and those sciences wherein they are commonly taught, but more especially to learn them the *great end* and *real business* of living."[1]

To fulfill this mission, a single "preceptor," occasionally aided by an assistant or two, instructed forty or fifty boys and young men. These students probably ranged in age from ten or eleven to the early twenties, with the majority clustered in the middle teenage years. Virtually all of them lived in or around Exeter. They came from a variety of economic circumstances, but that did not matter to the Academy, which was funded entirely from the original donor's generosity. There were no entrance requirements and no tuition, although students or their families paid a modest "tax" for firewood, candles, and other essential supplies. The students arrived on foot or horseback early each morning, six days a week, at a small, two-story wooden schoolhouse on Tan Lane for a six-hour day that began and ended with prayers.[2] In between, they sat on hard benches, studied, and recited their lessons under the watchful eye of the preceptor or his assistant. There was no organized athletic activity, but it is hard to imagine that the day did not include some time for the students to stretch, fight off boredom and drowsiness, and channel excess energy.

The Academy was open virtually year-round and, although it did not issue diplomas, most students expected to stay for several years until they were "ready" to move on. Many of them were headed to college, and if so, almost certainly to Harvard. With this goal in mind, these spent more time on Latin, Greek, and mathematics than their schoolmates whose formal education would end at the Academy, and for whom the "practical" subjects of English, logic, and geometry comprised the principal course of study. The college-bound students were perhaps preparing for a career in the ministry, or possibly in medicine, law, or teaching. But all of the students aspired to positions of leadership in Exeter or the nearby communities in which they would eventually settle. In all likelihood, those aspirations would be met.

How that distant Phillips Exeter Academy evolved into today's complex and diverse institution is a complicated story that, viewed from a distance, divides into three eras.[3]

The first era began with the Academy's founding and extended about nine decades. During this period, the Academy adhered closely to its eighteenth-century origins, preparing boys and young men for leadership and civic responsibility in a New England setting still dominated by small towns and an economy still based on agriculture and small business.

In the second era, which ran from about 1870 to about 1930, the Academy responded to major social and economic changes locally and across the nation, as well as to competition from public education and new demands from colleges and universities for students with deeper, more diverse preparation. The response evolved into an adaptation, as the Academy changed its character from a free "public" school that served students from Exeter and nearby communities, whether they were headed for college or not, to a more specialized private school supported by tuition and with many boarding students. In this second period, the Academy drew students from across the United States and prepared them specifically to enter the best colleges and universities in the nation, especially in the East.

These first two eras are covered in this chapter. The third era, which begins with the Harkness Gift in 1930 and covers the Academy's growth as a self-contained, primarily residential community offering a superior education to academically gifted students, is examined in detail in the remainder of this book.

THE ACADEMY: 1781–1873

By the census of 1775, wrote town historian (and Exeter resident, former governor of New Hampshire, and Academy trustee) Charles H. Bell more than a century later, the town of Exeter "had become practically the capital of the State, the seat of government, and the centre of all civil and military activity in New Hampshire."[4] One should not infer too much from this impressive description, however. As a British settlement, the town already had a history that stretched back nearly 150 years, but it also had a population of just 1,741 souls, and the state of New Hampshire was not yet even a fact in 1775. It was still a Royal Province, though that status would change soon enough.

Bell's description nonetheless indicates that Exeter, despite its size, merited a certain standing in the 1770s and 1780s. It was indeed one of the biggest towns in New Hampshire and the locus of much patriotic fervor. It featured two Congregational meetinghouses, a town hall, a schoolhouse, over two hundred residences, and several taverns. The town's economy depended upon lumber, much of which traditionally had made its way to the Royal Navy but was soon diverted to the service of the colonies. During the Revolutionary War, other industries emerged, including a powder mill (converted in the 1780s to a slitting mill for nails) and a paper mill. These enterprises helped diversify the economy and prepared the way for a future of light manufacturing that still undergirds the town. In these years, Exeter also sheltered the colonial government, which relocated from Portsmouth, a Tory bastion. In January 1776, a provincial congress meeting in Exeter adopted a new constitution for the state of New Hampshire. On June 11, the two houses of the new legislature endorsed a declaration of independence from Great Britain. These two acts, wrote Edward S. Chase, Jr., the town's most recent historian, accorded Exeter "the honor of being the site of the adoption of both the first state constitution and the first declaration of independence from Great Britain."[5]

The town of Exeter had built its first schoolhouse during the first decade of the eighteenth century.[6] There is no surviving account of what schooling was like in colonial Exeter, though it probably typified the experience of other "Latin grammar schools" in the region. Like others of its ilk, and virtually all publicly supported schools in New England, the school in Exeter catered exclusively to boys. (Girls, if educated formally at all, were taught privately, but it is worth remembering that most education in this era occurred outside of schools anyway, in the family, the church, or through informal arrangements.)[7] Consider the following account of a Massachusetts schoolboy's life in the middle of the eighteenth century:

> Starting at about the age of seven, he would attend school six days a week for the next seven years. His schoolhouse was a rude one-room building, perhaps 20 feet by 20 feet, with a fireplace at one end as the only source of heat in the winter. If he was lucky, the windows would have panes in them. He would sit on a hard oak bench hour after hour being drilled by a young Harvard graduate who served as master. Much of the master's time would be taken up teaching the three R's to students who had no college ambitions. A few of the older boys would be spending most of their time with classical authors. The day would be started with prayer and closed by having an older boy recite the Lord's prayer in Latin, and occasionally the master would deliver himself of some remarks on Christian virtue, for he took

seriously his responsibility for molding the character as well as the minds of his charges.[8]

By statute, towns in Massachusetts and New Hampshire that included more than one hundred families were supposed to have both an elementary and a secondary school, but many that qualified, including Exeter, did not comply. In 1780, a boy from the town who wanted schooling beyond age fourteen or to prepare for college at Harvard had several options. He might arrange to stay on in the local elementary school, subject to the schoolmaster's approval. He might enroll at a secondary school elsewhere, such as Boston Latin, or in the two private schools between Exeter and Boston: the Dummer School (founded 1763) or Phillips Academy in Andover (founded 1778). Most likely, he would arrange for private tutoring. Soon, however, he would have a much better option close to home, thanks to the generosity of local merchant John Phillips.

The founding of Phillips Exeter Academy in 1781 — like the establishment of Phillips Academy in Andover three years earlier — represented the leading edge of a wave of private secondary school foundings that would roll across America between the Revolution and the Civil War. In the 1850s, by one count, there were nearly 6,200 academies in the United States. These institutions were a diverse lot: some catered to boys, some to girls, and some were coeducational; some included elementary schools and some were practically colleges. Yet two features distinguished them: an administrative structure featuring a board of trustees and relatively private control, and a somewhat broader, more practical curriculum than found in Latin grammar schools. Although privately chartered, most academies accepted public funding in the form of gifts or subsidies rather than tax-generated revenue. Their trustees typically included prominent public figures. Most academies offered their services for free or only a modest charge, although they might be exclusionary along religious, gender, or racial lines. Many academies organized their curriculum in two divisions: a "classical" course that prepared a handful of students for college, and an "English" course that taught practical subjects to everyone else. For approximately a century — from about the 1780s to the 1880s — the academies filled a need not met by other institutions of the time by providing relatively open and cost-effective instruction to the mass of American youth.[9]

The Founding and the Founder

Phillips Exeter Academy was incorporated by an act of the General Assembly of the (five-year-old) state of New Hampshire on April 3, 1781. The school's

"Original Deed of Gift," dated May 17 of that year was signed by Exeter merchant John Phillips and his second wife, Elizabeth. The document is worth quoting at length because it has been cited often and extensively throughout Exeter's history and remains a vital source today. Heavily indebted to the similar deed of gift that had established Phillips Academy in Andover three years earlier, its rounded periodic sentences resonate with the time and place of its creation, mixing Enlightenment values, Calvinist theology, and capitalist ideology characteristic of late colonial New England. The preamble (a single sentence) opens:

> When we reflect upon the grand design of the great Parent of the Universe in the creation of mankind, and the improvements of which the mind is capable, both in knowledge and virtue, as well as upon the prevalence of ignorance and vice, disorder and wickedness, and upon the direct tendency and certain issues of such a course of things, such reflections must occasion in thoughtful minds an earnest solicitude to find the source of those evils and their remedy; and a small acquaintance with the qualities of young minds, how susceptible they are of impression, evidences that the time of youth is the most important period, on the improvement or neglect of which depend the most weighty consequences, to individuals themselves and the community.

The Deed of Gift went on to specify the properties the school would own and outlined its structure of governance, as well as its mission and values. A board of trustees, including a president, treasurer, and clerk, would meet at least once a year, to oversee the Academy and approve appointments of instructors, in which "regard shall be had to qualifications only, without preference of friend or kindred, place of birth, education, or residence." On the other hand, "applications [for employment] will be in vain where the daily worship of God and good government is not said to be maintained." The founder himself reserved the right to name his own successor as president of the trustees and to appoint the first instructor, who also served as the "principal instructor," or simply the "principal." In the future, this person was required to be "a member of a church of Christ, in complete standing," and "also of exemplary manner, of good natural abilities and literary acquirements, of a natural aptitude for instruction and government." Phillips added, "a good acquaintance with human nature is also much to be desired."

The Deed declared that the Academy "shall ever be equally open to youth of requisite qualifications from every quarter," with the only qualification stipulated as the ability to read English well. As a "public free school," the Academy would not charge for its services, but as it grew, Phillips hoped that those "who reap some advantage" by its education would "cheerfully assist" in meeting its financial obligations, "so that poor children of promising genius may be introduced, and members who may need some special aid may have it afforded to them."

As for values, the Deed emphasized an amalgam of Protestant Christian and capitalist virtues: piety, daily worship, discipline, economy, cleanliness, "an habit of industry," manual labor to help offset the costs of running the school, and "the several great duties" that individuals "owe to God, their country, their parents, their neighbors, and themselves." A resounding summary proclamation ran:

> it shall ever be considered as a principal duty of the instructors to regulate the tempers, to enlarge the minds, and form the morals of the youth committed to their care. They are to give special attention to the health of the scholars, and ever to urge the importance of an habit of industry. . . . But, above all, it is expected that the attention of instructors to the *disposition* of the minds and morals of the youth under their charge will *exceed every other care*; well considering that though goodness without knowledge is weak and feeble, yet knowledge without goodness is dangerous, and that both united form the noblest character and lay the surest foundation of usefulness to mankind.

The principal signatory to the Deed of Gift, John Phillips, was born in Andover, Massachusetts, in 1719, two days after Christmas—a holiday that his family, being good descendants of the New England Puritans, probably did not observe.[10] His parents, Rev. Samuel and Hannah (White) Phillips, educated him at home, evidently quite well. He entered Harvard at the age of eleven and was "precocious enough as a Freshman to write on the flyleaf of a textbook a note asking Tutor Davenport to step up to his chamber for a glass of ale." After graduation, he continued to read and study before returning to Harvard in 1738 to earn a masters degree. During these years and for a time after leaving college, he taught in classical schools in Andover and Exeter, home to his cousins and where he was listed on the town tax rolls as a resident in 1740.

In 1743, Phillips married Sarah Gilman, the widow of his mother's first cousin and with whom he had boarded in Exeter while helping to run the household and estate. His new wife, sixteen years his senior, possessed an abundant estate worth £75,000, including a general store and several African slaves. Phillips showed an aptitude for business and not only expanded the store but also diversified into other interests, including the import and export of food, manufactured goods, and lumber; investments and speculations in real estate; and lending money at what one school historian called "the pleasant rate of twelve and fifteen percent."[11] By about 1760, shrewd investments had made Phillips the richest man in Exeter and one of the biggest holders of wilderness property in New Hampshire.

According to Joseph G. Hoyt, who taught at the Academy between 1840 and 1859 and is the source of much information about the founder, Phillips "was conscious of his position in society, and was not unwilling to receive the homage of youth or age."[12] The middle years of his life teemed with accomplishments and honors. From 1752 onward, he held public offices in town, colony, or state capacities. He served as a militia captain, a judge, a member of New Hampshire's General Assembly, and a deputy to the Provincial Congress. In 1765, Sarah died, and Phillips took the loss hard. Two years later, however, he remarried, this time to Elizabeth (Dennett) Hale, another widow and member of a prominent, although not particularly prosperous, Exeter family. During the Revolutionary War, he stayed neutral, hoping that differences between the colonies and Great Britain could be ironed out short of American independence. When independence came, however, he remained a prominent figure in Exeter, in 1778 serving as moderator of the town meetings. The founding of the Academy, the only secondary school within twenty miles, perhaps further enhanced his standing in the community.

Throughout his life Phillips observed daily religious devotions at home and attended church services regularly. He sympathized with the evangelistic impulses of the Great Awakening, and in 1744 he and several cousins led a secession from the First Church in Exeter to form the Second Church. The experience of separation apparently was bruising, and many years later Phillips sought to heal old wounds by rejoining the First Church.

As neither of Phillips's marriages produced children, he found other ways to pass on his fortune during his lifetime, in this respect foreshadowing Edward S. Harkness. Phillips was especially inclined toward education, and his spontaneous gifts helped several needy young men through school and college. He made many substantial gifts to Dartmouth College, where he served as a trustee for two decades and received an honorary doctorate of letters. In 1776, he joined with his brothers William and Samuel to donate $1,000 to Princeton, at the time the biggest single gift in that institution's history. Two years later, Phillips contributed more than £1,600 toward the establishment of an academy in Andover in partnership with his brother Samuel and nephew Samuel, Jr. John Phillips remained a trustee of Phillips Academy for sixteen years, including serving the last three as president, and he left the institution a third of his estate. The successful launch of Phillips Academy also spurred him to found a similar institution in his home town.[13] Between 1781 and his death in 1795, Phillips gave land, cash, and other assets to Phillips Exeter Academy totaling more than $60,000 — more than $4 million in today's currency. These gifts included two-thirds of his estate at the time of his death.[14]

A Rocky Start

Phillips Exeter Academy greeted its first students in May 1783 in a modest two-story structure with four rooms on Tan Lane. (Later known as the First Academy Building, it has been moved several times, most recently in 1999, with several additions built on. Now at No. 12 Elliot Street, it is still in use as the residence of the dean of the faculty and is called the E. S. Wells Kerr House.) Fifty-six students enrolled during the first year. They were taught by William Woodbridge, a recent graduate of Yale with a few years of teaching experience in grammar schools. "There was no regular course of study," wrote an early historian, "but the pupils pursued such branches and formed such classes, as were found most convenient."[15] Woodbridge provided a glimpse of the Academy's daily life in his diary:

> the students were called to the Academy at one half after five in the summer, and before sunrise in the winter. Prayers were attended, and morning lessons recited before breakfast. The other six hours as usual were attended. Wednesday P.M. was recess, also Saturday P.M., yet prayers were always attended. Saturday and Sabbath mornings and evenings was a moral or pious lecture.[16]

This was a grueling schedule, and although Woodbridge was usually assisted by a young Harvard graduate, he was not long up to the task. Enrollments had plunged to thirteen students by 1788. That year, beset by ill health, the recent tragic deaths of his wife and infant daughter, and worn down by "all this Herculean labor," Woodbridge gave up and submitted his resignation.[17] In recounting this story, Hoyt later inferred "from some floating traditions, that, though the Trustees wished [Woodbridge] well at his departure from Exeter, as Christian men should, yet they economized their tears on the occasion, and proceeded in a business-like way to elect his successor."[18]

Stability

In an eighteenth-century context, "business-like" did not necessarily mean fast. The trustees took two years to choose Exeter's third preceptor: Benjamin Abbot, a twenty-eight-year-old graduate of Phillips Academy in Andover and Harvard, where he had delivered the Salutatory Oration. By 1790, Abbot had been teaching at the Academy for two years and was established as a resourceful and energetic teacher—everything, in short, that Woodbridge was not. Hoyt, who later met the aged Abbot, is the source of much lore, all of it positive, about Abbot:

> ... His pupils feared him, but not half so much as they loved him. . . . They knew that he was their friend, great-hearted and strong.

> ... His mind was a fountain, not a reservoir. . . . He breathed his own spirit into the worn text-books of the recitation room, and the mystic page glowed with his inspiration.

> ... Few men were so deeply versed as he in that most abstruse of all studies, *the human nature of boys.*

> ... He had the faculty of making his classes believe that the particular subject on which they were engaged was the most important and attractive branch of study in the world.

> ... He knew how to govern. It is not every man whose name is tasselled with an A.B. that is able to manage boys.

> ... Reducing equations and reducing rebellions are very different things. If of the various attributes of a teacher Dr. Abbot had any one in pre-eminence, it was the attribute of imperial authority—the *auctoritas* of Cicero.[19]

Abbot proved a good choice as preceptor and (after 1808), principal: he led the school for half a century, during which "the aspect of things . . . changed." Enrollments climbed back above fifty students per year and averaged between seventy and eighty each year between 1790 and about 1825. By 1794, the school had outgrown its quarters and the trustees hastily approved construction of a new Academy building. As described by an admiring visitor who saw it soon after it opened, the new structure was built "of wood, 76 feet in length and 36 in width, raised on two courses of hewn stone, and has on the top an elegant cupola. The whole is executed in a style that does honour to the institution, and to the taste of the gentlemen who planned it." This observer also noted that "the school room is calculated for about ninety [students]; and for neatness and convenience is thought to exceed all others known in the country. The second story forms a spacious room for exhibitions, and a small one for a library."[20]

In the Deed of Gift and other writings, Phillips had anticipated that the Academy might eventually prepare candidates for the ministry, and he even spoke of the school as a "Seminary." In 1791, the Academy attempted unsuccessfully to attract a professor of divinity, and the matter was postponed. About a decade later, Phillips's successor as president of the trustees, John Taylor Gilman, and Abbot revived the idea, arranging grants and buying books for divinity students. But there was little urgency in their efforts, and they made little headway. The situation at Phillips Academy in Andover provided a sharp contrast. As the Unitarian strand of New England congregationalism gained ascendancy at Harvard, the Andover trustees, who remained orthodox Trinitarians, were horrified. In 1808, they formed Andover Theological Seminary, and Phillips Academy all but severed ties with Harvard for nearly three-quarters of a century. At Exeter, the Academy retained a more tolerant, latitudinarian spirit. In 1817, it finally appointed a "Theological Instructor": Rev. Isaac Hurd, minister of the Second Parish in Exeter. Although Hurd taught at the Academy for more than twenty years, it was a part-time commitment, and when he at last retired, he was not replaced.[21]

The Academy's growth during the early nineteenth century reflected continued focus on secondary school education and a growing population in the region. There is evidence that the Academy was doing its job well. During Abbot's time (1788–1838), 1,991 students enrolled at the Academy from seventeen states and five foreign countries. Four hundred seventy-four of these graduated from college, but probably many more received at least some higher education. Of the college graduates, nearly half (231) attended Harvard, with Dartmouth (112) a distant second choice, and the remainder scattered among Bowdoin, Yale, Brown, and other New England colleges.[22] Predictably, the Academy trained leaders in New Hampshire and Massachusetts, and many of them attributed their success to their schooling. Several alumni — Daniel Webster, George Bancroft, Edward Everett, Lewis Cass, and Jared Sparks — gained prominence on a national scale. Webster was so fond of Abbot, at whose feet he had sat in the 1790s, that forty years later he insisted that Abbot teach his son, Edward. Bancroft later contributed $2,000 to the Charity Foundation, which supported boys from poor families at the Academy.

In 1818, the trustees voted to divide the Academy's curriculum into two parts: the Classical Department for students heading to college, and an English Department for those finishing their formal education in Exeter. The former offered a course in Latin, Greek, mathematics, ancient history, and English grammar and composition. There was also a small "Advanced Class" for students wishing to stay longer or to pass directly into the second year of college—an early instance of advanced placement. On the other side, the English Department covered a far wider range of subjects: English grammar "including exercises in parsing and analyzing, in the correction of bad English, Punctuation, and Prosody," arithmetic, geometry, algebra, plane trigonometry, something called "Mensuration of Superficies and Solids," ancient and modern (including U.S.) history, logic, rhetoric, English composition, forensics, and declamation, surveying, navigation, "elements of chemistry and natural philosophy with experiments," and astronomy. Students also received daily instruction in writing and, for spiritual uplift, courses in theology and sacred music.[23]

To house additional classrooms and meeting space, in 1822, wings were built onto the Academy Building. The Classical Department commanded the attention of Abbot and other permanent faculty, which included two other members, a professor of mathematics and natural philosophy (1808), and a professor of ancient languages (1822). These faculty members also covered some courses in the English Department, but the balance was taught by young assistants who remained at the Academy for a few years before moving on.

Growth and Change

In 1838, Abbot was succeeded as principal by Gideon Lane Soule, the first Exonian (class of 1813) to hold the position, and also the first professor of ancient languages. His election as principal was deemed a natural transition. As Myron Williams, a twentieth-century Academy historian put it, "It is little exaggeration to think of Dr. Abbot's term of fifty years and Dr. Soule's of thirty-five as one of continuous administration of eighty-five years."[24] Although Abbot is recalled as an outstanding teacher, Soule is remembered as an administrator and disciplinarian. "Rather tall, but well proportioned," he "had a finely-shaped head, an ample brow, and dark, searching eyes, which, as one of his pupils once said, 'took a boy in at a glance, from his boots up.'" His bearing was often described as "dignified" or "stately," and his manner seemed "business-like." On one occasion, when he was interviewing a new boy, he asked, "How old are you? The boy began to answer, 'I shall be . . .'"

when Soule interrupted him and said, "'No! I wish to know how old you are *now*.'"[25] Richard Montague, class of 1871, recorded another incident that revealed this aspect of Soule's personality. One day, a small earthquake rocked Exeter. Soule, who was leading a class, "stood it (the earthquake) better than we did, but, at last, even he rose from his seat and looked out the window. Then he saw that Abbot Hall was still standing and the trees were growing as they had been growing the day before, and, resuming his seat, he said calmly, 'Foster, construe that next sentence.'"[26]

Academy historians often treat Soule's long tenure as uneventful — a view that was undoubtedly influenced by what happened next (see below). In fact, Exeter made a series of dramatic changes starting in the late 1840s. The establishment of a public high school in Exeter in 1847 obviated the need for the Academy's English Department, which offered the practical curriculum for students not heading to college. The following year, the trustees voted to shut down the department, noting that classes had shrunk and that during the previous seven years not a single student had stayed the full three-year course. The trustees also took account of a faculty complaint that students "whose bad habits or want of capacity" caused them trouble in college preparatory classes had tended to end up in the English Department, making it "liable to be filled up with the idle and stupid."[27]

The Academy's narrower concentration on preparing students for college sparked many additional reforms during the 1850s. First, to offset the decline in enrollments caused by the elimination of the English Department, Professor Hoyt presided over a reform of the classical curriculum, dividing it into three principal years — junior, middle, and senior — with a definite progression toward enabling students to match college entrance requirements. The Academy also featured a small "preparatory class" for boys not yet ready to do the work of juniors, and at the other end, a bigger "advanced class" that equipped students for sophomore standing in college. This structure replaced the old system under which boys had arrived at various points in their schooling and remained until they were "fitted for some college class."[28]

A second momentous decision was to build a dormitory. Since the Academy's earliest days, some students had roomed with families in and about Exeter. Rising costs and uneven supervision were persistent problems, however, especially for "Foundationers," students who received financial aid after the Academy had instituted tuition charges in 1809. During the 1840s, Exeter experimented with voluntary "clubs" to provide room and board. Older boys managed these clubs, which rented facilities, employed matrons to cook and clean, and accepted boarders for about $2 per week. The success of such experiments led the trustees in 1852 to commit $17,000 toward building the first Academy-owned dormitory and dining hall. Opened three years later, Abbot Hall provided living quarters for about fifty students, who were charged $1 per year.[29]

A third consequential change followed in March 1857, when the trustees voted it "expedient to constitute the Instructors a faculty." Later hailed (especially by the faculty) as Exeter's Magna Carta, this vote, it was said, established the Academy as "a faculty-run" institution. Exactly what the trustees meant by the action, however, was not elaborated. The change was probably made to recognize the Academy's increasing scale, its assumption of responsibility for boarding students in Abbot Hall, and the faculty's growing involvement in disciplinary cases and its influence in the determination of scholarship and prize awards. Writing soon after the decision, Hoyt described "the internal economy of the school" as "not unlike that of a well-ordered college. The teachers constitute a faculty, in which are vested the government and instruction." Somewhat later, Bell described the faculty (defined as the permanent members of the board of instruction) as holding "regular weekly meetings, and after consideration and deliberation together, decid[ing] all questions of discipline."[30]

The fourth major change during this period transpired in 1858, when the trustees approved a recommendation from the faculty that it be "authorized to excuse pupils from attendance at the Academy except during recitation hours." This vote had several significant effects. It freed the faculty from the tedious duty of supervising the students as they prepared their lessons. It increased the students' responsibility to manage their time and develop a sense of punctuality. It also reinforced an emerging view of students as independent, self-reliant, young gentlemen. (It was at about this time that Soule became famous for saying at the start of each school year that "the Academy has no rules—until they are broken.") Finally, it freed up space in the Academy Building that could accommodate growing enrollments and additional faculty.[31]

In combination, all of these changes reversed the decline in enrollments, which had dipped to 69 after the abolition of the English Department in 1848. A dozen years later, they had soared to 151, a general rise that would continue until the early 1890s.[32] This growth was sufficiently robust that the trustees in 1857 could reject a proposal to expand the Academy by admitting girls.[33] A striking proportion of entrants arrived from all over the United States. Many of these students were undoubtedly attracted by Exeter's capacity to take on boarders, as well as its continued close ties to Harvard. Such was the case with one of the Academy's most famous students, Robert Todd Lincoln, firstborn of Abraham and Mary Todd Lincoln, who arrived in Exeter in 1859 for a year of preparation before moving on, his parents hoped, to Harvard. In this and many similar instances, Exeter did the job: after a year "devoid of excitement, and full of hard work," young Lincoln entered Harvard in 1860.[34]

New students may also have chosen Exeter because of its expanding ability to provide financial assistance. Although tuition charges rose sharply to accommodate the rising costs of running a bigger institution, reaching $45 per year in 1870, an increasing number of donors emerged to supplement the original Phillips bequests. Between 1862, when the family of John L. Sibley contributed $300 to the Charity Foundation, and 1873, five more donors appeared to make substantial gifts. By far the biggest was more than $42,000 from the estate of Jeremiah Kingman in 1873. These funds enabled the Academy to subsidize still more students, and the continuing growth in enrollments prompted the trustees to acquire a second dormitory. In 1872, the Academy purchased Swamscott House, a former hotel located on the corner of Court and Front Streets, and renamed it Gorham Hall, after David W. Gorham, M.D., a trustee and Abbot's son-in-law.[35]

In December 1870, the Second Academy Building burned to the ground, causing the 74-year-old Soule much grief. "It is said that, as he looked at the blazing and falling timbers, he wept like a child." In response to the fire, a group of alumni launched a subscription campaign to raise $100,000 for a new building. The effort rapidly succeeded. Ground was broken the following spring, and the new building was opened about a year later. Dedicated on June 19, 1872 — an occasion that also marked the principal's fiftieth year on the faculty — the Third Academy Building was a fitting symbol of how far Exeter had come under Soule. Although it was modeled on its predecessor — that is, a main building with two wings attached — it was much bigger and better made. Frank Cunningham, class of 1883, who wrote an informal history of the school published in the year of his graduation, described the new structure in clinical terms:

> It is built of pressed brick with trimmings of gray sandstone, and consists of a main building seventy-two feet front by fifty-five feet deep, to which are added two wings having a front of thirty-two feet and a depth of seventy-two feet. The wings have roofs, somewhat of the Mansard style, but more sloping, and having their otherwise severe outlines broken here and there by dormer and gabled windows.

The whole structure could accommodate more than three hundred students. It included six classrooms on the first floor, two in the central building, and two each in the wings. There was a great hall or lecture room measuring 69 feet by 43 feet on the second floor of the central building. This featured a small platform or stage and many rows of narrow benches, and was used for morning religious services, lectures, assemblies, and exhibitions. In August each year it was used for "the dreaded preliminary and final examinations for entrance to Harvard University."[36] The second story of each wing also featured usable space: on the western side, the library, and in the eastern wing, rooms for the Golden Branch Literary Society, a student group founded in 1818, and the Christian Fraternity, a Sunday evening Bible study group founded in 1856. The basement was also put to use, offering "an apology for a running track" until the first gymnasium was built in 1886.[37]

The building projects of the end of Soule's administration — the new Academy Building and the renovation of a hotel to provide additional rooming space — suggest the direction of change at the Academy. The institution was becoming bigger and more complicated, and it was providing a greater array of services than John Phillips had imagined in 1781. These would prove the dominant trends in the second era of the Academy's history.

THE BOARDING SCHOOL: 1873–1930

During the half century after the Civil War, the United States was transformed from a largely rural and agricultural society of separated "island communities" into an urban, industrial nation in which local and regional markets blended into an enormous mass market.[38] Rapid population growth and accompanying social and economic changes wrought havoc on many traditional institutions, and for the most part, academies failed to negotiate the transition. A few numbers tell the story. In 1870, there were only about 500 public high schools in the United States, and the vast majority of the nation's 80,000 secondary school students attended academies or other privately supported schools. By 1910, there were more than 10,000 public high schools, and only 11 percent of the nation's 1.1 million secondary school students attended private schools.[39]

The same years saw a similar transformation in higher education that resulted in the emergence of the modern university. Before the Civil War, most colleges were small institutions that taught essentially more of the same curriculum as the classical academies offered and provided little professional training except in divinity and medicine. The new industrial economy of the late nineteenth century strained the capacity of these institutions to provide leaders for a rapidly expanding society and forced a series of changes. By World War I, the modern research university had developed in a recognizable form: dozens of specialized and relatively autonomous departments; a mix of traditional liberal arts and newer "practical" subjects; a broad elective curriculum; an honors program; and professional schools for law, graduate education, and business, as well as for divinity and medicine. Many of these changes were initiated at Harvard under Charles William Eliot, who served as president between 1869 and 1910. But Eliot had many powerful contemporaries who joined in fashioning the new world of higher education at Princeton (James McCosh), the University of Chicago (William Rainey Harper), Johns Hopkins (Daniel Coit Gilman), Cornell (Andrew D. White), and many other leading institutions.[40]

For Phillips Exeter Academy, the fundamental social and economic changes swirling around it, competition from public schools, and the new demands of colleges and universities called for an adaptive response. The challenge of finding a response fell to a succession of principals, including Albert C. Perkins (1873–1883); Walter Q. Scott (1884–1889); Charles E. Fish (1890–1895), and, most especially, Harlan Page Amen (1895–1913). In their efforts they were not only aided but also impeded by the school's trustees, who themselves groped for solutions to unprecedented problems, and by its faculty, dominated for much of the second half of the nineteenth century by two powerful figures: George Albert "Bull" Wentworth, professor of mathematics (1858–1892), and his friend and Harvard classmate Bradbury Longfellow Cilley, professor of ancient languages (1859–1899).

Turbulent Times

When Soule retired in 1873, the Academy was a cozy little community, with a full-time faculty of six, including the principal. Soule had been partial to both Wentworth and Cilley and had leaned on them heavily during his final years. Both were gifted teachers and strong personalities, to whom adjectives like "blunt," "gruff," and "severe" were often attached, along with — to be fair — "warm-hearted," "kind," and "generous." In addition to his standing within the community, Wentworth was also renowned as an author. He made himself a textbook factory and a wealthy man, producing, during his long career, more than thirty math texts popular in secondary schools across the country and the source of wide acclaim.

When Soule announced his retirement in 1872, many expected that one of the younger men, probably Wentworth, would succeed him. However, both Wentworth and Cilley failed one of John Phillips's constitutional tests: although they attended church services regularly, neither was a member of a Christian church. Thus the trustees were obliged to recruit a principal from the outside. They found Perkins, a graduate of Phillips Academy in Andover and Dartmouth College, and most recently a principal of a public high school in Lawrence, Massachusetts.[41]

From the beginning, Perkins faced a host of challenges. An outsider, he had to win over — if he could — the allegiance of a closely knit, inward-looking faculty dominated by two strong figures. The trustees made the problem more difficult by declaring that "all questions of discipline, determination of the merit or demerit of the students, and recommendations of candidates for situations on the Charity Foundation be settled by vote of the Faculty." That ruling significantly diminished the principal's ability to govern the school without the full backing of the faculty. Perkins's task was not made easier by his rustic manner. "On his first appearance in Exeter, the new principal did not make a very favorable impression," wrote one of the school's historians. "He was large, ungainly, wore cowhide boots inside his trousers, and, as one of his admirers said about him, had a breath of the country about him."[42]

Perkins had also to contend with two other serious issues. First were the changes under way at Harvard. One of Eliot's first acts as president of the college was to raise the entrance requirements to include preparation in "useful" subjects such as the sciences, history, and modern languages. At Exeter, the trustees asked Perkins to teach physics and botany, which he agreed to do, and Cilley to teach French and German, from which he begged off. That necessitated hiring a new faculty member, the first of several added in the ensuing decade, as the Academy also began offering courses in modern and physical geography, soon adding U.S. history and other subjects. This trend of growing specialization increased the faculty's size and rendered Wentworth and Cilley, who were not sympathetic to the changes, even more disruptive. These changes, moreover, raised costs and led to a 25 percent increase in tuition just at the time when free public schools provided a viable alternative for many families.[43]

In 1875, the trustees compounded the Academy's problem by accepting a bequest from Woodbridge Odlin, class of 1817. An Exeter resident who was evidently unimpressed by the public school in the town, Odlin mourned the passing of the English Department and its service to young men not bound for college, and he sought to reinstate it. Although the trustees initially viewed this prospect without much enthusiasm, Odlin repeatedly raised the size of his intended donation until, at \$20,000, he arrived at their price. The money endowed a professorship, permitted hiring additional instructors to teach a growing variety of courses, and provided scholarships for as many as ten students a year. Although the new English curriculum was more coherent than its earlier incarnation, it nonetheless altered the character of the school. As a modern historian put it, the Academy "was becoming, by the 1880s, a junior college."[44] Its focus on the fundamental questions began to blur. Whom was it supposed to serve? What was it supposed to teach? And to what end? The change also opened up the Academy to nearly two decades of turmoil and strife between and among the faculty and students who were keenly aware of the status differentials between the two programs.

Perkins's efforts to grapple with the challenges facing the Academy were repeatedly undermined by Wentworth, who continued to sway the faculty in matters concerning discipline and the dormitories. There is no surviving evidence of overt confrontation between the two men, but Wentworth proved a constant irritant. Both he and Cilley permitted a boy whom Perkins had dismissed for poor academic performance not only to remain in their classes but also to attend graduation exercises. On another occasion, Wentworth advised a student that he could violate an Academy rule "so long as he kept out of sight as much as possible."[45] Such incidents were not lost on other students, and disciplinary problems soon became rife — especially among boys in the English Department, for whom the consequences of misbehavior were less drastic than for those who hoped to go on to college.

By the early 1880s, Perkins had had enough. He stayed on through the official observation of the Academy's centennial anniversary (of the start of classes) in 1883, and then abruptly resigned. Caught by surprise, the trustees made Wentworth acting principal for a year while they conducted a search. The next principal, Walter Scott, fared little better than Perkins. During the Civil War Scott had seen extensive service and marched with General Sherman to the sea. He later served as a Presbyterian minister, a faculty member at Lafayette College (his alma mater) and the College of Wooster, and as president of The Ohio State University. None of this, however, prepared him for the challenges of leading the Academy.[46]

Scott made progress on several fronts, strengthening the science curriculum, hiring new faculty — including George Lyman Kittredge, who subsequently had a distinguished academic career at Harvard — instituting lectures to vary the pedagogy, and raising funds to build a laboratory and gymnasium.

In 1888, he began the tradition of awarding diplomas at graduation, and thereafter Exonians were identified not by the year in which they entered, but by when they graduated. Scott also instituted an honors program. But he had no more luck than Perkins in winning over students and faculty. Although he persuaded the trustees in 1886 to invest supervision of the dormitories in the office of the principal, thereby wresting control from Wentworth, this measure proved insufficient to stem the tide of disciplinary problems. Students continued to flaunt rules and, when contemplating mischief or already in trouble, continued to turn for advice and protection to Wentworth. The professor himself was also becoming more difficult. He began showing up late to his classes, sometimes greeting them when they were half over.

Scott's attempts to assert control proved clumsy and often backfired. On one occasion, for example, after consultation with the town selectmen, Scott banned the annual bonfire that had long marked the close of school each June. The students defied the order and attempted to build the bonfire anyway. Scott called in the police, and, predictably, a riot ensued, with townspeople cheering on the students. In the aftermath, Scott was persuaded to restore the annual tradition, but only after further polarizing the community. Meanwhile, brawls and riots continued to erupt, all gleefully reported in the local and Boston press. After one such incident, Scott was forced to ask for police protection — a humiliating circumstance for a figure supposedly in command.[47] In a last, desperate attempt to quell the flames, Scott turned to the students themselves. In 1888, the students elected a student council which sought to establish self-discipline. When that experiment produced no discernible effect, Scott gave up and resigned.

The breakdown of order at Exeter was symptomatic of deeper changes in the town and the Academy. No longer an isolated rural village by 1890, Exeter had become a bustling "semi-industrial" town, with a population of 4,284. Many of its inhabitants were recent immigrants employed at machine works, cotton mills, brass works, pottery and drain-tile factories, and a carriage manufactory. A dozen different churches, reflecting Protestant denominational splits, as well as a growing population of Roman Catholics, contributed to the town's diversity. An excellent transportation network added to the transience of the community. In 1883, six trains daily ran between Exeter and Boston, a journey that could be completed in just over an hour and a half.[48]

Although a private institution, the Academy was not a cloistered community but integrated into the town itself. Students roomed at locations all over Exeter, and finding appropriate households and providing reliable supervision were problems made worse by the school's pronounced growth during the second half of the nineteenth century — from enrollments averaging between eighty and ninety before 1855 to more than 300 in 1887. In the latter year, only about eighty boys could be accommodated in dormitories, leaving the Academy to scramble to find housing for many of the rest. As a result, some students ended up in — or chose — inappropriate circumstances.[49]

Into this situation, after another Wentworth interregnum in 1890, arrived Exeter's fifth principal, thirty-five-year-old Charles E. Fish. Another graduate of Phillips Academy in Andover and Harvard, he had most recently served as head of a private school in Worcester, Massachusetts. His mandate was clear, wrote Laurence Crosbie, class of 1900, an English master between 1903 and 1942, and author of the best account of the Academy's first 150 years: Fish "was told to clean the Augean stables, and he set about the task with a will."[50] The trustees removed a major obstacle by persuading Wentworth to take leave during the initial year. While he was traveling in Europe, they induced him to resign his professorship — evidently with great delicacy. Wentworth was fifty-five and still vigorous when he left the faculty. He returned to live in Exeter and remained devoted to Academy, even serving as a trustee. He also bequeathed several major gifts to the school, including an endowed professorship of mathematics.

Fish set about his task efficiently and with the best intentions, but also with a demonstrable lack of tact. One of his first acts was to raise appropriate standards for private households boarding Academy students. Along the way, he disqualified some current landlords without giving reasons, thereby incurring the wrath of the local citizenry. Fish also alienated students by abolishing secret fraternities, expelling troublemakers, and dismissing students with poor academic records. These were unpopular measures but the right thing to do. He negated the benefits of these actions, however, by hiring a private detective to ferret out disruptive students, then denying the deed, and then getting caught in the denial. Another mistake echoed one made by Scott: during a disturbance Fish took refuge behind police protection, a sure sign of weakness. He became so fearful of an assault that he began wearing brass knuckles, an unseemly sight on the head of a school. He also disappointed some followers one year by removing several incompetent teachers and then decamping for the summer to Cape Cod, leaving the surviving faculty to cope with the aftermath.

The forces arrayed against Fish eventually proved overwhelming and, in 1895, he resigned. Several of his accomplishments proved significant and enduring, however, and he deserves more credit than he generally is accorded in Academy lore. His clumsiness notwithstanding, he started the Academy on the road to regaining control of rooming arrangements and hence of discipline. He made further progress by persuading the trustees to build a new dormitory; opened in 1893, the new Soule Hall housed fifty-two students. It was designed so that each room occupied its own level and opened to its own small landing in the stairwell; this design was deliberate and believed (incorrectly) to be "roughhouse proof."[51]

Fish also struggled to restore high academic standards. He instituted a new marking system and obtained the trustees' approval to expel students who failed to maintain a "C" average "or in the judgment of the Faculty . . . did not offer decided promise of rapid improvement. . . ." The result was a wave of expulsions during the next few years. After much difficulty and negotiation, Fish also persuaded the trustees to cut back the English Department, the source, he believed, of many of the Academy's disciplinary woes. The trustees swallowed hard in assenting to this measure, because it meant turning over to the town of Exeter Odlin's $20,000 bequest.

Still another fateful change followed Fish's decision to take advantage of a new educational consulting service that Harvard's President Eliot had established. Called the Schools Examination Board, the service consisted of a committee of Harvard faculty who visited secondary schools to review their policies and curricula. In 1892, Fish arranged for the Board to come to Exeter. The ensuing report found the Academy deficient in the quality of its instruction in English, history, and modern languages, and it also recommended the use of an entrance examination to screen applicants and help ensure higher uniform quality in the student body. Armed with such authority, Fish won the trustees' support to fire a language instructor and hire a new instructor in history. The Academy also purchased new books and maps and adopted the entrance examination requirement.

In combination, all of Fish's actions—good and bad—reinforced a precipitous decline in enrollments—from 355 in 1890 to 123 in 1894—that proved his ultimate undoing. The Academy simply could not afford to sustain such a trend, and it sought new leadership. The answer to their prayers was 42-year-old Harlan Page Amen, who had attended the Academy as a scholarship student between 1872 and 1875. Inevitably, Amen had also graduated from Harvard. From there he had made a noteworthy career at Riverview Academy in Poughkeepsie, New York, starting as an instructor in Latin, mathematics, and English and rising swiftly to become co-principal in 1882. When approached by the Exeter trustees with an offer to take charge of his old school, the proposition included a 50 percent pay cut. Under these circumstances, the trustees allowed him to name his other terms, which he did — an immediate 25 percent increase in tuition (to $100 per year); a promise to raise faculty salaries as soon as an increase was affordable; a commitment to build yet another dormitory within a year; a free hand to hire and fire instructors; and, curiously, a promise that he would not be required to speak at gatherings of the alumni or the public.[52]

Transformation

Amen's eighteen years as principal thoroughly reshaped the Academy. He began by building on the foundation begun by Fish. Unlike his unfortunate predecessor, however, he set about his work with considerable skill and diplomacy, and as a result accomplished vastly more. Amen's resolve to raise faculty salaries won over an important constituency and soothed anxiety about his equally felt determination to build a strong faculty, even if it meant letting go of some current teachers. He invested much of his time in recruiting new faculty members and working closely with the ones he already had. "Neither imposing buildings nor extensive grounds alone make a school great or efficient," he wrote, explaining:

> The essential feature is a band of able instructors joyfully consecrated to their work; strong, thoroughly trained men who are natural leaders of boys; men of large minds and hearts, whose sympathies go out to boys and whose cultured minds, good sense, and manly ways win or compel youth to their best effort."[53]

Amen had a knack for saying the right thing at the right time, for including constituencies that felt isolated or uncomfortable, and for finding common ground when matters threatened to pull apart. When debates about educational philosophy raged across the campus during the early twentieth century, for example, some faculty adhered to the standard curriculum and methods, while others advocated drastic changes. Amen steered a clear course between them, acknowledging both the power of tradition and the imperative of change:

> We are doing our utmost to keep alive in the school the best of the things which made the Academy's reputation in the past, and yet to lay hold of anything that is really good in more modern methods of instruction and

discipline. The earnestness and independence which have always characterized the Academy are precious relics of the past, and we shall maintain
them at any cost. . . .[54]

He took similar pains to win over the students. He was evidently a gifted
teacher—in Academy lore he is ranked with Abbot, Hoyt, Cilley, and other
greats in the classroom—and he made it his business to know every boy
by name. He set up a system of faculty advisers so that each student had a
teacher to guide him through the curriculum. He promoted organized athletics. He reintroduced fraternities but mandated that faculty closely supervise
them. Although a firm disciplinarian and prompt to dismiss "boys who prove
vicious or weak," he was almost always regarded by students, their families,
and faculty as acting fairly.[55]

In time, Amen overcame his anxiety about public speaking and energeti-
cally reached out to the alumni. He was an indefatigable correspondent, and
the surviving letters—only a portion of the total—from his eighteen years as
principal number nearly 30,000 pages. In the early years, he drafted most of
these in longhand, although he later hired a typist. The alumni were pleased to
be involved in the Academy and relieved to see it revived and in good hands.
In return, they proved generous. During Amen's tenure, the endowment of
the Academy nearly tripled, from $475,000 to $1,371,450. Scholarships, gifts,
and prizes multiplied. Amen raised $250,000 for the Teachers' Endowment
Fund to support salaries, purchase of books and other supplies, research,
and travel.

In November 1913, Amen's unflagging devotion to work finally overcame
him. Early in the morning on the day of the Andover football game, he suffered a massive stroke. He never regained consciousness and hence did not
learn that the Academy had defeated Andover 59 to 0. He died the following day. To Crosbie, the loss was incalculable: Amen "had the foresight of a
prophet, the educational zeal of a Loyola, the vigor of a Hercules; and he used
those gifts to bring success to his school."[56] Crosbie went on to tote up some
of Amen's contributions between 1895 and 1913, a period when most indica-
tors, like the endowment, soared: enrollments from 123 to 572; faculty from 10
to 33; the teacher-student ratio that averaged about 1 to 40 during most of the
late nineteenth century, to 1 to 15; real estate from fewer than 20 acres to more
than 400, including the Plimpton Playing Fields; and the number of buildings
from 9 (including Academy-owned private houses) to 32 (including new dormitories, a dining hall, and a library).[57]

As Eliot was to Harvard, so Amen was to the Academy: the leader of a complex institutional transformation. That transformation had roots that began well before his time and branches that extended well past it. It also was aided by faculty, trustees, alumni, students, and other stakeholders. But Amen's tenure marked an era in which Exeter ceased to be an eighteenth-century academy and became a twentieth-century college preparatory boarding school. It fell to his successor, Lewis Perry, to preside over the Academy's next great change, though its eventual magnitude would not become apparent until midway through his tenure.

Sustaining Momentum

Perry's hiring in 1914 at age thirty-seven proved the start of another long administration, this one lasting thirty-two years.[58] The youngest child of a Williams College professor of political economy, Perry was educated at Lawrenceville Academy and Williams. After college, he taught at Lawrenceville and Princeton, where he earned a masters degree, before returning again to Williams in 1900 as an instructor in English. It was there in 1914, as a professor of English, that the trustees of the Academy recruited him to become Amen's successor.

Perry's tenure began inauspiciously. On July 3, just two weeks after his election, the Third Academy Building was destroyed by fire. That catastrophe established one of the first priorities of the new administration: erecting a replacement. An insurance settlement fell far short of covering the damage but provided enough for work to begin on the Fourth (and present) Academy Building while Perry and the trustees worked diligently to raise additional funds to complete the job. The money streamed in—an early indication of Perry's fundraising prowess—and the new building was ready for occupancy by the fall of 1915. The architects, Cram and Ferguson of Boston, felt free to depart from conventions that had framed the Second and Third Academy Buildings and designed a structure "Colonial in style, modified by late Georgian." Befitting the Academy's growth and increasing specialization, the building featured thirteen classrooms, a large assembly hall, and several conference rooms that later served as the headquarters of the academic departments.

During his early years, Perry focused on getting to know the Academy and its constituents. To understand better the world of independent schools, he cultivated friendships with Dr. Samuel Drury, rector of St. Paul's School in Concord, New Hampshire, and Alfred E. Stearns, principal of Phillips Academy in Andover, who became regular correspondents. He also relied on veteran faculty including Joseph S. Ford, George B. Rogers (a Williams alumnus who was Perry's closest friend at the Academy), James A. Tufts, and Frank W. Cushwa, Odlin Professor of English, for advice and counsel. An excellent teacher, entertaining speaker, and terrific raconteur, Perry also possessed great personal warmth and charm. Yet another advantage, noted William G. Saltonstall, who saw Perry from multiple perspectives — as a student, faculty member, successor, and biographer — was his wife. Margaret Perry "worked as hard as her husband, memorizing names of students, entertaining members of the faculty and alumni, and getting to know people in town. It was a magnificent team effort."[59]

During the 1920s, Perry settled into a genteel working routine. His day began with chapel at 7:45 each morning. He spent from 8 to 1 P.M. in his office, greeting students, faculty, and visitors and attending to correspondence. From 1 to 2 P.M. he usually napped, then walked about the playing fields between 2 and 4 P.M., before returning to his office for the last two hours of the day. In leading the school, he maintained the course set by Amen, insisting on high standards for students and faculty alike. Over time, he relied increasingly on a handful of close associates on the faculty for administrative support: Ford as director of admissions, Rogers as director of studies, historian Corning Benton as treasurer, and English professor Wells Kerr as "recorder" and eventually dean of the Academy. Perry also worked closely and well with a small group of trustees, including George A. Plimpton '73, Jeremiah Smith, Jr., '88, and his classmate Thomas W. Lamont '88, men whose long careers on the board overlapped with most of the principal's tenure.[60]

Perry sustained Amen's drive to expand the Academy's facilities and endowment. During his first dozen years, three more new dormitories, an infirmary, gymnasium, swimming pool, and tennis courts were added to the campus. The Academy also acquired Phillips Church in 1922. Although he professed ignorance of money matters, Perry had few peers as a fundraiser. Part of his success was thinking big. In 1919, he launched a $2 million capital drive. Although it fell well short of its target, the campaign added $600,000 of much needed funds to the endowment. The following year, Perry started the Christmas Fund, an annual giving appeal. He formed close associations with several wealthy alumni and philanthropists who made substantial gifts to the Academy. Isabel J. Gale, wife of Edward F. Gale '54, gave the land for the Inn at Exeter. William Boyce Thompson '90 evidently bore no animus toward Walter Q. Scott or Charles E. Fish. Between 1915 and 1918, he donated $300,000 for the gymnasium and other athletic facilities. A decade later, Thompson followed with an astounding $1 million gift that provided for a new science building, administration building, and baseball cage.

As noted in the prologue, philanthropist Edward S. Harkness also proved a bountiful supporter of the Academy. In 1920, he persuaded his friend Perry to accept the first of four large gifts to the Academy: $300,000 toward the endowment of teachers' salaries. Two more donations brought the total up to $445,000. And then, in November 1930, he made a breathtaking commitment of nearly $6 million to institute revolutionary changes to the Academy and the delivery of its education. That gift enabled Exeter to become a self-contained and primarily residential community with a distinctive pedagogy and manner of operation. It thus ushered in the third and most recent era of the Academy's history.

As the Academy approached the 150th anniversary of its founding bequest, it possessed ample reasons to be both proud of its achievements and optimistic about its future. With an enrollment of approximately 600 boys and a faculty of 46, Exeter was a healthy, successful institution, thanks in large measure to its most recent principals. Harlan Page Amen had led Exeter through difficult times and given it stability, direction, and renewed purpose. Lewis Perry expanded on this foundation, adding new faculty and facilities and rebuilding a depleted endowment. Yet there was also much unfinished business. Exeter was not yet a fully residential school, and though it enjoyed an excellent reputation, it was not truly distinctive among leading independent schools. The Academy's leaders expected the Harkness Gift to help address these matters, though it would also prompt change in unexpected ways.

Governing a Faculty-Run School

The Harkness Gift wrought a profound transformation at Phillips Exeter Academy. The anticipated changes were evident soon enough on campus, in construction for new and remodeled classrooms and dormitories as well as in the presence of many new young teachers. As reviewed in the next chapter, the delivery of an Exeter education quickly came to realize Harkness's hopes. Classes became smaller and more intimate, the distance (real and metaphorical) between teachers and students diminished, students took a more active role in learning, and discussion of topics on the table became more vigorous and open. All this was expected. What Harkness and the leaders of the school had failed to anticipate — or, at least, had failed to discuss explicitly — was the equally profound impact of new ways of teaching and learning outside the classroom. A fresh spirit of inquiry and dedication to open discussion, examination, and analysis began to work its way into Exeter's fundamental operation, including its governance. In addition to a revamped campus, a much expanded faculty, and a new way of teaching, the Harkness Gift presented the Academy with principles and a process for guiding ongoing institutional change.

Harkness principles and practices of open discussion and debate fell on fertile soil at Exeter, where the traditions of New England town meetings and congregational church governance had made the institution already decentralized and democratic. In the 1930s, an official publication portrayed "the government of the Academy" as

vested in a Board of Trustees, not more than seven and not less than four in number, including the Principal, the majority to be laymen and not residents of Exeter. The Trustees, in turn, grant to the Principal and the Faculty very large powers.

One of the most distinctive features of the Academy, indeed, is the Faculty government. Like the school itself, its government is completely democratic. On Tuesday afternoons, at meetings of the Faculty, are presented all cases for disciplinary action of any sort, as well as measures of Academy policy and action. Often divergent views are expressed, on occasion recommendations by committees or administrative officers are reversed, and all action is decided by vote of the assembled Faculty. It is perhaps needless to add that these decisions are wholly free from political or religious bias and influence.[1]

The varied perspectives, experiences, and expertise of the trustees, administration, and faculty proved essential to meeting the diverse and complex challenges that Exeter faced after the 1930s. The central problem in managing a modern school is one of alignment: of ensuring that the needs and interests of the principal stakeholders — students, parents, faculty, staff, graduates, donors, and college admissions officers — are addressed and balanced. In Lewis Perry's time, the interests of these groups were closely matched around delivering a high quality, traditional education in a residential setting to (almost exclusively white and mostly well-heeled) boys who were likely to advance to a small number of prestigious colleges and universities. Over the years, however, the interests of some of the Academy's stakeholders began to diverge as it became more diverse and the outside environment imposed greater demands. In response, the trustees, administration, and faculty were obliged to rethink their roles and responsibilities and to reconfigure the relationships among them. The result is a partnership among a professional and specialized administration, an unusually active board of trustees, and a faculty deeply involved in educational policy and affairs. Harkness principles have greatly strengthened this partnership through the years.

EXPANDING FACULTY, EVOLVING ROLES

Lewis Perry stepped down as principal instructor of the Academy at the end of the 1945–1946 school year — the same time that longtime friend and supporter Thomas W. Lamont '88, a trustee since 1917 and president since 1935, also retired.[2] The twin retirements ended an era. No subsequent principal remained in office half as long as Perry, and no subsequent trustee president came close to matching Lamont's influence on the Academy's affairs.[3]

The roles commemorated at the retirements of Perry and Lamont had evolved significantly since the Academy's founding and early years. During most of its first century, Exeter employed fewer than ten people, and the principal ran the school, assisted by a part-time treasurer who was a member of (or appointed by) the trustees. The principal made final decisions about academic policy, admissions (including "charity cases" or scholarships), discipline, and hiring. The trustees, fixed by charter at four to seven members (including the principal), met two or three times per year to allocate financial resources, record gifts, approve actions and recommendations of the principal, and occasionally address policy matters such as whether to offer (or abolish) a program of courses for students not intending to attend college. The trustees also selected the principal, although, as noted in chapter 1, that duty was performed rarely during the school's first century. In the 1850s, curricular changes and the opening of Abbot Hall increased the responsibilities of the faculty. As a body, it met to discuss changes of the curriculum and many areas of student life, including discipline, previously the exclusive domain of the principal, who still retained final say in these matters.

In 1873, however, the trustees expressly gave power to decide discipline cases to the faculty as a whole. This step, unexplained in the official minutes, perhaps reflected a sense among the trustees that such matters were best handled by those who knew the students well—namely, their teachers. In any event, this action marked the true beginning of Exeter as a "faculty-run" school, because it meant that the faculty not only directed academic and student life, but also controlled the membership in the community, from admissions through graduation. A symbol of the change and the growing volume of business before the faculty was the appointment in 1889 of the first secretary of the faculty, James Arthur Tufts, an English teacher who would occupy this office for nearly four decades.

During the long tenures of Amen and Perry, the faculty's involvement expanded into administrative and institutional affairs. Amen, for example, appointed faculty members George Rogers and Joseph Ford as successive assistant principals with particular responsibility for admissions and scholarships.[4] Amen also created the position of "recorder," installing mathematician George H. Selleck into a position responsible for maintaining student records. Finally, Amen discontinued the long tradition of having the principal serve as clerk to the trustees—a position eventually filled by faculty members.

For his part, Perry also increased the faculty's role in the administration, appointing historian Corning Benton as business manager in 1918 and four years later persuading the trustees to elect him treasurer of the Academy. Perry later surrounded himself with a small group of faculty members who remained in key posts for decades: in addition to Benton, who served as treasurer until 1951, Perry's "cabinet" included Rogers as director of studies (with responsibility for academic advising and college placement and some coordination of the curriculum); Ford as director of admissions; and E. S. Wells

Kerr, who became recorder in 1926 and four years later was appointed the first dean of the Academy, with oversight of all student matters. When Professor Tufts retired in 1928, Kerr became secretary to the faculty, and this subsequently became part of the dean's responsibilities.[5]

Perry placed great faith in his close associates and trusted them fully with day-to-day operations at the school. He also had great trust in and respect for the faculty, most of whom, by the end of his administration, he had personally hired. A sign of this trust and respect—as well as of the growth of the faculty following the Harkness gift—was a proliferation of faculty standing committees. In 1928, for example, there were seven: an executive committee, plus committees for problems (discipline), scholarships, studies (curriculum), social life, senior council, and admissions. During the 1930s, as the size of the faculty nearly doubled and its scope changed with the completion of the school as a residential community, new committees were added virtually every year. By 1939, there were twenty-one standing committees, ranging from those charged with mundane matters such as dances and the radio station, to those with loftier responsibilities: Educational Aims and Practices, the Library, Public Manners, and Statistics and Testing.[6]

During the 1930s, the basic structure and organization of the faculty also changed. Previously, instructors had been grouped under "the somewhat informal aegis of whoever was then the senior man in the field."[7] Chemists met independently of physicists, Greek teachers of Latin teachers, and French teachers of German teachers. Following the Harkness Gift, academic departments formed under chairmen typically chosen on the basis of seniority and without prescribed term. An anecdote describes the power of department chairs during this era:

> Some years ago at the beginning of the fall term, during a meeting of an academic department, the new instructors were told—and old members reminded—that matters of policy were democratically settled by majority vote. The members were also told that decision on the subject under discussion could not be made "because the 'majority' has not yet arrived." The majority, in this case was Norman Lowrie Hatch, Chairman of the Department of Latin from 1939 to 1961.[8]

The department chairs held primary responsibility for making teaching assignments and recruiting new faculty.

Meanwhile, as might be expected during the half century the Academy ran well under Amen and Perry, the trustees receded into the background.

As a group, they were dominated by their president. Nonetheless, the period marked significant changes in the composition and work of trustees. Amen's aspiration to transform Exeter into a national school and his and Perry's ambitious building programs required a new order of financial and legal acumen. As a result, with Amen's encouragement, the trustees deliberately undertook a gradual shift in character. As positions opened up, they were less likely to be occupied by local grandees and more likely to be filled by wealthy alumni from the business and legal establishments of Boston and New York — men such as George A. Plimpton '73 (1903–1935), Jeremiah Smith, Jr., '88 (1907–1935), and Thomas W. Lamont '88 (1917–1946). All of these men became close friends of the principals and generous benefactors to the Academy. In addition, lifelong friends and fellow classmates Smith (a Boston corporate lawyer and third-generation Exeter trustee) and Lamont (a Wall Street banker) served as successive presidents of the trustees between 1920 and 1946. (The pair was known as "Tom and Jerry," an appellation that predated the famous cartoon characters but nonetheless later evoked smiles at Exeter.) During this period, trustee meetings were crisp and businesslike and generally confined to legal, financial, and budgetary matters, real estate transactions, and property maintenance issues. During Lamont's presidency, for example, most trustee meetings took place at the Union Club in New York City, where he was famous for wrapping up the sessions within three hours. During much of this period, some trustee work was parceled out to an executive committee and three other standing committees that dealt with the Academy's budget, endowment, and buildings and grounds.

During the fall of 1934, in recognition of the growing institutional significance of the alumni, the trustees voted to constitute an Alumni Advisory Committee (later called a Trustee Advisory Committee) of a half-dozen members, including the president of the Phillips Exeter Alumni Association. This body was created "to counsel with the Trustees and to serve in any other capacity that might prove useful to the Academy and agreeable to the members of the Committee."[9] During the next decade, members of the Advisory Committee attended meetings of the trustees and several standing committees, but they did not vote.[10] Nonetheless, the Advisory Committee served as a training ground for future trustees: after the death of Jeremiah Smith, Jr., in 1935, for example, committee member Francis T. P. Plimpton '17 (a Wall Street lawyer) was elected to fill the vacancy; when Plimpton's father, George A. Plimpton, resigned soon after, Advisory Committee member John A. Cowles '17 (from the Des Moines, Iowa–based family publishing empire) succeeded him.[11]

Throughout these changes, however, the trustees kept their hands off of academic policy and student affairs, entrusting these matters entirely to the faculty. By the time Perry and Lamont retired in 1946, "more and more the school was being run by its faculty," noted the author of a portrait of Perry that appeared in the *Atlantic Monthly*. The author added:

> The government was democratic, in form rather like a constitutional monarchy headed by a Prime Minister, but actually conducted on the principle of a New England town meeting. No one is the hero. Faculty committees do most of the work; the list of committees is staggering, but the work gets done. It gets done at the cost of a lot of talk, which is the price of democracy. On occasion, the Principal will be voted down on an issue he wants to carry. After one of these defeats his remark was: "I had that comfortable assurance of being right which ought to have warned me that I was wrong." His faith is the ultimate rightness of the democratic decision, that the collective judgment evolves from the group a wisdom which is better than any individual dictum. This creates an atmosphere in which wisdom can grow.[12]

CONTINUITY AND THE STIRRINGS OF CHANGE

Lewis Perry's successor as principal was forty-year-old William G. Saltonstall '24—"Bill" to his colleagues and friends and "Salty" to the students, though not to his face. During his seventeen years at the helm, Exeter began to change in dramatic ways, attracting growing numbers of boys from outside the northeastern United States and from nontraditional backgrounds. (See chapter 5.) In the fall of 1946, after only a few months on the job, Saltonstall led the first major reform of Exeter's curriculum in many years. His speech urging the abolition of the Latin requirement helped carry the day for a deceptively simple measure that had profound consequences for the school because it opened the door to expanded course offerings in science and history. (See chapter 3.) But the main legacy of his tenure was the modernization of the Academy's governance. This took the form of a bigger, more professional administration, the beginning of periodic, formal reviews of the Academy's operations and affairs, and the emergence of an expanded, working board of trustees.

Saltonstall hailed from an old and distinguished Massachusetts family. His ancestor, Sir Richard Saltonstall, a former Lord Mayor of London, had sailed to America with John Winthrop on the *Arbella* in 1630. Since then, the family had produced many leading citizens, including U.S. Senator (and former

Massachusetts governor) Leverett Saltonstall, the new principal's first cousin. The family also had long ties to Exeter, with the first Saltonstall enrolled in 1796 and at least two others members of subsequent classes. Bill Saltonstall, however, prepped first at Milton Academy in his hometown. After finishing there in 1923, he took a fifth year at Exeter, drawn, he later said, after hearing a lecture by Lewis Perry.[13] He next headed to Harvard, where he majored in history and lettered in football, hockey, and crew, and stayed on to earn a master's degree. Following a stint as an instructor at the William Penn Charter School and a year traveling in Europe, he was recruited to Exeter in 1932 as part of the expanded Harkness faculty. A tall, angular man with a friendly, gracious manner, he proved an excellent teacher and won the respect of his colleagues. His wife Kathryn Watson Saltonstall also won over the community with her charming and outgoing manner. In 1940, Saltonstall became chairman of the History Department and many people began to talk of him as a likely successor to Perry. And but for World War II, which beckoned him into the U.S. Navy, that transition would probably have occurred sooner. When the time came for Perry to step down, the trustees apparently gave little thought to choosing anyone else.[14]

The Exeter community greeted the new principal enthusiastically. When the appointment was made public on June 2, 1946, a cluster of students gathered in front of Saltonstall's new home on Pine Street for a spontaneous celebration. By then, many students viewed Perry as a grandfatherly figure from a distant past, and they were delighted to see a popular, energetic teacher take over.[15] Saltonstall underscored the change by maintaining a lifestyle quite different from that of Perry: he was the first principal since Amen (in 1899) to teach a full-time course, and he also helped coach the football team, an intramural hockey team, and watched the crew closely as it sculled on the Squamscott River.[16]

The principal's vigorous lifestyle notwithstanding, most members of the Exeter community believed that the transition from Perry's leadership would be smooth and natural. After all, Saltonstall's closest advisors—Corning Benton, Wells Kerr, Myron Williams, and Pike Rounds—had closely advised his predecessor. The new trustee president, Thomas S. Lamont, had served on the board or on the Trustee Advisory Committee since 1935 and was the son of the previous board president. Yet the Saltonstall administration embarked in new directions almost immediately, making significant headway in a burst of energy. In addition to the drive to establish Exeter as "a national high school," symbolized by the appointment of Hammy Bissell as director of scholarship boys, and changes to the curriculum, Saltonstall sought to elevate the Academy's role in national educational affairs. That meant developing a better understanding of Exeter's distinctive strengths and improving relations between the Academy and other secondary schools, including public high schools.

Saltonstall took office against a backdrop of fundamental changes in the school's governance, including an expanded role for the trustees. In June 1945, at the same meeting at which Perry announced his intention to retire and Bissell was formally appointed to oversee scholarships, the trustees voted to raise tuition from the "flat rate" set in 1934, with a $200 increase effective in the 1946–1947 academic year. Several years earlier, the treasurer and business manager had projected that the school would face operating deficits after the war as a result of the needs to accommodate returning faculty, pay higher wages to a growing staff, undertake maintenance deferred during the war, and tackle such long-delayed projects as the renovation of the dining halls.[17]

The tuition increase would partly defray increased expenses, which Benton calculated at $1,700 per student. To help pay the balance and avoid further tuition hikes that might jeopardize the scholarship program and new efforts to attract boys from middle-class families, the trustees laid the groundwork for a capital campaign. As a first step, they voted to expand the board's size. In addition to the principal and the six "charter" members, the six members of the Trustee Advisory Committee became "term trustees," with full voting rights for five-year terms. One of the term trustees remained the president of the alumni association and served while occupying that office; the other terms were staggered so that a new member would be chosen each year. The original charter trustees remained lifetime appointments. The trustees subsequently added two new standing committees: the Nominations Committee, to identify potential new members, and the Committee on Faculty Matters, to study faculty salaries and living and working conditions.[18]

Exeter launched its capital campaign in the spring of 1947, with a goal of reaching $5 million in new contributions by commencement of the following year. (See chapter 8.) Although the campaign ultimately surpassed its goal, its success was both deceptive and the result of hard struggle. This outcome prompted several actions in response. First, in an effort to improve alumni relations, Saltonstall devoted increasing attention to alumni affairs and strengthened the responsible administrative office. Second, although the new endowment income helped Exeter to balance the books after five consecutive years of deficit between 1943–1944 and 1947–1948, the trustees remained sufficiently concerned about the Academy's finances to commission an extensive study of the school's operations by the management consulting firm Cresap, McCormick and Paget. This study, which was coordinated with a similar Cresap engagement at Phillips Academy at Andover in 1950, resulted in more than sixty recommendations to change policies, systems, and organization at Exeter. The measures eventually adopted ranged from making small improvements, such as realizing savings by purchasing of milk in bulk rather than in bottles and more efficient management in the dining halls; to bigger matters such as better utilization of facilities and the abolition of maid service in the dormitories; to bigger still reforms to modernize and upgrade the Academy's administrative systems for planning, budgeting, and personnel management.[19]

The consultants also viewed the school's administrative organization with a critical eye, noting the overburdening of the principal with too many direct reports and responsibilities that were too scattered. These problems, moreover, seemed magnified by Saltonstall's continued insistence on teaching and coaching, as well as indications of his "preference toward being a school teacher rather than a strong executive." The consultants recommended that the principal's role be redefined as that of a chief operating executive and urged that the impending retirements of Benton and Kerr become opportunities to support the principal by hiring officers with administrative experience and shifting some responsibilities to them.[20]

In due course, the school carried out this advice. In the fall of 1950, Exeter recruited James Griswold to succeed Benton as treasurer. Griswold brought appropriate credentials to the job: the younger brother of a well-known Harvard law professor (and later dean of Harvard Law School), he was a Harvard MBA with nearly a decade's experience in college finance, including four years in his most recent post as business manager of Park College in Missouri.[21] Griswold proved a successful, activist treasurer for seventeen years. Saltonstall's initial choice to replace Wells Kerr fared less well. Robert N. Cunningham had joined the English Department in 1932, the same year that Saltonstall had come to Exeter. Cunningham left Exeter in 1939 for other pursuits and eventually became headmaster of St. Louis Country Day School. In 1953, Saltonstall brought him back as Exeter's new dean. He remained just three years, however, before resigning. Cunningham was replaced by Robert W. Kesler, a German teacher, who proved a strong and tough disciplinarian. As the 1950s wore on, Griswold and Kesler assumed increasing control of the direction of the school. Together with Pike Rounds, director of admissions, and Myron Williams and Herrick Macomber, successive directors of the office of studies, the group (including Saltonstall) was referred to by some faculty as "the Kremlin" (a shorthand name for the autocratic ruling elite in the Soviet Union) for its tight control of executive authority.

With management of the school in capable hands, Saltonstall increasingly devoted his attention to Exeter's role and position in its community and in the nation at large. In 1947, at the principal's behest, the Academy settled a twenty-year-old tax dispute with the town of Exeter by compromising on the valuation of the Academy's property. The following year, the Academy launched a Program for Adult Education under history teacher Phillips E. Wilson. The program ran a series of evening courses taught by faculty from the Academy and Exeter High School and by clergy and business people in the town and included such diverse offerings as "Chemical and Atomic Energy," "Effective Speaking," "Famous Men," "Goethe," and "Amundsen."[22]

Saltonstall also labored to redefine the Academy's position in the world of education both locally and on a national stage. He headed a survey of Exeter's public schools, lobbied the New Hampshire legislature against spending cuts for public education, became a member of the Advisory Committee of the Division of Secondary Education in the U.S. Office of Education, joined the board of the Shady Hill School in Cambridge, and served as president of the New England Association of Colleges and Secondary Schools. He promoted an exchange program that allowed Exeter faculty to gain experience at other schools while bringing in outsiders to teach at Exeter. He encouraged faculty to participate in a Ford Foundation study that resulted in the formation of a nationwide advanced placement program. Finally, Saltonstall proved receptive to new educational theories and ideas emerging in postwar America, and he supported the contributions of psychiatrists and developmental psychologists in independent schools.

In 1951, Saltonstall turned his focus to Exeter itself, inviting a dozen prominent educators and professionals to become a task group or visiting committee to study the school and ascertain whether it was living up to its aspirations.[23] The task group met for three days in Exeter in October and considered broad questions such as the role of the private school in a democratic society and how Exeter might measure its contributions to society and its success in achieving its goals. The task group came up with no specific conclusions, but left behind a mandate to continue study that a faculty committee subsequently took up.[24] The result of this high profile effort was published as the *Report to the Principal by the Exeter Study Committee* (March 1953), better known as *The Exeter Study*.[25]

An extraordinary, wide-ranging endeavor, *The Exeter Study* probed into most aspects of the school's affairs, including such expected areas as student life and the state of the curriculum, but also the administrative reforms proposed earlier by Cresap, McCormick and Paget. And here, the tone of the study became decidedly critical. In particular, noting staff reductions and turnover in the dining halls, faculty members worried that the pursuit of administrative efficiency may have come at the cost of employee loyalty and morale. "In a more general way," the authors continued,

> we suggest that the size of the budget should not blind us to the fact that we are not a business institution, but an educational institution: our end product is not a salable item of merchandise, but rather an aggregate of attitudes, understandings, appreciations, and skills which, we maintain, can not be achieved by quite the same methods that assure industrial efficiency.[26]

The Exeter Study went on to examine the role and responsibilities of the principal, agreeing with the Cresap report that the office was overburdened and opining that "it would seem unwise" for Saltonstall to continue "to subject himself to the demands of a regular teaching schedule." But the faculty authors placed greater emphasis than the consultants on the principal's responsibilities to the faculty—to aid its effectiveness and improve its morale. *The Exeter Study* also highlighted the need to clarify roles among the senior administrative officers and shift some responsibilities among them—from the director of studies to the dean, for example. As for appointments to such positions, the study urged that, "whenever possible, administrative officers should be appointed from the Faculty."

> Such a policy can encourage teachers in their work and keep alive their interest in the general policies of the Academy. It can increase the bond of fellowship among the administration, department heads, and members of the teaching staff. It is much easier, too, for a man to acquire a thorough familiarity with Exeter's standards if he has been a classroom teacher here.[27]

Among the study's many recommendations, the most important that were eventually implemented reinforced initiatives already under way, including the advanced placement program and the appointment of the school minister. The study's significance transcended these impacts, however, by reaffirming the faculty's involvement in virtually every aspect of the Academy's governance. As such, it fueled emerging tensions among the parties responsible for governing Exeter, especially as younger men joined the faculty and trustees.

Generational Changes

Saltonstall's relations with Exeter's faculty were outwardly cordial. Certainly the faculty approved of the Anniversary Teaching Fund Campaign, which raised $2 million in endowment funds in the mid-1950s to augment teachers' salaries. The principal also enjoyed personal and professional friendships with many faculty members. "Bill Saltonstall was impossible to dislike, and Kathie Saltonstall was impossible not to love," recalled long-time faculty member Henry F. "Ted" Bedford.[28] Bedford went on to note that Saltonstall's effectiveness with the faculty reflected his ability to

preside over what was a fairly chaotic group in a way that made everybody feel pretty good about it. . . . I thought that was not a bad [definition of a] head of school. If you had a complaint you went in and talked to Bill, you didn't get what you wanted, necessarily, but you felt better about it when you left. The fact that he rode his bicycle to school, the fact that he rowed out on the river, the fact that he played with kids. . . . all of that seemed to me to be what a school was supposed to be about. . . .

Over time, however, some faculty grew disenchanted with Saltonstall's leadership. Some older members resented the principal's sustained and eventually successful efforts to convert the department chairs from a lifetime appointment to a rotating five-year term. Another source of contention was housing assignments. Saltonstall disliked making these decisions because they inevitably disappointed some people, sometimes bitterly. Over time, he delegated such matters to Griswold, who then became a focus of discontent. In addition, Saltonstall often seemed indecisive and appeared to dislike making decisions under any sort of time pressure. "Bill was one of those wonderful people, who always said [when presented with a proposal], 'I'll sleep on it,'" remembers veteran math instructor Donald C. Dunbar. "It was said he had the lumpiest mattress in town."[29]

In the late 1950s, some younger faculty displayed signs of frustration with what they perceived as the slow pace of change at the school.[30] Led by Richmond Mayo-Smith, a charismatic and ambitious biology teacher, these "young Turks" (as they were known) were taken with emerging theories of adolescent psychology and group dynamics. Such work, it seemed to them, bore relevance not only to the provision of psychological counseling services, which began in the 1950s, but also to teaching around the Harkness Table, which could benefit from new social science techniques.

Saltonstall initially supported the young Turks and funded consultants, training programs, and research in areas of interest to them. Encouraged, in 1960 the group sought a bigger and more formal commitment, proposing that the school launch an extensive longitudinal study of Exeter students and graduates with the aim of discovering "more effective ways of understanding and counseling" them.[31] When Saltonstall and several older faculty members proved cool to the project, Mayo-Smith tried another tack. In a letter to Saltonstall that Mayo-Smith mimeographed and distributed to the faculty, he urged that the school required the infusion of "a new spirit of urgency and strength" to "erupt through a crust of comfort and ineffectual concern." He pointed out that some members of the faculty "have the imagination and daring to move Exeter ahead," but noted "forces — the age distribution of your Faculty, the concept of education held by your administrative officers" — that threatened to block progress. He then proposed a way of moving ahead: The office of the director of studies, which was supposedly concerned with both curriculum development and college placement, focused virtually all of its activity in the latter area. As a result, Mayo-Smith argued, Exeter had no one in charge of improving the curriculum — a duty that ought to be the responsibility, he believed, of a new, full-time officer. Then, in a move he later admitted was "cheeky," Mayo-Smith indicated that he would resign unless Saltonstall agreed with him.[32]

Saltonstall shot back a quick reply, also mimeographed, declining the offer, while regretting that his decision meant that "we shall lose your services."[33] In the spring of 1961, having negotiated a sabbatical (from which most people understood that he would not return to Exeter) and amid wild (and unsubstantiated) rumors that the younger faculty were prepared to resign *en masse*, Mayo-Smith delivered his farewell address in a series of three chapel talks enthusiastically covered and later published in *The Exonian*. Mayo-Smith took his theme for the talks a line from Robert Frost — "I gave up fire for form 'til I was cold." — and exhorted students to nourish sparks of innovation lest they be smothered by the weight of tradition and the inertia of institutions. No one in the audience missed the point.[34]

In the end, Mayo-Smith's departure did not trigger an exodus. But there were simultaneous signs that the trustees, also including younger men, were seeking more aggressive leadership of the school. At the end of 1956, after ten years as president, Thomas S. Lamont stepped down but remained a member of the board. His decision, in part, reflected differences with the principal, whom he thought too unassuming as a leader. Other trustees fretted about declining standards and rigor at the school and believed that the Admissions Office was falling down on the job of finding the brightest student body—as evidenced, in their opinion, by shrinking enrollments at Harvard. The Mayo-Smith affair fed still other concerns that the school was not creating enough opportunities for younger faculty to assume positions of responsibility, and that too few older faculty moved on to other schools or positions in education to help spread Exeter's influence.[35]

In the early 1960s, Saltonstall's incipient plans to mount another major capital campaign highlighted some strains in his relationship with the board. Both Andover and St. Paul's had recently received major gifts, which were announced with great fanfare. At Exeter, trustees wondered why the Academy did not appear to be doing as much to demonstrate leadership in American secondary education. Saltonstall responded by working with faculty groups to outline a new fund drive to expand Exeter and assert its influence in independent education. Proposals under consideration included the construction of a new library, gymnasium, and other facilities, as well as the establishment of a year-round curriculum. Based on a prospective gift from educational philanthropist Edward C. Simmons, there was even talk of founding an entire school based on Exeter's principles, perhaps in Albuquerque, New Mexico, where Simmons owned a sizable tract of land. Although the idea of replicating Exeter had been discussed from time to time, the trustees proved skeptical, partly because they worried it would be difficult to attract and keep the best faculty in New Hampshire if a comparable warm weather alternative were available.

In the winter and early spring of 1962, Saltonstall refined plans for the capital campaign, hoping to raise as much as $14 million. As he discussed these plans with the trustees, however, he found that he did not enjoy their complete support. Dudley W. Orr '25, recently elevated as president of the trustees, posed a blunt challenge. "During your administration as Principal," he wrote to Saltonstall, "it has not been clear to me what you think the Academy should become." Orr went on to add:

> We know that people will give money for academic excellence. They will give it for other things, too. In Exeter's case I do not see clearly what these other purposes are. Most of us have good reason to think that Exeter is the best secondary boarding school in the world and that, as such, it does as

much for the country as it does for the boys lucky enough to matriculate. We now contemplate an addition of $14,000,000 during perhaps the next ten years to the capital of the richest school in the world. Why?[36]

Orr's question was pointed and sharp, and ultimately Saltonstall chose not to answer it. For some time, he had been contemplating a move into public life, and there were rumors that he would run for governor of New Hampshire. He declined that pursuit, but in March 1963, at age fifty-seven, he accepted an offer from Peace Corps Director Sargent Shriver to become director of the Peace Corps Mission in Nigeria. Saltonstall's resignation as principal became effective at the end of the academic year.[37]

Saltonsall is remembered fondly by Exeter alumni and for good reason. He was warm and personable, and during his tenure the Academy grew in important ways, reaffirming the aspiration to become a national high school while introducing significant innovations such as the advanced placement program. Saltonstall also set the Academy on a path to apply Harkness-style inquiry and analysis to its long-range future through *The Exeter Study*. Nonetheless, he faced difficult challenges rooted in unsettled relationships among the trustees, administration, and faculty. The faculty was becoming more restive, while the trustees were asserting themselves in Exeter's affairs in ways not exercised since the tumultuous years before Amen's arrival in 1895. Saltonstall's resignation was the first indication of many rapid changes in the school to follow.

DISCONTINUITY

Bill Saltonstall's decision to leave Exeter prompted the trustees to attempt, for the first time, a formal national search for a new principal. In early March 1963, Orr appointed a three-person search committee to identify and screen candidates to become principal.[38] At about the same time, Saltonstall appointed a faculty committee to advise the search committee on the qualities a new leader of the school ought to possess. Although the faculty advisors met at least twice with the search committee, the latter evidently moved according to its own dictates and at its own rapid clip. At the recommendation of influential trustee Hugh Calkins, the committee quickly decided on their man: Richard Ward Day '47, headmaster of Hawken School in Cleveland. In May, the trustees approved the choice, electing Day as Exeter's tenth principal.

Day's appointment apparently caught the Academy's faculty by surprise. The faculty advisory committee was simply notified of the appointment, accepted the news without comment, and promptly disbanded.[39] A second surprise was that Day would not take over until June 1964 to enable him to remain at Hawken while overseeing the final phase of that school's expansion. During the interim, assistant principal and Latin master Ernest Gillespie '29 would serve as acting head of the school.

Many teachers of the Harkness generation look back on this interim year as a high water mark of faculty influence at Exeter. Gillespie, like Saltonstall before him, was a faculty member first and an administrator second. Gillespie, moreover, had Exeter in his genes: his father had taught at the school, and he had spent virtually his entire life on campus. Colleagues regarded him almost as a family member — which he almost was to many faculty who had watched him grow up. (Gillespie's wife was the daughter of Rev. Robert S. Wicks, the retired chaplain of Princeton who served as Academy minister from 1956 to 1960.) During 1963–1964, Exeter continued to run smoothly under the same officers — Gillespie, Kesler, Griswold, Rounds, and Macomber — who had helped to lead the school for many years.

Principal Day possessed an altogether different leadership style, one shaped by the military and refined in independent schools with strong executive heads. The son of a medical professor at Harvard and Tufts, he had been educated at several private day schools in the Boston area before attending Yale. In college, coincidentally, he became a good friend of Sargent Shriver, with whom he spent a summer abroad. After graduation, Day pursued a Ph.D. in history at Harvard, financing his way by teaching at St. Paul's and Choate. The coming of World War II interrupted his plans, and in 1941, Day joined the commandos and trained as a combat parachutist at Fort Knox. While there he attracted the commandant's notice and remained in Kentucky as a top aide throughout the war. In 1945, he finally went overseas with occupation forces in Japan, where he remained two more years. When he finally left the service, Day returned to graduate school and the world of independent schools, completing his Ph.D. and teaching at St. Paul's. Subsequently, he published his dissertation, a biography of Henry Franklin Cutler, the longtime, powerful headmaster at Mount Hermon School.[40] In 1952, Day was appointed headmaster of Germantown Academy near Philadelphia. Four years later, he moved to Hawken School, where he proved a skillful fundraiser and administrator. During his tenure at Hawken, the school doubled in size, acquired a new 240-acre campus, and expanded from a nine- to a twelve-grade program. (Hence Day's decision to remain at Hawken during 1963–1964 to preside over the graduation of the school's first senior class.)[41]

At Exeter during the interim year, with Day's encouragement and occasional involvement, a Faculty Task Force began a two-year planning process designed to review the school's programs and indicate new directions for the future.[42] Both the trustees and Day sought to reenergize the school and enhance its reputation in the world of independent education. For Day, reaching such goals would require unusually ambitious actions, and he was impatient to get started. Donald C. Dunbar, a member of both the task force and its successor, the Academy Planning Committee, recalls Day pushing for results. "He kept saying, 'I want to have a big idea. I want a big idea.' We'd say something about coeducation or something. 'Well, other schools are doing that. I want a bigger idea.'"[43]

In addition to a sense of urgency, Day also revealed his decisiveness. Not long after his arrival, he reversed some initiatives begun under the previous administration. Although Saltonstall's tenure is not remembered for additions to the physical plant, he had relied heavily on faculty input to design the Music Building and McConnell Hall, a dormitory opened in 1961. Saltonstall also had appointed faculty committees to plan several other projects, including a new library, dormitory, and gymnasium. In the fall of 1964, Day summarily halted these projects, although the school had already spent a significant sum on the design of the library. While Day continued to solicit faculty participation and comment on building projects, he made it clear that he would be the final decision maker, subject to the trustees.

To Day, the opportunity to erect new buildings became the occasion to express "big ideas." In February 1965, Day scrapped plans for an addition to the gymnasium in favor of building a comprehensive new athletic complex designed by the Boston architectural firm of Kallman McKinnell and Knowles, which was noted for its *avant garde* use of concrete and glass in the designs of Boston City Hall and other buildings. The following year, Day persuaded the trustees to engage renowned Philadelphia architect Louis I. Kahn, who had recently designed the Jonas Salk Institute near San Diego, to undertake a wholly new plan for the library, as well as a new dining hall. The eventual result was the impressive—and expensive—library that occupies the center of the campus today, and the less impressive—but still expensive—dining hall next to it. When the library was dedicated in 1972, it was the biggest secondary school library in the world, housing 100,000 volumes and rivaling the collections of some well-endowed small colleges. (Today, the Library retains its position as the biggest secondary school library in the world, with a collection of approximately 250,000 volumes.)

The gymnasium, library, and new dining hall were the most visible manifestations of one of Day's biggest ideas: a major capital campaign that would underwrite more new construction, as well as the renovation of many buildings on campus. In March 1965, Day announced that Exeter had received a bequest of $7.3 million from the estate of Edward C. Simmons. The gift was no longer tied to building an Exeter-like institution in New Mexico. Rather, of the total amount, Simmons's will stipulated that $5 million would be used to fund scholarships, with use of the remainder unrestricted. The announcement of the Simmons Gift dovetailed with Day's inclinations to launch a major capital campaign—a prospect enthusiastically endorsed by several younger trustees. During the following year, plans took shape, and in May 1966 came the announcement: Exeter would attempt to raise $21 million over a four-year period, including $13 million for construction and the rest for additional endowment resources. The rubric for the campaign was "The Long Step Forward."[44]

During the late 1960s, in anticipation of proceeds from the fund drive, Exeter launched on its biggest building boom since the Harkness Gift, adding not only the athletic complex, library, and dining hall, but also two new dormitories, Fisher Theater, and the renovations of Jeremiah Smith Hall and many other buildings. Among the latter, one of the most controversial was an expensive makeover and expansion of Gilman House to become the principal's residence. The project overran its budget several times and became a sore point with Day's critics, who regarded it as an ostentatious contrast to the traditional white frame house at 27 Pine Street where Saltonstall had lived.

With the support of the trustees, Day also revamped the school's administration. His first step was to hire Charles M. Rice, formerly a colleague of Day's at Choate and most recently president of Athens College, to succeed Pike Rounds as director of admissions. Next, as had occurred early in the Saltonstall administration, the trustees turned to outside experts to review Exeter's organization and administration, engaging Booz Allen & Hamilton, a management consulting firm where James Newman '33, was a managing director—and about to become an Exeter trustee.

The consultants delivered their report in the fall of 1965. Written in understated, diplomatic language, the report nonetheless advocated significant changes at the Academy. In particular, wrote the consultants,

> not only has administrative responsibility been divided, but the decision-making authority of both Principal and faculty has not been clearly

defined. . . . This has served at times to discourage decision-making and to inhibit the implementation of decisions which would be advantageous to the school. . . . The net result . . . has been a situation in which a new Principal finds that he does not control the means and instruments whereby he can exert his positive, comprehensive leadership decisively and with reasonable dispatch.[45]

The report went on to criticize the school's *ad hoc* tradition of planning, the informal and casual manner in which it set standards for administrative performance and appraised the results, the "lack [of] a strong sense of cost consciousness," and the persistence of "many operational practices which for years have been obsolete in business and government."[46] The consultants identified the office of the treasurer as a particular problem, noting that "over the past 15 years or more, there has been a steady concentration of business and other nonacademic affairs under the jurisdiction of the treasurer." The report concluded with a series of recommendations that added up to bolster significantly the authority of the principal, whom the consultants explicitly characterized as a "chief executive officer." This change required reinvesting decision-making authority previously shared with the faculty and reassigning many administrative responsibilities previously the domain of the treasurer.[47]

Day used the Booz Allen report to revamp the school's administration. He moved Gillespie from the position of assistant principal to the new office of dean of the faculty, with responsibility for faculty recruitment and development—a major concern given the anticipated retirements of many teachers who had arrived following the Harkness Gift. Gillespie served in this position until his death in 1967. His successor, classicist Robin Galt, held the position for two years, then turned it over to historian Ted Bedford, with the expectation that it would become a five-year rotating assignment.

It took several years longer for Day to round out a new administrative team. In 1969, Bob Kesler shifted to a new position as vice principal and the office of the dean of Phillips Exeter was restructured as the office of dean of students. Don Dunbar served as the new dean, a five-year rotating assignment.[48] The position of director of studies changed in 1970, when the incumbent, Herrick H. Macomber, chose to retire early.[49] His job then passed to classicist David Thomas, on a five-year rotating assignment.

At the end of 1965, Day accorded Griswold a leave of absence, during which many duties formerly attached to the treasurer's office were transferred to a new assistant principal for administration, history teacher Colin F. N. Irving '41. When Griswold returned, he retained the title of treasurer but devoted himself to a new assignment as executive director of development and alumni affairs, a fundraising position necessitated by the Long Step Forward. In September 1968, Griswold left Exeter to become president of The Chandler School in Boston, and Irving became the Academy's new treasurer. Because this position was specified in the 1781 act of incorporation and reported to the trustees, it remained an office designated without term.

After 1966, some of the treasurer's former duties were assigned to other new administrative recruits. Spencer F. Martin arrived as assistant principal for alumni affairs and development to take charge of the Long Step Forward. A more controversial newcomer was Walter Devine, a director of business affairs from a psychiatric hospital in Hartford, who in turn brought along a full complement of new assistants, among them a comptroller, a purchasing agent, and a personnel supervisor. Dunbar described the faculty's bewilderment at the new arrivals:

> They were not the type of co-workers to which we were accustomed. Devine's mentality was right out of Harvard Business School. I mean it was unbelievable to us hicks up here in New Hampshire to suddenly see these guys arrive and begin operating according to the business practices that all of us basically had shunned when we decided to go into teaching. There was tremendous antagonism. If you can believe it, they came up here and brought a shredder to Phillips Exeter Academy![50]

The new business manager did not remain long at Exeter. The reforms he championed took root, however, and increasingly the school's administration became the province of professional managers. This became a source of resentment among some older faculty who had been content with previous arrangements under which their colleagues—and friends—had filled key administrative posts. The trustees' decision, with Day's support, to lower the mandatory retirement age from sixty-eight to sixty-five further fueled resentment among some senior faculty.[51]

Meanwhile—as also occurred at the outset of the Saltonstall years— the trustees undertook their own reorganization. During the late 1950s and early 1960s, many veteran members of the board retired, and their successors tended to be alumni in the middle of the careers, schooled by the Harkness faculty, and already prominent in their respective professions, primarily in law, business, and medicine—people like Calkins, Newman, F. William

Andres '25, Brent M. Abel '33, Frank A. Augsbury '43, Philip C. Beals '38, Calvin H. Plimpton '35, and others. These were highly accomplished and ambitious people who were uninterested in being trustees unless they could have a significant impact on the school. While they were respectful of the president, the principal, and the faculty, they were hardly deferential to them.

Among its other recommendations, the Booz Allen report had urged that the school should abandon the distinction between charter and term trustees and that all trustees be elected for five-year terms, renewable once.[52] This step proved a tough sell among the charter trustees, but they were eventually won over, in part because Dudley Orr, the senior member of the group, approved of the change and declared himself ready to step down.[53] In 1965, the change took effect, and Orr's old friend, Boston lawyer Andres, became the new trustee president. Andres admired Day and supported him strongly until he left the board in 1972 to become president of the trustees at Dartmouth.[54]

Day manifested an enormous capacity for work, and there were many challenges that required his sustained attention in the late 1960s: the makeover of the administration, the impending retirement of many Harkness-era faculty, the building boom, the Long Step Forward, the end of required church attendance, and the advent of coeducation (see chapters below.) The strain of all this work caught up to him, and in the summer in 1969 he suffered a heart attack. He recovered and during his six-month convalescence, he vowed to delegate more to colleagues such as Bob Kesler. Nonetheless, upon his return, Day quickly reengaged with the issues facing the Academy and resumed a demanding pace of work. He found, however, that circumstances were changing in ways that complicated his ability to hold the Academy's most important constituencies in alignment. Strains developed and then became amplified in his relationships with students, faculty, and trustees.

Early in his tenure, Day had enjoyed considerable popularity with students. The class of '68 overlapped his first four years and at graduation made him an honorary member. Robert N. Shapiro '68, president of the Student Council and the top student in his class (and later an Exeter trustee), admired Day for his commitment to high purposes and wrote about him with admiration and affection in an essay published in 1990.[55] Some of the goodwill Day earned from students stemmed from decisions to increase student participation in the governance of the school. Before his arrival, for example, he had asked the Student Council for its recommendations about Exeter's future. Some suggestions were predictable and quickly dismissed — i.e., "de-emphasis of grades" — but Day accepted others, including expanded options for independent study and permitting student representatives to sit on some committees with faculty. Other Exeter initiatives that proved wildly popular among the students were the abolition of the church attendance requirement and the coming of coeducation. Both of these changes, in the eyes of students, reflected well on the administration.[56]

In the early 1970s, however, much of the goodwill Day had cultivated among the students began to dissipate. The problem was discipline, and in an era of campus unrest, anti–Vietnam War protests, and widespread and growing experimentation with marijuana, discipline became a big problem indeed. Many students came to perceive Exeter's rules as archaic and their enforcement as arbitrary and unforgiving. Student anger spilled over to Day himself following an incident in January 1971. The precipitant was a decision by the officers of *The Exonian* to run an editorial aggressively critical of the school's handling of student housing as new dormitories opened up and older ones were renovated. The editorial slammed the administration's policies, attacked a faculty member by name, and issued a call to arms: "What we need is a strong student union which would have the power to call the student body out on strike and force the Faculty to make some fundamental changes."[57]

With Kesler's support, Day responded swiftly and harshly. He summoned the president of the newspaper, William A. Hunter IV '71, into his office and, according to Hunter, offered him the choice of resigning from the paper or being dismissed from the school. As it happened, Hunter chose both outcomes: he resigned, and because he had already completed his requirements for graduation, he decided to leave anyway. News of Hunter's resignation reverberated across the campus. Fourteen editors and officers of *The Exonian* resigned from the paper, which suspended publication for two weeks, and a group of students took over an assembly to protest Hunter's treatment and air other student grievances. When passions eventually died down, Day's reputation with the students was seriously damaged.[58]

Meanwhile, Day's support among the faculty and the trustees began to erode. The halting progress of the Long Step Forward became an increasing source of concern in both constituencies. A year after the campaign started, the costs of construction began to soar and a trickle of delays became a torrent. The goal escalated to over $25 million, while contributions during the first year totaled just over $1 million. In the summer of 1969, more than three years into the fund drive, less than a year left before its scheduled completion, and coincident with Day's heart attack, the Long Step Forward drive was still only 60 percent along the way toward its target. A change in the campaign's leadership and direction — including the appointment of Daniel K. Stuckey '37 (son of the Exeter classics teacher who had penned the words to the school hymn) as assistant principal for alumni affairs and development, the advent of coeducation, and a massive escalation of effort during 1970 — eventually brought the campaign to a successful conclusion. Nonetheless, the struggle raised questions among the trustees about Day's abilities as an institutional leader and a fundraiser. These issues also bothered the faculty, who saw the promise of the Long Step Forward to improve their compensation and benefits apparently disappear as the proceeds were eaten up in expensive buildings. A jittery stock market and a national recession in 1971 heightened worries about the school's financial health.

At the end of 1972, Day lost a key ally when Andres resigned from the Exeter board to become chairman of the board at Dartmouth. His successor, Calvin Plimpton, had recently stepped down after eleven years as president of Amherst College, and he did not regard Day as favorably. Indeed, Plimpton believed that Day had made some monumental mistakes in the building campaign, most notably the library, which to Plimpton seemed extravagant beyond the school's needs and means.[59]

The conclusion of the Day administration was not long in coming. In February 1973, upset by projections for salary increases in an era of rising inflation and unhappy about recent administrative appointments, a dozen teachers met to organize a grievance committee. These faculty subsequently mobilized broad support for the creation of a Faculty Agenda Committee to discuss a wide range of issues facing the school. By April, the committee was meeting with Day on a regular basis, and some trustees began to worry that they might have an incipient teachers' union on their hands.[60] Meanwhile, some faculty members privately approached selected trustees to state that Day had lost the confidence of the faculty. As the trustees discussed matters among themselves, a consensus developed that it was time for a change. When presented with these circumstances at the trustee meeting in May, Day promptly agreed to resign and arranged to leave at the conclusion of the following academic year. He went on to serve as headmaster of the recently merged Kimberly-Montclair Academy in New Jersey until a second heart attack killed him in 1978 at age sixty-two.

In his brief letter of resignation, Day wrote: "I think of the years 1964–1974 as a transition period between the Harkness school and the school of the Long Step Forward."[61] He did not elaborate on this statement, but there is no doubting that the Academy began to change in fundamental ways and at an accelerating pace during his tenure, an era coinciding with turbulence and upheaval in American society. The direction and control of the school passed from the Harkness faculty to a new generation of faculty and professional administrators; the advent of coeducation and the increasing diversity of the student body and staff began to stir adjustments in the workings of the community; and the building and fundraising programs called for a new order of involvement from the trustees.

The implementation of change on this scale inevitably proved painful, especially as compounded by Day's views of the principal's role and his decisive management style. Looking back on these years, Don Dunbar drew a sharp contrast between Day and his predecessor: "This is an oversimplification, but Bill Salty was a principal who took the wishes of the faculty to the trustees. Dick Day was really a headmaster who took the wishes of the trustees to the faculty."[62]

EQUILIBRIUM REGAINED

Day's departure marked the beginning of a new era at Exeter in which the responsibilities and duties of the school's leaders — trustees, administration, and faculty — were redefined and the three parties came to a new understanding of how to work together more in keeping with Harkness principles. This process began almost immediately after Day's resignation in the search for a successor. The trustees appointed a search committee consisting of two trustees (James A. Newman '33 and Robert D. Storey '54), two faculty members (C. Arthur Compton '45 and André R. Vernet), and a representative of the alumni (James R. Sloane '39). These men were assisted by Booz Allen (where Newman was an officer, and which then included one of the biggest executive search practices in the United States) and an advisory committee consisting of thirty-one members representing alumni, parents, current and retired faculty, students, and friends of the school. The search committee took an exceedingly broad view of its assignment, "looking for a man between 35–45 years of age with a background in education."[63]

In March 1974, the search process finally yielded Exeter's eleventh principal from just beyond the upper end of this age range: forty-seven-year-old Stephen G. Kurtz, dean of the faculty at Hamilton College in New York. The new principal's background bore similarities to that of Lewis Perry: both had experience in independent schools as a student and teacher but had made their careers in higher education. A graduate of the Stony Brook School and Princeton, with a Ph.D. in history from the University of Pennsylvania, Kurtz was a recognized authority on the American Revolution and the early national period of U.S. history. Following graduate school, he taught history at the College at Wabash in Indiana, where he also served as dean of the faculty between 1964 and 1966. While at Wabash he received occasional feelers from independent schools. He was a finalist to succeed Frank Boyden as headmaster at Deerfield Academy before withdrawing at his own request. In 1963, after Saltonstall's resignation, he was also interviewed as a candidate at Exeter. When he left Wabash in 1966, however, it was not for a school but research, editorial, and eventually top administrative positions at the Institute of Early American History and Culture in Williamsburg, Virginia. Six years later, he returned to college life as dean of the faculty of Hamilton College in New York. It was there that Arthur Compton, one of the faculty representatives on the search committee, phoned him a year later to inquire about his interest in the principal's job at Exeter. "I remember exactly what I said," recalls Kurtz. "I laughed, and said, 'Mr. Compton, it's very nice of you to call, but you ought to look in your records. I was an unsuccessful candidate shot down in one round in 1963, and I'm ten years older, ten pounds heavier, and no smarter. Do you still want to talk to me?'"[64]

Kurtz's warmth, lack of pretension, relaxed manner, and sense of humor appealed not only to the search committee, but also, after his arrival, to the Exeter community at large. Compared with Day, said one faculty member, Kurtz was "much more sympathetic to people and softer in his approach with them, and a kindlier, gentler person. And he did go at things differently, I think it would be fair to say. Not more leniently . . . [but] more tolerantly."[65] A trustee noted that "almost overnight, [there] was a sense of relief, that we weren't at war with the faculty, which [had been] a terrible feeling."[66]

Kurtz's immediate charge was to make the school a happier place — to resolve the lingering discontents between the administration and the constituents it supposedly led, especially the faculty and students, and to rebuild morale. Another top priority was to reexamine the school's disciplinary and counseling systems, which were proving inadequate in the face of a restive generation of students. (See chapter 4.) Still other major tasks were to oversee the progress of coeducation, including the belated appointments of women to responsible positions in the faculty and administration and the continuing drive to make Exeter a more diverse community. (See chapters 5 and 6.) But, along with the trustees, Kurtz was simultaneously forced to confront another unforeseen challenge: the school's rapidly deteriorating financial condition. His appointment coincided with the first oil crisis of the 1970s, a 300 percent surge in the price of energy that triggered the deepest recession in decades in the developed countries. Inflation, which had begun to inch upward before the oil crisis, suddenly leaped into double figures. At Exeter, the oil crisis registered a triple shock, depressing the value of the endowment, triggering a steep rise in operating costs, and heightening faculty concerns about loss of purchasing power.

Kurtz met these challenges with the assistance of new leadership among the trustees. In November 1974, Plimpton stepped down as president of the board and was replaced by Jim Newman. This move was deliberate and intended not only to take advantage of the friendship and familiarity between the new principal and the head of the search committee that found him, but also to accentuate the break from an unhappy past.[67] Subsequently, Kurtz worked closely with Newman and his successors Charles H. Toll, Jr. (a law partner of Dudley Orr's who served as president between 1978 and 1981), and Michael V. Forrestal (1981–1988). These men and a handful of others whose tenures coincided with Kurtz's formed an inner circle of trustees on whom the principal came to rely heavily.[68]

Kurtz also took advantage of Bob Kesler's retirement and the job rotation cycle established under Day to appoint a new administrative team: Donald B. Cole as dean of faculty; David E. Thomas as dean of students; and Thomas C. Hayden as director of college placement. Together with Colin Irving and Daniel Stuckey, who remained as treasurer and assistant principal for development and alumni affairs, respectively, these men constituted the top leadership of the school. The group worked together well, in part perhaps because four of the six — Kurtz, Cole, Hayden, and Irving — were members of the History Department.[69]

Kurtz's first year on campus contrasted markedly with that of his predecessor. Whereas Day had begun making bold and sometimes controversial decisions and appointments soon after his arrival, Kurtz modestly announced that he was "content to listen and to learn where my background in scholarship and small college administration and teaching is helpful and where it is not."[70] He attended classes and extracurricular events, took time to meet individual faculty, met regularly with his staff, and traveled extensively to meet alumni.

Kurtz carried away several impressions from his year of getting to know Exeter. The school possessed obvious strengths and advantages. These included a widely shared mission, derived from the founder, of being "a purposeful school," one that could, with appropriate leadership, serve as a model of "excellence without arrogance." Yet Kurtz also noted "a kind of malaise over the place." He summarized the attitude of students as: "We work hard. We party. Then we get kicked out. Nobody talks to us. [We don't] know how to approach the faculty." The faculty fretted about inflation and remained unhappy that so much of the Academy's resources was consumed in buildings. Many faculty also complained about housing costs, uncertainty in the tenure process, and the demands on their time represented by "triple-threat" responsibilities of teaching, dorm duty, and coaching. Turnover among younger faculty in general and female faculty in particular seemed unusually high.[71]

In addressing these issues, Kurtz took advantage of the beginning of planning among the alumni and trustees to observe Exeter's bicentennial in 1981. These plans eventually included a three-year period of official celebration, starting in the fall of 1978, featuring conferences and symposia devoted to teaching and moral education, publications, and other special events and activities. The bicentennial also provided occasion to launch another major capital campaign to be conducted under the rubric of the Third Century Fund. Invited to state his initial goals for the campaign, Kurtz emphasized continuities with the past, quoting Lewis Perry and Thomas W. Lamont in 1941 on the aims of an Exeter education:

> that intellectual excellence should be demanded and expected of each student, that regulation of a student's life should be kept to a minimum in order that he might learn to be self-reliant and independent, and that the student body must be both national and democratic in character — drawn from all sections of the nation and from all walks of life as a protection against narrow parochialism and snobbery.[72]

Kurtz budgeted for some new construction, including what eventually became the Mayer Art Gallery and a renovation of the science building. Given the uses of the money collected during the Long Step Forward, however, he hoped to apply most of the proceeds of the new campaign to endow ten new professorships, increase scholarship aid, and provide greater benefits to faculty and staff. Unfortunately, these hopes were dashed as the school's financial woes ate up most of the funds finally raised.

Kurtz's style of management proved as unassuming as his philosophy. Nonetheless, three important episodes during his administration signaled important shifts in how Exeter was governed: the debate over discipline during the late 1970s; the resolution of the financial crisis; and the development of new policies about faculty housing and benefits in the early 1980s.

When Kurtz arrived, he later recalled, discipline "was the thing that was tearing Exeter apart."[73] Essentially unchanged since the 1930s, the school's system for dealing with discipline was proving inadequate for dealing with the increasingly complex demands being put upon it. The problem was both a rising volume of incidents and divisions among the faculty as to what to do about it. Many older faculty were convinced that the school had to uphold its strict rules by firing students caught with marijuana, while many younger faculty urged leniency and probationary sentences. As the number of major offenses rose in the 1970s, the faculty spent more and more of its time discussing disciplinary cases, with weekly meetings often turning into lengthy debates about the proper course of action. Meanwhile, the process yielded inconsistent outcomes—a fact that led to widespread cynicism and distrust among students and fears among trustees about potential liability. Indeed, in 1978 the parents of a student fired by the Academy sued for his reinstatement. The suit did not succeed, but it was an ominous sign of more legal challenges to come. But Kurtz believed that more than the disciplinary process was at issue. "I thought the system had an ill effect on the whole institution, and [especially on] the relationships between kids and faculty," he explained.[74]

Urged by concerned faculty members to take action, in 1976 Kurtz authorized the hiring of the school's first full-time counselor, Joseph E. (Jef) Fellows III '62. He also appointed an *ad hoc* faculty committee on discipline to review Academy procedures in dealing with violations. The following year he appointed a second faculty committee to review the penalty system at Exeter and at least three other schools. The committees garnered input from faculty, students, and trustees and took a hard look at recent trends and cases. In the end, they offered compelling arguments to modify the system, including statistics revealing that the percentage of students expelled for major offenses was far higher at Exeter than at comparable independent schools[75]—a fact attributed both to the lack of alternative punishments and the tendency of large groups to make conservative decisions. But many faculty ardently believed that participation in disciplinary cases was an essential part of their duties and were reluctant to give it up. The debate was finally resolved in 1980, when the faculty agreed to test an alternative approach that would transfer all disciplinary matters and petitions to a faculty Executive Committee.[76]

During the two-year trial period, the new process for managing discipline proved successful, and with little change or fanfare it was adopted as standard practice. (See chapter 4.) Most members of the Exeter community credit the new disciplinary process for improving relationships between students and faculty. But as significant as this outcome was the process by which it was reached: a prolonged period of research, study, and analysis by faculty and administrators with student input, periodic reviews and discussions of emerging findings, and, finally, the building of consensus behind an experiment in change. Such a process subsequently typified Exeter's approach to other issues and concerns that affected the community as a whole.

The second significant episode of Kurtz's tenure that affected Exeter's governance was a financial crisis in the 1970s. (See chapter 7.) The chief long-term impact of the crisis was a fundamental change in the attitude of the trustees toward management of the school and a new willingness to become involved in the details of its operation. At the same time, faculty representatives became more intimately familiar with the school's budget, and a new set of professionally trained administrators assumed day-to-day responsibility for financial affairs.

The trustees' 1977 directive that the Academy must balance its books within four years prompted several immediate actions. The board's Budget and Investment Committee worked closely with the administration to develop and update five-year projections of income and expense. A faculty-student Budget Review Committee also met with the treasurer and principal's staff to help establish priorities and participate in the process of controlling costs.[77] As the deadline to balance the budget approached, Kurtz appointed an *ad hoc* committee of faculty and administrators to consider ways to cut expenses. The Committee on Institutional Priorities met regularly from April to September 1979 and attempted "to delve into every possibility or question that has been raised about Academy finances in recent months." Minutes of the meetings were kept and distributed to the faculty, who naturally followed the discussions anxiously. The committee investigated a wide range of matters and eventually reported back with about two dozen conclusions that ranged on the expenditure side from cutting some staff positions, to new measures for energy conservation, to requiring students to furnish their own linens and blankets. Such recommendations went a long way toward reducing the 1978–1979 operating deficit of about $212,000. To avoid "changes in program of a serious kind," the committee believed, it would be necessary to raise new sources of revenue.[78]

The Third Century Fund capital campaign, steady rises in annual giving, and significant tuition increases met the need for greater revenue. These factors, in turn, resulted from more active oversight and involvement in the school's affairs by the trustees. Initiatives led by John R. Chase '45 on the revenue side, and by Richard J. Ramsden '55 on the expenditure side, resulted in the improved value and performance of the endowment and significantly better understanding and control of budgets. At the same time, a new set of administrators arrived to attend to the school's finances: James M. Theisen as director of development (1981); Jef Fellows (who after his stint in counseling had earned an MBA at Dartmouth's Amos Tuck School of Management) as treasurer and business manager (1986); and Don J. Briselden as director of facilities management (1987). All of these administrators brought professional training and experience to the task of managing the Academy's finances and physical assets.

The election of Michael Forrestal '45, a Wall Street lawyer, as president of the trustees in 1981 marked still another important change in the aftermath of the financial crisis. Forrestal recognized the need for the trustees to assume a new level of engagement in the school's affairs, recalls former trustee Frederick Mayer. Committee work became more intensive and forward-looking in an effort to anticipate and deal with problems and issues before they became critical. Forrestal also paid close attention to the nominating committee's efforts to recruit new trustees and urged a more professional approach to identifying the specific qualifications, expertise, and commitment necessary to augment and complement the existing board and attend to the school's affairs. The recruitment of Chauncey Loomis '48, a professor of English at Dartmouth, signaled to the faculty that the trustees wanted to broaden membership and perspective beyond the legal and financial professionals typically elected to the board.[79]

The trustees' new, more activist role in the life of the Academy was illustrated in the third key governance episode of Kurtz's tenure: the resolution of long-standing controversies about faculty salaries and benefits, including housing. Inability to defuse these issues had fueled controversies during the Day administration, and matters only worsened in the difficult economic climate that followed. Although Kurtz continued to meet with the Faculty Agenda Committee during these years, the budget crisis forestalled making significant improvement in the faculty's purchasing power. The issues were further complicated by the faculty's changing composition and expectations: the arrival of female teachers and some Ph.D.s and advanced graduate students who had begun their degree programs in hopes of landing a job in higher education raised questions about the continuing viability of the faculty's "triple-threat" responsibilities. Some of these new recruits found it difficult to combine teaching with coaching and dorm duty, and morale and turnover became serious problems. On the other hand, many older faculty believed that triple-threat responsibilities were integral to the life of the school and to moral as well as to academic instruction. They also resisted changes to rules and expectations they themselves had lived by. Finally, a tight housing market in Exeter made it difficult for any faculty without independent means to find suitable housing near the Academy.

This was a volatile mixture of concerns, and Kurtz and the trustees chose to address them in stages. In the fall of 1979, the principal appointed an *ad hoc* faculty committee to investigate dormitory life and housing policy. Chaired by English teacher Jack Heath, the committee reported back the following spring by affirming dorm duty as a central responsibility of Exeter faculty, and the committee recommended that new faculty spend "a substantial number of years in dormitory residence." At the same time, the committee urged that the Academy recognize "the heavy burden carried by dormitory faculty in advising students, in shaping student morale, and in providing personal presence throughout the day" by limiting outside responsibilities such as faculty committee work and departmental assignments. The committee also recommended changes to the Academy's housing policy, and asked that some proceeds of the Third Century Fund be used to increase faculty salaries.[80]

Kurtz accepted and implemented many of the committee's suggestions and referred others to the trustees. To prepare for eventual trustee action, Forrestal appointed another committee consisting of three trustees and two faculty members to investigate the broader issues of faculty housing and compensation.[81] Chaired by trustee Robert D. Storey '54, the committee actively solicited faculty comments and also engaged Cambridge Associates to survey the faculty and compare Exeter's policies and benefits with those of other leading independent schools. The committee concluded that Exeter's salaries and benefits were "not adequate in light of today's economic conditions" and that, in addition, the school's housing plan was "no longer adequate." The committee then recommended a five-year program to raise faculty salaries in real terms and the replacement of the school's mortgage plan with an annuity plan designed to encourage savings and facilitate the faculty's eventual purchase of a home, should they wish to do so. The trustees duly voted to accept these recommendations, and Kurtz and the administration, in turn, announced the changes in a series of policy statements during the spring of 1983.[82]

The specifics of these policy changes were no more important than the manner in which they were reached—a process that engaged faculty, trustees, consultants, and that yielded a considered outcome. The benefits of such a process were apparent in a new period of consensus among the administration, faculty, and trustees as the fortunes of the economy and the school picked up in the mid-1980s.

Exeter's new mode of governance came at a high cost to the person most responsible for making it work. By the mid-1980s, the duties of the principal's office and the process of gaining consensus among parties with disparate interests, involving long meetings and countless hours of discussions, had exacted a toll on Kurtz. His duties and schedule were both grueling and isolating. To help offset the strain, he met periodically with Theodore Sizer, his counterpart at Andover, as well as with the leaders of other independent schools to discuss common issues and challenges.[83] Nevertheless, in the spring of 1987, Kurtz informed the trustees that he believed the school was in good shape, and that it was time for him to move on.[84]

FORGING A PARTNERSHIP

Kurtz's decision to retire prompted another massive, coordinated campaign to find a successor. The new search featured still closer collaboration between the trustees and the faculty. Although formally the two constituencies maintained separate committees to carry out the search, these committees quickly merged in a single group of three trustees and six members of the faculty. "From the beginning," wrote trustee search committee chair Chauncey C. Loomis, "receiving and screening nominations and applications, these two committees operated essentially as one committee." The work began in the summer of 1986 with the assistance of an executive search firm. By Thanksgiving, a list of about one hundred nominations was narrowed to thirteen candidates, who were interviewed by combinations of trustee and faculty representatives. In January 1987, the list was whittled to three finalists, who visited the campus during the spring and participated in interviews with faculty, administrators (including Kurtz), and alumni/ae.[85]

The final vote occurred in New York in February. The choice was 43-year-old Kendra Stearns O'Donnell, special assistant to the president of the Rockefeller Brothers Fund. She had just completed a decade in the world of academic philanthropy with responsible positions at several major foundations, and she also bore an impressive résumé by traditional academic standards. She had attended Radcliffe and Barnard Colleges and held a Ph.D in English literature from Columbia, where she wrote her dissertation on Shakespeare. In 1971, she joined the English faculty at Princeton, where she subsequently became the first woman to be named to the ceremonial post of University Marshal. After six years at Princeton, she joined the John and Mary R. Markle

Foundation as a program officer, the first of a sequence of foundation jobs that led her eventually to the Rockefeller Brothers Fund. O'Donnell was also well acquainted with independent boarding schools. She had attended the Emma Willard School and later served as a trustee. In 1981, she was elected president of the Emma Willard board, a position she still held when Exeter beckoned.[86]

O'Donnell's appointment stirred notice because she was the first woman to lead a major coeducational independent school in New England, although that had been a minor factor in her selection. The trustees had sought a principal with a commitment to secondary school education, experience in boarding schools, knowledge of fundraising, and demonstrated ability to lead a complex institution. In O'Donnell, they found their strongest candidate. Although she lacked experience in running an institution, she would prove a strong institutional leader. If one of Kurtz's biggest achievements was to bring the constituents of the community together and launch a process of healing and working together, one of O'Donnell's signal contributions to Exeter was significant improvement in the process of decision making and in the implementation of those decisions.

O'Donnell came to Exeter as the first principal since Lewis Perry without immediate and obvious problems to fix. Hence she was the first principal in decades with the ability to define and set her own priorities. She placed a commitment to diversity at the top of her list and presided over the Academy's continuing adaptation and accommodation to the changing demographics of the national — indeed, international — population that it serves. She hastened the long and continuing process of making Exeter more truly coeducational by appointing women to key positions in the administration (including the new office of associate dean for multicultural affairs), leapfrogging some women over senior male colleagues as department chairs, and funding a day-care center. (See chapters 5 and 6.) Science teacher Lynda Beck, whom Kurtz had appointed a vice principal, was given increasing authority under O'Donnell, especially in representing the Academy in legal matters and with the outside world — a burgeoning responsibility in an increasingly litigious era.

O'Donnell's talents as a leader became evident at the start of her tenure. She enjoyed the support of a highly capable administrative staff that she fashioned into a collaborative working team. Her immediate staff included the vice principal (Lynda Beck); treasurer and business manager (Jef Fellows); dean of the faculty (Andrew W. Hertig); and the dean of students (Susan Herney). O'Donnell met weekly with these administrators, involving them in all major decisions. She also worked closely with other Academy officials, including the director of admissions (Richard D. Schubart); the director of college placement (Thomas E. Hassan); the head of the development office (Jim Theisen), the director of alumni affairs (Harold Brown, Jr.); and the director of facilities management (Don Briselden).

In collaboration with her administrative colleagues, trustees, and faculty, O'Donnell pursued several significant initiatives. She opened a new channel of communications with parents, instituting a newsletter that went out three times per year. On the administrative front and following the lead of a trustee committee, the Academy began budgeting for deferred maintenance of its buildings and properties. This step, in turn, enabled the administration to develop a comprehensive master plan to guide the renovation and renewal of the campus on a systematic and orderly basis over a defined period of years.[87] O'Donnell also drafted the school's first comprehensive management plan. Updated periodically, the five-year plan provided a dynamic tool to anticipate operating issues and manage the principal revenue and expense categories in the budget.[88]

O'Donnell displayed remarkable ability as a fundraiser. During her tenure — an era coinciding for the most part with a bull market — the value of the endowment soared from $121 million to nearly $289 million. The trustees, the treasurer's office, and the development office collaborated to develop a major gifts program to seek gifts on an ongoing basis as an alternative to time-consuming, expensive, and difficult capital campaign drives every decade or so. Between 1987 and 1997, the Academy received nearly two dozen gifts of $1 million or more — as compared to four in the entire history of the school before then. The proportion of alumni/ae participating in annual giving climbed to 55 percent, an all-time high and nearly double the level of the early 1980s. Under the principal's leadership, Exeter also sought to balance spending between bricks and mortar on the one hand, and human resources on the other. New structures built during O'Donnell's administration included the Grainger Observatory, the William G. Saltonstall Boathouse, and the Forrestal-Bowld Music building. Many other buildings, including the stadium and several dormitories, underwent significant renovations. In the mid-1990s, the Friends of the Library raised funds to computerize its holdings. The Academy also undertook a massive project to rewire its campus with fiber optic cable, an essential step in bringing the Academy into the information age. The Academy also applied the income from $10 million of new endowment funds to sustain faculty salaries and benefits at competitive levels. Still more new money was applied to scholarships so that an Exeter education could remain affordable to middle-class families.

During her early years at Exeter, O'Donnell attempted to forge a new consensus among the faculty and trustees about the direction of the school. The vehicle she chose was a new mission statement that gradually worked its way through committees and reviews to emerge in 1991. The new statement resonated with the language of John Phillips and affirmed once again the goal to unite knowledge and goodness in Exeter's students. But the statement also included two other noteworthy elements: a strong public commitment to diversity, declaring that it is "required" to enrich an Exeter education; and an emphasis on admitting students "of proven academic ability." In combination, these two elements pledged that while the makeup of the Academy would continue to change, its intellectual standards would remain constant. Exeter would seek to serve the best and brightest students, whatever they happened to look like, or wherever they happened to come from.[89]

Because Exeter's academic curriculum had recently been reviewed under Kurtz, O'Donnell focused more attention on "the other curriculum": the delivery of moral education. The outcome of this effort was neither a new set of courses nor a new way of teaching, but rather a better understanding of the way the Academy functions as a "total institution," training and acculturating its members not only in the classroom but in the dining halls, on the playing fields, and in extracurricular activities."[90] As a first step toward building this understanding, O'Donnell persuaded the trustees in 1991 to sponsor an intensive and extensive survey of Exeter students. The study reflected the Harkness "bias for informed decision making": rather than depend on casual analysis or anecdotal evidence in the formulation of new policies, she wanted fresh data that was rigorously collected and analyzed to serve as the basis of policy making.[91] Directed by Michael Diamonti, a member of the counseling staff, and psychologist Edward Hallowell '68, a new "Exeter Study" systematically questioned students, faculty, staff, and parents about their habits, lifestyles, expectations of, and frustrations with, the school. The result was a detailed composite picture of the Exeter community that revealed convincingly that students who operated in a supportive "social context," who were well connected with their peers and with adults — rare traits, unfortunately, in adolescents — flourished at the school. This conclusion seemed to contradict the age-old presumption at Exeter that self-reliance and individual striving were keys to success.

O'Donnell and the faculty used this information in many ways, making subtle changes to the discipline process and augmenting counseling services. In the mid-1990s, O'Donnell followed up the Exeter Study by appointing an *ad hoc* committee of faculty to examine residential life. The outcome of this work was further changes in policy to provide a more supportive experience for students outside the classroom to enable them to realize the full benefits of an Exeter education. As a result of these efforts, O'Donnell's tenure is regarded as a time of warming and humanizing Exeter without compromising its academic rigor.[92]

O'Donnell's relationship with the board evolved through stages, with a turning point in 1992. Prior to then, O'Donnell had worked with the board closely but rather formally in areas under the purview of the board committees such as finances, budgets, key appointments, buildings and grounds, and long-term planning. A significant change came in the summer of 1992, when O'Donnell acted decisively to dismiss a popular teacher found to be in possession of a significant cache of child pornography. Her handling of the incident brought about a new, closer relationship with the board, in part because it clarified the principal's role as the official most responsible for representing, protecting, and preserving Exeter's institutional interests. Because the case broke during the summer, O'Donnell was obliged to respond quickly without the opportunity to consult formally with either the faculty or the trustees as a body. She did consider options and alternatives with her administrative team, with individual trustees, and with legal advisors before taking action. She chose immediate dismissal on the grounds that the teacher's behavior and actions violated the community's trust and threatened the moral environment of the school. This action was perceived as hers alone, and for some weeks she occupied an unusually exposed position, while some critics wondered whether she had acted arbitrarily or had denied the teacher due process.[93]

An unusual level of apprehension and questioning greeted the opening of school in the fall of 1992. Fortuitously, however, the trustees had scheduled a weekend retreat in Exeter during the fall. Participants described the session as "cathartic" and noted that the principal and the trustees reached a new level of mutual respect, candor, and trust as a result. In the end, the trustees not only backed O'Donnell's handling of the child pornography case fully and formally, but they also voted to send president John Chase to the next meeting of the faculty, where he read a letter strongly supporting her action and the reasons for it.[94]

Looking back on the matter, O'Donnell saw it as "a catalyzing event" that significantly altered her relationship to the board. The episode taught her "how

... crises are opportunities for the pace of growth and change to increase" and "how I felt free to exercise a different kind of leadership as a result."[95] For their part, the trustees sensed a need to become more engaged in the life of the school, not only to provide better support to the administration but also, more importantly, so that they could provide better service as trustees. They also expressed a need to know one another better so as to function better as a team. At the retreat, several trustees voiced frustration at being inhibited from pursuing certain lines of inquiry by the board's formal procedures and the committee structure, which tended to box discussions into compartments. One trustee also noted a tendency to talk around certain topics rather than talk through them, drawing the distinction between "talking about baseball" and "talking baseball." That metaphor caught on. Subsequent meetings of the board included a baseball, which was passed around to trustees who wished to—and now felt free to—speak their minds about any important issue facing the school. In sum, the retreat helped make the entire board part of the old inner circle that had previously dealt with the "real issues."[96]

In 1994, the board's role underwent another significant change with the election of new leadership. The new president, Ricardo A. Mestres, Jr., '51, a managing partner of a Wall Street law firm, agreed to take on the position only if he could share duties with vice president K. Tucker Andersen '59, a partner in an investment firm. This new partnership arrangement became a model for the entire group, described by one trustee as "a Harkness table for 19." Explained Andersen, "At Exeter, our long-term goal is to create a partnership which extends to all elements of the school community—faculty, students, administration, parents, and alumni/ae." The result, said former trustee Robert N. Shapiro '68, is "an intricate web of governance rather than a straight-down hierarchy." At the same time, the trustees restructured the agendas of their on-campus meetings to allow more time for informal visits with students, faculty, and staff and more room for general discussion.[97]

When O'Donnell announced her resignation in May 1996, effective at the end of the following academic year, the new partnership model of governance was put to the test in the selection of a new principal. This time, a single search committee consisted of an equal number of trustee and faculty representatives. The committee dutifully engaged an executive search firm, solicited input from all constituents of the Exeter community, combed through scores of résumés, interviewed the strongest candidates, and arranged for the finalists to visit the school. In February 1997, the committee reached a unanimous choice, which the trustees unanimously endorsed: Tyler C. Tingley '51, previously head of The Blake School, an independent coeducational day school in Minneapolis, would become Exeter's thirteenth principal.

EXTENDING AND STRENGTHENING
THE FOUNDATION

A graduate of Kingswood-Oxford School in West Hartford, Connecticut and holder of three degrees from Harvard (A.B., Ed.M., and Ed.D.), Ty Tingley had spent his career in independent day schools before coming to Exeter. A few months after his arrival, he acknowledged being drawn to the Academy for three reasons, two of which reflected its status as a self-contained residential community and the third its distinctive pedagogy. "This school is so magnificently diverse," he noted. "I see one of the most important things in education at this moment in history is to prepare kids to build relationships of trust with people who may be very different than they themselves are, and I don't know a better way to do that than by living together." Second, he admired "the intentionally moral and ethical component" of Exeter's curriculum and an "ethos that operates 24 hours a day." Third was "the Harkness method and the extraordinary faculty that teaches it," which "has got to be, if not the finest, then one of the finest faculties in the country."[98]

The equal representation of trustees and faculty on the search committee that had recommended him indicated to Tingley "that the trustees believe in this business of a faculty-governed institution, and that it was not not simply rhetoric but in fact was the real living, working philosophy of the institution."[99] Meanwhile, he also clearly understood the importance and ubiquity of Harkness principles at Exeter — that, as he put it, "the skills of dialogue you learn around that table are eminently portable."[100]

Grateful that the challenges looming ahead — "unlike most school situations" — were "academic, conceptual, philosophical, programmatic, not financial," Tingley set about extending and strengthening the foundation he inherited."[101] As his immediate predecessors had done, he formed collaborative working relationships with top administrators, including, among others, Jef Fellows, who continued as treasurer, and historians Jack Herney and Barbara Eggers, who served successively as deans of the faculty. Similarly, he worked closely with the trustees, including new president James G. Rogers III '63, who had headed the search committee, and vice president Julie Ann Dunfey '76, as well as with their successors, Charles T. Harris III '69 and Paul D. Goldenheim '68. The partnership between trustees and administration that had grown so close during the O'Donnell years remained intact.

Following discussions with the trustees, Tingley sought to amplify the strategic planning process begun by Principal O'Donnell and develop a comprehensive master plan for the Academy.[102] Addressing the faculty in January 1998, he outlined a process for an Academy Master Plan that would begin with "establishing broad institutional goals and working backward from those goals to the present. This will free us from the time-consuming exercise of taking stock of the present through extensive analysis of current policy and collection of data, and point us immediately toward the future, toward where we want to be." The first step, he pointed out, was "to assert goals on which we can all agree," and he named three: (1) to have the finest high school faculty we can assemble; (2) to have the finest student body we can find; and (3) to offer an academic and residential curriculum that would most effectively meet the educational goals articulated in Exeter's mission statements.[103]

During the late 1990s and early 2000s, Exeter, as a community guided by Harkness principles, undertook comprehensive studies and developed action plans in each of these areas. The planning process itself was by now well worn at Exeter: begin with general debate and discussion; empower representative steering committees to begin detailed analysis; solicit and take account of input from multiple perspectives; deliver periodic reports and updates on progress; and synthesize and ultimately decide in meetings of the faculty as a whole.

In looking at the future of the faculty it was immediately apparent that it would undergo another generational change early in the new century, as the replacements for the original Harkness generation of teachers would themselves retire. By the end of the first decade, half of the faculty would have less than ten years' experience at the school. Working with department chairs and faculty committees, the administration developed new guidelines for faculty recruiting, compensation and benefits (including housing), and training and career development. Projections revealed that maintaining and cultivating a first-rate faculty would require significant additional financial resources, especially to raise the percentage of faculty living on campus and thus integral to the Academy's learning environment.

In examining the student body, the planning process suggested a need to consider reducing the school's enrollment to maintain ideal teacher-student ratios while simultaneously increasing the applicant pool by drawing from some nontraditional schools and regions. Another important objective was needs-blind admissions. Like efforts to ensure a continuing high quality faculty, ensuring a continuing high quality student body would require significant investment.

Such was also the implication of inquiry into improving the learning environment at the Academy. Several older dormitories, in retrospect, had been designed to accommodate too many students to offer "a nurturing dormitory culture that respects the individual and provides a sense of community and identity."[104] Another concern was the lack of a student center on campus, a place where students could gather and meet to pursue social and extracurricular interests. This was a particular problem for day students.

Meanwhile Exeter made rapid headway on multiple fronts in the late 1990s and early 2000s. In 1997 an unrestricted gift of $7.5 million from trustee Rick Smith '66 was applied in a major drive to revamp the science curriculum and erect a new science facility to replace the aging Thompson Science Building (see chapter 3). Opened in 2001, the Phelps Science Center ultimately represented more than $38 million in investment to bring Harkness teaching and principles to the sciences and into the age of information. Once the new facility was complete, the Academy turned to a major renovation of the Thompson building to transform it into a new student center, which opened in 2006 as the Elizabeth and Stanford N. Phelps '52 Academy Center.

In 1999, the Academy kicked off a new curriculum review under the rubric of developing "the next curriculum." The review likewise proceeded as an extended Harkness discussion, with faculty, administrators, and trustees afforded multiple opportunities to contribute to the process and eventual outcome. (See chapter 3). Another project involved the renewal of the Academy's landscape, including a plan to establish a "continuous tree canopy and ground plane to unify the campus and make it a more welcoming place."[105] At about the same time, plans were drawn up to renovate the Academy's biggest dormitories and restructure them into smaller residential communities.

While the master planning process and these initiatives were under way, Exeter also launched several programs to reach traditional constituents through new channels and extend its reach to entirely new constituents. A new director of communications, Julie Quinn, collaborated with the Alumni/ ae Affairs and Development office to issue a steady flow of publications between the Academy and parents through both print and web-based media. The *Bulletin*, the *Parents Newsletter*, and *Non Sibi* (not for oneself — a publication sharing "stories of vision and philanthropy" at the Academy) were available in print and online, while the Academy's webpage (www.exeter.edu) also became a font of news and information. The electronic Exie-Net also sought to strengthen bonds between the school and its graduates. New summer programs, the Exeter Humanities Institute, the Shakespeare Institute, and Access Exeter, sought to introduce teachers and young students to the Academy's approach to teaching and learning.

All of this activity required investment, and to pay for it the administration and trustees announced in 2004 a major capital campaign that anticipated raising $305 million over five years (see chapter 7). Called the Exeter Initiatives, the campaign kicked off with $150 million in pledges already in hand and expected to raise the resources to ensure Exeter's continuing success well into the twenty-first century.

CHANGE, HARKNESS-STYLE

By the late twentieth century, Harkness principles of open discussion and analysis of problems and issues had thoroughly infused the Academy, triggering far more than a pedagogical revolution in the classroom. Leaders of the Academy used Harkness-style gatherings to tackle major challenges from changing admissions policies, to curriculum reviews, to reform of the discipline process, to faculty development, to upgrading housing and improving residential life, to adopting new technology, to launching and managing large-scale capital campaigns, and beyond. Harkness principles and practices addressed the Academy's most pressing needs as it grew larger, more complex, and more diverse by enabling complicated issues to be broken down into constituent pieces with broader understanding of how these pieces interrelate and interact. As an aid to such understanding, Harkness inquiry and discussion proved remarkably effective. The same principles and practices also deliver another important benefit: of bringing together multiple stakeholders around an important decision or action. Everyone is heard, all points of view are patiently listened to, the contributions of all participants are taken into account. Many issues brought into focus via Harkness discussion are and remain controversial, but rarely do they provoke sustained dissent. That is because even disappointed stakeholders respect the principles and trust the process.

During the seven decades and counting since the Harkness Gift, the Academy learned how to use Harkness discussion to great effect, changing how the institution itself changes and facilitating its adaptation to new social, economic, and demographic circumstances. This was a difficult lesson for Exeter's leaders to learn during the initial decades of the Harkness Plan, when older traditions and role definitions still prevailed and the trustees, faculty, and administration were less closely aligned. Once embraced, though, the Harkness principles and process guided the Academy through a series of significant transitions and shifts in its external environment, as the following chapters reveal.

3 Enlarging the Minds

Ten uppers entered Rex McGuinn's classroom to the strains of blues — mood music for the assigned reading of the week, August Wilson's *Two Trains Running*.[1] Taking their seats around the large oval table, they directed their attention to writing paragraphs about the play, an exercise they engaged in at the beginning of every class. Ten minutes later, McGuinn opened the discussion with a question, which met with brief answers from two students. Another gave a detailed interpretation based on the text, which one of the original students queried. A fourth student then spoke up, and after her two more offered alternative interpretations. All that occurred in the first ten minutes of discussion. By the end of the fifty-minute class, only one student of the ten had remained silent. All had listened intently to the discussion throughout; none had looked at their watches or shifted in their seats. McGuinn occasionally asked a question about the text to direct the class to a point they had missed, and at the end he emphasized the bigger picture, summarizing the play in the context of the others the class had already read.

This class is an example of Harkness teaching — Phillip Exeter Academy's distinctive pedagogy and the manifestation of a major turning point in the school's long history. The premise of this book is that Edward Harkness's major gift in 1930 touched off a transformation of nearly every aspect of the Exeter experience. These changes began first and foremost in the classroom. By enabling the school to hire many new teachers, reduce the size of classes, design new classrooms, and institute seminar-style teaching across the curriculum, the Harkness Gift had a profound impact on the delivery of education: as two eminent faculty members put it, the gift helped convert the classroom from a teaching to a learning environment.[2] The shift in focus to the individual students in turn led to major changes in the school's curriculum, which began to accommodate individual needs as well as evolving expectations about the purpose and content of secondary school education.

From there, the impact of the Harkness Gift rippled outward, altering the school in ways that no one could have anticipated. It changed Exeter's attitude toward change itself, an attitude evident in the school's continuing adaptations in the current "age of information."

CHANGES "OF A FUNDAMENTAL NATURE" IN TEACHING AND LEARNING

In bestowing his major gift to the Academy, Harkness sought pedagogical innovations "of a fundamental nature—so sweeping and so different" from traditional methods that they would change not only Exeter but also secondary education generally. As it played out, the gift produced the desired effects at Exeter and then some, although, because it requires substantial resources, it fell short of igniting a wider educational revolution.

The magnitude of changes in teaching and learning that the Harkness Gift triggered is apparent in the contrast with the Academy's traditional pedagogy—which was similar to that in many other public and private secondary schools. During Exeter's first hundred and fifty years, most classes followed the same basic format—lectures and recitations. Accepting traditional views on pedagogy and cognitive development, the Academy believed its job was to teach students facts; college would teach them how to reason from those facts. For the large majority of students, the classroom afforded little, and only formal, interaction with the instructor or with each other. The usual setting was a room featuring rows of desks, with the teacher perched on a platform in the front, to be looked up to by the students while simultaneously looking down on them. During class, or recitation, as it was called, he (all teachers were male until the 1960s) would lecture some twenty-five to fifty students. Whenever he paused to ask a question, a barrage of snapping fingers would assail him from students competing to give the answer. Most faculty called on their students using their last names, although some teachers also used a mildly politer form of address, prefacing the name with "Mister."

These circumstances made for a highly competitive classroom, but also one in which shy or lax students could become anonymous. "The casual visitor to a recitation in the Academy," observed Lawrence Crosbie in 1923,

> is always startled and sometimes shocked by the old Exeter custom of snapping the fingers. If the boy hesitates in his recitation, a fusillade of snaps from those who know or think that they know rings out. It is often disconcerting to a new boy, but he soon learns to stand to his guns, no matter how fast the musketry rattles about him.[3]

Giving the correct answer — generally recapitulating something memorized — was the way to gain recognition in a class where written exercises were rare. Appropriately enough, those who succeeded in this environment were called "sharks." Students who had difficulty keeping up would receive private tutoring until they were ready to join the fray.[4]

Consistent with the conservatism that generally marked its attitudes, Exeter was quite content with this mode of education. So too were the colleges and universities where its graduates matriculated — approximately one-third of every graduating class went to Harvard, Yale, or Princeton. With that kind of record, there was little incentive for change. Exeter's faculty could reasonably believe that their students received an excellent education, one of the finest available. But as Harkness recognized, there was also nothing especially distinctive about Exeter's pedagogy. Nor did it meet the needs of many students at the Academy. Harkness designed the gift to remedy both of these shortcomings.

Recruiting New Faculty

Soon after the Harkness Gift was made public, the Academy launched efforts to make the changes the donor had envisioned. Although the level of excitement ran quite high, few realized at the time how dramatic these changes would be. Altering the architectural setting of the classroom would change the way teachers taught and students learned. It would transform the delivery and eventually the content of an Exeter education.

Construction on new dormitory and classroom buildings began during the summer of 1931, as did efforts to hire new faculty. The prospect of increasing the number of teachers by nearly half prompted much discussion of the qualities required in the newcomers. A faculty committee report suggested:

> The selection of new men is made on the principle that the men should be young enough in years and spirit easily to take up and carry out the conference method of instruction, and old enough to have a sufficient background and experience in life to give substance and authority to their instruction. The teacher (1) must be the right kind of man in character and personality; (2) he must know thoroughly his subject and the art of teaching; (3) and — what would naturally follow — he must command the respect and confidence of his colleagues and students.[5]

Finding over two dozen men of that description in a variety of disciplines was, thanks to the Depression, not difficult to do. "The Academy hired a lot of men from colleges," recalled Charles M. Swift, a mathematics instructor who came to Exeter at the end of the decade. Swift noted that colleges were dropping off personnel because of their budgets, and Exeter was able to pick up men who were highly qualified in their fields. These were scholars and added greatly to the academic strength of the Academy.[6] A number came straight from graduate study or teaching positions in the Ivy League, such as the English teacher Chilson Leonard (Yale), the classicist Henry Phillips (Harvard), and the mathematician H. Gray Funkhouser (Columbia).

The infusion of new blood — an expansion of the faculty by over 50 percent — had an immediate impact on the way people at the Academy thought about teaching. "This flood of new, young people brought a lot of pedagogical ideas into the school at the time," recalled Richard F. Niebling, an English teacher and one of the new recruits. The school heralded their arrival as the beginning of an exciting new era. Many of the older instructors, however, were unenthusiastic. Although they were happy to have the size of their classes cut in half, the transition to a seminar format proved difficult for some who had been content with the old style of teaching. It did not take long for a generational divide to develop. "When I first attended faculty meetings," Niebling recalled, "there were some older members of the faculty who were grudging in their acceptance of the new people who were here. The old system . . . had to be abandoned. But some of the older men said it didn't make a great deal of difference. . . . There was a lot of good teaching going on here before the Harkness Plan."[7] More teachers joined the faculty over the course of the 1930s, and, by 1941, the Harkness teachers constituted nearly half of the eighty-three-man faculty.[8] As the older members retired, their younger colleagues assumed a greater role in faculty decisions. The Harkness teachers, said Niebling, "were the dominant members of the faculty for years and years. I was the youngest in my department for any number of years because this group continued teaching. Many of them stayed for their entire career."[9] That was a long time: the last of the Harkness hires, Charles M. Swift and Alan H. Vrooman, retired in 1978.

From Teaching to Learning

As the new teachers entered the ranks, the "Harkness Plan," as it came to be called, began to take root. Harkness had hoped to convert virtually all teaching to the new method as quickly as possible. Progress came gradually, however, because the faculty had neither models to follow nor a clear idea of how to reach the goal of individualized instruction. Although the donor had made certain suggestions concerning class size and teaching methods, these were matters the faculty wished to determine themselves. "We believe that the whole plan would have to be experimental and subject to experimental verification," noted one faculty report, "for we could not bind ourselves *in advance* to a certain fixed number in all sections in all subjects in all years."[10] Three elements, however, were deemed desirable: small classes where every student could participate; a different type of classroom, with a conference table modeled on a design by historian and treasurer Corning Benton, which would allow students to see their classmates' faces and to be on eye-level with their teachers; and sections organized in terms of ability, which would permit slow, average, and bright students to proceed at their own respective paces. Under these conditions, teaching and learning would occur through discussion rather than lecture and recitation. Exeter would have the advantages of a small school — small classes and personal supervision — in a large school setting.[11]

Practical rather than pedagogical considerations determined which classes first sat around the table: classicist Robin Galt, one of the early Harkness recruits, recalled that classics and mathematics classes were the only ones to adapt the seminar format in 1931 because they were taught in the Academy Building, the only building in which renovated rooms were ready in time for the start of the school year. The recently finished Thompson Science Building had been built with more traditional classroom and laboratory space in mind. English, History, and French adopted the seminar method with the completion of Phillips Hall the following year. By 1935, the remaining departments had followed suit, except for Science, which would make a full-scale change in the early 2000s.

The new classroom configuration had immediate results. One teacher, Henry S. Couse, described his impressions during the first term of Harkness teaching:

I had not suspected that a merely physical change in the classroom could so influence our work as it has done. Sitting in a group about a table instead of in formal rows of seats has abolished almost completely the stiff duality which used to obtain between instructor and class, when, I am afraid, his elevation on a platform tended to hedge him about with too much dignity and make him somewhat unapproachable, even to the fearless curious student; and which certainly did tend to make the student still less articulate. The very naturalness of the new arrangement, besides being more comfortable, has in good part wiped out that class-consciousness. Now, there is a freedom of discussion, an eagerness to participate, that I never saw before, the value of which to both student and instructor is incalculable. And it comes mostly from sitting about a table.[12]

Taking the teacher off his pedestal was important; the change in the method of instruction, even more so. The seminar method became the pedagogy of choice, the teacher asking questions that required not the regurgitation of memorized facts, but thoughtful discussion. The eminent historian Arthur M. Schlesinger, Jr., '31 recalled:

> We sat around tables and talked back to the master; education became, not a performance, but a process. Also the standards were high. I barely passed in my first term and thereafter set to work. I had never worked so hard in my life. When I went on to Harvard later, everything was easy. So far as the training of the mind was concerned, Exeter could hardly have been more effective for me.[13]

Compelled for the first time to engage actively with the material at hand, students worked harder. Grades rose at once—after only three years, reports showed 12 percent more As, Bs, and Cs and 6 percent fewer Ds and Es.[14] This was not grade inflation, the school's analysis revealed, but real academic improvement. Learning replaced teaching as the primary activity in the classroom.

Harkness had hoped that classes would include no more than eight or ten students, but the average class size in the 1930s was twelve—a number that has remained relatively constant ever since. The advantages of such small classes were obvious. They not only demanded more of the students, but also enabled teachers to give them attention in a way that large classes did not. Teachers could see who was keeping up with assignments and who was coasting, who was reading intently and who was just skimming. In short, the teacher got to know the students as individuals. At the same time, students could develop closer relationships with teachers.[15]

Perhaps the greatest advantage of the small class was that it allowed the teacher to read his students' papers with care—it facilitated the teaching of writing. Not surprisingly, at the inception of the Harkness Plan, teachers immediately began assigning more written work. Vrooman, an instructor in English from 1937 to 1978, recalled:

> The way to teach writing, I soon discovered, was to cause the students to write—give them plenty of opportunities to write—look at their work

carefully. We used to write a weekly theme, but then we decided it was better to have them write perhaps a somewhat more ambitious paper every other week, but write at least once a week in class — fifteen to twenty minutes.[16]

This became a common practice in the English Department, Niebling noted:

I would come into class and say, "Assume the angle," and they'd pull out these slides on the Harkness Table. And I'd give them a question and they'd have to write for the hour, often on extemporary topics, because we felt — Chilson Leonard, George Bennett, and a number of others did this — we felt it was very good to have them respond in writing immediately. They got to be awfully good at it: being able to lay out an answer that was pretty well organized and mechanically good, considering they were writing in class. It was a wonderful discipline, and very important.[17]

Other departments soon followed suit, instructing students in the types of writing specific to their disciplines.

As expected, Harkness teaching caught on quickly in humanistic disciplines like English and history, but it also proved effective in math classes, where a student could be called upon to explain his solution to a geometric problem at the blackboard. The class could use the problem to formulate a theorem, much in the way a history class could use Thucydides to formulate conclusions about the Athenian Empire. "A mathematics is quite different from a foreign language class," explained Jackson B. Adkins, mathematics instructor from 1939 to 1970. "The drill is as essential, but it goes at a different speed. It's a mixture of the teacher talking and engaging the kids in saying, 'Well, do you think somebody can answer the question in a reasonable fashion?'"[18]

Although small class size and the conference method were generally popular innovations, the dividing of sections according to ability met with a more mixed reception. "Fast" sections were an instant success among students and teachers alike; "slow" sections, however, were abandoned after few years because of a general lack of enthusiasm for teaching less able students as well as a decline in the number of students who fit this classification. Since the inception of the Harkness Plan, "track" sections have gone in and out of fashion. In the mid-1980s, the faculty established "standard" and "intensive" sections in certain disciplines to meet the needs of students from diverse backgrounds.[19]

From the outset of Harkness teaching, each instructor had considerable autonomy in running the class. Each had a personal classroom, and each imbued the class with his own personality. The predominant style in the first days of the Harkness plan — stern and demanding — was epitomized by classicist Norman Hatch. Known as "Booby" Hatch around campus, he was famous for boxing students' ears and throwing erasers. Herrick H. Macomber '26, who taught at Exeter from 1936 to 1970, recalled that:

> Hatch's method seemed to be to scare the kids to death. . . . One boy reported that he'd skipped class because he got all ready to go and he'd be so scared, he wouldn't go. The young fellow went into the office of Pike Rounds, who was Director of Admissions at the time, and he said, "Sir, I want to change my courses. I want to drop a subject." And Pike asked him what it was he wanted to drop, knowing full well who it was. "Mr. Hatch's Latin class," the boy said. "Well," Pike said, "you know Mr. Hatch, he has these ways which take a little getting used to, but by the end of the year the boys just swear by it. He is very strict and very insistent that the work be thorough, but he would *never* ask the students to do something that he wasn't doing himself only ten times more." Pike said, "Has he torn up a book yet?" The boy said, "No." He said, "He will." About two weeks later, the boy came back all excited, and said, "He did it! He did it today! He took the boy's book whom he suspected of using a crib and just tore it apart!" Maybe it was cruel and unusual punishment, but the end product was likely to be pretty good.[20]

As admired as the Hatch method of motivating was in its day, it was challenged later by instructors with a new philosophy of education, the most prominent being biology instructor Dick Mayo-Smith. In 1960, Mayo-Smith led the faculty's Research Planning Committee in the Academy's first serious psychological research project. Employing theories of adolescent development current in that period, the committee identified and analyzed the forces affecting the Exeter student's capacity for intellectual and emotional growth. The study found that these forces — which it termed the "oblique education of the boy" — appeared in forms ranging from explicit rules to unwritten codes (for example, the pressure to conform). They acted through the student's relationships with other people in the classroom, on the playing field, in the dormitory, and away from school.[21]

Mayo-Smith's provocative views triggered a revolutionary change that continued even after his departure in 1961.[22] When the Harkness generation began retiring later in the decade, their successors — an equally large wave of new teachers—arrived at Exeter with a different understanding of developmental psychology and more attunement to adolescent needs, perhaps because memories of their own adolescence were fresher. Methods of motivating and engaging students changed accordingly. In general, the new teachers preferred discussion and counseling to the sterner style of confrontation and humiliation.

Changes in individual disciplines made a difference in the way teachers conducted their classes. In the 1950s, the History Department replaced the single textbook with a number of works used in conjunction with primary sources, so students could evaluate both the evidence and modern interpretations of it.[23] In the mid-1990s, the Mathematics Department replaced textbooks with problem sets in all but the very advanced courses, with successful results. Techniques derived from research in learning theory and cognitive science helped students articulate in nonverbal ways; Margaret McGuinn, for instance, had students in her English classes create visual projects to supplement oral and written discussions.[24]

Throughout its evolution, the Harkness system has consistently screened for good and dedicated teachers. Explained Chauncey C. Loomis '48, "Most of the teachers then and most of them now are people of intellect who care about the material they're teaching, as well as about the kids, and that's crucial. They take great pleasure in the material. When I taught there in 1988, one of the things that pleased me was that a lot of the conversation those teachers would have was not just about the kids, but also about what they were teaching."[25] Loomis remembered his own experiences as a student of George Bennett, one of Exeter's great English teachers:

> He was my favorite teacher. I admired him a great deal—his intellect, his voice—I loved his voice. His whole approach to things. There was a moment in one of his classes where he read aloud, and he had a beautiful voice, and I was aware of the focus that he had on what he was doing. I was aware of the room itself and all of us sitting around that table. I was aware of the light in the room; the sun was coming in. It was a combination of the voice and the general sense of that man caring a lot about the literature he was teaching. I suddenly thought, "My God. This is terrific." That was a very important aspect of my time at Exeter.[26]

Interestingly, the Academy has not typically provided sustained instruction for its regular faculty in the art of teaching. (The only teachers who receive formal instruction are the Faculty Interns, student teachers with one-year appointments.[27]) What some viewed as pedagogic freedom others viewed as neglect. Vrooman remarked:

> One of the things that appealed to me at Exeter was that teachers were pretty well left to their own devices. But perhaps I was left too much to my own devices when I came. I got no help at all. I had never been a teacher! All I knew was the way I had been taught. It was a sink or swim place. I did my best to keep my head above water. The first year was tough.[28]

According to Charles Swift, "If you were capable of being here, you got it. You got it quickly by osmosis and by asking your own questions of other faculty. And if you did ask questions and learned, you got along. If you didn't, you tended to disappear."[29]

Perhaps the reason why the Academy does not provide formal instruction on how to teach is that there is no preferred way to lead a Harkness class. Pedagogic philosophies and methods vary from instructor to instructor. "The way I go about teaching European history is quite different from other people in my department," history instructor Stephen C. Smith explained. "There is no single correct approach."[30] The students, the other half of the equation, vary just as widely — in intellect, home environment, and the preparation they received before coming to Exeter. Experience in the ways of the Harkness classroom also plays a role. In a class of preps or lowers, all eyes tend to be on the instructor, who guides the students to the issues to be considered. In classes where students are more accustomed to sitting around the table, there is a greater tendency for them to direct their questions and responses at each another, and the ensuing discussion forces them to think rapidly. Here, the teacher is more of a peripheral figure, speaking up to prevent the discussion from going off on an unfruitful tangent, or to elicit a response from a taciturn student. There are times when a teacher sits and says nothing at all, and there is a popular anecdote about one who left the room unnoticed by the students absorbed in discussion. But it would be a mistake to think that the teacher is not playing an active role — or that there is any one ideal type of class. And even a class that was a great success one day can fail the next — if students are tired or unprepared, if the teacher is not adept at using the students' observations, or if the chemistry simply is not there.[31] For all the variations in teaching and learning, however, classes at the Academy share common pedagogical goals: students learn to interact with teachers and fellow-students, and they learn to ask questions — two crucial skills, regardless of discipline.

THE HARKNESS PLAN AND A CHANGING
CURRICULUM, 1930–1990

Although the Harkness Plan focused primarily on the "how" of teaching, it also had a profound impact on "what" was taught. Harkness himself did not give much thought to how his gift might affect the curriculum, but the new pedagogical methods that ensued produced lasting changes in the content of the Exeter education. Since its founding, the Academy had structured its curriculum with two goals in mind: preparing its students for college and providing them with the best education possible. In the nineteenth and early twentieth centuries, these goals were complementary, and Exeter altered its curriculum only when the universities its graduates attended, especially Harvard, revamped their own curricula or admissions requirements.

The introduction of the Harkness Plan changed this pattern considerably. The new emphasis on individualized instruction caused the school to grapple for the first time with difficult curricular questions. At the heart of the Academy's numerous debates were three interrelated questions: (1) whether the school should teach skills or content; (2) what courses should be required and the balance between these and courses students could choose to take; and (3) whether it was better for students to give them exposure to a wide variety of fields or have them focus on fewer, each in greater depth. These debates proceeded in various ways over time in response to social pressures, educational trends, and the changing population of the Exeter community. The inquiry, debate, and discussion characteristic of the Harkness Table increasingly influenced deliberations among the faculty, as evidenced in three periods in the post–World War II era: a prolonged debate over the Latin requirement culminating in its abolition in 1946; an era of incremental changes to the curriculum during the next four decades; and a major curriculum review in the mid-1980s.[32]

The End of the Latin Requirement

The first post-Harkness debate over the curriculum concerned the requirement that each student take two years of Latin. This debate played out over twelve years — extended by World War II — and passed through three distinct phases. In 1936, Exeter first considered the question of whether Latin should continue to be a required subject. When the debate was resumed in 1941, the focus shifted to meeting the needs and aptitudes of individual students. Following World War II, when the school addressed the Latin question for a third and final time, circumstances had changed considerably. With vigorous new principal Bill Saltonstall at the helm, flush with the nation's postwar optimism, the Academy was ready to make the decision it had talked about for so many years. The debate was ostensibly about Latin, but the real issue ran deeper — whether students should have more choice in the subjects they studied at the Academy. By deciding to give students that choice, Exeter not only opened the door to further curricular change but also began to modify the way it approached such matters.

Like other New England boarding schools, the Academy in the 1920s offered the traditional liberal education, the classical curriculum of ancient languages and mathematics combined with "modern" subjects like English and history.[33] The four-year Exeter student was required to take four years of English, three of mathematics, two of Latin, two of a modern language, a third year of either Latin or a modern language, and one year of history (mostly ancient). In his upper and senior years, he had the choice of four electives in advanced English, advanced mathematics, advanced language, additional history, or science. This heavily humanistic program prepared students for advanced study at the Ivy League colleges and universities, as well as at other leading institutions. But this education also came with costs, as Donald Ogden Stewart '12 reflected a half century after his graduation:

> most of it never had a real connection with the world we lived in. Ancient History, Latin, Greek, French, German, Physics, Chemistry — these were mainly "to discipline our minds" and to pass the dreaded College Board exams. And probably, for our age group, this was the best that could be demanded of the faculty. We had entered as boys. Now that we were men, it was up to the colleges to direct these well-trained minds into their real understanding of the world about them.[34]

This criticism, however, came long after the fact. Although individual instructors from time to time may have replaced Cicero with Catullus, or Milton with Melville, as trends and tastes dictated, the school engaged in major curricular reform only when absolutely necessary — the last instance having occurred in the mid-1890s to harmonize with changes in Harvard's entrance requirements.

The onset of the depression in the early 1930s brought a questioning of many of the old assumptions about the purpose of education. As the bread lines grew, the traditional classical education came under fire across the United States from those who argued that schools had an obligation to educate their students in ways that would better enable them to contribute to modern society and its industrial economy. Science and history, not Latin and Greek, it was claimed, deserved greater attention. Students should have freedom to study these subjects in depth, an outcome that at most schools and universities could only be achieved feasibly by modifying or abandoning the ancient language requirements. A prominent advocate of these progressive views was Harvard president James B. Conant—himself a scientist—who, upon taking office in 1933, eliminated most of the university's traditional language requirements.[35]

The national debate resonated at Exeter, where the Harkness bequest was beginning to transform attitudes toward education. Lewis Perry and George Rogers returned from their trip to Britain in early 1930 with ideas from the public schools they had visited, including the idea of giving science a more prominent place in the curriculum. That idea lay behind the decision to use some of the recent Thompson bequest to erect the first building on campus dedicated to science. The Thompson Science Building was completed just as the first Harkness teachers arrived on campus. Among them was John C. Hogg, recruited as chair of the new Science Department. Creating a viable program out of an assortment of physics and chemistry courses, he then directed his attention to expansion.[36]

Many of Hogg's young colleagues hailed from the nation's top universities, and they infused the school with fresh perspectives on education. The Academy began to question seriously what constituted an appropriate secondary education. The problem consisted of two related issues: whether students should have greater freedom in the selection of courses, and more specifically, whether the two-year Latin requirement should stay on the books. Advocates of change argued that this requirement made little sense for boys who lacked linguistic interest or ability and also made it difficult for them to take advanced courses in science or history. Allowing students to study disciplines that interested them made sense in light of the Harkness pedagogy's tighter focus on individual education.[37]

Elimination of the Latin requirement was not such a radical idea—Andover had dropped Latin in favor of history and science requirements a few years earlier[38]—but the old guard at Exeter was not ready for it. Latin, defenders of the requirement contended, provided a strong foundation for learning modern (i.e., Romance) languages and understanding the evolution of Western civilization, while its mastery also required discipline and refined skills in logic, grammar, and expression. After considerable debate, the traditionalists carried the day, although they permitted a compromise. As an experiment, a small number of boys were to be "released" from the Latin requirement to take a two-year combined course in physics and chemistry. The experiment proved a success and increased pressure for change as the Science Department sought to introduce more new courses, including biology.[39]

Although the faculty as a whole laid the question of curricular reform to rest for a while, some departments did not. Saltonstall, for example, had joined the faculty in the second year of the Harkness Plan as a history instructor. He took it as his mission to bolster the position of "the social studies," by which he meant particularly history, in the curriculum. This discipline, he believed, was especially well suited to the Harkness classroom. When he became chair of the History Department in 1940, he translated his views into concrete action. Under his leadership, the number of instructors and course offerings rose substantially. "The History Department strengthened itself greatly under Salty," Vrooman recalled. "He brought in some young men who stirred things up."[40] Thanks also to interests stirred by the war, history soon became one of the most popular subjects on campus.

With these changes in the works, the faculty was ready to reconsider the possibility of curricular reform in the spring of 1941. Now ten years after its implementation, the Harkness Plan had clearly moved beyond the experimental phase to become as central to everyday life at the Academy as the Phillips Deed of Gift. The debate centered on the same issues as before — the merits of requirements vs. electives — only now with the Harkness perspective more firmly rooted in the faculty. The curriculum, it was argued, should be flexible enough to fit the aptitudes of individual students, help them discover what these aptitudes are, and make it possible for them to take sequences of courses in a variety of subjects. Although these objectives implied the need for a major remodeling of the program, financial constraints would not allow for more than some minor adjustments.[41] By the time the matter came to a vote in November 1941, the school, bracing itself for war, was even less inclined toward change, especially since it was clear that Principal Perry would retire within a few years. When the question of the Latin requirement came up, the faculty voted overwhelmingly to retain it, although Greek was now deemed an acceptable substitute.

After Pearl Harbor, impetus for reform waned as the Academy turned its attention to various emergency measures — hiring replacements for the dozens of faculty who left for the armed services and preparing students for special training and officer training programs. The so-called Anticipatory Program enabled students turning eighteen to complete their education before enrolling for the draft. The program, which ran from June 1943 to February 1944, offered courses recommended by the armed services: mathematics, physics, English, and history.[42] Adjusting the regular curriculum as well, the school emphasized mathematics and physics, taught now with a practical slant that some faculty, accustomed to the more theoretical bent of Harkness teaching, found disconcerting. The few new courses offered in this period — preflight aeronautics, navigation, and radio — were similarly practical.[43] During this period, the History Department brought the students in touch with current events at home and abroad and picked up still more devotees.

Following the war, Exeter was ready, willing, and able to resume the curricular debate. Momentum for change came from various sources: on the university level, increasing specialization and the expansion of the natural sciences; on the secondary school level, an opening up of attitudes toward education; and at Exeter, from Saltonstall's election as principal.[44] The so-called "Eight-Year Study," a comprehensive report of the most important curriculum experiment of the period, had concluded that successful preparation for college did not depend on preparation in certain prescribed subjects in secondary school; equally important, it encouraged secondary schools to continually develop and evaluate their educational programs.[45] In 1942, the College Entrance Examination Board had also decided to widen the focus of its examinations, a move that further encouraged secondary schools to broaden their curricular offerings.[46] At Exeter itself, a rise in science and history enrollments substantiated theories of individual aptitude and strengthened arguments in favor of elective choice. An additional and not insignificant factor was the initiative launched at the end of the war to diversify the student body — which strengthened the need to cater to a wider range of talents and interests (see chapter 5).

Another powerful force added to the gathering momentum for change. In the fall of 1945, a committee of distinguished members of the Harvard faculty published a study entitled *General Education in a Free Society*. Nicknamed the "Red Book" because of its crimson cover, the study devoted three-quarters of its attention to public secondary school education. Rejecting specialization in favor of a return to the more traditional liberal arts education — although without the customary emphasis on the classics — the Red Book spoke of the need to educate the increasingly diverse student body in a common cultural tradition and proposed a core curriculum built around English, the humanities, science, mathematics, and social studies. This report was the most influential of several produced in the postwar years and prompted many institutions of higher learning to develop general education programs.[47]

The Red Book received special attention at the Academy, and for good reasons. John Finley '21, the vice chairman of the Harvard committee, was a distinguished classics professor and Exeter alumnus; Thomas W. Lamont '88, a member of the Harvard Corporation, was the president of Exeter's board of trustees; and Charles Wyzanski '23, a Harvard Overseer, was also an Exeter trustee. The imprint of Exeter on the Red Book was unmistakable. What the Harvard study saw as the most important goals for the nation's high schools—to teach American youth to think, communicate, and make relevant judgments—Exeter teachers were already achieving around the Harkness Table. Several Red Book suggestions for the improvement of particular disciplines—for example, mathematics—were already in practice at the Academy. As Mathematics Department chair Philip E. Hulburd noted, "With the publication of the Harvard Report on General Education, in 1945 . . . we found that we were already a good way along the right path, since our program seemed to include most of the recommendations made. . . ."[48] However, the Harvard study was suggesting something Exeter was not doing—offering a balanced curriculum that included science and history but not Latin.[49]

The advocates of change thus had powerful arguments on their side, as well as the advantage of Saltonstall's support. But they faced the significant obstacle of a long classical tradition and a still-influential older generation who supported the requirement. When the members of the Academy Committee on Educational Aims and Practices convened in the autumn of 1945 to discuss the curriculum, they knew they were in for a long and difficult debate. Addressing the easiest task first—the various criticisms of the curriculum voiced during the past decade—they listed the problems that needed correction. Course requirements seemed heavy on the linguistic side, making it difficult for students to take a three- or four-year sequence in science or history, which had become important disciplines in their own right. Nor was there much opportunity to take courses in the arts. After several months of discussion, the committee agreed on a few requirements: four years of English, three of mathematics, three years of one foreign language, and a year of American history. Cutting down the linguistic requirement from two languages to one would give students the opportunity to take more courses in history or science. In late October 1946, the committee presented its plan to the faculty, which immediately fell into heated discussion on the issue of whether there should still be a two-year Latin requirement, with the traditionalists proposing an amendment to that effect. Finally, in mid-November, the matter came to a vote. Up to this point, Saltonstall had stayed out of the debate, preferring that the faculty make the decision themselves. Realizing, however, that the committee's proposals now faced the possibility of rejection, he spoke up:

> I shall not feel that I am being honest with my colleagues or with myself, if I maintain a judicial silence in this discussion of the curriculum. I do not wish to wait for a vote without making my position clear. Like most of you, I have thought about this question long and hard. Like many of you, I have had moments of doubt. Like nearly all of you, I have made my decision. I oppose the retention of the two-year requirement of an ancient language.
>
> I do not in any sense mean that the student at Exeter should know less of his inheritance from Greece and Rome. He should, on the contrary, know more of the art, science, thought, politics and literature of the ancients, if he is to be truly modern. My experience as a teacher does not, however, persuade me that the study of an ancient *language* should be required of all boys at Exeter. Nor do I feel that the ancient languages can fairly lay claim to any monopoly of the means of teaching disciplined thought. They have their important place in this respect, but they must share it with modern languages, mathematics, the arts and the social studies.[50]

Saltonstall's words had the desired effect. The faculty rejected the amendment 53–29 and the following week ratified the original proposal by an overwhelming majority.[51] Latin would now be an elective, along with advanced courses in science or history.

The Latin vote was more than a debate on the ancient language requirement: it was a debate on the question of whether Exeter should follow the growing trends of elective choice and specialization. Accordingly, the tally reflected the generational divide between the pre-Harkness and Harkness instructors. Interestingly, most students favored the old ways, and *The Exonian* printed an open letter to the trustees calling on them "to re-define Exeter's goals and to re-establish Exeter upon its rightful course."[52] Although the abolition of the requirement held, enrollments in Latin and Greek remained steady over the next ten years.[53]

An Era of Incremental Change

Following the vote on the Latin requirement, the Academy entered a period of incremental changes to the curriculum. New courses and departments were added to the existing framework as incoming faculty and rotating department heads brought their interests and ideas to their disciplines, and as outside pressures dictated. The expansion of the elective system did little to change the school's position on key curricular issues. But it did change its attitude toward the faculty that taught the curriculum—an attitude reflected in the creation of institutional support for faculty and in a more professional approach to faculty recruiting. The sum total of these changes was an Academy that more closely resembled a liberal arts college than a secondary school that prepared its students for one.

The postwar transformation began with a marked expansion in elective course offerings, which kept pace with growth in the student body and faculty. By 1955, the faculty numbered ninety members—more than twice its size in 1930. Regenerated by returning servicemen, some of the more "traditional" disciplines directed their attention to completing program revisions begun before the war. The Mathematics Department developed a unified series of courses that covered the subjects of algebra, geometry, and trigonometry simultaneously.[54] Science grew in popularity and enrollments reached 70 percent of the student body by the mid-1950s—a noteworthy development, considering there was no science requirement at this time.[55] Interest in other "practical" fields grew as well—Romance languages, for example, bolstered by the elimination of the Latin requirement, and history, owing to the new prominence of the United States in world affairs. The Academy became the first secondary school in the country after the war to offer a course in the history of the Far East.[56]

By the late 1940s, every major department was offering a college-level course to its top students, anticipating by several years the development of the Advanced Placement Program elsewhere. (Exeter, along with Andover and Lawrenceville, played a prominent role in the establishment of the AP program.) These courses raised the level of academic performance, resulting in "more independent work, more analysis, and more understanding."[57] Interest in minor fields rose during this period also. The transformation of the old Alumni Hall into the Lamont Gallery and new studios in the early 1950s led to a great boost in the size of the Art Department and the popularity of the visual arts on campus.[58]

Although individual departments embraced reform in this period, the school as a whole proved somewhat more reluctant to make any significant changes in the curriculum. Of the numerous reforms recommended by the Exeter Study Committee in 1953 (see chapter 4), the faculty adopted only one of major import, the appointment of a school minister—a move in line with a growing resurgence of interest in religion nationwide.[59] It was a conservative response in keeping with conservative times.

When the Cold War and Sputnik emphasized the need for national expertise in scientific fields, schools and colleges everywhere poured money and attention into developing bigger and better math and science programs. At Exeter, enrollments in science continued to grow. Yet Academy scientists refused to jump on the bandwagon, instead upholding the principles on which the department had been founded in the 1930s. Science teaching at its best, they argued, was not an elementary introduction into professional technology, but a mental discipline that taught the student how to make deductions from observable fact. They held firm to the belief that the combined physics/chemistry course then currently offered did more to promote interest in science than programs emphasizing industrial application and technology.[60]

Although Exeter chose not to expand its science program in this period, it made important innovations in some humanistic fields. In the late 1950s, the school formed a Department of Religion, giving the discipline academic legitimacy; the emphasis here, as in schools nationwide, was Judeo-Christian. In the late 1950s and early 1960s, the Department of Romance Languages expanded, adding the study of Italian as a minor course and merging with the German Department into the new Department of Modern Languages. Russian and an experimental program in Chinese joined the roster — responses to developments in the outside world.[61] These same years also witnessed the beginning of the foreign studies program — Schoolboys Abroad, a joint venture initially with Andover and later involving St. Paul's, with programs in France and Spain. Eventually, students would have the choice of studying at institutions in England, Germany, Mexico, Ghana, Russia, and China. However, Exeter's overall curriculum experienced little change at this time. It wasn't until 1962, for instance, that the school adapted a recommendation made nearly ten years earlier and added a requirement in art, music, or religion — an acknowledgement of the growing importance of these fields.[62]

As the Academy expanded and developed its elective system, it focused attention almost exclusively on the needs of its students. The other important (indeed, crucial) constituent in every classroom — the teacher — received far less attention. This was a strange oversight, considering that Harkness himself emphasized the need to provide for faculty. A portion of his gift, designated the Harkness Fund for the Advancement of Teaching in the Academy, was intended to support faculty study or travel, as well as visits to Exeter by distinguished teachers. The money, however, was used for other purposes, and the program was not implemented until after World War II.[63]

When Dick Day became principal in 1964, he knew that he would be devoting the next several years to two major undertakings critical to Exeter's future, a building program and a major capital campaign. An equally urgent problem was the fact that during the next decade the school would lose most of the Harkness generation — approximately one-third of the faculty — to retirement. As Day was well aware, it would be more difficult to replace these teachers than it had been to hire them in the first place. Faculty recruitment had changed considerably since the days of Perry, who found teachers by calling a friend or circulating an ad at the best Ivy League colleges. Donald Cole, who joined the History Department in 1947, noted, "Before I came, you would just call a few friends at Harvard or Yale and get teachers that way, or you would get teachers you knew at other prep schools."[64] As time passed and horizons continued to broaden, Exeter undertook national searches, extensive interviews, and other procedures characteristic of modern recruiting.

Meanwhile, the Academy faced another, equally challenging situation. As the Exeter community and curriculum expanded after the war, so had the faculty's needs, but without an adequate administrative structure to deal with them. Saltonstall did what he could in individual cases, but his attention was fragmented by the need to meet multiple demands.[65] The dean of the academy took care of the student, but the school lacked an equivalent leader to take care of the faculty. In 1966, Day created the position of dean of the faculty (and renamed the preexisting position the dean of students), naming classicist Ernest Gillespie as the initial occupant. The dean of the faculty became responsible for the supervision of faculty recruitment, remuneration and grants, as well issues related to teaching and advising. Over the course of the next twenty years, the dean of the faculty established various programs, including funding for faculty members to pursue additional graduate study.

During the turbulent years of the late 1960s, schools and colleges across the country tried to relate their programs to the significant social problems of the day. These efforts did not involve major curricular renovations but *ad hoc* modifications intended to meet the demands of an increasingly diverse student population. Interdisciplinary programs such as Afro-American studies and the open classroom — programs that combined learning with community service — were two of the more important outcomes of this trend. Exeter followed suit with courses on black literature and history and two programs: the Washington Intern Program, which placed a group of seniors on Capitol Hill, and the Independent Study Program, which opened up the spring term of senior year for a project of the student's choosing.[66] In addition to these electives, a full-year science requirement entered the curriculum in 1969–1970.[67]

The next step was to consider larger educational objectives. People began asking how the Academy could better prepare students for the changes society would see in the next thirty years. In its report to the trustees in May 1970, the Long-Range Planning Committee argued that Exeter needed to continue providing a broad humanistic education that emphasized not only the acquisition of information but also the ability to obtain, assess, and use information in an imaginative way.[68] It believed that skills were every bit as important as content and should receive proper emphasis in the curriculum. At a faculty meeting the following September, Dean of the Faculty Henry F. Bedford urged:

> Content, we maintain, is our business and for years it was our only business. Content is the key to classroom control, since teachers can ask questions and then approve the answers. It has been an unnerving experience to discover that increasing numbers of students, parents, politicians, columnists, and other busybodies do not accept the sovereignty of content any longer. They have brusquely declared both questions and answers irrelevant, thereby at a stroke wiping out what we have dedicated ourselves to for years. . . . For better or worse, education in the United States has chosen to appeal to the public as a useful enterprise; that is what the kids call "relevance." And the public, and their children, are no longer willing to accept uncritically some teacher's designation of what is useful. Which suggests that we ought to rethink our objectives. . . . The need to be clear about objectives and priorities, then, begins in the classroom, on the fields, and in the dormitories, where student-faculty contact begins. . . . The product must be more than formulas, forms, and facts. It must be education, and we had better know what we mean by that word.[69]

The time for a curricular review had come. Taking charge in his usual decisive way, Day established a new committee of the faculty "to decide what skills and content students at Exeter ought to learn, and then shape curricular requirements to meet those objectives."[70] During a two-year period, the Curriculum Committee addressed a number of difficult issues: whether to help students gain a learned body of information or educability, whether students should have choice in the fields they study, whether it was more important for students to gain exposure to a wide variety of fields or to do advanced work in a small number, and how to integrate the learning that takes place in the classroom with the learning that takes place in the dormitory and on the playing fields.

In 1972, the committee offered a fresh interpretation of the issue of choice vs. requirements. It recommended that the school should not only encourage choice, it should, ironically, require it. Course requirements would become the tool to ensure that every student would acquire skills and content and, at the same time, follow a program with both breadth and depth. "Basic" requirements would help students develop the fundamental cognitive skills of each discipline — reading, writing, numerical literacy, research methods, and so on — whereas "depth" requirements would encourage them to do advanced work in at least two fields of their choice. The committee also introduced two interdisciplinary programs that would emphasize skills: basic training in word and number skills for preps, and the fundamentals of verbal communication for first-semester lowers. On the other end of the interdisciplinary spectrum was the Senior School, in which participating seniors would live in one dormitory and, with faculty aid, create their own program for the year.

Although the faculty voted to accept the report of the Curriculum Committee, the reforms it advocated proved relatively minor when implemented. The school was not ready, and the faculty had not been sufficiently prepared, to consider more radical actions. These circumstances would change in a later curricular review.

The New Curriculum in the 1980s

During the late 1970s and early 1980s, concern grew nationwide that secondary schools and colleges were not preparing students for the world that awaited them upon graduation — a world characterized by rapid technological change, pollution of the environment, dwindling supplies of energy, cultural conflict, and globalization. Rather than continue to apply piecemeal measures to the overgrown elective system that had evolved since the late 1940s, educators advocated a comprehensive and balanced reconstruction of the curriculum. Leading the way in this "back to basics" retrenchment, Harvard adopted a "core curriculum" that aimed to help students to think and write effectively, understand methods for gaining knowledge, be informed about other cultures and other times, gain insight into moral and ethical problems, and attain some depth in a field of knowledge. Students would have to fulfill requirements in five basic areas: literature and the arts, history, social and philosophical analysis, science and mathematics, and foreign languages and cultures; there would also be a compulsory component in expository writing. The

program, a reaction against increasing fragmentation and compartmentaliza-
tion of knowledge in the university, marked a return to the general education
curriculum Harvard had espoused in the 1940s — with a modern slant.[71]

At Exeter, a similar story unfolded. In 1983, Principal Kurtz asked the Curriculum Committee "to create a new curriculum, not to approach the task
with revision of the present curriculum in view."[72] This was a tall order: the
Academy had not done a major curricular reassessment since 1946, and much
had changed in the interim. The composition of the community had changed
radically, with the predominantly white, Christian, and male population giving way to a group that was coeducational and racially and ethnically diverse.
College choices had become equally diverse, expanding from the narrow con-
fines of the Ivy League to more than seventy institutions across the country.[73]
The composition of the faculty had changed as well, though less pervasively.
More important, the teachers hired in the late 1960s and 1970s had views
about education quite different from those of the Harkness faculty they had
replaced.

The task of curricular reconstruction would have been difficult enough in
a school with less history behind it. But at Exeter it was nothing short of arduous. In urging the committee to start from scratch, Kurtz was asking for new
answers to the issues the school had been debating for the past fifty years —
skills vs. content, requirements vs. electives, and breadth vs. depth. "Kurtz's
charge was unusual, in that he stipulated that the proposal could not be taken
apart," explained historian E. Arthur Gilcreast, who chaired the curriculum
review. "Everything [together] had to be voted up or down. That put a real
burden on the committee."[74] At the same time — and in contrast to Day —
Kurtz favored a more open, collaborative approach to the review and allowed
it ample time — four years — for completion.

Realizing that it would be impossible "to escape 200 years of tradition and
the force of a successfully working system," the committee sought instead to
strengthen the strong elements in the curriculum and eliminate the weak.[75]
"This committee did not meditate on ideas from Mt. Olympus," Gilcreast
noted. "We spent an enormous amount of time in the first year talking to
faculty members one on one, and many of the ideas came from this process.
We drafted a proposal and circulated it among the faculty, and then spent six
months discussing it. The proposal went through three separate faculty votes."
What emerged from these discussions were some new ideas and some old
ones — a plan that addressed the needs of a diverse community while upholding the traditions of individual education and a faculty-run school.

Using language strongly reminiscent of the Harvard core proposal, the Curriculum Committee made its position clear:

> We support a return to the "basics," but we mean by that a return to a broad, liberal arts education for all students. . . . By "basics," the Committee first of all means skills. We believe our graduates should be able to read, write, speak, and listen effectively. . . . They should be able to apply mathematical and experimental methods of analysis, to identify and understand historical problems, to ask ethical questions, and to comprehend languages and cultures other than their own.[76]

Like its Harvard counterpart, the Exeter committee was critical of the lack of attention paid to the instruction of basic skills. Dedicated, however, to the tradition of individual education fostered by the Harkness Plan and sensitive to the ever-widening range of student needs, the committee was reluctant to do away with the elective system. "The school had a strong tradition of electives," Gilcreast explained. "We did not want to injure the electives system and the small departments which had become an important part of the curriculum."[77] The solution to this dilemma was a compromise to ensure students would gain a broad exposure to a variety of disciplines while allowing them some elective choice.

The committee proposed to restructure course requirements to adjust the balance in a program that still put most of its emphasis on English, mathematics, and foreign languages. It proposed to increase science and history requirements by a full year and to add lesser requirements in the arts and religion. The course load for seniors would be increased from four courses to five each term. To help them synthesize what they had learned in their years at Exeter, the committee recommended creating a Senior Studies program that would require a major interdisciplinary research project of the student's choosing. To help younger students, the committee proposed fall-term courses for preps (Junior Studies) and lowers (Lower Studies) to address imbalances in preparation and develop academic skills in an interdisciplinary context. The committee also proposed a health education course for preps that would cover subjects such as the physiology and psychology of adolescence, alcohol and drugs, exercise and fitness, and sexuality.

To accommodate all the new course requirements while retaining some choice in electives, the committee believed, it was essential to adapt a trimester calendar. The flexibility thereby gained would enable instructors to offer a variety of new courses, including a group of options open only to seniors in their last term (an attempt to remedy the so-called "senior slump"): courses on "The Beats," "Imperial Russia," and "The Greek Views of Life," to name a few. Flexibility also provided the rationale behind the creation of a daily schedule that allowed instructors to meet their classes for different lengths of time and to eliminate Saturday classes occasionally.[78]

Complementing these reforms was an administrative change. To help simplify what had become complex arrangements, the committee proposed to augment the responsibilities of the post of director of studies and to create standing faculty committees responsible for curriculum development, scheduling, and academic advising. These structures were intended to help dissolve the departmental ties that prevented the faculty as a whole from discussing and resolving curricular issues. In Gilcreast's words, they were "a way of enabling the faculty to see the whole Exeter student and the process of learning, rather than to see the student only in relation to a single discipline."[79] It was hoped that these committees would enable the faculty to consider curricular changes on an ongoing basis rather than in the massive review held each decade.[80]

After prolonged Harkness-style discussion and debate, the faculty endorsed the new curriculum in 1985, and it took effect in the 1986–1987 academic year. Some significant changes took root immediately. Science became one of the most popular subjects on campus. The school came to recognize the importance of health education and, thanks largely to Dean Susan J. Herney's emphasis on the importance of psychological health, formed a Department of Health and Human Development.

Other reforms proved less successful, however. The Senior Studies program did not flourish because it "proved difficult to staff," Gilcreast noted. "Another hope that has not materialized are the administrative reforms. The standing curricular committee was intended to keep discussion of the curriculum alive. It has been difficult to maintain because of politics, the cumbersome nature of the committee system, and the high amount of turnover. The director of studies position was designed to provoke constant questioning, but it is hard to go against the autonomy of the different departments."[81]

One reform proved particularly controversial: the trimester calendar, the glue holding the new system of requirements and electives together. While some teachers praised the schedule for giving students exposure to more courses and instructors, others complained that it gave them less time with their students and made each term seem rushed and hectic.

Although some unhappiness with the New Curriculum lingered through the administration of Principal O'Donnell, she resisted pressure to launch another major curricular review so soon after one just completed and focused instead on "the other curriculum"—teaching goodness (see chapter 4) and a reevaluation of residential life. Nonetheless, the review process played out better than it had in the early 1970s, in part because it proceeded in a spirit and at a pace more consistent with Harkness principles.

THE HARKNESS PLAN IN THE
AGE OF INFORMATION

In the 1990s, the declining cost and increasing power of new information technologies posed new challenges and opportunities for educators. Simulations, software packages, multimedia, the Internet, web casting, videoconferencing, and other tools for distance learning heralded fundamental changes in the organization and delivery of education. Every educational institution felt the impact, and it became possible for growing numbers of students to earn high school, college, and professional degrees based almost entirely on electronic-mediated learning. In the United States, home schooling—a phenomenon fueled by information technology—became the fastest growing segment in secondary education. Some pundits predicted that traditional schools and universities could become obsolete and that, at the least, the institutional shape of education in the future would look radically different from that of the past.[82]

The Academy's leaders did not agree that new technology would create significant alternatives to an Exeter education anytime soon. As Principal Tingley put it, "there are some skills, some human intelligences, that really are not addressable through electronic media, and require human interaction. These will raise the value of what we do around the Harkness Table."[83] On the other hand, Academy leaders also believed that the new technology constituted a powerful tool to enhance the Exeter experience. The Academy set about to justify this belief by following Harkness principles, as illustrated in three episodes: the introduction of information technology to the campus and classrooms; the "completion" of the Harkness Plan with curricular reforms in the Science Department and the construction and opening of a new science building; and yet another thoroughgoing curriculum review launched in the late 1990s.

The Impact of Information Technology
on Campus and in the Classroom

The first step in 1995 was the formation of a Technology Steering Committee (TSC) consisting of faculty and staff. Drawing from many sources, the TSC formulated a five-year plan to develop new services for phone, voice mail, and data connectivity for every student, faculty, and staff member. In 1998, a new associate dean, math instructor Susan Keeble, was appointed to serve as the senior Academy official responsible for technology and special projects. By the dawn of the twenty-first century, more than 850 Academy-owned and -maintained PCs were stationed across the campus. All administrative, academic, and dormitory buildings except the stadium and boathouse had been wired and every academic department was connected to the campus-wide network.

While Exeter proceeded deliberately to connect the community, it also developed polices to govern "acceptable use" of the technology. In many respects, said Dean Keeble, this was a simple thing to do. "If you excised the word 'technology' from the acceptable use policy," she notes, "it could apply equally well to any other matters on campus." The policy recognized the same norms of civility, tolerance, and respect emphasized in other official statements and expected students and other users of the system to behave responsibly. Students, for example, were reminded that "E-Book [the Academy's official policy book] rules and disciplinary responses regarding behavior such as hazing, harassment, and plagiarism are applicable to network use as well."[84]

On the pedagogical front, Exeter initiated a series of experiments with technology in the classroom. In 1995, an anonymous donor gave $500,000 to the Academy to establish a Technology Incentive Fund to underwrite experiments by faculty members. At first the fund helped individual faculty to pursue small-scale tests of new hardware and software. By 1997–1998, however, proposals were originating from whole departments "looking closely at the Harkness philosophy and examining how technology can be used to enhance that philosophy."[85] The Modern Languages Department, for example, sought support to develop new curriculum materials that could be revised and edited in the classroom and shared instantly with other classrooms. The result was a high level of collaboration among faculty as well as new materials that could not only be used at Exeter but also shared outside on the Internet. The History Department used an incentive grant to set up a computer lab in one classroom. Students could access on-line maps, visual aids, and documents that could be projected on a screen for discussion around the Harkness Table. The History and English Departments worked with software to foster collaborative research and writing. The Art Department acquired digital imaging equipment to complement its cameras and darkrooms. Expressing "a strong desire to share the materials and techniques they have developed with the world outside of Exeter," the Science Department launched a series of workshops for public and private schools in New England.

By the late 1990s, Exeter was making creative and increasingly intensive use of information technology to support its educational mission. The Academy's intranet home page posted community-wide news and schedules of upcoming events, with links to more information on particular topics. Departmental and faculty web pages carried class assignments, schedules, and news. Exeter's public web site provided a welcoming introduction to the school to prospective students and their parents and offered a wealth of information about the Academy and its activities. The public web site, along with efforts by the Science and Modern Languages departments (among others) to share learning and applications with other schools, evoked Exeter's old dream of establishing sister academies elsewhere, perhaps in the West, an inner city, and even overseas. A "virtual Exeter" was beginning to manifest the school's influence in the outside world in a more accessible and cost-effective manner. This was but a start. Predicted Principal Tingley, "we may in fact discover new markets opening up around the world as a result of our technology, once our web presence and our interactions with the rest of the world technologically become more advanced than they are now."[86]

Meanwhile, as faculty, staff, and students became more experienced and comfortable with email, the ties binding together the community on campus grew tighter and stronger. So, too, did the links between the school and the wider community. The Alumni Affairs and Development offices gained a powerful new mechanism for connecting with alumni and donors. The Admissions Office could communicate more easily with prospective students and their parents. The Communications Office could inform the public about news and events faster and more readily provide frequent updates. With email and cellular telephones, students could more easily communicate with their parents about activities, accomplishments, and frustrations. Faculty and staff noticed that feelings of homesickness among students seemed to dissipate faster than in earlier years.[87]

Looking ahead, Dean Keeble saw new technologies—wireless Internet access, electronic site security (access cards instead of keys, video monitoring, alarms and motion detectors), digital video, electronic registration, online grading and advising, electronic submission/receipt of funds, relational databases, and electronic imaging and archiving—as posing new challenges and opportunities for the Academy. And some challenges will continue: finding the time and means for faculty to explore new technology; providing and sustaining a consistently high level of support to users; and responding to new frontiers advanced or discovered by the students — "they're always a step ahead of us," says Keeble. "The changes are coming so fast," she notes, "that it's hard to keep up with them, much less budget for them." Meanwhile, Exeter will proceed using Harkness principles of inquiry and discussion and according to its own timetable. "We don't necessarily want to be on the cutting edge of new applications," says Keeble. "We want to have a technology plan that is well thought out and applications that are tested before we take a big plunge."[88]

Harkness Teaching Comes to the Sciences

In the late 1990s Exeter reaffirmed yet again the central place of the Harkness Table in the Academy's life by incorporating its principles into the design of the first major building project of the new century: the Phelps Science Center. As noted above, the Science Department was the last major frontier for Harkness teaching to penetrate, the delay due in part to the architecture of the Thompson Science Building, which had been erected just before the Harkness Plan took shape.

Featuring three large classrooms and three open space laboratories, the Thompson Science Building accommodated six instructors and about 275 students per term. It was an impressive structure, but it was not designed for Harkness teaching and, two years after it opened, too modern to renovate. This consideration combined with the science faculty's preferences for traditional, lecture-based instruction to impede the spread of Harkness teaching in the sciences. For many more decades, science education at the Academy consisted of "chalk talk" and demonstrations to students seated in rows, supplemented by weekly laboratories with individual projects.[89]

Over the years, pedagogical methods in science teaching changed with the arrival of new generations of faculty and students. Some faculty, for example, temporarily rearranged the rows of chairs to form a circle for discussion. Still, the Science Department did not formally embrace Harkness teaching. The renovation of the Thompson Science Building in 1978 modernized the classrooms (now numbering six) and laboratories but still did not redesign the space around Harkness principles. By then, the Science Department had grown to a dozen faculty members teaching the modern curriculum of physics, chemistry, and biology.

In the late 1980s and early 1990s, new information technologies prompted a fresh appraisal of science teaching at Exeter and the continuing viability of the Thompson Science Building. The first stirrings of change originated among the physics faculty. "When I arrived at Exeter in 1991," recalls physicist Scott Saltman, "we had four Macintosh computers in an open laboratory in the Science Building. Students used them for crunching numbers and some modeling of experiments," but the computers had limited impact on how physics was taught.[90] That soon changed with the advent of cheaper PCs and new interface devices—probes and sensors—to enable the computers to gather and monitor data on experiments in real time. It became possible, for example, to measure force and motion with great precision while graphing results in a matter of minutes. That, in turn, enabled teachers and students to spend more time analyzing and discussing results rather than collecting and presenting them.

In the mid-1990s, the physics faculty arranged for a bank of PCs to be installed in an open laboratory. Each instructor had access to the computers and many began routinely to devote a portion of class time to performing and interpreting experiments. Many problems were structured so that two or three students could work together around a PC and discuss results. Gradually, Harkness principles were catching on in the department.

The use of computers in teaching physics proved popular with students, and enrollments began to climb. Meanwhile, instructors in chemistry and biology also began redesigning their curricula to take advantage of the PCs. Chemistry labs, for example, could collect precise measurements of the acidity, temperature, and color of solutions; in biology, students used electronic microscopes to examine organic samples. In each instance, the technology facilitated small group discussion. Enrollments in chemistry and biology courses also began to soar.

In the winter of 1994, the Science Department faculty met with the trustees to discuss their cramped quarters and future needs. The trustees encouraged the faculty to begin planning for a new science building—a process that unfolded in a typically Exonian manner. The Department retained a consultant and met weekly for two years to review the science curriculum and consider changes. This work culminated in a new mission statement (January 1995) and program statement (May 1997). The mission statement strongly affirmed Harkness pedagogy: "The department considers the laboratory and the field to be its Harkness Table, and experiential learning to be its unifying theme."[91]

A thorough review of the science curriculum then followed. Courses were tested against the new standard of the mission statement and, if found wanting, redesigned to emphasize "the process of scientific inquiry . . . hands-on learning . . . [and] more group and cooperative learning, in keeping with the Harkness tradition." These principles, in turn, illuminated requirements for new teaching facilities: more classrooms (so that each instructor would have his or her own), larger and more flexible space, and common labs to accommodate group experiments.[92]

Impressed by the Science Department's work, the trustees in the fall of 1997 authorized the Academy to develop specific plans for a new science building. Exeter engaged Centerbrook Architects and Planners LLC to guide the process and design the building. The starting point was the mission statement, program statement, and commitment to the Harkness approach to teaching science. Once again, planning proceeded in the distinctive Exeter manner, with frequent meetings and discussions between the architects and an Academy steering committee that garnered inputs from faculty, administrators, and students. A prototype classroom featuring a Harkness Table was built in the Thompson Science Building. Representative instructors in physics, chemistry, and biology taught in the prototype space, and all of them "commented on the increased level of engagement and enthusiasm among their students as a result of having a Harkness Table in the classroom."[93] In addition, as plans took shape, a steering committee invited comment and feedback from the wider Exeter community, including alumni and trustees.[94]

Meanwhile, plans for the new facility were fairly complete, and Harkness principles informed the fundamental design of the whole building. The optimum size of the classrooms, for example, was ascertained by calculating the room needed to accommodate a Harkness Table, as well as necessary lab space. These dimensions, in turn, determined the footprint of the building as a whole.[95] It would feature twenty classrooms, with common lab space for each of the three disciplines, as well as a general multi-science lab, an open lobby, a large auditorium, and additional space for a computer science center, technicians, and specialized instrumentation. The design called for a three-story, four-level structure with the auditorium and computer science center extending from the first floor through a mezzanine. The second floor would be devoted to biology and chemistry in respective wings. In each wing, five classrooms would be grouped around a common laboratory big enough to hold two classes at once. The chemistry lab would require plumbing for water and natural gas, as well as a hooded area where students could work safely with fume-producing chemicals; the biology lab would feature a large aquatic tank to allow students to study and observe marine life. This general design was repeated on the third floor, which would house physics in one wing and a multi-science space in the other. All told, at 72,000 square feet, the new structure would be slightly larger than the Academy Building and the biggest building project on campus since construction of the Class of 1945 Library three decades earlier.[96]

The next step was to secure funding, with a budget for construction and future operating expense estimated at more than $38 million. In 1997, an anonymous donor had made an unrestricted gift of $7.5 million that was now applied to the project. Hundreds of gifts, large and small, soon followed. Peter Durham '85 donated funds to underwrite the computer science center. In 1999, Stanford M. Phelps '52 completed the campaign with a $15 million gift. An extraordinarily generous benefactor, Phelps had also funded major renovations of the stadium (1996) and Phillips Church (1998).[97] Following this gift, the new science building was named the Phelps Science Center. Construction began in 1999 with the relocation of the Wells Kerr House to Elliot Street and formal ground breaking on October 2. The Phelps Science Center opened at the start of the 2001–2002 academic year. (Phelps family generosity to Exeter continued. As noted in the next chapter, Phelps and his wife became major donors to the new student life center. The Elizabeth and Stanford N. Phelps '52 Academy Center opened in 2006.)

Deciding Not to Change

A third illustration of the continuing vitality of the Harkness Plan in the age of information unfolded in the late 1990s and early 2000s, when the faculty deemed it time once again to examine the content, process, and organization of an Exeter education. In this instance, Harkness-style inquiry and discussion yielded an informed choice against making major changes.

By the late 1990s, Harkness principles had further permeated the curriculum, not only in the Science Department but also in evaluating the effectiveness of classroom teaching generally. During the 1997–1998 academic year, for example, the faculty approved a student-initiated program to "afford students and teachers the opportunity to discuss a class before the end of the term in order to improve the teaching and learning environment." Called the Midterm Effort to Improve Classes (METIC), the program featured a Harkness discussion to assess how the class had functioned while there was still time left in the term to make changes. During the subsequent term, the Student-Faculty Relations Committee hosted a follow-up meeting to enable faculty and students to share their experiences and address specific issues.[98]

METIC proved an initial step on the path to a much more ambitious review of the curriculum. "Given the extent to which the world had changed since 1985," noted English instructor Ellen Wolff, "it seemed like an excellent opportunity to reflect deliberately on the work we do with our students."[99] Thus the Academy embarked upon a multiyear process to determine the shape of "the next curriculum." The initiative involved an open, thorough, and sustained investigation of "the many facets of learning in general, and learning at Exeter in particular—from what other secondary schools teach, to how the brain works, to the historical roots of the structure of schools today."

The initiative kicked off formally in 1999. It adopted a very broad definition of the curriculum—"all of the experiences students have under the guidance of teachers"—while focusing on such topics as "life before PEA"; curriculum and pedagogy at other secondary schools; the perspective of college students, faculty, and admissions officers; "learning about learning"; "curriculum mapping" (understanding schoolwide, week-to-week patterns in student workload); Exeter's unique culture and values; and "the structure of time" (schedules and the ways students spend their time at Exeter and other secondary schools). Participants in these inquiries were broadly representative of the community as a whole, engaging members from all departments, most offices, and a variety of backgrounds and experiences.

During the next several years, study groups prepared background papers, and committees readied a set of proposals to modify the curriculum in light of social, economic, and technological changes in the wider world. Some proposals, for example, aimed to make the curriculum more global, to take greater account of foreign cultures. Others sought to boost student exposure to computer science as well as to ecological issues and concerns.

In the spring of 2004, the faculty considered the proposals but in the end decided against making major changes. Principal Tingley pointed out that while the curriculum review did not alter the basic structure of the curriculum, it did stimulate fresh thinking about new courses and new content. Innovations and experiments are bubbling up across the departments. The Science Department, for example, developed a course called "Environmental Science and Society," while the Religion and History departments expanded coverage of Islam, and Modern Languages offered Arabic. A course in "algorithmic thinking" in Computer Sciences became a new diploma requirement.[100]

Reflecting on the initiative, historian and former dean of the faculty John D. Herney noted that "sometimes the best decision is not to change." Such an outcome is a perfectly valid result of Harkness inquiry, he added. "The curriculum review didn't result in significant changes to what we teach. But this was an informed choice. We looked at other places and listened to and considered lots of ideas and in the end, after lots of discussion, we didn't change much. But that's OK."[101]

THE CUMULATIVE IMPACT OF
HARKNESS TEACHING

In 1988, Chauncey Loomis '48, an English professor at Dartmouth, used a leave of absence to return to Exeter to reexperience the Harkness Table. What he found and subsequently recounted in *The Exeter Bulletin* stands as a ringing affirmation of Harkness teaching and learning and its benefits both to students and to the Academy. "In secondary school," he wrote,

> the lived life and the intellect should begin to come together. At age sixteen, most of the Uppers in my class, without realizing it themselves, had made the connection between the intellect and their daily lives: they were not merely smart, they also were becoming thoughtful about the phenomena of their lives — including their studies, which perhaps to their own surprise had become a vital part of their existence. That sort of thoughtfulness (as against mere smarts) is the most precious thing a school can give to a student — and also the most precious thing a student can give to a school.[102]

At the same time, it became apparent to Loomis that the power of the Harkness system lay not in a single class, course, or year. Rather, it was the cumulative impact of Harkness teaching across discipline and through the years that made the critical difference:

> Many of the public high school students I've taught at Dartmouth are as natively smart as the best Exeter students, a fact that some Exeter graduates find hard to swallow. Few, however, have had the advantage of going to a school in which virtually all of their teachers treat them as persons capable of an intellectual life, and in which virtually all their classes offer them the chance to engage themselves fully in their own education. When I taught my splendid Uppers, I was benefiting from the work done by the Exeter teachers who had taught them before me.

Finally, he noted,

> To argue well, you also have to listen well, and my Uppers did. As pleasing as their intellectual vitality was their civility. I could sense some per-

sonal animosities in the room, but they were always suppressed for the sake of maintaining discourse. A sometimes forgotten benefit of the Harkness System is that it cannot flourish unless students almost instinctively learn civility — concern for others, and at least apparent respect for what they think. I can think of no better training for civilized discourse than the classroom at Exeter, and civilized discourse must be at the core of all good education and all full lives.

Loomis's reflections distill the essence of Harkness teaching and learning, which has permeated the Academy deeply and shows no signs of abating influence. If Harkness himself could visit an Exeter classroom in the early 2000s, he would surely recognize what he had sought in making the gift: active learning, which comes from engagement with the subject at hand. Writing a short story, constructing a mathematical proof, conducting a biology experiment, or playing a Mozart sonata, the student learns the skills of reading, writing, listening, and critical thinking. Because the Harkness Plan has remained focused on the individual, it has worked regardless of the backgrounds of teachers and students or the modes of particular academic disciplines. Remarkably adaptive to the challenges of different generations, the plan has survived — and in fact, has aided in — the great expansion and diversification of the Exeter community and curriculum.

4 Forming the Morals

Each year hundreds of Exonians participate in nearly fifty clubs and projects sponsored by the Exeter Social Service Organization (ESSO). From teaching Headstart preschoolers, to delivering meals to the elderly, to serving as "best buddies" to youngsters with significant special needs, to donating blood to Red Cross drives, students on a daily basis apply the moral lessons taught at Exeter to life in the real world.

Even in the new millennium, John Phillips's statement about the union of goodness and knowledge remains the most quoted portion of the Deed of Gift and a vital part of the school's philosophy. Yet what constituted moral education and how it should be delivered changed in response to trends in religion, developments in the field of adolescent psychology, and changes in the composition of the community. The path was a difficult one, involving the reconciliation and balancing of values that often seemed at odds with one another — how to foster caring and concern for others without sacrificing the academic rigor Exeter was famous for, and how to nurture self-reliance and independence while fulfilling the guiding role that is the obligation of every boarding school. Over time, instruction based on explicit Christian precepts and coupled with an unforgiving disciplinary system evolved into a more secular and tolerant approach based on everyday living in a residential community.

EARLY APPROACHES TO GOODNESS

The only remedy for a world beset with ignorance and vice, John Phillips fervently believed, was the "improvement of youth." This "improvement" involved the imparting of "useful knowledge" but, Phillips emphasized, such instruction must be subordinate to promoting "virtue and true piety." It was important to teach youth English, Latin, and other academic subjects "but more especially to learn them the great end and real business of living." Many of the lessons of living were learned outside the classroom: teachers were expected to be models of behavior, and were liable for misconduct, and only families of "good character and licensed by the trustees" could board students. Students who misbehaved were expelled "to preserve this Seminary from the baneful influence of the incorrigibly vicious."[1] Although Phillips did not found Exeter as a church school, Puritan tenets—work hard, shun evil, and go to church—were emphasized in daily prayers and in lectures on morality or piety given every Saturday and Sunday.[2]

Although Phillips envisioned a religious appointee leading the school's efforts at moral education, the position of "Theological Instructor" was not established until the early nineteenth century, and it lapsed after only twenty years. Student demand for religious and ethical instruction remained, however, while the school's responsibility increased after the completion of the first dormitory building in the mid-1850s. Still, the Academy was slow to establish a formal advisory system of any kind. In 1856, students at Exeter established their own support system in the form of the Christian Fraternity. One of its founders later recalled, the nine student founders "were seeking at Exeter mental equipment for the work of life. They also felt the need of spiritual power to overcome in the conflict with sin; they were convinced that their religious strength would be augmented by Christian fellowship, with united prayer and religious effort."[3]

The Christian Fraternity came together each Sunday night for a meeting filled with prayer and the discussion of Bible passages. During the 1890s, the popularity of these occasions grew enormously, and it was estimated that nearly half of the students on campus attended at some point, an increase in interest "due to no sensational methods and to no official pressure, but to a natural growth of religious feeling."[4] Convinced of the need for formal religious instruction, the Academy instituted Bible classes. Over time, the Christian Fraternity evolved into a more secular organization known for its lecture series, and close to one hundred students would come regularly to hear speakers on a range of nonacademic topics: "The Right Use of Time," "Self Control," "What You Can Do for the School," and "What We Owe Our Parents."[5] In 1896, the Fraternity produced the first E-Book, a guide to rules and regulations at the Academy as well as a directory of faculty, staff, and personnel. In the early twentieth century, the Fraternity gradually expanded its focus to include life outside the school, with members teaching English to foreigners and doing volunteer work in the town's Boy Scout chapter and a mission in the West End of Exeter. Membership also expanded, reaching nearly 20 percent of the total enrollment, "quite regardless of creed."[6] After World War I, the Fraternity channeled energy into fundraising, and the proceeds went to charities all over the world, and closer to home, to the Academy's Davis Library. Catalogues of the 1930s described the Fraternity as "a group of students interested in unselfish service to the school. . . . It develops the habit of helping; in short, it stands for the fullest expression of Christian life within the school."[7] But there was no denying the increasing outward focus of the organization, which, by World War II, was devoting its efforts to sponsoring career conferences and advising students on how to find a job.

The development of student interest in moral guidance in the mid-nineteenth century also led to important changes in Exeter's disciplinary system. In 1858, as noted in chapter 2, the faculty voted that students were no longer required to study in the recitation room monitored by an instructor, but could now study on their own in their rooms. It was during this period that two enduring Exeter expressions came into vogue. The first is attributed to Principal Soule: "the Academy has no rules—until they are broken." The second, "The student bears the laboring oar," was probably the aphorism of a notoriously tough instructor. Whatever the provenance of these expressions, their message was clear: students were expected to know how to behave, just as they were expected to do their work. Left on their own, boys learned independence, discipline, and responsibility, the values that would make them into men.

The second change of critical importance came in 1873, when the trustees, wishing to ensure that disciplinary decisions were consistent, decided that the faculty rather than the principal would handle all such matters. Exeter became a faculty-run school. Although students were responsible for running their own lives, teachers were to correct lapses whenever they occurred.

The Academy took pride in giving its students more freedom than many other schools—a fact it promoted in its literature. But there was little time to exercise this freedom, thanks to the so-called "tyranny of the daily schedule": classes six days a week—a program followed since the school's founding— along with various athletic and extracurricular activities, which multiplied in number during the late nineteenth century. The 1870s and 1880s witnessed the beginning of many important Exonian institutions, including the first football game with Andover (Exeter lost), the first Exeter orchestra, and the first publication of *The Exonian*, the oldest student newspaper in the country.[8]

For some Exonians, the Academy's notion of independence had less to do with student freedom and more to do with the general absence of adult guidance. Eventually, old boys took it upon themselves to advise newcomers and, in 1904, began publishing helpful hints in the E-Books. Entitled at different times "A Word to New Students," "The Exeter Spirit," and "Points for

New Men," these instructions exhorted Exonians to "uphold the Academy's standards" and "make Exeter proud."[9] The E-Book of 1911–1912 proclaimed that "Exeter has few rules, no petty ones"[10]—an assertion that was, however, more fictitious than factual. The Academy had had extensive lists of "laws" and "customs" since its early days. "Laws" were major regulations and were to be observed to the letter; for example, "No scholar shall, in term time, go out of town without liberty obtained of the Principal, or in his absence, of the Assistant, or one of the Trustees." By contrast, "Customs" pertained to manners and were to be observed as the student saw fit: "No scholar shall, in any place, or at any time, except in wet weather, address an Instructor or Trustee with his head covered. The same respect shall be paid to all gentlemen and Ladies of distinction."[11]

From a faculty perspective, however, the classroom provided students with all the guidance they needed. As a description in 1913 put it:

> speaking generally, the Exeter class rooms . . . are in their spirit both ethical and religious. They place character above knowledge. They train while they instruct. Accuracy, the supreme virtue of a scholar, is demanded with an insistence that will not be denied. Fundamental virtues like honesty, industry, punctuality, and courtesy, are taken for granted; and an offense against any of them is punished with rigor and severity. The moral worth of the habit of clear thinking is appreciated. Slovenliness in all its forms is lashed until it smarts. Both in the class room and in the general administration of the school there is a rigidity of standard which is ethical and at the same time religious. . . . The authorities in a school like Exeter are not only *in loco parentis*; they are, in a measure, *in loco dei*.[12]

Boys who lived up to Exeter's high academic and behavioral standards thrived there and needed little guidance. Upholding ideals of strength and virility that had become popular in the late nineteenth century, the school prided itself on providing "the kind of atmosphere in which a strong, manly boy thrives and is happy."[13] This type of student worked hard on the playing fields as well as in the classroom. On the other hand, students who were less successful scholastically, or who broke the unwritten code of rules, did not last long in a disciplinary system that was harsh and unforgiving. Boys who could not make the grade (literally or figuratively) found higher-ups generally unsympathetic. "It was not a coddling school," history instructor S. Percy Chadwick noted. "At that time there was no regular pre-consideration of cases of discipline by a committee, and, if decisions were sometimes handed out in a rough and ready way . . . there was an honest striving to be just."[14] He explained:

> It has been the belief that Exeter has a special type of training, prepara-
> tory for the larger liberty of college or life. When a boy shows he cannot
> respond to that training, cannot fit into our system, restraints remind him
> of his failure and after continued failure he is removed from our midst. In
> such cases, it is my understanding that the boy has not succeeded in the
> Exeter type of school, not that the school or the system is at fault in most
> cases. . . . All boys cannot succeed in a school of large responsibility.[15]

Once again, an Exeter epigram emerged to explain the Academy's position on discipline: "liberty, tempered by expulsion."[16] Not surprisingly, more than a few boys looked for escape — physically and mentally — from a system they regarded as oppressive. Accordingly to Corliss Lamont '20, the most common infraction in those days was leaving campus without permission, with nearby Hampton Beach a perennial favorite.[17]

While drinking alcoholic beverages and possessing firearms were banned and cause for dismissal, smoking presented a more complex challenge and forced the Academy to choose between values it held equally dear. As early as 1918, a committee formed to study the matter pointed out that smoking was antithetical to Exonian standards of discipline and achievement, but pro-hibiting the habit would violate the school's long-standing tradition of free-dom.[18] Eventually, the school established a common room in each dormitory where students were allowed to smoke. The "butt room" soon became a place of escape from the adult world where students let off steam, exchanged anec-dotes, and engaged in intense discussions. Some viewed these rooms as dens of iniquity, where nonachievers sat around talking and wasting time. For oth-ers, however, the butt rooms answered a need — in the absence of a student center — that the school had not managed to fill. As evidence of the hazards of smoking accumulated in the early 1960s, the faculty "moved in the direc-tion of discouraging it" by tightening restrictions and forbidding boys under 16 to engage in the habit.[19] The popularity of butt rooms dropped, and in some cases they were converted into social rooms — a metamorphosis that occurred campus-wide after smoking was banned in 1987.[20]

As the number of boarding students grew in the 1920s, the faculty took a more active stance in disciplinary affairs, lowering the curfew from 10 P.M. to 8, and publishing the Academy's rules in the E-Book as "a few of the regu-lations . . . which may be of interest to students." Concisely stated, the rules covered a wide range of topics, including "Minimum schedule," "Permissions to leave town," and "Dishonesty."[21]

By contrast, the Academy's attitude toward moral instruction — outside of Phillips Church and daily Chapel (see below) — remained rather passive. Teaching by example seemed to be the preferred method, occurring when circumstances allowed. Corliss Lamont '20 recalled an incident, during his time at the Academy, when he informed Principal Lewis Perry that the baseball coach was baking the baseballs the night before the game to give the Exeter team an advantage. Perry called the coach into his office and demanded an explanation. The coach said, "Well, I tried to win the games, Mr. Perry, and I did win them," and Perry fired him on the spot.[22]

THE HARKNESS PLAN, RESIDENTIAL LIFE, AND MORAL INSTRUCTION

The hands-off approach to moral instruction that the Academy had employed for 150 years suddenly came under scrutiny in 1930, when the Harkness Gift forced the school to revisit many of its assumptions about education in general. Although the gift is most often associated with discussion-based learning around oval tables, it also had profound implications for life outside the classroom. By completing the transformation of the Academy into a school principally of boarders on campus, the Harkness Gift prompted Exeter to reexamine its responsibilities toward its students. Consequently, the school redefined the values it wished to instill, and its faculty's role in instilling them.

When Harkness told Perry that he wanted to fund a change that would have an enormous impact on education at Exeter, he had in mind "the forgotten boy" who was lost in the shuffle of the secondary school experience. Although the plan that eventually met with his approval concentrated on changes to individualize instruction in the classroom, it recognized the need to improve instruction outside the classroom as well. A substantial portion of the $5.8 million gift was allocated for student housing, including the four new dormitories and renovations to those existing, as well as the removal or remodeling of several wooden houses. In five years, the construction was completed, and the last of the students boarding in town moved on campus. There were altogether thirteen dormitories, housing between thirty-five and seventy students each, and eight houses, where from three to fourteen students lived. For the first time, there were accommodations for instructors with families. The number of day students dwindled to less than 10 percent of the enrollment. The Academy had become a full-fledged residential community.[23]

Now that the great majority of students were living on campus, the school had to develop and enforce consistent standards for supervision that had previously been the responsibility of the boarding houses in town. Recognition of this obligation was apparent in the so-called "House Plan" whereby each dormitory became a self-contained residential unit with resident instructors, one for every twelve to fourteen students. Preps — ninth-graders — resided in two dormitories, Dunbar and Webster, where they could be watched more carefully.[24] They would spend subsequent years in another dorm where they would have a bit more freedom and responsibility. The aim of the new advisory system was to encourage the development of a close relationship between the student and his adviser, whose role in the dormitory became as important as his role in the classroom. "As the teacher deals with separate *parts* of the boy's body and mind, the adviser should deal with him as the individual *whole*; he should be concerned about the boy's intellectual, moral, and social welfare."[25] While the new classroom configuration prepared Exonians for the college classroom, the new housing configuration similarly prepared them for residential life in college.

Recognizing that parents needed not only to guide children in their paths but also to correct them when they strayed, the Academy strengthened its disciplinary system. In 1930, Perry appointed E. S. Wells Kerr, an English master and the school's part-time recorder, as the first dean of the Academy. This full-time position was to be concerned with all student matters, including housing, morale, and discipline. Instructors were to report to the dean students who were experiencing academic difficulty or who had committed a misdeed. The student would then be summoned to the dean, who as chair of the Executive Committee would talk to him and review the matter with the two other administrators and two faculty members on the committee. In the case of major infractions, the committee would recommend a course of action to the faculty, which would make the final decision on the matter at one of its weekly meetings.

On the eve of construction of the new dormitories, the *Phillips Exeter Bulletin* assured alumni that the proposed changes would not jeopardize everything that they had known and loved (or hated) about the school:

It need not be feared that under the new system the ancient virtues of the school will be impaired. "The seriousness of living and of learning; the difficulty of learning and the willing acceptance of this difficulty; reverence for duty as the spring of all our actions; a respect for work as such; a scorn of softness; a belief in discipline, in strictest justice, and in individual freedom." This is our creed, our working principle, and we believe, our greatest asset.[26]

In September 1935, the last of the new dormitories opened its doors, and the new advisory system was up and running—but not doing what its engineers had projected. Attempts to draw students and faculty closer together were not very successful—the key reason being, ironically, that the teachers hired with Harkness money were by and large professionally trained scholars keener about academic than moral instruction. "Every student had an advisor who was always available," Herrick M. Macomber '26 explained, "but more or less the attitude was you're on your own."[27] Henry F. Bedford '48 captured what the experience of facing one's advisor was typically like: "You'd show up at the master's door and say, 'I'm having trouble with my Latin,' and he would reply, 'The thing to do is work, and the time to start is now,' and close the door. That was the tradition."[28] Students in need of a sympathetic ear often turned to the faculty wives, who were on the spot (though not the payroll) to provide sympathy.[29]

The disciplinary system was more of a success, largely because of the man running it. Kerr was, paradoxically, a warm, gracious man who disciplined students with an iron rod—a combination of qualities essential for the job. Dubbed "the Dick" (1930s-era slang for a policeman) by students, he summoned miscreants with slips of paper, "Dickie slips," that struck terror in every boy's heart. Many parents found Kerr difficult and uncompromising. After a run-in over the firing (the Exonian term for expulsion) of his son, one father walked away muttering, "Kerr by name, cur by nature." But the rules were spared for no one, including George A. Plimpton '44, who was fired three months before graduation for, as he later put it, "a multitude of sins, both academic and secular," including possession of an antique firearm. His father, influential trustee Francis T. P. Plimpton '17, pleaded with Kerr to readmit the youth but the dean was adamant. "Francis," he reportedly said in a story now part of the Academy's lore, "if you're speaking as a parent, go to Hell. If you're speaking as a trustee, I quit."[30]

During this period, overt moral instruction remained essentially religious. The relatively small number of students who came to the Academy as preps were compelled to take a course in Bible. For most students, exposure to ethical and moral issues occurred in Chapel, schoolwide meetings held six mornings a week, and in the services held at nonsectarian Phillips Church, where

visiting clergy representing various Protestant denominations delivered sermons every Sunday.[31] (Church attendance was mandatory, although students
could, if they preferred, attend services at one of the other churches in town.)
Frank W. Cushwa, a powerful teacher in the English department and a regular
visitor to the pulpit, delivered a sermon that Perry believed best summarized
the philosophy of the Academy:

> [I]n this school you will find that the goals which you will hear most about
> from us are not riches and honor and mastery, but the one that Solomon
> chose, a wise and understanding heart, understanding to discern judg-
> ment — or as we put it — the ability to think honestly, clearly, wisely, to use
> sense, to apply reason to life, to know human nature, to know yourself.
> This, we have come to believe, is a part of the rock-foundation of our edu-
> cation, that foundation on which only you can durably build.[32]

For all the talk about morals and the right way to conduct one's life, ultimately the school left it to students to figure out what it all meant. Cushwa's
favorite expression, "Every student hammers out truth on his own anvil," said
it all. Boys were expected to teach themselves about goodness — not unlike
the way the way they taught themselves about knowledge via the Harkness
Table. As one graduate explained:

> The unique character of the Academy was the never expressly stated prem-
> ise that we were expected to find for ourselves a workable personal phi-
> losophy which was rooted in our study of the best things in our common
> inheritance. It was entirely up to us to hammer out our own answers, if we
> chose to. The school did not hold up to us a formal or contrived set of rules
> which we were urged to follow; it hoped that we would find a fit and com-
> fortable standard of morality in our appreciation of our own past. We were
> singularly fortunate in our search that our presiding guides and mentors,
> Lewis Perry and Wells Kerr, were also fit models to copy.[33]

When Pearl Harbor intruded upon the idyllic world of the Academy, the
institution was ready to stand up and be counted. Thirty-three faculty members volunteered for service, among them William G. Saltonstall, and those
who stayed behind were eager to do their part as well. "In late December 1941,
I informed the Academy that I was resigning to join the armed forces," *emeritus* instructor Ransom V. Lynch '32 recalled. "I was immediately told that
there would be a position waiting for me when I got back."[34] Perry corre-
sponded with General George Marshall on the issue of whether Exeter should

conduct military drilling to prepare boys for service.[35] Students contributed in a variety of ways, raising money for Red Cross drives, donating blood, and purchasing Liberty Bonds. To solve the local labor shortage, more than seventy-five volunteers helped farmers harvest apple and potato crops, and many others chopped wood. When a heavy snowfall in January 1943 threatened to close down the Boston and Maine railroads, Exonians by the dozens shoveled the railroad yards hardest hit — one of many wartime scenes captured by John W. Knowles '45 in *A Separate Peace*. "At Exeter," the *Bulletin* proclaimed,

> the classrooms are no longer so removed from the problems and work of the world. While learning history, languages, mathematics and science, a boy may be participating in adult life and carrying his share of the load. This may go far in developing in him the perspectives and self-reliance that frequently remain dormant in less arduous times.[36]

ACTIVE APPROACHES TO CULTIVATING GOODNESS

Saltonstall returned from the war to find Exeter — and the rest of the country — in a very different frame of mind from that which prevailed when he went overseas. When he succeeded Perry as principal in 1946, postwar optimism was already beginning to give way to fears of communist subversion as American-Soviet relations deteriorated and polarized. Public schools everywhere girded themselves against the threat of infiltration, requiring teachers to sign loyalty oaths or pledges to promote patriotism.[37] Although Exeter was spared the horrors of red-baiting, the school responded to the changing climate, turning its attention formally to questions of moral education again for the first time in a decade. Taking to heart Phillips's words about the need to prepare youth to be good citizens, the Academy continued to encourage the traditional values of independence, achievement, and responsibility but expanded the definition of these concepts to prepare students to be responsible members of the community. To make this happen, the school itself took on more responsibility, increasing the amount of moral instruction through religious venues, expanding the advising system, and involving students more in the life of the school.

Each school year under Saltonstall began the way it had in past eras, with a Chapel in which the principal read from the Deed of Gift and talked about the importance of knowledge and goodness. He then went on to read the list of the offenses that could result in expulsion: hazing, cheating, and — the famous one — "reprehensible conduct with girls." During the year, Saltonstall would

address the school at Chapel once or twice every week, often discussing topics of moral import, and he would end the year in much the same way he
had started it. These were not empty rituals, explained William T. Loomis '63.
"The repetition of the message over four years really sank in."[38]

But for Saltonstall, that was not enough. He felt that the Academy needed
to strengthen and expand its methods of moral instruction:

> We are particularly interested at present, while we maintain our pursuit of
> excellence in the subject matter fields such as Latin and Art, in discover-
> ing more effective ways of teaching and measuring some of the important
> intangibles which really make a "good man and true." We are preparing
> boys for a world assailed by propaganda, prejudice, witch-hunting and
> crime. Exeter will not be worthy of its part, if it fails to help boys stand firm
> and confident in times when standards waver, when democracy is imper-
> iled by apathy, when initiative and enterprise give way to the demand for
> security.[39]

In the hope of discovering what those ways were, Saltonstall had already
set in motion three different investigations into student life outside the classroom. In his first months as principal, he had appointed a Committee on
Counseling to establish a college and career counseling program. The following year, he appointed a Committee on Student Responsibility and Faculty Relations, which recommended ways in which students could be granted
nonacademic responsibility — in the dormitories, athletics, and student organizations — that was proportionate to the near-total academic responsibility
they already enjoyed. And in 1948, the Committee of Aims and Practices at
his behest studied the advising system and reported that students felt the lack
of personal understanding and guidance.

The only concrete outcome of these endeavors was a pamphlet that Saltonstall published for advisers, a list of instructions on duties that ranged from
"improving conduct and taste — in language, in reading, in room decoration,
and in personal cleanliness and general appearance" to visiting students in
the infirmary. "The Adviser," he wrote, is not "a policeman, a big brother or
a father confessor; he is an understanding friend to whom a boy can readily
turn."[40] The choice of words — "friend" rather than "parent" — was telling.

This first attempt to provide guidance for advisers had a limited impact on
the interactions of advisers and students: resident faculty for the most part
continued to be supervisors, not counselors. Donald Cole, a history instructor
from 1947 to 1988, recalled, "In my early years in the dorm, I spent more time

enforcing the rules — from check-ins at breakfast to bed-checks at night — than I did befriending students. And I made sure students knew what the rules were."[41] Advisers were as likely to write to parents about a student's problems as talk to the student himself.[42] In this period, as in earlier times, athletics provided the best opportunity for students in search of a supportive adult, as well as valuable lessons in competition, teamwork, and sportsmanship.[43] Coaches like Ralph Lovshin and Ted Seabrook — the former memorialized by the track bearing his name, and the latter by John Irving's prose — proved immensely influential on generations of Exonians.

The Rediscovery of Religion

The Academy needed to provide moral instruction not only in the dormitories, but also in other facets of school life. The men who conducted the Exeter Study in the early 1950s expressed this sentiment clearly and cogently:

> Our school will maintain a firm belief that learning without character is dangerous, and it will therefore regard the development of character, based on religion and ethics, as being of central importance. To this end the school will emphasize moral and spiritual values in the classroom, from the pulpit, and throughout daily life. The student will be given an awareness of moral responsibility to himself, to his community, and to God. It will not be sufficient merely to develop healthy attitudes: the attitudes must harden into convictions that will lead to responsible action.[44]

While people all over the country were rediscovering religion, the Academy made an effort to return to the more religious ways of its past. The essential first step in this process, the appointing of a school minister, was not a new idea. As early as the mid-1930s, the trustees had encouraged Perry to hire one, but he never seemed able to find the right person for the job. Ironically, the matter was taken care of by Saltonstall, who as a Unitarian did not himself satisfy the Deed of Gift requirement that the principal instructor be a member of the Church. A firm believer nonetheless in the importance of Christian education for the development of character, Saltonstall fulfilled the trustees' vision and in 1952 appointed the Academy's first school minister, the Reverend George E. Beilby, Jr., of the Congregational Church at Williams College.[45] While providing religious leadership for the Academy community, this appointment announced to the outside world that Exeter was still a Christian school.

With the arrival of Beilby on campus, the Academy resumed a religious fervency it had not known since the late nineteenth century. In addition to making the morning Chapel service a more religious experience, the school maintained and strictly enforced the church attendance requirement. In 1953, the school established the Benjamin Abbot Society, a religious discussion group that met with faculty members and visiting preachers.[46] It was hoped that the return to religion would prepare Exonians for life in the real world. For Beilby, it was "very appropriate that the Academy, at this time of international crisis with its resulting feeling of fear and insecurity, pursue with a renewed vigor the task of confronting students with the articles of faith so necessary to the heart and mind of a people born to be free."[47]

The students, however, did not see it that way. Few signed up for Bible classes, and many complained of the unduly demanding church attendance regulations. Beilby, the *Exonian* opined, "never became more than the titular center of Exeter religion . . . because the loose, intellectualized Exeter community is not receptive to organized religion."[48] When Beilby resigned in the spring of 1956 to assume a church position, the Academy found a successor more accustomed to an academic environment. The Rev. Robert R. Wicks, former dean of the chapel at Princeton, urged the school to expand its concept of religious instruction to include academic study of the subject. Under his aegis, the school supplemented its Bible offerings with courses on Judeo-Christian ethics, entitled "Biblical Thought in Relation to Modern Problems" and "Greek and Hebraic-Christian Understanding of Human Values." In 1958, Exeter established a Department of Religion with Wicks as chair — a move that gave religious instruction the same legitimacy as the more traditional academic disciplines.

Although most of its efforts to strengthen the delivery of moral education were focused on religious venues, the Academy also made its first foray into the field of professional counseling during this period. At the urging of school physician James T. Heyl, in 1949 Exeter appointed its first psychiatrist, a resident-in-training in the Harvard medical system who visited the campus once a week to meet with students. The following year, the Academy hired clinical psychologist Lovick Miller, who introduced the faculty to the concept of group dynamics, providing new insight into the way personalities affected the functioning of a class. The focus of the new "psychiatric program" was not limited to boys who were having difficulty in school or otherwise seemed troubled. Its aim, rather, was "to help in every way to make the Exeter experience of maximum benefit to every boy — from the point of view of his scholastic growth, physical, social, and emotional growth."[49] The founding of the Senior Counseling program in 1955 added a new element to the program—the student. Functioning as a counselor to three or four new students in his dormitory, each participating senior would reassure homesick new boys, alert faculty advisers to potential disciplinary problems, and keep an eye open for dormitory disturbances. The program thus provided support for new students while instilling a greater sense of responsibility in the seniors who took part.[50]

Counseling took another step forward in 1958, when Heyl, wishing to improve the overall quality of health care and, at the same time, to make Lamont Infirmary eligible for payment from parents' insurance plans, convinced the trustees to have it converted into a licensed hospital. When writing the by-laws, he expressly provided for the confidentiality of medical and psychiatric records—and became the first faculty member at the Academy to be granted this privilege. "The trustees were very supportive," Heyl recalled. "They encouraged me to make sure there was some place for boys to go."[51]

Heyl's efforts to establish a counseling program at the Academy dovetailed with a burgeoning of interest in developmental psychology nationwide. During the late 1950s and early 1960s, scholars and counselors such as Jean Piaget, Lawrence Kohlberg, and William G. Perry, founder and director of Harvard's Bureau of Study Council, proved increasingly influential in shaping new views of adolescence and moral development. Their work incited a group of forward-minded instructors at Exeter to search for ways to provide better support for students. Led by Richmond Mayo-Smith, the Counselling Committee met several times in 1959–1960 with Harvard's Perry.[52] That same year, the Research Planning Committee, also led by Mayo-Smith, conducted case-study research that provided new insight into the pressures students had to contend with in the academic and nonacademic spheres of life at Exeter.[53]

Despite growing recognition that adolescents were not young adults, Exeter found it difficult to adjust its standards accordingly. Its leaders realized that the school's arduous regimen and high standards were responsible for much of the pressure and unhappiness students felt, but they found it difficult to abandon or modify the work ethic that had become thoroughly engrained in the institution. As students were fond of saying, the words inscribed on the Academy Building, "*Huc Venite Pueri, Ut Viri Sitis*,"[54] meant "Come here, boys, so that you may become weary." In lieu of lightening the workload, the school unwittingly provided a safety net for times when it was too much to handle. The night before a paper was due, students feeling particularly oppressed could check into the infirmary, along with their notebooks and typewriters. Lying on their beds, they would hold their thermometer to the reading lamp that had been provided long enough to get a temperature of 101 or so — which enabled them to skip class the next day and use the time to complete the assignment.[55]

In general, the Academy took a dim view of students who did not live up to its strict standards — standards embodied in its dean, Wells Kerr, for nearly twenty-five years. Respected by faculty and revered by students, Kerr proved a hard act to follow. His successor, Robert N. Cunningham, who became dean in 1953, was decidedly less authoritarian, favoring a more lenient system in which counseling was as important as discipline.[56] Despite pervasive dissatisfaction with Academy life — an attitude labeled "negoism" by Exonians of the period — students still wanted a Kerr-like dean. Tensions came to a head one spring morning in 1956, when they shouted Cunningham down in the middle of a Chapel address, forcing him to relinquish the podium to Saltonstall. Cunningham resigned shortly thereafter, and some believed this event contributed to his decision.[57]

The next dean, Robert W. Kesler, came from the mold that the old guard knew and liked. The embodiment of moral rectitude, he often read aloud and discussed Biblical passages in morning Chapel. "He had a great stentorian voice which was perfect for that sort of thing," Loomis noted. "He talked about Jonah and the Whale certainly more than once during my time there. Over the four years, those sermons — the beauty of the language and the cadence with which he delivered it — made a real moral and cultural impression on me."[58]

Kesler was best known, however, for his role as school disciplinarian. His no-nonsense approach inspired concern and fear in students, regardless of the seriousness of the misdeed — whether it was failing to complete math homework or returning from vacation smelling of beer. "Kesler was totally moral and ethical," noted the Reverend Edward S. Gleason '51, school minister from 1967 to 1971, "but he couldn't communicate with the students the way Wells Kerr could."[59]

During Kesler's deanship, the school made a few notable attempts to involve students more in the disciplinary system. In 1961, the Academy established the Senior Proctor Program, the disciplinary equivalent of the Senior Counseling Program. The following year witnessed the formation of the first student-faculty committee, the John Phillips Committee, which devoted its efforts to encouraging the development of civic responsibility in the Exeter community.[60]

Kesler had some serious disciplinary problems to keep him busy, with alcohol consumption heading the list. According to the Attrition Book, an official record of student departures, in the late 1950s and early 1960s, approximately half of the students fired for disciplinary infractions had been caught inebriated or with liquor on their breath. Other "major offenses" (infractions deemed serious enough to result in expulsion) that were popular in those days were gambling and going out of town without permission, with occasional firings for plagiarism or cheating on an examination.

Although the list of major offenses was set in stone, the treatment of minor infractions was a source of continuing debate in meetings of the faculty and student council. A major issue during the Perry and Saltonstall administrations was the regulation banning radios in students' rooms. Beginning in the early 1930s, discussions of what constituted a radio and why phonographs but not radios were permissible filled many a Student Council docket. Student protest of the prohibition hit its stride during the late 1950s and early 1960s — not coincidentally, the blooming-time of rock and roll — and the Academy finally conceded in 1963. "We had to give in on that because students were so clever at secreting the radios that we couldn't catch half of them," Cole recalled. "The very day we made the announcement, half the students had them in their rooms."[61]

During the Perry and Saltonstall administrations, the Academy readjusted its thinking on moral education in significant ways. As the school assumed more responsibility in forming the morals of its students, the advisory system born of the Harkness Plan came to include career and psychological counseling for students, advising for faculty (albeit on a small scale), and a program in which students did the counseling. The findings of adolescent psychologists inspired thoughts on how the system could be improved, though it would take an entirely different set of circumstances for these thoughts to bear fruit.

CRISES AND SOLUTIONS

In the 1960s, with new actors on the scene and amid growing social unrest and activism across the United States, the terms of the debate on moral education began to shift at the Academy, where the church attendance requirement was the focus of discussion. By accommodating the demands of its students to abolish mandatory church, the Academy avoided the rebellions that shook several other prep schools in this period. What some viewed as a temporary expedient also had more profound consequences, forcing the school for the first time to assume full responsibility for fostering goodness in its students.

The Church Attendance Requirement

The shifts in attitude that culminated in the church attendance controversy date back to the early 1960s. When Mayo-Smith left Exeter in 1961, the interest sparked by his committee's findings left with him. It would take another two years—and prodding by an outside source—before Academy officials paid serious attention to the implications of his research. In June 1963, the Harvard Health Services organized the first Counseling Institute for Independent Schools, held at the Northfield School for Girls. The Northfield Conference's emphasis on the need for adolescent counseling raised important doubts about long-standing Academy traditions: Did the policy of "liberty tempered by expulsion" help students to mature faster? Did the faculty work so hard to encourage self-reliance that students came to believe them to be cold and indifferent?[62]

Predictably, Exeter's response to the questioning of its traditions was to adjust and expand them to suit the times. Science instructor C. Arthur Compton noted,

> We have a long and great tradition of individual responsibility. But we have not been so forward looking in our concern for the collective areas of life. In this sense we, in my opinion, have fallen behind. . . . Man must, after all, live in society and his own worth depends upon his ability to resolve his own needs with those of his society.[63]

Making student responsibility a top priority, Acting Principal Gillespie gave the Student Council authority over all extracurricular activities as well as "the right to serve as arbiter in student problems."[64] The newly empowered Student Council soon extended the scope of its activities, and in 1964 helped establish the Student Judiciary Committee. "Stud Jud," as it was called, functioned mostly as an advisory body to students who had committed disciplinary infractions.[65]

When the Academy Planning Committee (headed by Compton) studied the various facets of school life, it laid special emphasis on the importance of fostering goodness.

> Exeter's traditional emphasis on academic excellence must be maintained but better balanced by more effective attention to the boy's non-academic life. The student finds new meaning in education as he comes to realize that academic success is not its sole or even main purpose. To reach this understanding, he must have the satisfaction of an increasing sense of participation and responsibility in the community.[66]

One way of fostering responsibility, the APC suggested, was to create programs like the Academy Student Service Program, a work program in which students would do light maintenance work in dormitories or on campus grounds, and "Quarter Off," a program which would allow a student to spend a term off campus doing social service work. The APC also made some amendments to a program in which the entire school took part. It proposed, for example, that the school rename its daily meetings, from "Chapel" to "Assembly" — a change that the trustees eventually approved (see below). This was one of many signs of Exeter's growing secularization. Removing religion from moral instruction, however, was an entirely different — and inconceivable — matter. Convinced that corporate worship was essential for giving knowledge an ethical framework, the Committee upheld the church attendance requirement.[67]

The APC proposals charted the course of moral education that Exeter was to take over the next few years. A strong supporter of public service, Principal Day worked with Colin Irving and other administrators to figure out ways to teach social responsibility.[68] The first step was to create role models, and Chapel soon became a showcase for people doing good deeds in the outside world. The school also established the prestigious John Phillips Award to honor alumni who, in their service to society, best exemplified the selflessness embodied in the motto *non sibi* (not for oneself).

Then came the second step: creating opportunities for social service. Tapping into student interest in the growing urban crisis, in 1966 the Academy started a tutoring program in inner-city Boston, the Roxbury Wednesday Program. The following year, students established a much larger program based at the Academy itself, the Exeter Student Service Organization (ESSO — subsequently Exeter Social Service Organization). With the school minister as its sponsor, ESSO revived many of the Christian Fraternity's programs and created several others. Over the years, the number of programs and participants would grow rapidly, and by the early 2000s, ESSO would have more participants than any other organization on campus. Once a term, ESSO sponsored an assembly dealing with some aspect of community service, and school minister and ESSO adviser the Reverend Robert H. Thompson '72 spoke on the importance of volunteering. "ESSO provides the best opportunity to put into practice what Exeter teaches," he later noted. "This is very important to communicate to students."[69]

While the creation of social service programs was something everyone at the Academy agreed on and participated in, the APC's proposals concerning the church attendance requirement inspired reactions of a quite different order. As activists on college campuses challenged the Establishment and its values, students at Exeter challenged the assumption that religious instruction was essential to a moral life. Opposition to mandatory church had been building since 1961, when the Student Council Religion Committee began looking for acceptable alternatives.[70] The APC report was a signal that it was time to try again. Soon after its publication in early 1965, the Student Council petitioned the faculty to give all students, not just upperclassmen, a choice of church services. In the spring of 1966, the Student Council Religion Committee polled students and reported that more than 80 percent of the student body was opposed to the church attendance requirement, and "the great majority" of the more than fifty faculty interviewed were "sympathetic and concerned about the problem."[71] Arguing that the church requirement was too narrowly Judeo-Christian in its focus, the student committee urged the school to abolish it entirely.

Concerned that this tide would rise too high,[72] Day at once established a committee of faculty and seniors to study the issue. After much discussion, the committee, led by school minister Frederick Buechner, a Presbyterian minister and an avid supporter of the church requirement, reaffirmed the Academy's commitment to exposing students to Judeo-Christian traditions. Those proved Buechner's final words on the subject, as he left the Academy the following year to devote more time to writing. His replacement, the Reverend Edward S. Gleason '51, an Episcopalian minister, took a more liberal view of the church requirement. As turmoil over similar requirements at Andover and St. Paul's, threatened to engulf those schools,[73] Gleason persuaded Day that Exeter should not sit idly by. "He gave me the support I needed to prevent a revolution," Gleason recalled, "but he also made it clear that if I failed, I'd be fired that same day." Day's solution was simple: "All you have to do, Ted, is create services the kids want to attend."[74]

At Gleason's suggestion, Day appointed two faculty-student committees, one to study the state and place of religion at the Academy, and the other to address the question of worship and liturgy at Phillips Church. After deciding in favor of abolishing the attendance requirement, the committee on religion turned to the more serious issue at hand: the need to bridge a yawning "generation gap" and restore a broader sense of community. The successful interactions of the members of this committee over the course of the year led to, and were a model for, Human Rights Day on May 1, 1968, a day set aside for faculty-student seminars in the wake of the Martin Luther King assassination (see chapter 6).[75]

Later that month, trustees followed the Religion Committee's recommendation and put an end to mandatory church attendance, replacing it with voluntary participation in worship geared to student needs and the further development of an academic religion curriculum.[76] At the same time, the trustees voted to rename Chapel as Assembly and reduce meetings from six to four times a week, "to improve communication and encourage relevancy." Meanwhile, renovations to the hall in the Academy building increased capacity to hold 1,000 people.[77]

Ironically, while many students referred to the elimination of the church attendance requirement as "abolishing religion," it actually led to increased interest in spiritual matters. In 1968–1969, an average of 200 of the 825 total student body attended the weekly service in Phillips Church, whose architectural renovations — pews moved to face each other — enhanced a sense of community. The Deacons, student leaders of the church, played a major role in planning and conducting the services, and the school minister provided spiritual, ethical, and personal guidance. The church was now a parish. That year, some 200 students enrolled in courses like "Ethics and Modern Society," "Ethics and Selected Social Problems," and "Major Themes of Biblical Faith."[78]

No less important, Phillips Church became a forum for views on salient political and social issues. "One of the greatest days was 15 October 1969, when there was a national moratorium held against the Vietnam War," Gleason recalled. "Classes were canceled and the students fasted, held a service, and maintained a silence all day — activities that all emanated from the church."[79] Like the Academy as a whole, Phillips Church was adapting to the demands of a new era.

When Gleason left the Academy in 1971 to become headmaster at Noble and Greenough School, Day found a replacement who would keep the Academy moving in the same progressive direction: Daniel W. P Morrissey, a Catholic priest who had spent years in various university settings before coming to Exeter as assistant minister in 1970–1971. Morrissey's initial appointment was not controversial at the Academy, although his promotion raised some issues, including the Deed of Gift's stipulation against hiring non-Protestants, and the old guard's objections against "moving in a direction that was not Exeter." While Day was ready to ignore the wishes of his more conservative colleagues, he could not ignore those of the founding charter. So determined was he to make this appointment that he considered having the Deed of Gift amended by the New Hampshire legislature — a move that, thanks to the state's anti-discrimination laws, turned out to be unnecessary.[80]

During the early 1970s, in the attempt to create opportunities in the weekly schedule for spiritual reflection and contemplation, the school started setting aside a thirty-minute period on Thursday mornings for voluntary "services" at Phillips Church. Initially a traditionally religious session with prayers and hymns, "Meditations," as they came to be called, soon became a time in the week when individual faculty members read aloud an account of an extremely personal, often profoundly spiritual, experience. (The same period also witnessed the beginning of the nondenominational Tuesday Evening Prayer.) In the 1980s, Meditation "speakers" came to include adults from the broader Academy community and members of the senior class. Attended by 100 to 150 students and adults, Meditations provided an opportunity for the Academy to encourage the values of "clear cogent expression, observation and contemplation, respect for others, and a sense of the complex interrelatedness of humankind."[81]

Disaffection, Drugs, and Discipline

With the end of mandatory church in 1968, students breathed a sigh of relief—a sigh that was not, however, shared by faculty and administrators, as they now faced anew the question of what constitutes moral instruction and how it should be delivered. It soon became apparent that there were no easy answers. Devised in simpler times for inculcating boys with traditional virtues, the existing advisory and disciplinary systems proved inadequate to deal with the social, political, and moral issues of the late 1960s and early 1970s. At the same time, the advent of coeducation raised new questions about the school's role in fostering goodness (see chapter 6).

Although the debate over the church attendance requirement occupied the minds of faculty and administrators in the mid-1960s, they gradually became aware of the development of another problem that had the potential to rend the fabric of the community and that proved far more difficult to solve. Like adolescents everywhere, Exeter students had proved adept at finding ways to escape the pressures of school and flout authority. In the 1950s and early 1960s, there were the "negos"—the Academy's equivalent of the Beat Generation—disillusioned and dissatisfied students who sought solace from the trials and tribulations of daily life in the local butt room. Some students chose alcohol as a means of escape. In the late 1960s, however, increasing numbers began experimenting with marijuana, LSD, and other mind-altering substances.

The more widespread the problem became, the more it challenged traditional methods of advising and discipline. For over thirty years, the academically oriented Harkness generation had perpetuated the values of independence and self-reliance and the hands-off approach to advising that helped foster those values. During the mid-1960s, the Academy Planning Committee and consultants from Booz Allen had suggested the Academy place more emphasis on advising—the former stressing the need to find and train teachers to be effective advisers, and the latter stressing the need for hiring professional counselors. These suggestions, however, went largely unheeded. Principal Day and many senior faculty, recalled school physician Heyl, did not agree that Exeter ought to provide more counseling.[82] Thus the Academy continued to deal with drug and alcohol cases through the disciplinary system.

Students caught with drugs or under the influence were fired. In the course of the 1960s, the number of expulsions rose dramatically. And it was clear that many more transgressors went undetected: as a poll taken in 1968 revealed, 28 percent of Exonians schoolwide (40 percent of seniors) had tried marijuana on or off campus.[83] In true adolescent fashion, students treated the stringent disciplinary policy as a challenge and devised ways and places to indulge without being caught.

Such behavior caused serious strains in the community, as some students lied to peers, teachers, doctors, and therapists—anyone who could report them to authorities. Advisers found themselves in a difficult position. According to Heyl, they wished to observe "the posture of trust and consequent obligation . . . [and] to respect the word of a student even if he chooses to lie in order not to incriminate himself."[84] Students in search of someone they could really confide in could go to Reverend Gleason, one of the few faculty members not compelled to report them to the dean's office. Not all who sought his advice were involved in the drug scene. "I became a focal point for students who wanted to do something responsible for their friends," Gleason recalled. "This way they could talk to an adult about it, and I would allow them to go off and work with their peers to get them to stop using drugs. A lot of that happened in a quiet and very responsible way."[85]

Gleason's work provided the impetus for an institutional response. In 1968, a subcommittee of the Counseling Committee reviewed the school's "authoritarian" advising and disciplinary systems with "the aims of improving communication between faculty and students and giving students more responsibility."[86] The committee's proposals resulted in various sorts of innovations, including programs in drug and sex education, an expansion of the Stud Jud's role in the disciplinary process, and instruction for faculty that went beyond the "Handbook for Advisers." The school also made hazing first on the list of major offenses because, unlike other infractions, it inflicted harm on other people. But the reform with the greatest impact was the Discretionary Rule, which gave faculty the authority to decide which infractions to report to the dean's office.[87] Students hailed the Discretionary Rule as a major breakthrough, and communication on campus, especially in the dormitories, improved immediately.[88]

But a single rule could not work miracles. The firing of three prominent athletes in 1970 for drinking once again underscored the need for the school to take a more active role in the realm of moral instruction. In its report to the trustees that year, the Long Range Planning Committee issued the most far-reaching statement yet:

> In the purposes of Exeter the component of "goodness" is harder to define, but it will surely assume a greater relative importance in the future than in the recent past. Exeter has tended to assume that a loose rein, rigorous intellectual training, and a mandatory program of competitive athletics were enough to build character, if not actual "piety and virtue." This assumption has undoubtedly been correct as far as it goes. Hard work will always have a part in the formation of character. In the future, however, the Academy will have to apply the same resources, the same effort, the same careful planning to the development of character as it does to the field of intellectual training rather than simply assume that one inevitably follows the other. It is actually here that the greatest challenge lies, the greatest opportunity for the Academy to do something unique in the field of education in the years immediately ahead. We shall be seeking ways to teach young people to find the modern equivalents of "piety and virtue," to find them early in life rather than after years of painful trial and error.[89]

Teaching virtue was the greatest challenge, primarily because no one could agree on what that meant. To Arthur Compton, it meant applying the same standards of excellence as those applied to academic achievement:

> This is an extraordinary school; and if we begin to accept ordinary patterns of behaviour [sic] or normal levels of performance, we will have lost our justification for continued independent existence in a society that cannot afford exclusive education unless it provides something unique and positive. We must remember that this cannot be the right school for everyone. And if we try to make it so, we will simply reduce it to nothing.[90]

Translated into practical terms, this attitude led many faculty to advocate continuance of the policy of immediate dismissal for students who used drugs. But this policy came under fire from post-Harkness teachers, some of whom had tried drugs in college and were more tolerant of the practice. Faculty discussions of drug cases became rife with generational conflict. The only point on which everyone could agree was that the school had a real crisis on its hands. As Heyl later recalled,

> There was panic at the top. Parents worried at a distance and the administration worried that this is going on in this school. There were disturbed faculty members, but they were disturbed at the level of irritation or, "Is it my role to do this? Must I snoop in this room at night? Am I a detective instead of a dormitory man?" The rebellion was a very real one. Drugs were the instrument as much as anything else.[91]

The faculty explored various alternatives, including a "one mistake" policy that would make it possible for the student to learn from the misdeed.[92] At the urging of Dean of Students Donald C. Dunbar, in the early 1970s Exeter modified the disciplinary process in some important ways. From then on, all underclassmen placed on disciplinary probation had to write their own accounts of the behavior that caused them to be placed on probation and a list of reasons why they should be permitted to return to the Academy the following year. Second, students appearing before the Executive Committee to discuss their cases could bring in a friend — often a student proctor — and a faculty member — often their adviser — to speak on their behalf, whereupon the committee would present the case to the faculty. Third, the Executive Committee now consisted of seven teaching faculty, and its chair, rather than the dean of students, presented disciplinary cases to the faculty at large. "As a result of these reforms, students began to feel that they would have a fairer go in the disciplinary process," Dunbar explained. "At the same time, the faculty now had the feeling that it was *their* Executive Committee and their vote counted. The administration no longer dictated what happened."[93]

The advising program fared less well. Despite the admonitions of the Long Range Planning committee, the Academy did little to strengthen its advising program at this time. In fact, as financial pressures mounted in the mid-1970s, the already inadequate counseling program was the first to be cut — a sign of institutional priorities that was impossible to misread.[94]

Meanwhile, another development, the advent of coeducation, introduced new challenges. In the fall of 1971, the disparity in the male and female dress codes became a major source of student dissatisfaction. Following in the foot-steps of Andover students, whose protests a year earlier had led to the elimi-nation of the coat-and-tie requirement,[95] Exeter's Student Council proposed various alternatives, all of which the faculty resoundingly vetoed. When plans for a student boycott raised the specter of crisis, Day appointed a joint trustee-faculty-student Special Committee on Shared Responsibility "to dis-cuss student-faculty communication" and "to define and seek out areas in which students may share responsibility for the daily life of the Academy"—not the first time a committee had been set these tasks.[96] They quickly reached a solution—informal dress for Sunday dinner—a way of soothing passions without sacrificing a rule the school was determined to retain.

A second issue was larger in scope and its ramifications took somewhat longer to resolve. As soon as girls arrived on campus in 1970, it became appar-ent that existing visitation rules were obsolete. In addition, students needed a place to socialize outside of the dormitories.[97] Although the concept of a social center was by no means revolutionary, the reasons behind it at Exeter were. To make coeducation work, the Academy needed a common meeting place where large groups of boys and girls could mix and mingle. It needed to make "a distinction between formal academic instruction and informal personal development," argued Associate Dean of Students Thomas C. Hayden. It was important to have a place "for boys and girls to meet apart from . . . the Hark-ness classroom" and for "the faculty and students to come together as equals . . . in a time of flux and uncertainty."[98] In 1972, the old Davis Library became home to the new Student Center. Housing a game room and the headquar-ters of various student organizations like *The Exonian*, *Pean*, and Stud Jud, it provided a place for casual social interaction as well as structured activities like coffee houses, folk concerts, and poetry readings.[99] According to Susan J. Herney, then associate dean of students, the creation of the Davis Student Center marked "increased awareness of the importance of student activities in the life of the school."[100]

Although the Academy devoted a great deal of energy to improving moral instruction during the late 1960s and early 1970s, meaningful change and progress proved slow in coming. Attempts to improve the advising and dis-ciplinary systems made little progress due largely to disagreement among the faculty and administration about what needed to be done. In this period of discontent, many people recalled Acting Principal Gillespie's parting words to the Class of '67: "It is nearly time for you to be off," he had said. "You have a lot to do. This is no time to concern ourselves with nostalgia. As a matter of fact,

I don't believe anybody ever made the claim that Exeter is a warm nest."[101] Widely misquoted and misinterpreted, the phrase "Exeter is not a warm nest" became the rallying cry of advocates of change, and defined a central issue for the next administration.[102]

WARMING THE NEST

In 1974, the trustees charged Day's successor, Stephen Kurtz, to make Exeter "a happier place." Professionally and personally, Kurtz was the ideal candidate for the job of warming up the Academy. A scholar of early American history, he revered the Deed of Gift as a historical document vitally relevant to modern times. A religious man who once considered a career in the ministry, Kurtz viewed his role as principal as "a kind of lay ministry without the collar" at a time when the church's role in many students' lives was on the wane.[103] Committed to providing students with emotional and moral support, this "new man" of the 1970s — sensitive, emotional, and empathic — also wanted Exeter to stop taking itself so seriously, pursuing academic rigor to the exclusion of moral education.[104] "Knowledge without goodness," he later recalled, "was in need of attention."[105]

Shortly after arriving at the Academy in the summer of 1974, Kurtz wrote a letter asking the faculty one question: If Exeter were to go broke, what is the one thing they wanted to see preserved at any cost? The vast majority of the eighty-seven responses indicated that the faculty wanted to preserve the school's academic standards at all cost and did not want to see that excellence slip in any way. Kurtz realized that his first task — albeit a large one — was to promote "an attitude that promoted achievement without sacrificing physical and psychological well-being."[106] He appointed a faculty-alumni committee to study the school's health services, and a student-faculty committee to study the role of students in the nonacademic life of the Academy.

While these investigations were in progress, events on campus gave the proponents of radical change an even greater sense of urgency. In December 1975, a lower-middler boy committed suicide and two others attempted it, stunning the community and prompting Kurtz to a fast response. He immediately appointed the Student Life Committee "to investigate the allegation that we have not recently achieved the same high standards in the quality of student life in the dormitories and in student-faculty relations as we have in the quality of academic achievement," and "to determine what may be done to improve the quality of life at the Academy without weakening academic standards."[107] This initiative was also in keeping with the times: the Watergate scandal and subsequent revelations of illegal corporate activities, *Newsweek* reported, have dealt the United States a shock comparable to Sputnik, "and this time educators have responded with demands for the teaching of morality in the classroom."[108]

During the course of 1976, the different committees appointed by Kurtz reached more or less the same conclusion: the Academy needed to put more emphasis on fostering goodness. For the Health Services Committee, this meant establishing a counseling program; for the Student Life Committee, it meant Saturday night visitation hours, educational programs on sex and drugs, training in counseling for faculty, and a revised Discretionary Rule that guaranteed confidentiality of student-faculty conversations on disciplinary matters. As in the past, however, faculty members who observed infractions still would be compelled to report them to the dean's office.[109]

Kurtz had heard all he needed to hear. At his urging, in the summer of 1976, Dean of Students David E. Thomas appointed Joseph E. Fellows III '62 the school's first full-time professional counselor. Fellows at once directed his attention to changing "the system that teaches that the student *alone* bears the laboring oar"—and providing support to students in need.[110] The demand for Fellows's services proved so great that a second counselor, Jill Nooney, was hired a year later. In addition to providing individual therapy, Fellows and Nooney set up dorm discussion groups, proctor workshops, and listening skills training groups. They also created a number of programs for teachers—workshops, support groups, and faculty-student discussion groups—to do what the Handbook for Advisers could not. It was hoped that these programs would "guide the faculty toward the new sensitivity."[111]

This would not be easy. The evaluation committee of the Commission on Secondary Schools of the New England Association of Schools and Colleges noted in the autumn of 1976 that:

> the quest for academic excellence sometimes crowds out the quest for moral excellence. . . . [There is] a strong tendency for faculty to assume that knowledge and goodness were almost completely interchangeable concepts and to restate any question about "goodness" as though it were a question about "knowledge." Indeed, academic excellence is taken by some as the equivalent of moral excellence. This is not the vision of Dr. Phillips.[112]

One way to redress the imbalance in perspectives and also signal institutional priorities was to use a mode of discourse familiar to academicians, the conference. In honor of the upcoming Bicentennial, the faculty and trustees decided to hold a series of summer institutes for teachers on subjects of critical importance. At Kurtz's insistence, the first, held in 1978, was to concern the teaching of morality and the communication of values. Organized by English instructor Charles L. Terry, the Bicentennial Summer Institute on Moral Education featured as speakers three leading experts on moral development — Theodore R. Sizer, head of school at Phillips Andover; Lawrence Kohlberg, director of the Center of Moral Education at Harvard; and Douglas H. Heath, a Haverford professor and prominent clinical psychologist — as well as instructors from Exeter and several peer schools. While providing the first extensive opportunity for reflection on the teaching of goodness, the institute highlighted two diametrically opposed but equally important methods for doing this. The first, the didactic — "direct teaching, usually in the form of structured classes or meetings" (usually schoolwide meetings) — stood in direct contrast with the second, the contextual — "learning that emerges from a deliberately designed environment, and the intentional, but implicit, educational messages emanating from it."[113] The Bicentennial Summer Institute, Kurtz later wrote, provided Academy faculty with a "sharpened awareness of the importance of dormitory living and the vital role that teachers play in instructing students outside the classroom."[114]

While it was important to talk about the teaching of values, the school also needed to ensure that its system of rules and punishments reflected those values. The disciplinary system, a creation of the 1930s, proved inadequate for dealing with the demands put upon it in the 1970s. Its three-tier penalty system (Restrictions, Probation, and Requirement to Withdraw) proved inflexible and unforgiving. As the number of infractions rose, faculty meetings were increasingly taken up with disciplinary cases that often turned into philosophical discussions, yielding inconsistent outcomes and much dissatisfaction among students. Convinced by a substantial number of senior faculty that reform was essential, in 1977 Kurtz authorized a lengthy review of the Academy's disciplinary system. The findings were compelling. In 1980, at the motion of instructor Al Ganley, the faculty voted to transfer all disciplinary matters and petitions to a faculty Executive Committee on a trial basis.[115] (As before, students brought up on charges had the option of consulting the Stud Jud before presenting their case to the Executive Committee.) The new approach passed with flying colors, and in 1982 became standard practice.[116] The faculty also reformed the penalty system, creating a fourth tier, "Restrictions with Review." Applicable to major offenses deemed not dangerous or malicious, it imposed the same limitations as "Restrictions" (lasting, however, four weeks instead of three), with a Review at the end of the period.[117]

Connected with this new approach to disciplinary problems was a new perspective on the role of the dean's office in such matters. When P. Richards "Rick" Mahoney became dean of students in 1980, Kurtz charged him with overseeing "the nurture of our students"—a radical departure from the Kerr-Kesler conception of the job. Handing his disciplinary jurisdiction to Associate Dean Susan J. Herney, Mahoney made dormitory life his central focus. "Kurtz felt very strongly that the responsibility of the dean of students should not be the administration of discipline," Herney explained. "This sent the wrong message to the student body and to the school as a whole. The dean should be responsible for taking care of students in their entirety, not just misbehavior for rule infractions."[118]

Although it had taken years to reform the system, the effects of the reforms were immediate and far-reaching. The transference of disciplinary cases to the Executive Committee liberalized the disciplinary process, affording more opportunity to investigate and understand the factors of each individual case. At the same time, the more forgiving penalty system gave transgressors the chance to straighten up and fly right. Between 1980–1981 and 1990–1991, the number of disciplinary-related firings dropped from twenty to five.

Not everyone was pleased with the way things turned out, however. Some faculty believed the school was growing soft, allowing behavior that should not be tolerated. Others lamented losing the role they had long played in defining and maintaining the values of the school; in their view, faculty meetings risked becoming little more than a series of announcements.[119] Some students also were dissatisfied, finding fault with a system that punished only those who were caught and treated the same infraction differently at different times. "Because the faculty tries to take into account all the details of each case, there is going to be inconsistency in the results," explained Kathleen J. Brownback, Mahoney's successor as dean of students. "But the process—the effort to really try to treat each case individually—is utterly consistent."[120] "A student with a lot of support may not get fired, and a student without it may," acknowledged Brownback's colleague (and eventual successor), Ethan W. Shapiro. "But the process is weighted very heavily in the student's favor."[121]

After the new disciplinary system was in place, Kurtz turned his attention to the other half of the goodness equation, the advising system. In May 1982, he appointed an *ad hoc* committee on counseling to do a thorough review of counseling needs and services.[122] "The school's principal deficiency in counseling," the committee reported, was the "disparate and therefore often unfocused response to problems affecting the health and emotional well-being of many students."[123] The school needed to integrate its various counseling resources—the professional therapists, health services, dean's office, school minister, dormitory advisers, and the college placement office. To this end, Kurtz appointed a standing faculty counseling committee—a statement of the school's new priorities. Over the next couple of years, the counseling program—now three full-time therapists—joined up with the department of health services and put greater emphasis on group therapy and mental health education in the attempt to address a broader range of needs. Students too got into the act, with the establishment of a peer counseling group called the "Student Listeners."[124]

In the mid-1980s, newly appointed dean of students Susan J. Herney continued the work of expanding student support services that her predecessor had begun. One of her first acts was to appoint psychologist Michael Diamonti as director of counseling services, to oversee the integration of counseling services with the many support services provided by the Dean's Office. Herney devoted much effort to establishing programs to assist faculty in dealing with adolescents, including workshops on racism, homophobia, eating disorders, depression, suicide, and drug and alcohol intervention.[125] She also put together an evaluation system through which dormitory heads gave the other faculty in their dorm feedback on their performance as advisers. "I thought it was vital that the residential part of the school had a way of validating the work the dorm faculty were doing," Herney explained. "And if there were problems, there needed to be a way to find where they were and provide faculty with the support and tools they needed."[126]

Ironically, although the school had always placed more emphasis on knowledge than goodness, it had never provided support for students with academic problems. As early as the 1950s, committees had stressed the need for an academic counselor, but the consensus had always been that existing structures—principally, the director of studies, college placement officers, and faculty—were more than adequate. As national awareness of learning disabilities grew in the early 1980s, the Academy gave the matter serious thought for the first time in decades. Although Exeter seldom had students who fit the technical definition of "learning disabled," some Exonians had "minor learning disabilities"—a term broad enough to include the poorly prepared or poorly functioning—and needed a support system.[127] Exeter, it turned out, was the only one of the twelve EISCAP schools that did not have an academic counselor.[128] Under the leadership of Associate Dean Anja S. Greer, the school established an academic support system with an expanded and upgraded peer tutoring program and courses in study skills.

Reflecting old and new currents of thought on fostering knowledge and goodness, the Curriculum Review of 1986 — the final accomplishment of the Kurtz years — reasserted the importance of the Harkness system in providing moral instruction as well as intellectual training.[129] But in the view of the Visiting Committee of the New England Association of Schools and Colleges, this was not enough: Exeter needed to meet the same standards residentially as it had academically. Although the faculty was less divided over the necessity of support systems than it had been ten years earlier, views on the role of the teacher outside the classroom still varied considerably. When the faculty as a whole relinquished jurisdiction over disciplinary cases, it also lost its forum for discussing questions pertaining to residential life. The time had come for the Academy to reassess its role *in loco parentis*.[130]

GOODNESS IN THE RESIDENTIAL COMMUNITY

When Kendra S. O'Donnell arrived on campus as principal in 1987, she inherited the unfinished task of "warming up" the Academy. In her first year on the job, this meant, above all, listening to what people at the school had to say. As the student body became increasingly diverse in the late 1980s, it became apparent that Exeter needed to adapt its values and methods of moral instruction accordingly. O'Donnell's answer was to put new emphasis on community living. The greatest opportunity for boarding schools, she said, "lies in creating pluralistic, multigenerational communities that work: communities where people share values and goals; where differences enrich; where people grow and are productive; where work is constructive."[131]

In the spring of 1989, O'Donnell launched a review of "The Other Curriculum," the first major initiative to improve life outside the classroom in many years. More than thirty groups of students and faculty studied and developed proposals for a variety of issues, including the dress code, disciplinary system, family life, telephones in the dorms, and the confidentiality policy.[132] On at least one occasion, the proposals spawned additional studies and, eventually, significant reforms. After a faculty-student *ad hoc* committee on discipline found that the disciplinary system was still perceived as cold and arbitrary,[133] it was decided that students should have a more active role in the disciplinary process. In the spring of 1991, the faculty adopted a Student Council proposal to add four students to the newly created Discipline Committee who would participate in discussion but not decision making, thereby eliminating the need for Stud Jud.[134] By moving students from a separate committee to one where they directly interacted with faculty, the reform created a Harkness Table environment for dealing with disciplinary cases—an important step in the evolution of a more tolerant, understanding disciplinary procedure.

"The Other Curriculum" had made a difference, but piecemeal reforms could only do so much. What was needed was a major overhaul of the school's environment. The first step, the trustees decided, was to develop a mission statement that would provide "a touchstone for planning for the future."[135] After meeting many times in small groups and as a whole, in 1991 the faculty produced the Academy Mission Statement:

> The founder of Phillips Exeter Academy defined its mission more than two centuries ago. "Above all," John Phillips stated, "it is expected that the attention of instructors to the disposition of the minds and morals of the youth under their charge will exceed every other care; well considering that though goodness without knowledge is weak and feeble, yet knowledge without goodness is dangerous, and that both united form the noblest character, and lay the surest foundation of usefulness to mankind."
>
> Exeter today continues the commitment to unite knowledge and goodness. It seeks students who combine proven academic ability, intellectual curiosity, and tenacity with decency and good character. At the Academy, exacting inquiry and thoughtful discourse foster the life of the mind, instruction and activity promote fitness and health, and the daily interactions of a residential school nurture integrity, empathy, and kindness. Because learning and growth at Exeter arise from each individual's engagement with others, the richness of education here requires diversity in all its dimensions; students and faculty value the differences they bring to the community they share.
>
> The challenges that students meet at Exeter and the support they receive have a common purpose: to stimulate their development as individuals and as members of society. Exeter seeks to graduate young people whose creativity and independence of thought sustain their continuing inquiry and reflection, whose interest in others and the world around them surpasses their self-concern, and whose passion for learning impels them beyond what they already know.[136]

Although mission statements had become fashionable in many organizations and subject to skeptical interpretations, at Exeter the exercise was taken very seriously and the actual statement debated by many people and stakeholder groups over many months. Meanwhile, as the mission statement took shape, Diamonti and child psychiatrist Edward M. Hallowell '68 set out "to gain a greater understanding of the current generation of Exeter students, both from their viewpoint as well as their parents' and teachers' viewpoints." While the overwhelming majority of students and parents sang Exeter's praises, they had critical things to say about the advising and disciplinary systems. The triple threat of teaching, residential advising, and coaching left advisers little time for their students. And since advisers also served as disciplinarians, students found it difficult to have a close relationship with them. While students on the whole did not object to rules and regulations (apart from the dress code and visitation hours), they did object to the lack of uniform enforcement and big differences of mode among the various dormitories.[137]

In addition to shedding much-needed light on the Exeter experience, the Diamonti-Hallowell study provided the impetus for improving student-faculty communication. In 1991, Exeter established the Academy Student Assistance Program to enable students to seek help confidentially for themselves or others at risk or struggling with serious problems — most commonly, substance abuse — without fear of disciplinary action.[138] Early the following year, the faculty endorsed a thoroughly revised Confidentiality Rule that encouraged students to speak to their advisers more freely about themselves.[139]

While most programs launched in the late 1980s and early 1990s dealt with fostering goodness on campus, Academy officials realized that the emphasis should begin at the true beginning of one's Exeter career, with the admissions process. In 1992, the school formulated an Admissions Statement that had much in common with the Mission Statement developed a year earlier:

> At Phillips Exeter Academy, we seek to enroll students who combine proven academic ability, intellectual curiosity, and tenacity with decency and good character, young people who welcome challenges and opportunities provided by a rigorous academic program within a diverse community. We seek students from a wide range of backgrounds — racial, geographic, socioeconomic, ethnic, religious, and cultural — in order to create a rich educational environment both in and out of the classroom. Because what happens in the classrooms, on the playing fields, and in the dormitories depends to an unusual degree upon student engagement with other students and adults, we look for candidates who demonstrate interest in and involvement with others. Above all, we look for students who have

the capacity to grow and who are likely to thrive at Exeter, whether they enter as four-year, three-year, two-year, or one-year students.[140]

The Academy had always screened for scholastic strength; it was now time to screen for strength of character as well. "Exeter is seen as the place — and I think accurately — where we ask more of our kids," O'Donnell noted. "We throw them out on their own much more than other schools. We select kids who can survive that, some who actually blossom that way. Once in a while a kid comes here who is overwhelmed and has to leave. But that's the rare exception."[141]

Prompted by the Diamonti-Hallowell study and the Academy Mission Statement to continue efforts to improve life outside the classroom, in 1993 the Academy launched the Residential Life Initiative, a complete renovation of the residential life structure. That fall, the Residential Life Steering Committee conferred with faculty and spouses, students, graduates, and parents on a wide range of issues — time and scheduling, dormitory personnel, living space for faculty and students, and student life.[142] The following spring witnessed the first-fruits of this labor, the Residential Life Statement:

> Exeter believes that academic life and residential life are united in purpose. The Academy's principles of goodness and knowledge must guide our lives beyond the classroom as well; there is no schoolroom where knowledge alone is pursued, no area of residential life where goodness forms the only curriculum. Exeter affirms that academic success is linked to the excellence of our residential life and we commit ourselves to pursuing that excellence in order to enhance the learning environment at the Academy.
>
> Exeter strives to create an environment that cherishes both the individual and a strong sense of community. We must teach civility, honesty, generosity of spirit and concern for others. Students must learn to make personal decisions regarding time, to care for their own physical and emotional well-being and to balance work and leisure. The opportunity to live together in a residential school should help students look beyond self concern to responsible citizenship and to the welfare of others.[143]

Aiming "to embrace the educational value inherent in a fully integrated residential community,"[144] the initiative focused on student-faculty relations, dorm life, and the relationship between extracurricular and academic programs. As associate dean and then as dean of students, Kathy Brownback focused on improving "dorm spirit," encouraging individual dormitories to hold meetings for discussing issues of concern or opportunities for relaxing together.[145] In 1995, the school established a Residential Life Council to coordinate the residential life program, much in the way the Curriculum Committee coordinated the academic program.[146] That autumn, the Academy observed its first Residential Life Day, a day set aside for special dormitory activities,[147] and it set a weeknight curfew hour for all classes to preserve "quiet time" in the dorms. In 1997, the Residential Life Initiative also examined other aspects of the nonacademic experience, with the dining halls and the frenetic daily and weekly schedules high on the list.

Two incidents during the O'Donnell administration put the school's philosophy to the test. First, in 1989, an unusually severe hazing incident that had led to the expulsion of four boys prompted her to call a special Assembly where students engaged in discussion and spoke their minds. Boys claimed that hazing created dorm unity and wanted to know which acts were permissible, while girls expressed horror and disbelief. One senior who had hazed in the past defended the rite as a way of building dormitory solidarity. The initiates were supposed to understand its importance and bore no grudge. "No," one of his prep victims angrily replied, "I have always hated you and resented what you did to me."[148] This session — in many ways a schoolwide Harkness Table — educated students and faculty alike on gender and generational attitudes toward hazing.

The second incident was the dismissal of a popular teacher for possession of child pornography films. O'Donnell acted decisively in the case, over the objections of some of the teacher's friends that he had never acted inappropriately with Exeter students — none were in the films — and that his privacy had been invaded. "There's a great deal of tolerance in the community for lives lived in a variety of ways," she stated, "but they have to be lived with integrity." After the teacher had been sentenced, O'Donnell spoke at a schoolwide Assembly of "a standard of adult behavior" at Exeter — a standard that condemned any sexual intimacy of any sort between an adult and a young person — while reaffirming that Exeter "educates against disabling prejudices" such as racism, sexism, and homophobia. "As in all crises, there are opportunities to talk about things," she later explained. "If I had gotten up there on the assembly stage and said that just out of the blue I'd have blown them away. But this was an opportunity to say, 'this is the way it works.' It's a message that you need to get out."[149]

Although the Academy by the 1990s and early 2000s had moved a great distance from its Calvinist roots, spiritual avenues to goodness still existed for students who wished to take them. Rev. Thompson used his pulpit to discuss Christian precepts on Sunday mornings, and moral issues of a more general nature at the voluntary Tuesday evening prayer meetings. "At those evening meetings, I choose readings that have to do with the acquisition of virtues and the way we live together," Thompson explained. "I also speak to the entire school at Assembly two or three times a year, and raise issues that have to do with their spiritual growth and development or their interaction with the Exeter community and the larger community."[150] In addition, Thompson, along with several members of the religion department, provided individual counseling to students who sought their advice in a time of crisis.

In the mid-1990s, the advent of technology posed a new challenge to the Academy's disciplinary system. The installation of telephones and data lines in every dormitory room suddenly afforded students limitless access to both the Exeter community and the outside world—and limitless potential for abuse.

As American society came to grips with the legal ramifications of the Internet, the Academy addressed the question of how to deal with technology transgressions. Deciding not to create a new list of rules specific for telecommunications, in April 1997 the faculty formulated the Acceptable Use Policy, which stated that students who accessed the network were "representatives of the Academy and . . . expected to behave accordingly"[151]—an invocation of the school's traditional guidelines for moral behavior. "The faculty said, 'We have standards of behavior and we will use the same standards of behavior and apply them to transgressions of technology,'" said Dean of Students Ethan Shapiro. "Our challenge is to educate students on how we expect them to use technology and interact as we expect them to in person and by mail. We want students to understand what is acceptable and what is not."[152]

GOODNESS IN THE NEW MILLENNIUM

In the early 2000s, the values that date back to the Academy's founding remain central to the school's educational philosophy. Interpreted differently at different times, Phillips's charge to unite knowledge and goodness was the driving force behind the delivery of moral education throughout the twentieth century. Although the change in the delivery of moral education was more incremental and cumulative than the revolution in teaching methods induced by the Harkness Table, ultimately, its impact on the Exeter experience is arguably as great. The Academy became a warmer, more nurturing institution, with a supportive advising system that attempts to respond to adolescent needs and an understanding disciplinary system that gives students the chance to learn from their mistakes. As counselors, listeners, and proctors, students came to play an essential role in the functioning of those systems.

In the new millennium, moral education continues to be one of the Academy's top priorities, with the understanding that it takes place everyplace in the community, in all the waking hours. The dormitories, playing fields, and activities and events are as vital to this mission as the classroom. "In the dorms," for example, as history instructor and dorm head Michael Milligan puts it, "students learn to live with different kinds of people. They learn to think beyond their own experience and to get along despite their differences. They make day-to-day decisions about how to live together. How do you treat someone who is younger than you are? How do you talk with one another? Joke with one another? How do you treat people who are racially and ethnically different?"[153]

Recent physical changes on the campus reflect this broad understanding of the Academy as a comprehensive learning environment for both knowledge and goodness. The renovation of six large dormitories was explicitly designed with the need to foster community by reducing the student-faculty ratio and by creating more common spaces. The most visible sign of this imperative is the Elizabeth and Stanford N. Phelps '52 Academy Center, the thoroughgoing renovation of the original Thompson Science Building into a multipurpose meeting ground. Opened in 2006, the Phelps Academy Center includes the grill and a convenience store, the post office, game rooms and lounges, music practice rooms and workrooms for projects and crafts, kitchens, clubrooms, meeting rooms, and offices, and a 200-seat forum for large meetings, lectures, movies, and concerts. "Exeter has always sought to bring together a diverse group of people and help them forge lasting connections in classrooms and dormitories and on playing fields," said Principal Tingley. "What the Phelps Academy Center offers us now is a new opportunity to expand upon these connections by seeking each other out in a central place that belongs to everybody."[154]

Meanwhile, the debate continues over how best to strike a balance between enlarging minds and imparting goodness. Some say that the warming up of the school has compromised academic standards and a rigorous work ethic, while others argue that academic demands allow little time for other endeavors and create an atmosphere that is unnecessarily stressful—a debate that assumes greater urgency in a world of increasingly competitive college admissions, where academic achievement is the coin of the realm. In all like-lihood, however, the Tingley administration and those that follow, like their predecessors, will continue to place a high priority on creating a supportive environment for both learning and moral development, the qualities needed for success at Exeter, in life, and in the world beyond.

5 The Composition of the Community

"The Academy shall ever be equally open to youth of requisite qualifications from every quarter," proclaimed John Phillips in 1781 in his original Deed of Gift. During the 227 years since then, leaders of Phillips Exeter Academy often quoted and reaffirmed this language, although what they meant by it shifted with time and circumstance.

At the time of the Harkness Gift, and indeed for most of the school's history, "youth of requisite qualifications" consisted predominantly of white Protestant boys and young men who came from a variety of economic backgrounds. Most students hailed from middle-class or wealthy families, although a significant number of boys on some form of financial assistance leavened the mix and reinforced Exeter's meritocratic values and aspirations. The complexion of the student body in the early twenty-first century could hardly be more different. Students of this era, boys *and* girls, trace myriad roots in different races, ethnic groups, religious affiliations, geographical and national origins, economic fortunes, and even sexual orientations. Paging through "The Photo Address Book"—better known as "the face book"—the most casual observer cannot help but notice this diversity.

As might be expected, the path between these markers—between the monochromatic Academy of 1930 and the multicultural Exeter of the early twenty-first century—proved full of twists and turns. The Academy repeatedly reexamined its concept of community in response to shifts in the world around it: economic crises, changing demographics, new social values and political movements. But some changes were deliberate. Each year the processes for admission of students and recruitment of new faculty, administrators, trustees, and staff help to define and redefine the terms of membership in the Exeter community. Over time, the definition has expanded to welcome people from diverse backgrounds. The changes at Exeter occurred in stages and at an uneven pace, and they accumulated to produce dramatic differences in the makeup of the school, as well as in its curriculum.

The transformation of the school, of course, mirrored changes in other, similar institutions. But Exeter's traditions gave it a distinctive course and generally enabled it to steer clear of bitter controversies and rancor that divided some other schools and colleges. The founder's enduring values, along with the dynamics of the Harkness Table and the rhythms and disciplines of residential life, helped to counter and balance the demands of those who sought too little or too much change, at slower or faster rates. Although it had to be reminded from time to time, for the most part, the school treated the members of its community as individuals rather than representatives of constituent groups. In the early 2000s, critics of the direction, pace, and extent of continuing change still exist, and Exeter continues to meet challenges in making its multicultural community work smoothly. But in looking ahead, the school maintains its trust in the traditions that have brought it thus far.

OPENING UP, 1930–1960

The process of opening up Exeter to "youth of requisite qualifications from every quarter" took distinctive shape soon after the Harkness Gift, when the school reexamined the meaning of John Phillips's great statement in troubled economic times. Reaffirming its commitment to socioeconomic diversity in the 1930s, the Academy broadened the meaning of "youth . . . from every quarter" in subsequent decades to welcome students from across the United States, regardless of their geographical origins, religion, and race.

Although the Harkness Gift greatly increased the resources at the Academy's disposal, the Great Depression followed hard on its heels. As the school sought to expand to fill its new classrooms and dormitories, ironically, it had dwindling ability to help students who could not pay their own way. Indeed, the school teetered on the brink of losing the most remarkable form of diversity it possessed: the variety of economic circumstances from which its students hailed. For many years a scholarship program had enabled poor boys to attend, side by side, with the sons of the region's wealthiest families. The students varied greatly in age, from fourteen to the mid-twenties. "Boys arrived from farm, factory, city, and business, and received a chance, no matter what their resources, to get an education at the Academy."[1] Yet just when the Harkness Gift offered hope that Exeter might grow into an institution of national prominence, a depressed economy threatened to turn it into a homogeneous school for the wealthy. How the Academy's leaders responded to this crisis helped prepare the way for Exeter to redefine its community and open its doors to a much wider public.

The Depression triggered drastic declines in the school's endowment and income. By 1931–1932 enrollment had dropped to 650 from the customary 700,

resulting in a budget deficit and making it increasingly difficult to accommodate the growing number of scholarship requests. To meet its financial obligations, the school was forced to favor applicants from wealthier families. Lewis
Perry appealed to the alumni and friends of Exeter for aid in finding "applicants of good caliber who can pay their way,"[2] while the "standards for admission . . . were adjusted to fit the times."[3]

In late 1933, the Academy accelerated the trend toward serving only those
who could pay by revamping its tuition policy. The previous year, tuition had
totaled $350 per year, and board $324; the room fee was determined by the
size of the room occupied and varied from $50 to $400. After a few minor
fees were added, the total charge ranged from $762 to $1,112, with an average
of $1,012.40.[4] Under a new "flat rate" tuition plan, each student would pay a
flat charge of $1,050, regardless of the size of his quarters. Because this hike
made it still more difficult for students of lesser means to attend, the Academy
established Foundation Grants, which were awarded by faculty vote on the
basis of need and character — the latter determined by academic preparation,
extracurricular activities, and maturity. These grants went to approximately
20 percent of the student body. Scholarships, determined by grades, supplemented grants for the very needy and provided the principal source of funding for "old boys," or returning students, after their first year.

By such means, PEA managed to overcome its enrollment problem. By the
late 1930s, it had far more applicants than it could possibly accept. But few of
these applicants were truly needy. Families watching their pennies were reluctant to commit themselves to private school education when they could not
be certain of receiving financial aid after the first year. Poorer boys who did
apply often could not compete with wealthier boys who had better academic
preparation. As a result, the grant recipients were generally younger and well-
to-do and, if not for the Depression, probably could have attended the Academy on their own resources.[5]

The price of this change was the loss of variety that had long characterized
the student population and, many believed, benefited the school. "The Academy has obtained a student body of a complexion much different from that of
thirty years ago," lamented trustee John Price Jones, reporting on behalf of the
Committee on Scholarships in 1938. He added that it was

a student body representing families of culture and fine background, [but]
It does not contain the wide varieties of American boyhood such as it had
years ago. While it cannot be said that the Academy will become another

St. Paul's or Groton, the question may be raised whether, even with a great number of boys getting Foundation grants and scholarships, the Academy may not lose some of the democratic complexion for which it has been famous—where the rich boy learns from the poor boy and where the poor boy is enriched and stimulated by his association with more fortunate boys.[6]

The economic conditions that had discouraged needy boys from applying to Exeter during the 1930s improved little as the decade came to an end. Perhaps hardest hit were those living great distances from the Academy, who had to contend with the expense and loneliness of travel in addition to high tuition. Applications from outside the Northeast declined steadily during these years. In the late 1930s, more than three-quarters of all students hailed from New England and the mid-Atlantic states.[7] Hoping to expand its geographical reach, in 1940 the Academy instituted Regional Grants—full scholarships for needy boys of exceptional academic promise who resided in Alabama, Kentucky, Mississippi, Tennessee, or west of the Mississippi.[8] But it was still difficult to attract more than a handful of students from distant locations.

The problem only worsened when the United States entered World War II. Because of restrictions put on travel, it was difficult for admissions officers to spread word of the Academy. In addition, many families were reluctant to send their sons away to boarding school when it was all too likely that they would soon be leaving for the armed forces. In September 1941, Perry wrote a letter to parents extolling the Academy as excellent preparation for military service, but this seems to have had little effect.[9] The decline in applications among the financially needy was so great that the Academy had trouble finding both Foundation and Regional scholarship boys.[10] To keep enrollments up, admissions officers concentrated their attention on bringing in the sons of alumni rather than locating new recruits. By late 1943, it was apparent that the school was in danger of becoming truly homogenized.[11]

Concerned by this state of affairs, the trustees urged Perry to pursue measures to make the student body more socially, economically, and geographically diverse. In the spring of 1944, Perry appointed the Special Scholarship Committee on the Awarding of Scholarships and Foundation Grants, which completely restructured Exeter's method of allocating financial aid. Under the new system, scholarship eligibility of "old boys" was determined not by grades but by need, academic attainment, and character. Boys who came to Exeter with financial aid could count on aid for the duration of their time there. This policy thus ensured a place for economically disadvantaged students at the Academy.

At the behest of the trustees, Perry went one step further — and an important step it was. In June 1945 he appointed H. Hamilton "Hammy" Bissell as the first Director of Scholarship Boys. "The position was created," Bissell himself recalled, "as a positive step toward insuring a broad geographic and economic distribution of scholarship students at Exeter."[12] He was to travel throughout the country and talk with alumni, parents, and adults involved in "boys' work" and scholarships such as the Boy Scouts, Rotary Clubs, and the Future Farmers of America. It was hoped that these contacts would recommend boys who satisfied three criteria: financial need, academic ability, and character, defined as "integrity, responsibility, the promise of social usefulness."[13]

A campaign of this sort was an expensive proposition in the best of times, and times were hard in 1945. Increases in costs of food, supplies, and maintenance had resulted in deficits for the years 1943–1945. To balance the budget and pay for the expanded scholarship program, the trustees voted to raise the tuition from $1,050 to $1,250.

Such was the situation when Perry handed the reins to Bill Saltonstall in June 1946. The new principal rose to the challenge with very clear ideas of how to make the Academy simultaneously more diverse and prosperous. As he explained in a letter to parents:

> Exeter will go on during the years ahead seeking to become a more truly national school. We are proud of our New England heritage, but increasingly desirous of attracting first-rate boys from the most distant parts of the country and the world. . . . No public schools and few, if any, private schools offer such an opportunity for "national living" as is available at Exeter.[14]

Anticipating that the tuition increase would further limit the economic and geographic range of the applicants already restricted by depression and war, Saltonstall launched a major publicity campaign, promoting Exeter as a "national high school." In the belief that people were willing to pay for prestige, he claimed the Academy was the best school of its kind, one that provided a unique educational experience to its students.

As Exeter's "national representative,"[15] Bissell traveled extensively each year combing the country for suitable boys. He encountered a variety of obstacles that made it difficult to reach qualified applicants. Perhaps the most challenging of these was the Academy's reputation as an upper-class, WASPish institution. "It is hard for most people to conceive of the amount of tolerance of individual backgrounds which exists at Exeter," he said. "Private schools are ordinarily associated with Protestantism, even occasionally with atheism; with capitalism and reaction in politics; and racially with only the Anglo-Saxon race."[16] Bissell, however, persevered with his task, and managed to establish contacts which in the years to come would send a stream of deserving scholarship boys to Exeter.

One of the largest sources of new entrants was the carrier networks of city newspapers. Bissell believed that boys who had newspaper delivery routes were industrious and responsible, the sort who could do well at Exeter. "What we look for in a prospective student is the combination of ability and responsibility which guarantees that he will eventually become a useful member of our society. It is easy enough from a boy's record to judge his academic ability. His sense of responsibility is a little more difficult to discover, and we believe that in no activity can a boy better show a sense of responsibility than in the carrying of a newspaper."[17] Bissell's tactic involved talking to a group of carriers about Exeter. Boys who were interested in the Academy would visit the school with their parents, with the newspaper often paying their way. It is hard to be certain, but the number of scholarship boys who came to Exeter as a result of this process was probably in the hundreds.[18] To raise money for these grants, in the summer of 1946 the trustees launched the Phillips Exeter Fund, a major capital drive. Between that drive and Bissell's efforts on the road, the Academy established seventy-five new grants by the time Saltonstall retired in 1963.

Bissell's involvement with the scholarship boys did not end with matriculation. Once they arrived on campus, they became virtually his wards. He followed them closely and supported them however he could. He even helped them obtain scholarships for college. In return for financial support, these boys performed four hours' work of service to the Academy each week without cash remuneration.

Bissell believed passionately in the importance of his mission. As he put it,

I have heard it said that education is America's magic. However that may be, it is apparent that the education of its talented youth is America's dream. I can't help feeling, however, that one important fallacy is evident in every scholarship program that I have observed. The fallacy is that no boy or girl is selected for further education until he or she becomes a high school senior. . . . I firmly believe that far too many of our best boys and girls never become eligible for any of these awards, because of circumstances which are outside their control and which operate on them during the years from fourteen to eighteen. All these scholarship programs are predicated on the belief that by a process of a survival of the fittest, the best boys and girls will show themselves at the end of their high school careers. I cannot believe that the fittest necessarily survive. I believe instead that the survivors are merely the "best fitted." Economic advantages, geographic advantages, social advantages, have been given to them and have been kept from other boys and girls during the high school period. . . . I believe it to be evident that adequate educational opportunity at the secondary level for exceptional boys and girls is inherent in the American educational dream. . . . Exeter . . . is a privately supported school which can fit into the over-all scheme of American secondary education by providing exceptional opportunity for exceptional boys."[19]

By the mid-1950s Exeter had a geographically and economically diverse student body. As the PEANs from the period attest, students hailed from nearly every state in the country and several foreign countries as well. Reflecting the school's geographic diversity were the social organizations that emerged in those days: the Southern Club, Midwestern Club, Pacific Coast Club, and International Club.

The efforts of Saltonstall and Bissell to restore balance to Exeter's student body coincided with another change: the opening of the Academy to increasing numbers of "minority" — i.e., non-WASP — students. Earlier such students were scarce, consisting of a handful of Catholics, Jews, African-Americans, and foreigners who attended. In the late 1930s there was only one African-American student at the Academy, Lucien V. Alexis, Jr., '38. Since he was not allowed to live in a dormitory, he lived with the track coach, Ralph Lovshin, who himself in some respects was a marginal member of the community. A Roman Catholic, Lovshin had come to the Academy in 1934, but was not considered a member of the faculty because of the literal interpretation of the school's Deed of Gift, which stated that "Protestants only should only be concerned with the trust and instruction of this seminary."

Robert Storey '54, an African-American and later a prominent attorney and Exeter trustee, recalls being the only black student in his prep year and one of six on campus during his entire four-year tenure. It was difficult for minority students to feel truly welcome, although Storey, an excellent athlete, became quite popular. As William I. Witkin, a Jewish graduate of the class of

'39, has observed, "Minority students . . . were occasionally asked to join [in student activities and organizations], but the likelihood was rare, unless he happened to have been a football or basketball player."[20]

Certainly, the Academy made little provision for students from nontraditional backgrounds. Everyone was required to attend daily morning Chapel and church on Sundays—policies that harked back to the days of John Phillips himself. By the 1950s, Chapel was no longer an overtly Protestant Christian ritual, but the church attendance requirement remained onerous for observant Jews and other non-Christians. At the beginning of the school year, the daily bulletin informed students of the rule:

> During the first two Sundays of the term, boys may attend either Phillips Church or one of the town churches. The church which a boy attends on the second Sunday of the term, October 1st, determines the church which he will attend for the rest of the term, unless he reports another preference to the Dean's Office before noon on Monday, October 2nd.
>
> Every boy attending Phillips Church must sign his own name on the card in his pew. *Do not* sign the name of another boy even though he is present.
>
> Boys attending town churches must give their names before the service to the monitor at the church they attend.[21]

In lieu of the nondenominational Protestant service at Phillips Church, boys could attend one of a number of different churches, from Catholic to Christian Science. But for many years there was no synagogue in the vicinity, and Jewish students generally "chose" to attend the service in the local Unitarian Church—a practice that tended to support Exeter's philosophy of assimilating, as opposed to accommodating, students of varied backgrounds.

Exeter's treatment of racial and religious minorities during Lewis Perry's tenure reflected the principal's personal beliefs. Quoting Booker T. Washington, he once expressed the opinion that it would be "a great mistake for colored boys to come to either Exeter or Andover." In his biography of Perry, Saltonstall does not mince words on the subject:

> Perry denied Exeter's democratic tradition in permitting limits on the numbers of African-Americans and Jews in the academy. He never specifically discussed quotas of any kind, but he did suggest that limits were advisable. He invariably treated individual African-Americans and other

minority members with utmost courtesy, but at the same time he thought the school "had to be careful in regard to Jews," although "some of the best boys have been Jews."[22]

In like manner, Perry opposed the abolition of exclusive fraternities on campus, although he finally relented in the early 1940s, when a faculty committee chaired by Saltonstall pushed for the change.

Saltonstall's role in the demise of the fraternities was indicative of his liberal views and policies. During his first year as principal, for example, he promoted Lovshin to the faculty.[23] In 1951, Exeter hired its first Jewish instructor, Gerald Strauss. Three years later, the school introduced a weekly Friday evening Sabbath service. Early in his tenure, Saltonstall summed up the Academy admissions policy as follows:

> The present policy of the Academy is to admit from the list of applicants those boys who give the most promise — as boys and as students. They may be African-American or white, Jew or Catholic, sons of alumni or boys with no previous Academy connection. They may be one-year applicants or four-year applicants, private-school boys or public school boys. By character recommendation, interviews, past performance and various tests the Academy selects the "best" candidates, regardless of class.[24]

This statement proved more aspirational than accurate. The Academy's contacts with groups like the Urban League and Boys' Club enabled African-Americans to attend, but few actually came. One entered in 1947, and there were none for several years after that. The numbers slowly crept up to twelve (out of about 250 new students) in 1959–1960 — still a very small percentage of the total student population. Catholics and Jews remained distinct minorities. The emphasis on Bible study and Christianity, in fact, was growing. In 1952, Saltonstall hired George E. Beilby, Jr., as school minister, thus ending a long tradition of faculty members and clergymen of various denominations preaching at Phillips Church. Five years later, the faculty established a Department of Religion to provide instruction on Biblical literature and theology.

The student body also featured clear class lines in this period. The scholarship boys had jobs — they waited on faculty tables, worked as assistants in the library, and served as tour-guides on campus — whereas boys from wealthier families did not. For some scholarship students, however, this was not problematical. P. Richards "Rick" Mahoney '62, later a faculty member and dean of students, spoke positively of his own experience as a scholarship boy. "[I]n some considerable sense, [it was] a source of pride, because you were thought to be good enough by Exeter not only to get into but to be worthy of their financial support."[25]

By the late 1950s, the Academy was clearly opening its doors to accept boys from unusual backgrounds who sought an Exeter education. Through Bissell's efforts, it was also beginning to pursue boys who, if left to their own initiative, were highly unlikely to consider attending a private school in small-town New England. During the following decade, Exeter reached out much more aggressively to find new students from varied backgrounds and disadvantaged circumstances.

REACHING OUT, 1960–1985

The early 1960s was a time of immense ferment and turmoil in American society, the era of John F. Kennedy's New Frontier and a burgeoning civil rights movement. Like virtually every other significant institution in the land, Exeter changed profoundly during these years and found itself a much more open and diverse community as a result. At the outset, the school sought to lead this change. In the process, however, the tide of events nearly overwhelmed it and forced it to adapt in ways scarcely imaginable in the era of the Harkness bequest.

In 1964, Richard Day became Exeter's tenth principal instructor. A man with close ties to the Kennedy administration — as noted in chapter 2, a good friend at Yale was Sargent Shriver, the president's brother-in-law and first director of the Peace Corps — Day embodied the optimistic spirit of the times, and he was determined that Exeter assert national leadership in many issues of the day. Thus, as Martin Luther King voiced the dreams and frustrations of African-Americans across the country, Exeter sought to join their struggle. At first, building on a foundation established by Saltonstall and Gillespie, these efforts were modest; later, under Day, they became more ambitious and comprehensive.

Even before Day's arrival, Academy officials proudly noted that the school had admitted African-American students as early as 1851, if not before.[26] "It is important to note this fact," said Acting Principal Ernest Gillespie in a Chapel talk in 1964, "that no one knows when the first Negro student came nor how many have come, for it shows that Exeter has had true integration. The Negro students were not distinguished from the others in any way." On another occasion Gillespie said,

There is no planning with faculty, students, Board of Trustees, or parents necessary. . . . the Negro students are accepted completely by the student body. There are almost no problems in these areas at all. It isn't that we have a great many of them, probably about a dozen in the average year, but they actually are accepted without any discrimination by the student body. Last year, for example, the colored boys were captains of the wrestling team, and of the basketball team. . . . We do search for qualified candidates with a good deal of intensity. We have found the Urban League and the various Boys Clubs around the country as excellent sources of recruitment. In general we have found that Negro candidates do not have as many advantages as others, and so we quite frequently accept Negro candidates whose aptitude scores are not particularly impressive, and in most cases we have found that they have been able to meet the competition quite successfully, provided there is strong evidence of motivation and character.

Although this language grates on the twenty-first century ear, Gillespie sincerely believed that the Academy was doing its part to help African-Americans, and it was prepared to do still more. During his year as interim principal, various leaders in the rights movement visited campus, including Ralph McGill, editor and publisher of the *Atlanta Constitution*, historian Herbert Aptheker, T. I. Atkins from the NAACP, and some Yale students who had served as "freedom riders" in Mississippi. Under Gillespie, and with Day's strong support, the Academy also made its first concerted effort to recruit African-Americans and other students from what it perceived as disadvantaged backgrounds.

The experiment began in the Summer School. In 1964 Academy officials increased the number of summer scholarships awarded to needy and academically able students of grades 8 through 12. They also established SPUR — the Special Program for Undeveloped Resources — a scholarship program for low-income inner-city students. Students who completed the eighth grade, had good (not necessarily outstanding) records, and had shown evidence of drive were eligible; they were expected to return to their home school after the summer at Exeter. The choice of acronym was not incidental: the sponsors of the program hoped that the experience would spur the students to pursue their education more ambitiously and that they in turn would spur other students back home. In the first year of the program, twenty students (fourteen African-Americans and six whites) came to Exeter from Atlanta, Cleveland, Pittsburgh, and St. Louis.[27] The numbers would peak in 1967, when the program had fifty students from ten cities. During the summers of 1966 and 1967, the reality of the national urban problem was made even more vivid for the secluded New Hampshire academy when riots broke out, first in Cleveland, then in Detroit, where one of the schools participating in SPUR was partly damaged.

When Day arrived in the fall of 1964, he accelerated initiatives launched earlier. The Academy opened the regular session to increasing numbers of African-Americans and other extremely needy students. Exeter's primary source of applicants was A Better Chance, a national minority assistance program established in 1964. "ABC identified underprivileged whites and minorities and offered support and training so that they could attend private schools, mostly boarding schools," Mahoney explained. "The kids applied to ABC, and ABC tried to place them in one of a variety of schools."[28] Thanks to generous funding by the Office of Economic Opportunity, ABC offered a six-week summer program to prepare students for boarding school, and it provided some financial aid to the school itself.[29] The number of African-American students rose at once. Between 1966 and 1967 enrollments jumped from eighteen to twenty-five. The numbers continued to climb over the next several years.

Exeter's aggressive recruiting policy proved controversial among faculty and alumni. Critics worried that the Academy could achieve diversity only by sacrificing its high academic standards. Proponents responded by noting that academic preparedness was only one of many criteria that should govern the admissions process. It was important, they argued, to look for boys who would contribute to other aspects of the Exeter experience. In the words of science instructor Robert F. Brownell, Jr.:

> The present policy of the Academy, as I understand it, is not to tie the admission process solely to objective evidence of superior intellectual promise, but rather to use this as a screen. Energy and vitality as shown by meaningful participation in sports, jobs, dramatics, debate clubs, and independent projects, etc., play a very large role in the selection of the student body. . . . Boys are not taken, however, who represent a great risk of being unable to cope with the curriculum. . . . A conscious effort has also been made to broaden the geographic, economic, and racial base of the student body to the extent permitted by scholarship funds.[30]

There was little doubt that the school was deliberately changing long-standing policies. This was perhaps the first time in Exeter's modern history that other criteria besides academic performance were given so much weight in the admissions process. Thus began a new phase in the history of admissions that was to culminate in the multiculturalism of the late 1980s and early 1990s.

Exeter's attempts to reach out to the African-American community were not limited to admissions. In late 1964 Day suggested that every Exeter student devote part of the school year to public service in the nation's inner cities. Along the same lines, he proposed in 1966 that the Academy establish an annex in a low income area of Washington, D.C., where students could learn about urban problems while doing volunteer work.[31] Although financial constraints forced Day to abandon the idea, his interest in community service survived in other forms, such as the Roxbury Wednesday Program, a tutoring program for disadvantaged children from a lower-income section of Boston. In 1967, the Academy founded the South End Summer Volunteer Program to give Exeter students the opportunity to spend a summer in a settlement house in another Boston neighborhood and learn about inner city life firsthand. The Academy also tried to educate students about blacks in other nations. In February 1965, various African students and specialists visited the campus to take part in "Africa Week," a five-day program of lectures and informal discussions on the emerging nations of Africa.

Achievements and Accommodations

During the late 1960s, the unrest that affected college campuses nationwide arrived at Exeter, where students started speaking out on issues like the Vietnam War and civil rights. The interest in civil rights directly correlated with the marked rise in African-American enrollments in this period. Like other minority students, African-Americans had long felt uncomfortable at the Academy. It was so vastly different from what many of them were accustomed to, and there were so few students like themselves with whom they could talk about their experiences. This situation changed with the near doubling of the number of African-American students in 1967–1968. Suddenly they had sufficient numbers to make an impact on the Exeter community.

Discussions of the need for an African-American student group resulted in the formation of the Afro-Exonian Society (AES) in late 1967. The original purpose of the Society as stated in its Proposal for Incorporation was to "educate the Academy Community to the needs and the values of African-American America." But AES soon found itself attending to the academic and social needs of African-American students, providing tutoring, sponsoring dances and conferences, and acting as a vehicle for students to discuss their difficulties in adjusting to Exeter life. At the time of its formation, some expressed the concern that other minority groups would follow suit and form separate organizations, thus splintering the Exeter community. This fear proved unfounded, however, probably because no other minority group had yet achieved self-consciousness or a critical mass: for example, in 1972, when the Academy began keeping statistics on its minority population, students of Asian descent represented only 3.3 percent of the total student body.[32]

In the meantime, strong philosophical fissures formed within AES, as they had among African-Americans nationwide. Many members believed the organization should help the African-American student who was having difficulty adjusting to Exeter. Some more militant members, however, opposed assimilation of any kind. As one student put it, "[we] refuse to give up [our] African-Americanness simply because [we're] at Exeter."[33] In early 1968 Theophus Smith, one of the cofounders of AES, spoke out on Black Power:

> I am the New Black. I will neither babble about how much I love Jesus, nor entertain you with sparkling, racial comedy. I will not eat with my fingers, nor go out of my way to sit down at a dining hall table with you. I will not flunk out of this place, but neither will I participate in the childish fanaticism of raving with you about your Math. test, or your Phy. Sci. lab, or your grade in English. I want neither to be your enemy, nor your friend. I don't want your love, nor your pity, nor your guilt, nor your fear. I demand only that you respect me.[34]

By and large, the students who embraced such views were younger and had recently arrived on campus; they brought to Exeter ideas currently gaining popularity in large cities across the country. For the militant blacks on campus, the purpose of the AES was to promote black identity and unity. They found support for their position in sources outside the Academy community, such as the newly formed Northeast Afro-American Society, an organization of African-Americans in private secondary schools.

In the winter of 1970–1971, the AES Society requested that the Academy establish an African-American Cultural Center "to educate the Exeter community to African-American culture through periodic cultural displays, seminars, speakers, films, a permanent library consisting of African-American history and African-American literature and other activities which are interracially oriented . . ." The proposal ran into opposition from the Academy Steering Committee because the Afro-Exonians wanted the Center to be closed to whites at certain times. After extended discussion, the AES agreed that the Center would be open to everyone in the Exeter community at all times. In early 1972 the African-American Cultural Center was established in the Davis Library, with an interracial student-faculty committee supervising its operation.

James A. Snead, an African-American student at Exeter in the late 1960s and early 1970s, recalled this period as "four years of on-and-off racial antagonism and mutual paranoia." Black students, he said, "questioned the motives of those who wished to befriend them and they were themselves as afraid of the differences between the races as some whites had been." And yet, Snead contended, "There were never any moments that I can remember when one member of the community refused to play with, eat with, room with, study with, talk with, or otherwise befriend another member simply for racist reasons."[35] Manifestations of racial misunderstanding were subtler. "How does it feel to be African-American?" and "Do you think you passed *this* time?" were questions all too often asked of African-American students.[36] Around the Harkness Table they were asked to give "the black perspective" on matters at hand, just as in the early days of coeducation girls would be asked to provide "the female perspective" (see chapter 6). The "traditional" Exeter approach regarded individuals from minority groups as representatives of a class, as if these classes were homogeneous.

African-American efforts to reach the Exeter community through culture made headway. A notable success was a singing group, the Precisions, formed in 1967. "We somehow grasped," Snead wrote, "that music was our only way to get through, to overcome, to say that we were somebody." The group consisted of five African-American singers and a back-up band that was all white except for Thee Smith, who played saxophone. Later, when Black Power was popular on campus, the Precisions renamed themselves the "Afro-Set Five." Snead replaced a white organist because "too much white skin in the back-up band didn't fit the ideology of the group."[37] He observed,

> The histories of the Afro-Exonians and of our singing group were curiously parallel, in that both, in line with the Civil Rights movement as a whole through its feud with Stokely Carmichael's "African-American Power" movement, grew increasingly radical in approach and rhetoric. . . . [There was] polarization, both between African-Americans and white and between African-Americans themselves. It was the first time I realized that Exeter and the real world were not so far apart after all.[38]

The black cultural movement produced strong reactions from white students at the Academy. Whereas some were stunned by militancy and found it difficult to understand what the African-Americans were saying, others were more sympathetic, realizing they needed to listen more closely. The assassination of Martin Luther King in April 1968 made some of the more sympathetic students realize that they must do more than just listen. Convinced by an AES-WPEA sponsored racial symposium that political action was the only way to change the status quo, a number of students joined members of the faculty and townspeople in circulating a civil rights petition throughout the state. Accompanied by a faculty member, three students — all of them white — took the petition to Washington, where they met with New Hampshire Senators Norris Cotton and John McIntyre, and Congressman Louis C. Wyman. The Academy both encouraged and supported these efforts — especially Day, who, in addition to his duties as principal, also chaired the New Hampshire Commission for Human Rights. On the first of May, the school celebrated Human Rights Day and held discussion groups on race relations all over campus.

The King assassination also spurred administration officials to pay greater attention to the needs of African-American students. Meeting two weeks after the assassination, Day, Vice Principal Robert Kesler, and Dean of the Faculty Robin Galt agreed on the importance of appointing African-American instructors. They were clearly skeptical of finding sufficient numbers of African-American teachers who could thrive in Exeter's environment, however. As Galt reported in a memo, they

> decided not to hire a Negro immediately, but that every effort should be made before Spring of 1969 to acquire a classroom teacher who will be able to conduct himself adequately in the classroom. Department Chairmen are to be informed that they have a definite responsibility in looking for such a person. . . . It was agreed that if a good Negro [teacher] can be found he might be signed up at any time for service in September, 1969. If he seems to be really good, he might even be added to the faculty as of September, 1968.[39]

Soon after this meeting, the Academy managed to locate its first black instructor, M. C. Utaegbulam of Biafra, who had spent the past few years at Yale Divinity School. He would spend the following year at Exeter while raising funds for the Biafran war effort. Two African-Americans came in 1969–1970: Earl Belton '65, an instructor in history and religion, and William H. Bolden, an instructor in English who became the first continuing African-American appointment; he remained at the Academy until his retirement in 1991. Dolores Kendrick, the first African-American female appointment, came in 1972 and taught in the English department for twenty-one years.

Officially, Bolden was instructor in English, admissions officer, and adviser to the Afro-Exonian Society. Unofficially, he gave what little free time and energy he had to members of the African-American community. "Bill cooked us Thanksgiving dinner," Harold Brown, Jr., '74, director of alumni/ae affairs, recalled. "There was no place on campus for African-Americans to have a party with their own music. Bill's house was always open to us." Brown added, "More than that, Bolden gave African-American students the nurturing and support they could not get elsewhere. He was instrumental to any success that Afro-American kids had at Exeter. Bill did as much to make the school a multicultural institution as Hammy Bissell did to get youth from every quarter."[40]

As the only African-American woman instructor at PEA for many years, Dolores Kendrick was keenly aware of the existence of racism and sexism at the school. She encountered prejudice from both colleagues and students — African-American students as well as white.

> You're talking about an African-American woman professional in a class-room of white affluent kids whose only association with African-Americans had been the women who worked in the kitchen. They didn't know what to do with me at all. The African-American students were having their own problems, but they had not come into contact with an African-American professional woman and even today people have told me that I probably was up against racism amongst my students at that time as well as what I was experiencing from my colleagues.

Kendrick devoted much of her time to helping minority students. For several years she served as adviser to the Afro-Exonian Society, and led efforts to improve campus life for students of color. She helped create the position of Dean of Minority Students and established the Listening Committee, a place to air professional grievances and seek advice, and the Becoming Invisible Group, a support group for faculty of color. "It was envisioned as a group in which people of color bond and empower themselves in the bonding so that they will be focused as one," Kendrick explained. "This ensures that their interests will be taken care of."[41]

The appointment of African-American instructors in the late 1960s and early 1970s improved the lives of African-American students appreciably, but it was only a first step. Among other concerns at this time was the need for courses to cover the achievements of African-Americans. Demonstrations at Harvard and other universities had resulted in the development of ethnic studies and Afro-American studies departments. The debate played out at Exeter in 1969, when Earl Belton went to Principal Day on behalf of the African-American students with a list of "non-negotiable demands," which included the addition of African-American studies to the curriculum. The following semester saw the addition of the "History of African-American Americans" and "African-American Literature," respectively, to the History and English departments' offerings.

In 1971–1972 the number of African-American students reached a peak of sixty-nine, and many milestones were marked. The African-American Cultural Center opened, and the senior class had three African-American officers—the first time in the school's history. Caucasian students attended meetings of the AES after a three-year hiatus, and African-Americans began participating in Student Council meetings—a sign, Snead noted, that they had "overcome their fears of inferiority or poor speaking ability and . . . [were] taking an active role in school affairs."[42] Although the problems that African-Americans encountered at Exeter were far from settled, the school seemed at last to be dealing with them head on.

Problems continued for other minorities at the school as well. Like the African-Americans, observant Jewish students were experiencing challenges of identity. From the mid-1950s on, the Jewish Congregation had provided a haven for them. "Jew-Cong" was student-run, and rabbis and rabbinical students from Harvard led the services.[43] But Jewish students still felt out of place in a school that continued to emphasize New Testament instruction and churchgoing, and displayed insensitivity to Jewish religious practices. In 1963, a clash arose between the administration and Jewish students over the school's refusal to excuse them from Saturday morning classes to attend services on Yom Kippur, the holiest day in the Jewish calendar, although the football team had been excused to play an away game on that day. The following year, the first day of school fell on Yom Kippur, but Jewish students again were not excused from classes. The president of the Jewish Congregation wrote a letter of protest to the *Exonian*, but the administration failed to respond.[44]

Jewish students were expressing their dissatisfaction with Academy policies at a time when Exeter students as a whole were beginning to voice their disaffection with required church attendance. In response to a Student Council petition in 1965, the Academy loosened the regulations concerning church attendance to allow students to attend any religious service they wanted in any given week. On some occasions the Jewish Congregation had considerably more non-Jews than Jews. As Lincoln Caplan '68 recalled, many non-Jewish students attended because they preferred a Friday night service to getting up early on Sunday morning.[45]

Students did not want to be forced to practice religion, especially one alien to their own, although they were more willing to study it. Protest against required church attendance was accompanied by demand for courses dealing with ethical concerns and religious issues. The Religion Department expanded its curriculum, first adding courses on Christian ethics, and then removing the explicitly Christian focus. Courses such as "Christian Ethics and Modern Society" became "Ethics and Modern Society," and covered issues of interest to African-Americans and whites alike, such as "lifestyles and problems of the Negro."

The relaxation of traditional rules regarding religion brought with it a new acceptance and respect for Jewish students at the Academy. In 1966–1967, Ira Helfand was president of the Student Council, and the following year Caplan was president of the senior class and Robert Shapiro was president of the Student Council. Shapiro went on to be class valedictorian, while Caplan was elected class orator. "In a really short time, the sense of struggle was supplanted by Jews making it," observed Caplan. "It is striking that many of the people who were seen as successful on campus were Jewish."

In May 1968, the trustees voted to abolish required church attendance, or, as the students put it, "Exeter abolished religion."[46] Not surprisingly, the number of participants in religious services plummeted at once, and the Jewish Congregation was no exception. Many Jewish students, however, continued to attend, having found an identity in the organization. "I went originally out of a sense of duty," Caplan says, "but eventually I gained a sense of appreciation for the community I found there. It was not a major commitment of mine, but something I looked forward to and took a sense of belonging from. It was at Exeter that I became a Jew."

By the end of the 1960s, Jewish life at Exeter was appreciably better than it had been a generation earlier, but certain problems remained. Although Jewish students constituted approximately 10 percent of the population, there was no rabbi in residence, and only two faculty members were Jewish. Many students found support in the Jewish Congregation's weekly Sabbath dinner and service. A second group, the Jewish Students Organization, was formed in 1980, and eventually took over the functions of the Jewish Congregation. One of its leaders, Judd Levingston '82, was so deeply affected by his experiences at the Academy that he became the first Exeter graduate to attend rabbinical school after college.[47]

Catholic students also had a difficult time at the Academy during the middle decades of the twentieth century, although their story reads somewhat differently. The number of Catholic students grew steadily after the 1930s, but the school did little to recognize them as a distinctive part of the community. They did not find a spokesman until 1969–1970, when Day managed to appoint Catholic priest Daniel J. M. Morrissey as school minister — an effort that included a petition to the trustees to change the Academy's charter. "Diversity mattered a great deal to Day," Morrissey recalled. "But others with more traditional WASP orientations saw the hiring of a Catholic priest as moving in a direction that was not Exeter."

As important a symbol as was Morrissey's appointment, however, it did not solve the problem perceived by many Catholics on campus. "Catholics were considered a minority even in the 1970s," Morrissey said. "They were not struggling or isolated as African-Americans, but there was little sense of a Catholic identity at the Academy. During my ten-year tenure, there was no Catholic student group on campus."[48] It would not be until the following decade that Catholic students would come into their own at Exeter.

Contrasting Experiences

Although African-American students had made great strides at the Academy, they too found the 1970s a decade of challenge. The achievements and advances of 1971–1972 proved a high water mark that, it turned out, would not be matched again for nearly three decades. In 1972–1973, African-American enrollments began dropping, until in 1979–1980 they plummeted to their lowest point in thirteen years. Some officials pointed to an increase in the competition for able African-American students, as more and more private schools launched aggressive recruiting programs. Others argued that the Academy was simply less interested and made less of an effort to bring African-American students to campus. In all fairness, however, a number of serious issues — financial woes, coeducation, and discipline — claimed the school's attention (and money) during this period.

But there were clearly other forces at work. In the early 1970s, Exeter's primary source for African-American students, ABC, lost federal funding and eliminated its summer preparatory program as well as scholarships. From that point on, the Academy had to provide financial aid for any students recruited through ABC. From the perspective of Exeter's finances, this could not have happened at a worse time. With the onset of the inflationary recession in 1974, fuel prices soared and other operating expenses followed not far behind, while the endowment, the main source of funding for scholarships, plummeted in value. To make ends meet, the Academy raised tuition every year and devoted a greater proportion of the budget to financial aid. (See chapter 7.) The number of funded students remained at 25 percent, but, as the recession worsened, more and more of these students were white: the number of minority students on financial aid declined from approximately 21 percent in 1972–1973 to 14.5 percent in 1979–1980.[49] As African-American enrollments declined, so did campus interest in African-American culture. By 1974–1975, courses on African-American history and literature had been removed from the curriculum, and the Afro-Exonian Society was functioning less as a political organization than as a social club.

Concerned by this state of affairs, Principal Steven Kurtz instructed the Committee on Admissions and Financial Aid in 1981 to examine the composition of the school to determine whether the Academy was following John Phillips's precept of making the school open to youth "from every quarter." The Committee recommended that the Academy increase the "socioeconomic diversity of the student body," meaning now the number of minority students, specifically African-Americans and Hispanics, as well as students from blue-collar families. To do this, the school sought to increase the percentage of students on financial aid. Admissions officers also focused on attracting students from public rather than private schools and deemphasized the pursuit of foreign students.[50]

To step up minority recruiting, the Admissions Office became part of several programs that focused on specific groups from certain parts of the country. Three programs came into existence in the academic year 1986–1987 alone. Prep for Prep targeted African-American, Hispanic, and Filipino students from the New York City public school system. The Hispanic Youth Group aimed at Hispanic students in the southwest. The Independent School South African Education Program recruited South African students who were victims of apartheid, in a program that enabled students to spend a year in an American boarding school before entering an American college. Prep for Prep was by far the most important of these programs. It provided two summers' worth of training and then placed the student in one of a small number of good boarding schools. "Prep for Prep," Mahoney explained, was "what ABC was in its heyday."

But Exeter's challenge was not simply to bring more minority students to campus. For a variety of reasons — academic, disciplinary, or emotional — 30 percent of the African-Americans who enrolled at Exeter in the early 1980s did not make it to graduation. The African-Americans who did stay too often withdrew from campus life. Small numbers participated in extracurricular activities. The Afro-Exonian Society was reduced to devoting most of its meetings to planning of soulfood dinners, trips to the beach, and dances. Like other clubs, it continued to sponsor four assemblies per year, but only a handful dealt with racial issues. During this period, the Academy brought a few prominent African-Americans, including James Baldwin, Jesse Jackson, and Boston activist Mel King, to campus, but otherwise offered little support to the African-American community. According to Reverend Robert Thompson '72, an African-American and the school's minister since 1986, "the school gave the blacks nothing else after the Black Cultural Center. There were very few faculty of color and no other support mechanisms. Graduates did not come back much, so there was little contact with them."[51]

Led by Dolores Kendrick, a few concerned members of the faculty established the Minority Support Group to provide support for African-American and other minority students. Realizing that the time for substantive change had come, in early 1984, Jack Heath, dean of the faculty at the time, insisted that the Academy institute an Affirmative Action program. This meant, among other things, that "at least 10 percent of the faculty hired (i.e. about one faculty member a year) will be members of minority groups until the percentage of minority faculty members approximates the percentage of minority students." But this proved no easy task. The common perception of Exeter as an elite white institution was off-putting to minorities. Moreover, there was the problem of living in a small town in New Hampshire where there are few people of color — a problem that persists to this day. "It's hard to get minority faculty to come to a state like this," acknowledged John D. Herney, dean of the faculty in the late 1990s.[52] The limited financial remuneration the Academy was able to offer was another serious impediment. With the great demand for teachers of color everywhere, Exeter had difficulty competing. The search began for African-American faculty, and, even more important, for a new administrative position devoted solely to minority students, the Adviser to Students of Color. It would result in the appointment of Reverend Thompson as school minister and Verna Mayo as Adviser to Students of Color in late 1986.

Meanwhile, support to minority students had to come from other sources. With this purpose in mind, the Minority Support Group sponsored "The American Dream Deferred," a symposium on racism held over the course of three months in early 1985. The response of the students, however, was hardly enthusiastic. Racial tensions flared noticeably at an assembly held in honor of Martin Luther King. Edmund Perry '85, an ABC recruit from Harlem, read the speech on African-American Power that Thee Smith had given in 1968. It was apparent now more than ever before that the support system for African-American students was inadequate. Instructors Kendrick and Donald Schultz urged the administration to appoint a special adviser for African-American students. Officials discussed the matter, but the decision took time in coming.

The issue came to a head in June of that year, when Perry was killed in an encounter with a policeman in Harlem. The incident brought to light the difficulties inner-city African-American students had in adjusting to life at leading prep schools — and intensified and accelerated the institutional response to the problem. The Academy at once launched efforts to find ways to improve the situation of African-Americans on campus. One step was to increase the number of minority students — in particular, African-Americans and Hispanics. But there was another bigger question to consider: Once they had arrived, what should the school do to support them in their new environment? In the autumn of 1985, Exeter launched the Sampler, a special pre-orientation program that gives the "non-traditional student" — who could be an African-American from the South Bronx, a white from Iowa, or an Asian from Hong Kong — the chance to spend a week at the Academy before the beginning of term to sample classes, activities, and life in New Hampshire. Under the guidance of Dean of Students Susan J. Herney and Associate Dean of Students Anja S. Greer, the school also established counseling and academic support services for all students. (See chapter 4.)

Although the Academy directed its attention to improving life for African-Americans on campus, another minority group became increasingly visible in this period: Asians and Asian-Americans. The story of the Asian experience at Exeter reads quite differently from that of the African-Americans. When there were sixty-nine African-American students on campus in 1971–1972, there were only thirty-two Asians. As a result of the globalization of the economy and the influx of immigrants from Southeast and East Asia, the number of Asian and Asian-American students at the Academy surged ahead. "This phenomenon did not occur everywhere, only at Exeter and a few other top-ranked prep schools, because of the importance the culture attaches to education," explained Mahoney.[53] In 1988–1989, the Asian students composed practically 20 percent of the population, and Eugene Yuan-Chun Shen '72 became the first Asian-American to join the board of trustees. The increase in numbers prompted the faculty to add courses of Asian content to the curriculum. By 1994–1995, there was a full sequence of courses in Chinese language (begun in 1982) and Japanese (begun in 1988); in 1995–1996, the English Department offered a course on "Asian Masterpieces" and included the poets Li Bai and Tagore in its course on "The World's Great Poems."

But the Academy proved less attentive to the needs of Asian students in other respects. Although the Asian students asked for space of their own, akin to the Black Cultural Center, the administration denied their request out of concern that other minority groups would ask for dedicated rooms as well. The existence of many different Asian organizations, which did not all cooperate in the request, was an additional handicap.

EXPANDING THE AGENDA SINCE 1985

Exeter's sensitivity to issues of diversity increased markedly with the appointment of Kendra Stearns O'Donnell as principal in 1987. O'Donnell came to the Academy at a time when pressure for change was building from all sides. In agreement with the trustees, faculty, and alumni/ae, she made diversity the Academy's top priority. At the Alumni/ae Council Weekend in the fall of 1990, O'Donnell explained why the issue was so important:

> We wish to become and we are becoming a more diverse community because we want to remain true to our mission. Our fundamental calling as a school is to educate young people who will be effective citizens in their future communities. . . . No matter what their scope, the communities in which we expect our Exonians to be effective citizens are likely to be multiracial, multicultural communities. . . . John Phillips . . . argues that we must educate youth who will change the downward slide of civilization. . . . Perhaps it is not too grand an aspiration to believe that we are educating the youth who will be the peacemakers for society in the future. In order to educate the peacemakers, we need to create for them and with them a harmonious environment which contains all the elements of diversity.[54]

In pursuing John Phillips's mission of uniting knowledge and goodness, O'Donnell maintained, the Academy ought to adhere to its traditional high academic standards, but at the same time, it should take responsibility for educating students about the world around them. She argued that it was important for students to learn about people whose way of life was different from their own in order to be free of prejudice, whether it be racism, sexism, or homophobia. This view was an extension of the philosophy developed in the late 1960s, when the Academy first redefined the kind of student it was looking for to include those with diverse interests and backgrounds. The aim in 1990, as in 1968, was to educate students in the ways of people different from themselves so that they could serve their communities well. As Kendrick recognized, "It is no longer feasible for kids to graduate from the old Ivy League and walk out into a world that is going to be WASP and Anglo-Saxon. It isn't there anymore, so it's up to us to prepare them for that world."[55]

O'Donnell's views struck responsive chords among Exeter's faculty, students, and alumni. With the support of Kendrick and Reverend Thompson, in 1988 alumni/ae of color founded the Subcommittee on Excellence through Diversity, with a mission "to promote the diversity needed to carry forward the founder's ideals."[56] In 1990 it was elevated to the status of an Advisory Committee of the General Alumni/ae Association[57] — a development that, in conjunction with the appointment of Harold Brown '74, an African-American, to the position of director of alumni/ae affairs, signaled the seriousness of the Academy's commitment to diversity. Over the next few years, the Advisory Committee on Diversity created a number of programs, including the Mentoring Program, which put minority students in touch with minority alumni/ae from their home cities, and the Fireside Chat Program, which established a dialogue between the dean of faculty and the Advisory Committee on Diversity to identify potential faculty of color.

The Community Support Group (CSG), a standing committee of faculty and students, also promoted acceptance of ethnic and cultural diversity on campus. The CSG sponsored Assembly speakers, student and faculty workshops, and continuing dialogue among faculty, students, and administrators, and various organizations on campus. In the fall of 1987, it hosted a Faculty Workshop on the Realities of Racism in the Residential School. In the early 1990s, the CSG sponsored publication of "Excellence through Diversity," a brochure addressed to minority applicants, and it regularly published *Multi-Cultural News Notes*, a newsletter with information about student organizations, academic and administrative departments, and library acquisitions and exhibits.

Among the most significant of CSG's accomplishments was the Multicultural Assessment Project, or MAP, conducted in 1988–1989 "to see how diversity in a school population can be used to enhance the educational program and to increase students' understanding of their history and culture and the history and culture of others."[58] The study expressed concern about several problems. There were too few minority students and far too few minority faculty on campus. The curriculum did not reflect the Academy's growing diversity. There was also continuing racial insensitivity, which appeared in various forms. Students and faculty in the late 1980s still had an "assimilate to us" approach, and minorities were expected to change in order to fit into the Exeter community. Students too freely still used racial stereotypes and slurs. Minority students were made to feel they must represent their entire race or ethnic group in classroom discussion. African-Americans were not permitted to play certain music at a school dance. The Academy as a whole lacked a proper vocabulary for discussing and understanding racial issues. In short, there seemed a general lack of understanding of other cultures.[59] Minority students were apparently reliving the same experience that James Snead had encountered two decades before.

In response to these findings, the faculty expanded the curriculum to include many multicultural course offerings. Instructors in the English Department introduced courses on various minority and ethnic authors, including "Afro-American Writers," "Caribbean Literature," "African and Caribbean Literature," and "American Cultures: Literature from the African-American, Asian-American, Hispanic-American, and Native-American Traditions." The History Department had recently introduced a course on "Africa in the Twentieth Century." At the urging of the MAP, it increased its emphasis on social history, delivering courses that paid due attention to the history of various racial and ethnic groups in American history. The Religion Department expanded its curriculum to include courses on Judaism, the Holocaust, Islam, Hinduism, Buddhism, and Zen Buddhism.

The Academy also made a concerted effort to bring more people of color to campus. The Admissions Office added some newly established recruiting programs to ABC and Prep for Prep. In 1990, O'Donnell appointed Gary M. Hill Jones associate dean, thus elevating the position of adviser to students of color. A year later, she gave the position wider authority, renaming it Associate Dean of Multicultural Affairs and appointing Nadine Abraham-Thompson. Individual departments also began recruiting faculty of color more aggressively, but, as in the past, it remained significantly more difficult to hire minority faculty than it was to recruit minority students. There were still the same factors that had discouraged people of color from coming in the late 1960s— geographical isolation, the school's elitist reputation, and uncompetitive pay compared with other residential schools. The Academy managed to recruit minority faculty through ventures such as a joint NAIS/ISAM People of Color job fair in Boston. But retaining them was another matter. In addition to a demanding schedule, they were expected to advise students of color. With over two hundred minority students and only a handful of minority instructors, the burdens seemed heavy.

The Office of the Dean of Students was also quite active. Thanks in part to a generous grant from the Dewitt-Wallace Reader's Digest Fund, the school held numerous assemblies on issues of diversity. Cornel West, Julian Bond, and Randall Kennedy visited the campus, as did Jong Koo Ahn, the Korean Consulate General in New York City. Ronnie Lupe, chairman of the White Mountain Apache Tribe and Santos Hawksblood from the Chiricahua Apaches spoke on Native American issues. The Buddhist photographer Galen Rowell gave a Tibetan slide show, and Lydia Douglas showed photographs of African-American women. Students attended performances by the Harlem Spiritual Ensemble, Blues Jazz with Earl Bethel, and the Inca Son of Peru.

Exeter's students themselves played an important role in the school's multicultural development. In the fall of 1989, the Afro-Exonian Society formed a subcommittee called the Racial Awareness Group. It provided (and still provides) a weekly forum for students to discuss issues of race, religion, sex, and sexual orientation. Encouraged to explore issues of racial, ethnic, and religious identity, students in the early 1990s formed a variety of groups celebrating their cultural heritage: the Hispanic Society, La Aliancia Latina, OLE (Organización Latinoamericana de Exeter), Chinese Culture Club, Chinese Studies Association, Korean Society, Japanese Club, Native American Society, Indian Society, Islamic Society, Hindu Society, Cuban Society, and the Unitarian Universalist Fellowship. Twenty-five years earlier some had viewed the formation of the Afro-Exonian Society as divisive to the Exeter community. Now the formation of such groups seemed evidence of a healthy multicultural environment. "It is a way for adolescents to get a sense of their identity," explained Dean Abraham-Thompson.[60]

As opposed to the other groups formed in the early 1990s, the Gay/Straight Alliance concerned itself with issues of sexual identity rather than ethnicity or religion. In this era the Academy came to believe that sexual orientation, like ethnicity or religion, was an important component of one's identity and should be accepted as such. In the past, Exeter's attitude toward its gay and lesbian population had hardly been so tolerant: students caught in homosexual acts were formally asked to leave the school. Things were not much better in the 1980s. Kelly Dermody '85 well remembered the difficulties gay and lesbian students encountered when she was a student:

Homophobic attitudes and anti-gay comments were often present and obvious in my Exeter experience. However, as I tried to navigate through my developing gay identity, the more subtle oppression of heterosexual assumptions pained me as much as, if not more than, explicit hostility. . . . Everyone at Exeter — teachers, dorm heads, coaches, and students — assumed heterosexuality in their speech and comments as a given for all Exonians. . . . For gay-identified students or those, like myself, who were simply beginning to develop questions about their sexual orientation, our minority experience entailed a different burden of prejudice and invisibility [from that experienced by ethnic and religious minority students]. . . . There wasn't any institutional understanding of the particular minority experience of non-heterosexual students.[61]

Fearful of rejection, gay students kept themselves carefully closeted. Nor were they alone: gay faculty members also were reluctant to have their sexual orientation known to the Exeter community. Christine Robinson, an instructor in the English Department since 1980–1981, recalled that she spent her first four years at the Academy closeted. "I came here and heard stories of men who left quietly. I internalized that as some kind of message." It was only when she joined the School Year Abroad program in France in 1984–1985 that she came out. But when she returned to Exeter the following year, she still did not feel secure enough to make a public statement.[62]

The climate started changing in the late 1980s, but not without some work on the part of the school. Susan J. Herney, then dean of students, recalled a girl who came to complain of the harassment of her gay and lesbian friends. "What are you going to do about it?" the girl demanded. The school responded at once, sponsoring a panel in early 1989 on "Sexuality, Homosexuality, and Homophobia." "Two of the participants, recent graduates who had come out at Harvard, spoke of the self-hate, the depression, and the near-suicidal experience they had experienced," Herney said. "The faculty were so touched by the pain. That made them much more educated and aware of what it's like to be an adolescent in that situation."[63] In this atmosphere of greater awareness and acceptance, Robinson came out at a Thursday Meditation in the early 1990s. This encouraged a number of students to open up to friends and adults, and in 1992 they formed the Gay/Straight Alliance and welcomed "any student or faculty member interested in combating societal discrimination in the stereotyping of people of 'different' sexual orientations."[64] This became one of the more active groups on campus, hosting a weekly forum and sponsoring assemblies. Gay and lesbian alumni/ae, historian Kevin Jennings, experts on HIV/AIDS, and a panel from the Names Project subsequently visited the school. In the mid-1990s, the English Department introduced a course on "Sexual Orientation in Literature." The greater acceptance of homosexuality was evident from the trustees' decision in October 1995 to extend faculty and staff health insurance to partners of same-sex couples.

The purpose of all student organizations based on some form of racial, religious, ethnic, or sexual identity was not simply to celebrate a particular culture. It was important for individuals also to relate to the community as a whole. The Diversity Council, representatives from the school's various religious, ethnic, and cultural clubs, played an important role in this regard. Advised by the principal, the Council formed a "link between these different organizations, support group for individual organizations, and a vehicle for joint activities." Every week it held discussions on Exeter's radio station, WPEA.

Outside events had also made the Academy more sensitive to racial and ethnic issues. In the summer of 1989, supporters of the Ku Klux Klan distributed recruitment pamphlets in the town, and the school learned a few months later that a town resident and member of the Rockingham County Sheriff's department was a local Klan organizer. The Academy immediately joined the town selectmen in denouncing the organization. At an Assembly the following year, Leonard Zeskind, a member of the Center for Democratic Revival, gave a lecture on the aims and methods of the Klan.[65]

Although the Academy was united against the KKK's threat, other issues remained divisive. The question of whether to make Martin Luther King Day a school holiday, for example, proved contentious. Congress had voted it a national holiday as of January 1984, and for years afterward the school celebrated the day with a special assembly devoted to race relations. As more and more states decided to make it a legal holiday (though not New Hampshire), members of Exeter's minority community began to press for this as well. The Academy, which did not celebrate any national holidays that fell during its regular academic calendar, avoided the issue until December 1989, when James W. Montford, an instructor in art and the adviser to students of color, decided to stage a hunger strike. After he had fasted for six days, the faculty held a heated debate and voted to observe the holiday. They then devoted much thought and organization to planning events that would make the day meaningful for students, including workshops, movies, and prominent guest speakers.[66] In this instance, as in others, Exeter was slow to institute change, but once it did, it expended great effort to make the holiday an important educational experience.

In the course of the late 1980s and early 1990s, Exeter made significant strides in its quest for diversity, but, as the Composition of the School Committee's report of early 1993 found, many problems lingered. The Academy needed to recruit African-Americans, Hispanic-Americans, and Native-Americans more aggressively. Equally important, the school had to make further changes to accommodate students of different backgrounds and abilities. Finally, it needed to deal with the persistence of intolerance, which ranged from racial and ethnic jokes to the hazing of girls, homosexuals, and minority students.

To address these problems, the school stepped up recruiting efforts and sponsored various workshops dealing with racism, homophobia, and sexism. Under dean Abraham-Thompson's leadership, the Academy addressed matters of diversity in a variety of ways, ranging from occasional assemblies on multicultural issues to finding money for students from disadvantaged backgrounds to buy textbooks.

CHANGES, CHALLENGES, AND CONTINUITIES

Exeter in the early twenty-first century is more diverse than it has ever been. The ranks of students, faculty, administrative staff, and trustees include individuals from many different racial, ethnic and religious groups. The student body has an increasingly global complexion, including citizens of nearly thirty nations, from Panama to Pakistan, from Bharain to Brazil, from Egypt to Estonia. The curriculum boasts a wide array of courses on Asian, African-American, Hispanic, and gay literature, African-American, Asian, and Latin American history, and eastern and western religions. Students seem quite knowledgeable about other cultures, with understanding and acceptance reinforced by workshops held throughout the year. They observe Kwanzaa, the Chinese New Year, and International Day. They celebrate their own cultural heritage in numerous clubs, and also share it with those of different backgrounds. New milestones and markers are reached, as with the appointment of same-sex couples as dorm parents in 2000 and the welcoming of transgendered students in the middle of the decade.

Behind Exeter's progress lies many of the Academy's distinctive traditions. "In the most ideal ways, the Harkness teaching method provides that level playing field we all strive for," observed Abraham-Thompson. "It makes it possible for a young Asian-American, Hispanic, African-American, or Caucasian

In 1832,
the Second
Academy
Building was
a notable
feature in
the town of
Exeter though
the Academy
itself had a
tiny footprint.

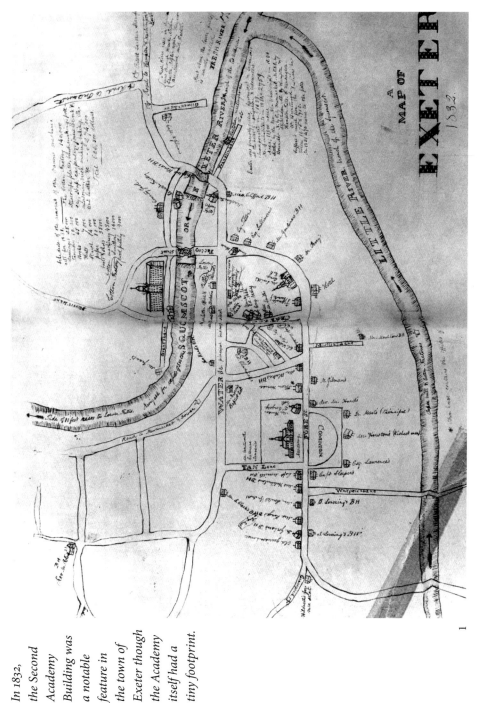

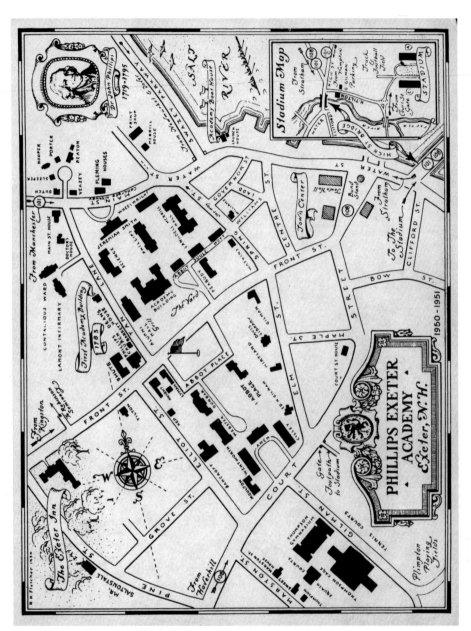

More than a century later, the impact of the Harkness Gift was evident in new classrooms and dormitories situated on a recognizably modern campus.

Today, the Academy spreads across more than 600 acres and maintains more than 125 buildings. Note the Class of 1945 Library in the center of the picture.

3

4

The founder of Phillips Exeter Academy, Exeter resident John Phillips, married well but left no heirs. He bequeathed a sizable part of his estate to establish a free academy in his hometown.

The First Academy Building housed classes between 1783 and 1794. Originally located on Tan Lane, the building now sits at 12 Elliott Street and is the residence of the dean of the faculty.

Benjamin Abbot began teaching at Exeter in 1788 at the age of 26. Two years later, he became preceptor and then, in 1808, principal instructor, a position he held for thirty years.

Of the Second Academy Building, an admiring observer noted that "the whole is executed in a style that does honour to the institution." It was destroyed by fire in December 1870.

The first Exonian to lead the Academy, Gideon Lane Soule (class of 1813) followed Abbot as principal and served for 35 years.

9

Dedicated in 1872, the Third Academy Building could accommodate 300 students. It, too, burned to the ground in 1914, just weeks into the tenure of Principal Lewis Perry.

10

The great hall on the second floor of the central wing of the Third Academy Building hosted religious services, lectures, assemblies, and exhibitions, as well as "the dreaded" college entrance exams.

Plus ça change: a commentary on dining hall fare, c. 1910.

11

The annual clash with Andover, shown here in 1911, became an important event on campus at an early date.

12

Harlan Page Amen led Exeter between 1895 and 1913, an important period in the Academy's growth and modernization.

Built in 1915, the Fourth (and present) Academy Building was expanded and remodeled extensively in 1931 following the Harkness Gift.

13

14

After the founder, philanthropist Edward S. Harkness left the largest imprint on the Academy, donating $5.8 million to inspire "something revolutionary" in secondary education.

15

Lewis Perry was 53 when notified by his friend Harkness of a major gift. By then he had already served as principal for 18 years and he would stay on to lead the Academy another decade and a half.

16

17   *Before . . . Before the Harkness Gift, classrooms in the Academy Building were organized in rows of seats to accommodate as many as 50 students for lectures and recitations.*

18

    . . . and After. Under the Harkness Plan, classrooms became more congenial to learning, reconfigured around the oval Harkness Table, which seated 12 students and the teacher.

19

The opening of school [here in the late 1940s] each year heralded nine months of nonstop activity.

20

For many years, dinner was served in the dining hall, with scholarship boys serving as waiters, as in this scene from 1955.

Three boys perch on a branch above the Exeter River before taking a plunge. Scenes such as this figured prominently in John Knowles's novel A Separate Peace *(1959), set at an academy modeled on Exeter.*

21

The butt room (for smoking) in each dorm served as a center of social life in the early post–World War II years. Pictured here: the butt room in Hoyt Hall.

22

23

Bill and Kathie Saltonstall frequently entertained students at their home on Pine Street. "Bill was impossible not to like and Kathie was impossible not to love," recalled a faculty colleague.

24

H. Hamilton "Hammy" Bissell '29 (Hon. '32, '36, '38, '42, '44, '45, '60, P '58, GP '95) helped implement principal Saltonstall's vision of making Exeter "a national high school." As director of scholarship boys from 1945 to 1961, Bissell recruited boys from all over the United States.

By the late 1940s, Exeter drew students from 47 states.

Exeter today not only attracts students from all over the nation but also from all over the world.

27

In 1964, the aged Lewis Perry (seated) met with his successors (L to R), Richard Ward "Dick" Day (1964–1974), Bill Saltonstall (1946–1963), and Ernest Gillespie, who served as interim principal during 1963–1964 and later as the first dean of the faculty.

The Exonian printed a special edition on February 27, 1970, to announce the trustee vote opening the Academy to girl students.

28

29

In 1995 — on the 25th anniversary of the decision to make Exeter coeducational — the trustees authorized changes to the lintel above the main door of the Academy Building. The original inscription, "Huc venite pueri ut viri sitis" ("Come here boys so that you become men") was bracketed between the year of the founding and 1970.

HIC QVAERITE PVERI PVELLAEQVE VIRTVTEM ET SCIENTIAM

30

On granite panels above the main entrance to the Academy Building, a new inscription appeared: "Hic quaerite pueri puellaeque virtutem et scientiam" ("Here boys and girls seek goodness and knowledge").

The coming of coeducation was the biggest but not the only big change at Exeter during the Day years. The Love Gymnasium signaled an end to pure Georgian architecture and heralded a new look for the campus.

31

An even bigger departure from tradition, as well as an enduring monument to Academy values, was the new library designed by renowned architect Louis I. Kahn. Opened in 1971, it was — and still is — the largest secondary school library in the world. In 1995 it was endowed as the Class of 1945 Library.

32

By the early 1970s, the growing diversity of the student body was a fact of everyday life. Pictured at center: Harold Brown, Jr., '74, later director of alumni/ae affairs.

33

Principal Stephen G. Kurtz (1974–1987) proved a soothing influence after a decade of dramatic changes at the Academy.

34

35

Exeter's 12th principal, Kendra S. O'Donnell (lower left), led the Academy between 1987 and 1997. Among her priorities were opening doors to students from many backgrounds, improving residential life, and "the other curriculum," to teach goodness.

36

Tyler C. Tingley came to Exeter in 1997 to guide the Academy into the twenty-first century. Leading a Harkness-informed master planning process, Tingley has presided over a building boom, the greening of the campus, and a soaring endowment.

The opening assembly each September (pictured here in 2006) launches the academic year with a reminder of Exeter traditions.

More than 75 years after the Harkness Gift, the Harkness Table remains the centerpiece of an Exeter education, a powerful source of learning through decades of continuous change.

39

41

40

Athletics plays an important role at the school, helping to develop body as well as mind, teaching teamwork, and providing outlets for energy and competitiveness.

42

Students collaborate on a mural.

43

44

The cast of South Pacific takes a bow.

45

The Academy's facilities to support the arts include the award-winning Forrestal-Bowld Music Building, which opened in 1995.

46

The Academy's Concert Choir performs in Phillips Church, another venue for performances.

Dedicated in 2001, the Phelps Science Center was designed with Harkness teaching in mind. The building includes classrooms, laboratories, and open spaces intended to inspire and facilitate learning.

47

48

In the early 2000s, the old Thompson Science Building underwent a major renovation and rechristening as the Phelps Academy Center, which houses the grill, post office, meeting and club rooms, an auditorium and recreational spaces.

49

Playing bingo in the grill.

50

51

Exeter is hardly all work and no play.

52

Making choices in the dining hall.

Building friendships in the dorm.

53

Getting advice.

54

55

When Annie Riley '03 sought to establish the first New Hampshire chapter of Best Buddies, a not-for-profit organization dedicated to helping people with intellectual disabilities, dozens of students signed up to help. Pictured here: Academy students and local teenagers at a bowling alley in Exeter.

56

Sharing ideas in the library.

*Enjoying
personalized space
in the dorm.*

*Relaxing and
reading.*

The Exeter Initiatives capital campaign kicked off in 2004 with an assembly featuring noted historian David McCullough at the Harkness Table.

Finish line: classmates and friends celebrate graduation.

61   *An Exeter education: brought to you by the faculty (pictured in 2007).*

student to have his or her say. The kind of learning that happens around that Harkness Table is priceless."[67] But that is only the beginning. "It is not enough to sit around the table," explained Randolph Carter, director of multicultural diversity at the National Association of Independnet Schools. "We must ask whether we are engaged in mutual inquiry. Multiculturalism has been a side issue and needs to be put in the center of the table. We cannot study the Treaty of Paris without asking what individuals were present when the treaty was made. That is the next step Exeter must take."[68]

The residential life program provided another support to multiculturalism. "What happens in the dorms is as important as what happens in the class-room," Abraham-Thompson explained. "Kids live together, they eat together, they sleep in the dorms together. They have to negotiate a lot of things. That kind of learning is going to change your life. If you are living with a young African-American woman you are going to learn a lot about her family, how she does her hair, what her needs are."

For all the progress the Academy has achieved during the past seven decades, however, in some respects it has traveled in a widening circle. Soar-ing tuition has raised anew the old concern that the school might lose its economic diversity. The middle class was less well represented in the early 2000s than it was forty or fifty years earlier, when Exeter was more affordable. In the attempt to make Exeter a more feasible option for middle-class fami-lies, the trustees launched a series of initiatives designed to slow the rate of tuition increase while adapting the needs analysis system to provide financial aid to middle-income families without penalizing traditional recipients. The affordability of an Exeter education for a middle-class family remains an issue today and is one of the priorities for gifts under the Exeter Initiatives capital campaign.

Racial diversity also has been a continuing focus, though the Academy is encouraged by recent progress. In 2006–2007, 38 percent of the students were people of color. After hovering at a relatively low level for decades, the number of African-American students on campus began to climb in the mid-1990s, finally passing the peak of 1971–1972. In 2006–2007 enrollments included eighty African-American students. Behind this rise lay renewed commitment and redoubled efforts to recruit minority students. Meanwhile, the numbers of Asians and Asian-Americans in the student body has oscillated in the range of 20 to 25 percent of the total.

The Academy has similar goals for increasing the diversity of its faculty. The school continues to recruit at the NAIS People of Color Job Fair, and began participating in two newer programs, New England Minority Network and Sphere. Money from the DeWitt-Wallace Foundation facilitated travel for recruiting faculty as well as visits by minority candidates to campus. But the problem was far from solved: of the 162 full-time faculty at the Academy in 2006–2007, only 4 percent were African-American, and 6 percent were Asian or Asian-American, including associate dean of faculty Ronald Kim.

Convinced of the need for more energetic recruiting, the faculty established the John and Elizabeth Phillips Fellowship to hire new teachers out of college or senior faculty from a racial or ethnic group that was underrepresented on the faculty.[69] "The fellowship lasts for one to three years as opposed to most fellowships, which last a year," Director of Alumni/ae Affairs Harold Brown '74 explained. "At a time when there are few tenured slots open, it gives minority faculty a chance to stay at the Academy for a while."[70] Heading the initiative was Stephanie N. Johnson '85, who would help identify potential fellows by establishing a network of contacts around the country — a network that would help Exeter locate minority faculty in the future.[71]

Realizing that true multiculturalism depends on more than admissions statistics, the Academy has understood the need to foster greater sensitivity to the needs of different sectors of the community. "Both students and faculty need to be made more racially aware," said Reverend Thompson '72. To this end, the school continued to hold assemblies and workshops dealing with racial sensitivity and multicultural issues.

Exeter's embrace of the multicultural ideal of the late twentieth and early twenty-first centuries changed the Academy in fundamental ways that most observers believe are much for the better. But it also created another set of challenges for the school to address. When it seriously took on the charge of educating students in those social-cultural areas, the problem arose of striking the proper balance between a multicultural definition of education and the traditional, academic one. The quest for multiculturalism placed added burdens on the residential faculty, requiring them to acquire sensitivity and skills rarely gained in the normal course of training of secondary school teachers.

The school also fought a drift into "political correctness," the tendencies to confuse the interests of individuals and groups and to suspend critical judgment for the sake of merely accepting all differences and distinctions among cultures. Exeter sought to walk a fine line, balancing the needs for personal identity with the interests of the whole community. The faculty periodically reevaluated the curriculum to determine what topics and interpretations were appropriate to teach, and what, because of their political nature, were not.

The Harkness approach, with its emphasis on tolerance and respect, has been invaluable in these endeavors. These have proved controversial matters, however, and, like society at large, Exeter will continue to debate them.

Exeter's journey toward multiculturalism has been long and unevenly paced, but there has been much continuity along the way. Consistent with the founding mission, the school has consistently reformulated its definition of diversity — economic, geographic, sociological, and multicultural — to mirror a changing world. The northeastern WASPish institution of the early 1930s has given way to a community of different nationalities, races, ethnic origins, religions, and sexual orientations. The gates are open to people of all backgrounds, to youth from every quarter. But the process of transformation has by no means come to an end. With many more applicants than can be accommodated, the Academy must continually make choices and grapple with the question of whom it is trying to serve. For now, this much seems certain: the answers it reaches will change as the society around it changes.

Coeducation: The Quiet Revolution

In 1995, a quarter century after Exeter admitted its first female students, Principal Kendra Stearns O'Donnell remarked that the coming of coeducation represented a "historical milestone, one not quite as ancient as the introduction of the Harkness Table, but at least as important" in the school's history.[1] That was a powerful and provocative claim, since the Harkness Table remains one of the Academy's most distinctive features. Yet there is no disputing the far-reaching impact of coeducation upon Exeter, which was O'Donnell's real point. As it adjusted to girl students and increasing numbers of women faculty, administrators, and staff, Exeter became a qualitatively different place from what it had been for nearly two hundred years. Most people who were part of the transition believe the school is healthier, happier, and more balanced than it had been as an all-male institution.

Today, girls and women are so integral to the school's identity that its long past as a male bastion seems remote and almost quaint. This outcome was scarcely foreseen in the 1950s when advocates and opponents first debated whether to admit girls, although they knew they were considering a significant change. Nor did it become clear once the first girls and women faculty arrived in the 1970s. Indeed, the full effects of coeducation upon Exeter were delayed in coming and manifested in a long sequence of accommodations to the needs, interests, and aspirations of girls and women. Harkness-style inquiry and discussion proved integral to this process, which played out unevenly across different segments of the community. Progress for girl students was swift and virtually complete by the early 1980s. The integration of female faculty took much longer, with some issues and concerns lingering into the early 1990s. O'Donnell's appointment as principal in 1987 itself marked a significant milestone for women, who also gained an increasing presence in the administration, on the board of trustees, and in alumni/ae affairs. This "quiet revolution" had run its course by the mid-1990s and indeed exerted a widespread and profound impact on the Academy.

SMALL STEPS TOWARD A BIG CHANGE, 1950–1970

Exeter thought about becoming a coeducational institution for nearly two decades before it made its decision. The process took so much time partly because of the Academy's by then engrained habit of examining and discussing every aspect of important matters thoroughly before committing to action. In this instance, the partisans were well aware that big issues were at stake, a circumstance that prolonged the debate. Everyone knew that "going co-ed" would be expensive and probably irreversible, that its effects on Exeter would prove far-reaching, and that there would be losses as well as gains in the transition. For momentum to build behind the move, much had to change at Exeter and in the world around it. And, over time, that is exactly what happened: a generation of opponents retired or gave way, new leaders emerged to promote the cause, and external pressures mounted markedly as one leading school and college after another committed to coeducation. By the late 1960s, these forces were irresistible, and they finally drove the Academy to its momentous decision.

Exeter first considered the question of whether to admit girls in the early 1950s, years before it became a focus of discussion at similar private academic institutions elsewhere. Considering that the Academy was extremely successful and proud of its traditions, this was remarkable, but it made sense in light of Exeter's aspirations under Principal Saltonstall to become a "national high school," one of the top secondary schools in the country. Initially, that meant recruitment of academically able boys from every economic level and region of the country. The next logical step, some suggested, was to move beyond being the best boys' school to be the best school for students of both sexes. During the 1952–1953 school year, interest in the possibility of coeducation was so great that the Exeter Study Committee considered it as part of its broad examination of the institution. Ultimately, the committee stopped well short of endorsing coeducation, however. The committee took note of philosophical objections and practical problems and recommended instead that consideration be given to building a separate but affiliated girls' school in the vicinity. This would be a long-term objective and the committee proposed no timetable.[2]

It was not long, however, before the issue surfaced again. In 1959, some faculty members proposed to admit girls to the summer session. The director of the summer program, Phillips E. Wilson, initially opposed the idea. He argued that girls would "distract" the boys in the program, and the trustees declined to pursue the possibility. Soon after, Wilson had a change of heart. Having in the meantime established a coeducational adult education program in the town, he decided it was important to open up the Academy. Wilson also had personal reasons for this decision. As his daughter, Susan "Tootie" Wilson Cole, explained, "He felt quite strongly about girls going to Exeter, since he had three daughters who could not." Wilson tried to drum up support for admitting girls to the 1961 summer session, but his colleagues were less than enthusiastic. "He had quite a fight on his hands," Cole recalled. "Some members of the administration and the faculty were very much against it."[3]

Wilson finally prevailed, and in 1961 the Academy took a small step forward by opening up its summer session to girls. The fourteen who attended that year were day students and most were daughters of faculty. Meanwhile, some members of the faculty continued to press for girls to attend the regular session as well. They proposed the matter not on its own — for it was clear it would meet a frosty reception in the faculty — but in the context of other issues Exeter was confronting at this time. By 1960 it had become apparent that the school was in need of several new major facilities, including a library and gymnasium. This naturally raised the question of enrollments. "We realized that we had to do a study to determine how large those facilities should be," explained treasurer and historian Colin Irving. "Should we build them for the current number of students, or make them bigger?"[4] Examining the question in detail, the Trustee Subcommittee on Faculty Matters reported in September 1961 that it would be in the Academy's best interests to increase the student population from 750 to 1,000. Following the suggestion of several members of the faculty that coeducation "might be a good way to increase the size of the school and was desirable as an educational pattern in itself," the subcommittee proposed the Academy conduct a separate study of coeducation "as an integral or coordinate part of the Academy."[5] And so the Committee on Possible Coeducation at Exeter came into being, the first in a series of formal groups to explore the subject.

While the committee went about its investigation, the summer school experiment took another small step forward. For unrelated reasons, the summer school became an autonomous entity independent from the Academy in September 1961.[6] Irving, who assumed direction of the summer school in addition to his other duties, expanded the program in various ways, the most important of which was to admit the first girl boarders, and the summer school committee immediately began recruiting girls as well as women teachers and dormitory proctors.[7] Irving was quite candid about his aims. "I regarded this as a practical experiment to see how dormitories and the gymnasium could be utilized," he said. "It was a great success. The [summer school] faculty, half of whom came from the regular faculty, were very pleased with the girls. We had minimum disciplinary problems. It was much more fun than the old summer school had been. I hoped that girls would eventually be at Exeter full-time."[8]

Despite the success of the summer experiment, when the Committee on Possible Coeducation at Exeter reported to the trustees in early autumn, it recommended against the Academy becoming coeducational. Girls would enrich the classroom experience, but outside the classroom their presence would create "problems," because girls "confuse" and "distract" boys. A better solution would be "the establishment of a good school for girls in or near Exeter. If funds became available for this purpose, the Academy might itself undertake the establishment of such a school, but no effort to obtain these funds should be permitted to divert attention and energy from current capital needs."[9] Fully integrated coeducation simply seemed out of the question.

The issue of coeducation lay dormant until the autumn of 1964, when Richard Day arrived as principal. Anticipating the change in leadership, the trustees had just appointed the Academy Planning Committee (APC) to conduct yet another study of the school. Chaired by C. Arthur Compton, the faculty committee examined the question of how "Exeter students can receive the best possible education *for their time*." Exeter, the committee found, should add 250 girls to the current total population of approximately 750 boys—a change that would strengthen the school's academic excellence and add a great deal to activities outside the classroom. But the committee deemed it important to limit enrollment to girls in the eleventh and twelfth grades because "at this age many girls would better adjust to our kind of boarding school life, and both boys and girls . . . would have the maturity to assume the responsibilities imposed by Exeter's freedom." For the longer term, the committee urged the Academy to consider building a separate girls' residential campus "close enough to the centers of school life to permit easy access by the girls, but peripheral enough to create a carefully delineated area easy to supervise. The establishment of coeducation would therefore impinge minimally on the freedom of Exeter boys." The committee also urged the administration to hire a few women to be on the faculty so that "boys can learn to appreciate the intellectual capacity of women." With these changes, it argued, Exeter "would become more nearly a national school."[10]

But the APC's endorsement failed to convince the trustees. As in the past, finances proved an obstacle. Plans for the Long Step Forward, the largest capital campaign to date, were already in the making, and they had nothing to do with coeducation.[11] A fundraising effort of this size consumed the attention of trustees and senior administrators. But even more important, it required tremendous support from the alumni, some of whom were adamantly opposed to coeducation. Day himself had little patience for that point of view. "It is fatuous," he declared, "to consider Exeter a national school unless it has girls as well as boys." Irving explained, "Conceptually, Day had always favored coeducation, but powerful forces — principally, alumni — were arrayed against him." Day went out of his way to avoid alienating these people, as did the other proponents of coeducation. Irving remembered a big fundraising dinner in Washington when one alumnus asked the question that was on everyone's mind: Was Exeter going to admit girls? Irving gave the official response: "It is the firm intent of the trustees that Exeter will not go coeducational." The audience shouted and cheered.[12]

The Long Step Forward began in 1967 with great fanfare and enthusiasm from all quarters. The administration was careful not to raise the subject of coeducation during the initial stages of the campaign, but interest in the possibility continued to grow both on and off campus. Polling Exeter students, faculty, and alumni for their opinions on a variety of current issues, Bruce K. Eckland of the Educational Testing Service found that 26 percent of the older alumni — those of the pre-Harkness generation — favored girls attending Exeter, in contrast with 88 percent of current students. The same held true for the different generations of faculty. Eckland summarized the results as follows: "As a whole, students, faculty, and alumni believe that Exeter should strongly consider a co-educational program in some form, such as the establishment of a separate but near-by boarding school for girls. However, there is a major split between the older, more conservative alumni and the younger generation. In fact, the difference in opinion is so large that it almost certainly represents a major change in social attitude towards the opposite sex."[13]

What Eckland observed from his study of the Exeter community was in fact happening all over the country, as increasing numbers of single-sex colleges and universities began considering the possibility of coeducation. At Yale, for example, officials were weighing the prospect of coordinate affiliation with Vassar. To many at Exeter, a coordinate girls' school was the perfect compromise — a way to put girls on campus without overturning traditions or jeopardizing the success of the Long Step Forward. In the spring of 1968, the board of trustees instructed Irving to undertake a financial analysis of a plan in which a girls' school of 200 to 250 students "maintains a separate identity, occupies a separate residential campus, and shares such common facilities with the Academy as are practical and mutually agreeable." Irving's report was extremely enthusiastic: "a coordinate school project is eminently feasible, and mutually advantageous [for both schools] from the financial viewpoint."[14]

Even with the financial go-ahead, however, the school's leaders were not ready to make a decision. Determined to resolve the issue, Day appointed the Coordinate School Philosophy Committee. The committee circulated a questionnaire to faculty and students asking if they wished to share classes, meals, clubs, and athletic activities with girls, and it held separate open meetings for students and faculty. Members of the committee also met with representatives from a number of private schools that were already coeducational or were actively considering it, including Milton Academy, Kent, Choate, Loomis, Taft, Westminster, Middlesex, and the National Cathedral School.

While this study was under way, pressure to embrace coeducation continued to mount. In the fall of 1968, two of Exeter's models made the move. A committee at Princeton had been studying the question of whether the university should undertake to educate women, and in late September the *Princeton Alumni Weekly* published the results. The report, generally considered the most thorough analysis on the subject, examined the desirability and feasibility of coeducation from a variety of perspectives. It found that admitting women would appreciably increase Princeton's attractiveness both to the best men applicants and to faculty recruits. In response to the argument that the presence of women would prove a distraction for men, the study said that it was a moot question because undergraduates spent many of their weekends traveling to visit their girlfriends or to socialize at women's colleges and coeducational institutions. Meanwhile, the study pointed out, as a national institution, Princeton had a duty to help educate the growing numbers of women who would occupy important positions in the workforce and in society. As to whether to proceed through coeducation or coordinate education, the committee argued the economic and educational advantages of the former but pointed out that if Princeton were to adopt the coordinate form, it would be as a step on the way to coeducation. The report concluded that "The quality of the educational experience at Princeton would be greatly enriched if women were admitted, that to achieve these benefits in full measure an undergraduate body including not less than 1000 women [i.e., 25 percent of the undergraduate body] is desirable, and that the arrangements should be coeducation rather than coordinate." As a result of this study, the trustees of the University decided that girls would probably be admitted to Princeton in the near future.

The reaction at Yale was more enthusiastic, with the students demanding in the fall of 1968 that the university implement full coeducation at once. The administration responded by scheduling "Coeducation Week" for early November. The students marched on President Kingman Brewster's house demanding the University admit women at once, and three days later presented him with a petition of 1,700 signatures. The following week, Brewster put the question to the faculty, which voted in favor of Yale's opening its doors to women the following autumn. These events received a tremendous amount of publicity, including television coverage and articles in the *New York Times*, *Life*, *Time*, and *Newsweek*. Soon afterward, the trustees of Princeton announced that the university also would admit women in the autumn of 1969. At about the same time, Harvard and Radcliffe announced they would merge, and plans were made for women students to live in the Harvard houses, starting in the spring of 1970. It was evident that the best way for a top college to remain competitive was to become coeducational.[15]

The news in the Ivy League reverberated at Exeter. In late January 1969, the Coordinate School Philosophy Committee submitted its report. The students and faculty, it found, generally favored coeducation rather than a coordinate system. The latter would be "educationally restrictive": with two boards of trustees, two administrations, and two faculties, it would be difficult for Exeter "to preserve the freedom of action which would insure the perpetuation of its educational ideals." Citing the Princeton study, the CSPC argued that a coordinate system with many capital expenditures would also be "fiscally extravagant," since it would inevitably result in full coeducation. Although the committee clearly believed coeducation preferable to a coordinate system, it recommended that "a detailed study be made of the two possible courses of action for the future."[16]

Students at the Academy greeted the report enthusiastically. The Exeter Student Council immediately petitioned the faculty for a two-week experimental exchange with girls' schools during the spring term. The faculty denied the petition, however, noting that the proposed exchange was not long enough and that there was insufficient time to implement the program. It proposed instead that the Academy investigate an extended exchange as well as the possibility of coeducation. Day announced in a Chapel talk a few days later that the Educational Affairs Committee of the Trustees supported an investigation of "the feasibility of a semester exchange, beginning in January 1970 and involving perhaps 100–150 boys and the same number of girls." He enjoined André R. Vernet, a member of the Modern Languages Department, to conduct this investigation. Vernet spent the next three weeks holding discussions with representatives from two girls' schools near Boston—Concord Academy and Dana Hall. But it soon proved difficult to find enough volunteers at Exeter, and the school decided to abandon the idea. The students were apparently uninterested in an experiment in coeducation. They wanted the real thing.

By this point, the issue had been escalating for nearly eight years. Eager to resolve the issue once and for all, in the spring of 1969 the trustees appointed the Coeducation Committee, chaired by trustee Calvin H. Plimpton '35 and composed of trustees, faculty, students, and the headmistress of the Dana Hall School, Edith B. Phelps, to conduct an exhaustive investigation of coeducation and make "a firm recommendation that such education *would* or *would not* be desirable for Exeter." Hedging their bets, however, they also authorized the purchase of the Benedetto farm, prime real estate in nearby Kensington that would, in conjunction with the Academy's holdings in that area, make it possible to establish a coordinate girls' school.[17]

Over the course of the next several months, the Coeducation Committee examined coeducation from a variety of perspectives—sociological, psychological, pedagogical, educational, and practical—and presented its findings at a special meeting of the trustees in mid-January 1970. Coeducation would result in a student body that was "more natural, healthier, happier, more diversified, and qualitatively superior." Classes would be more stimulating with the "feminine point of view." The admission of "able, highly motivated girls, perhaps replacing less qualified boys, will sharpen intellectual exchange, increase competitiveness in the best sense, and confirm the traditional value of hard work." Exeter had a responsibility to prepare its students for institutions of higher learning, where coeducation was fast becoming the norm. It was in the national interest to prepare girls as well as boys to be the leaders of tomorrow. Coeducation would draw better teachers and students—an important consideration, given the competition with the other boarding schools. The coeducational summer school had proved a great success. "The committee believes that coeducation would so improve the quality of education at Exeter that it recommends the admission of girls as soon as possible." After considering the various options of coeducation—exchanges with girls' schools, coordinate education, the admission of day girls, and the admission of boarding girls—the Coeducation Committee concluded that the optimal plan was to admit day girls in 1970, and boarding girls the following year. The goal would be to increase the size of the Academy to 1,000, with girls constituting 20 to 40 percent of the student body. "Fully integrated coeducation," the report concluded, should be achieved "in the shortest possible time."[18]

These arguments proved extremely compelling. At Day's urging, the trustees approved the proposal but postponed a final decision and public announcement "until key alumni and prospective donors could be visited during January and February." On February 27 the board made its decision public: "Exeter shall become a coeducational institution in the regular session with the admission of female day students in September 1970, provided that no significant capital expenditure be made unless funds to support coeducation become available. The administration is charged with the preparation of plans for admission of a limited number of boarding girls in 1971. In making this decision, it is the policy of the Trustees that the number of boys not to be reduced."[19]

After many years of deliberation, the Academy had decided to take the plunge: Exeter was to become coeducational at last.

WELCOMING GIRL STUDENTS: AN AWKWARD INTRODUCTION

Exeter now had to prepare for the arrival of girls. The first step was to send out a special Academy Paper on "Coeducation at Exeter" to all alumni, parents of students and applicants, and employees. Playing down the magnitude of the decision, the pamphlet claimed that "coeducation will not require capital construction or a reduction in the number of boarding boys." The trustees hoped this statement would allay the fears of alumni during the Long Step Forward.[20] But it also reflected the Academy's belief that nothing much would have to change—an attitude that was to complicate the process of assimilation in the years to come.

Meanwhile, Exeter began attending to the practical details—hiring women teachers, revising the regulations in the E-Book, assigning girls to dining halls, and arranging for the participation of girls in extracurricular activities. Despite these efforts, many problems would arise during the process of implementing coeducation, some completely unexpected and some humorous—from a distance, that is. By far the biggest problem the school faced, however, was its own ambivalence toward the change.

In September 1970, day girls arrived on campus, a total of 40 in a student body of 887. The following year, the Academy welcomed its first boarding girls, 80 in all, in addition to 48 day girls that year; there were 770 boarding boys and 53 day boys. The female boarders resided in two dormitories, Bancroft and Hoyt, situated on opposite ends of the campus.

Ironically, although the Academy had pondered the possibility of coeducation from every angle, it was poorly prepared to welcome the girls when they finally arrived. The physical plant was still that of an all-boys' school. Construction undertaken in the late 1960s, supposedly "designed with flexibility for future accommodation both as to numbers and as to sex," proved inadequate.[21] The new gymnasium's locker facilities for girls were quite small. The only direct access from the girls' locker room to the training room took them near the boys' locker room. To avoid running into boys wandering about in towels, one had to ascend a flight of stairs, walk the length of the building, and then descend the back steps. The new nine-story library, completed in November 1971, was little better: it featured only two bathrooms for girls.

As some of the first wave of female students remembered, there were other signs that the Academy was not ready for a change of this magnitude. There were few female role models — only the handful of women who had been hired in those early years. English and history classes alike gave short shrift to the accomplishments of women authors and activists. The school paid little attention to the physical and mental health needs of its new female residents: no women doctors were on staff, nor was there resident expertise in female adolescent development.[22]

And there were still other signs — less noticeable to some, but no less important. The first girls who graduated received diplomas worded as they had been since the school's founding, with masculine pronouns.[23] The locker room door said "Girls" instead of "Women" (its counterpart said "Men"). When it rained, the boys' tennis team had exclusive use of the indoor courts. "More than anything," Ellen A. Fowler '72 said, "we were running headlong into two hundred years of tradition. The change that had to happen was so fundamental, so deep, that we only stumbled over little indications of it."[24]

Another consequence of coeducation was the discrepancy in the dress code. Boys had to wear jackets and ties, whereas girls could wear whatever they wanted, with the exception of jeans. Interestingly, the boys reacted strongly to the reverse discrimination. "In the fall of 1971, they went on strike and put pillow-cases over their jackets to protest," Fowler recalled, "but nothing was done about it."[25] In 1974, the school relented, allowing boys to wear turtlenecks with their jackets. Jeans came later for both sexes, but the disparity between the dress codes was never fully corrected. The school finally formulated more specific regulations for girls in 1987, but did not insist on the same degree of formality as their male counterparts. Boys still wear ties or turtlenecks, and girls still have greater freedom of dress. While some see the looser code as an advantage, however, others believe it represents an institutional attitude — a tradition of grooming boys rather than girls for positions of leadership.

Some of the problems girls encountered in the early days of coeducation were due to sheer lack of numbers. In 1970–1971, girls' athletics were virtually nonexistent outside of physical education classes. "There were no girls' teams in that first year because of the small number of girls," explained Kathy Nekton, instructor in Physical Education and chair of the department for several years. The one girl who won a varsity letter that year had participated on the boys' ski team. That all changed the following year, when there were enough girls to form varsity teams in field hockey, basketball, swimming, lacrosse, and tennis. "It was a rather ambitious program," Nekton observed, "considering that there were only 126 girls in the school at the time."[26]

The first girls on campus were not a risky population. Many came from affluent families which had already sent their brothers to the school. Not surprisingly, they were scholastically every bit as good as their male peers. "The girls they selected for those initial classes were ones they thought were very safe bets," observed Judith Hall '71. "The girls as a whole were really dynamic people. If they hadn't been, they wouldn't have made it through the admissions process."[27] Five of the eleven senior girls who graduated in 1971 were members of Cum Laude, the school's honor society, and one received the prestigious T. A. D. Jones Scholarship at Yale.[28]

And yet girls had other problems in the classroom. Many of the older male instructors made it quite clear that they did not want girls at the Academy. "There were some faculty members who told me and some of my friends that they had voted against coeducation and really didn't think girls should be here," recalled Hall. "That really made you feel uncomfortable when you suddenly found yourself in the classroom with that person. You never were sure whether you were going to be given a fair shake and whether your intellect would be respected as boys' intellects were."[29] Even the instructors who had supported coeducation often did not know how to treat girls in an academic setting. "The teachers couldn't figure out what to call us," Ellen Fowler '72 observed. "They used to call boys by their last names. Now they wondered, should they call you 'Miss' and the boys 'Mister'?" Often there was only one girl in a class of twelve. "I felt I was always on display," S. Kimberly Welch '72 remarked. Instructors commonly asked, "What is the female point of view?" — even in French class, where students were asked for the "mademoiselle's point of view."[30] Boys often seemed at sea as well and made awkward attempts to praise their new classmates, with comments like "pretty good, for a girl."

As difficult as the academic experience was for those first girls, social interactions were not much easier. Hall recalled,

> We were very much aware of the fact that we were females in an all-male environment. When you walked into classrooms you were the only female and you looked for another female face because you felt more comfortable if there was one. In the dining halls, if you walked in without other females, you were made to feel very uncomfortable. Everybody looked at you to wonder where you were going to sit, and if you sat down at a table where there were males, depending on whether they had had much contact with females in the past, which many of them hadn't — particularly those boys who had been here for a number of years — it was a very strange situation. Most of the Exeter boys that had been at the Academy for a while were used to seeing girls their age at dances when the girls were shipped up on buses and they'd stay for a couple of hours and then were shipped back. And that was their whole way of dealing with females. They had never dealt with girls as equals in the classroom, on the playing fields, and in extracurricular activities, so you were always pointed out.[31]

This social awkwardness encouraged many girls to bond with their female classmates. "The Exeter girls moved in gangs across the campus, ate together at all-girl tables and fled, after classes, to the isolated study areas allotted to them," wrote Joyce Maynard '71.[32] For Joan Barrett Wickersham '74, the "consciousness of being a minority worked in a positive way. There was a lot of natural bonding just because you were female. I made very close female friendships [at Exeter] and there was an immediate identification with the other women in the class. It was almost a natural selection as far as making friends went."[33]

The number of girls grew steadily over the course of the 1970s, but the Academy accommodated their needs at an uneven rate. Nekton repeatedly informed the administration that the girls' locker facilities in Thompson Gymnasium were in need of expansion, but the problem was not fully corrected until the 1980s. Users of the boathouse were even less fortunate: although girls started rowing on the varsity crew in the mid-1970s, their facilities remained woefully inadequate until the completion of a new boathouse in 1990. The situation was not much better at the Academy Library, where the girls acquired additional bathrooms only after a librarian, frustrated at the inconvenience, co-opted the boys' room on the second floor. Even so, the two urinals were not removed from that bathroom, and they remained for many years. Although some men found this problem trivial, women had to deal with it every day. "People would laugh in '73, '74, '75 about the urinals in the girls' rooms, but by '77, '78 they were seen as a metaphor for Exeter's attitude toward coeducation," recalled English instructor Peter Greer '58, a member of the faculty since 1968. "We'd ask when we would become a really coeducational school. Things seemed worse in the mid-to-late 1970s than they did earlier. The novelty of being female at Exeter had worn off."[34]

No doubt nearly two hundred years of male exclusivity made it difficult for the Academy to anticipate and accommodate the needs of female students. The atmosphere began to change, as the number of girls steadily rose and the faculty of the Harkness generation began retiring, their places filled by younger faculty who themselves had attended coeducational schools and colleges. When girls constituted nearly 40 percent of the student body in the early 1980s, they started feeling at home at Exeter.

WELCOMING WOMEN FACULTY:
A THORNY PROBLEM

The process of assimilation proved lengthier and more difficult for female faculty than for female students, although the reasons for the difficulties were similar. Academy officials had agreed during their deliberations in the 1960s that women would play an important role in coeducation, but they apparently had given little thought to what the school needed to do to recruit and integrate women faculty into the community.

The first two women faculty members came to the school before the school became coeducational. Ann Cunningham taught Mathematics in 1968–1969, and Helen P. Twiss taught French in 1969–1970; both came on one-year exchanges rather than as part of a plan to bring in women faculty. When the first girls came in 1970–1971, they were joined by five women faculty — Carol France, Janet Kehl, Leslie A. Pederson, Marian I. Wassner, and Sage Dunlap. (There were 125 men on the faculty at the time.) Like all new appointments, they were soon overwhelmed by their responsibilities, the aptly named "triple threat" of teaching, coaching, and dormitory supervision. The teaching component entailed four classes that each met on the average of four times per week, Monday through Saturday. It entailed other obligations as well — weekly faculty meetings, conferences with advisees, and committee work. After class each instructor had to coach a team or supervise athletic activities that met for practice between three and five days a week. And then there was dorm duty, one to three times a week and every third or fourth weekend — depending on the number of faculty residing in the dorm.

The attrition rate of women faculty was quite high during the 1970s. Four to eight women came each year, but as many as seven left the following summer. A large number left after only two years. Research and analysis indicate that the attrition rate for men was equally high, though it is clear that women felt acutely stung by a number of factors. As demanding as the triple threat was for men, it seemed worse for women. The obligation to do committee work was particularly heavy because the same few women were called on to serve repeatedly. Men tended to enjoy the coaching requirement, but some women did not, explained Academy librarian Jacquelyn H. Thomas, who first came to Exeter as a faculty spouse, "since most were not brought up to be athletes in the same way men were."[35] Even dorm duty was a greater burden. "Some boys came to talk to us because we were women," observed Carol France. We were less formidable than some of the grand old men. Always four or five knocked on my door in a night. Sometimes the sessions were long, and sometimes in the middle of the night. One boy knocked in the middle of the night because he thought he was going to commit suicide, so you are up all night with a child. I had sixty boys in my dorm, and there were girls who, if they didn't like the woman in their dorm, came to you. That's dorm life. But I think we got more of it than the men because we were more open."[36]

Under such circumstances, women found it difficult to have much of a personal life. Single women felt stifled socially, and Exeter's geographical isolation did not make things any easier. Kehl recalled, "There was no private life for single women."[37] France added, "It was grim. I didn't even have a private entrance to my apartment. I opened the door and was in the hall with the boys." Married women had their own set of problems, since they had to balance the triple threat with their responsibilities as a wife and mother. "In a two-career family, the triple threat became a quadruple threat," observed one instructor, "because women — particularly those with small children — still had the primary responsibility at home."

The new women on the block — especially the younger ones — also had to deal with boys developing crushes on them, especially in the first year of coeducation. France recalled, "The women faculty were 25 and 26, very young for being put in this position. The school had 40 girls, who were gone after their last class. The most difficult emotional thing was that the boys who were 18 or 19 years old saw girls, and then they disappeared. So we all had to deal with a lot of 18-year old boys getting mad crushes on us. It was very difficult for everybody because it was such an abnormal mix."[38]

Women who came to Exeter in the 1970s faced some of the same problems as women who joined the corporate world in this period — many men did not take them seriously as professionals. It was a status of invisibility, explained Susan J. Herney, associate dean of students from 1972 to 1985. "I was not invisible as an individual, but as a young woman. Over and over at committee meetings I would bring up an issue and there would be no response. A man would bring up the same issue minutes later, as if it had never been spoken."[39] The institutional biases were subtle but persistent. Some men consulted women only when they wanted the "women's point of view," just as they asked female students for the "female point of view."

As these women discovered, their presence had done little to change the fact that Exeter was a male institution. Men continued to hold the key positions, and the school continued to have a male ethos. Women were expected to adapt rather than change the model. As a result of this attitude, women felt intense pressure to prove themselves — even beyond Exeter's high standards. "The younger women who were hired felt they really had to be better than their male peers," Herney explained. "It was difficult because there were not many mentors or role models for these women."

The wives of the faculty, meanwhile, faced an awkward change of status with the coming of coeducation. The wives were long accustomed to playing a vital if largely unacknowledged role in the life of the school. They hosted open houses and tea parties, planned and presided over birthday parties, and welcomed parents, even opening their bathrooms to mothers. They helped supervise dorm life and manage check-ins in the dormitories. And they volunteered for a host of assignments, assisting with costumes and makeup for theater productions — sometimes even directing — and helping to chaperone at dances.[40] Although the wives spent a considerable amount of time in these activities, they did not have the status of faculty. They could not attend faculty meetings, nor did they receive any remuneration for their work (the sole exception being tutoring). "No one even thought about getting paid," said Helen Stuckey.

The position the wives had enjoyed in those days changed dramatically when professional women arrived on campus. Jane Scarborough, a member of the History Department from 1970 to 1974, observed, "When women joined the faculty in the early years of coeducation, they displaced the faculty wives. They couldn't come to the faculty meetings, even though they often knew more than we did about the students from being in the dorms and counseling. When we came on board, we were legitimized in a way they were not. This difference in status divided us initially, so that we did not seek each other out."[41] Jacquelyn Thomas added: "I knew how it felt to be displaced as a faculty wife. I could take being a second-class citizen, but all of a sudden I was a third-class citizen." The change in status motivated Thomas to acquire graduate training and launch a new career.[42] In 1975 she was appointed acting Academy librarian and became the first wife to join the faculty full-time. Two years later Exeter began paying faculty wives for dormitory counseling in the summer school as a way to grant them professional recognition. Even so, some faculty wives remained dissatisfied and pressed the administration to acknowledge their roles and compensate them for carrying out certain duties.

Faculty husbands also felt out of place in the early years of coeducation. They were an unknown entity, and did not fit into one of the school's traditional social slots. "It was threatening to male spouses to come to an environment like this and be one of maybe three faculty husbands," mathematics instructor Anja S. Greer observed. "The school did not know how to respond to them. Functions often took place on Wednesday afternoons because there were no classes then. Many of the women spouses did not have a job and could go to these events. My husband at the time could not attend because he had a regular nine-to-five job. He tried for the first couple of months but it was hard for him to interact here. He left in November. Two other women came that year with spouses. Both of their marriages ended also. Exeter simply did not make any accommodations in the early years."[43]

As difficult as things were for the first women faculty, they often had reasons for leaving that had less to do with Exeter than with where they were in their lives. Young and in the first stage of their career, they had other things they wanted to do. Thomas observed, "They left to go to other schools, to get married, to further their education. When women came here it was not their final step. When men came here with families, they had been in another school. This was the final step, this was where they intended to finish their career."[44]

The high attrition rate prevented Exeter from increasing the size of the female faculty in any sustained manner. Few women stayed long enough to get tenure (which at that time was five years), let alone seniority. It is the custom at faculty meetings for the more senior members to sit at the front of the room. For many years, there was not a woman among them. Thomas recalled,

"You could not see a woman in the faculty photographs because we were all there in the back. We finally had our own photograph taken so that we could see our faces. During a trustee meeting, we got all the women—all ten of us—to sit together to show how small the number was. But no one noticed."[45]

There were men at the Academy who sympathized with the women's plight, but they had a hard time making themselves heard. In August 1972, Colin Irving returned from the Governor's Conference on the Status of Women to inform his colleagues that Exeter and most of the other 125 employers represented were "technically in violation of Title VII of the Civil Rights Act of 1965 in the matter of sex discrimination." The school needed to correct three major problems: an insufficient number of female employees, discrimination on the basis of sex, and inequality of pay and benefits. He urged the school to adopt an Affirmative Action program, but to no avail.[46] As a private institution, Exeter was not legally required to do this. And it was far from ready for so big a step.

Making Progress — At Last

During the accreditation process of 1975, the internal committee stated the need for more women faculty generally, while the external committee expressed concern for the kind of women the school was hiring. Female faculty members, it said, were not making a sufficient contribution to girls' athletics. The number of female teachers was disproportionately small, and they tended "to be more classroom specialists than their male counterparts." The committee recommended that Exeter hire versatile "school women," just as it sought to hire "school men." Moreover, the school should appoint a woman to a first-level administrative position to "strengthen substantially the position of women on the Exeter faculty and within the Academy community."

The calls for change came from within and without, but the school was slow to act. Taking matters into their own hands, Herney, Lynda Beck, Molly Plumb, and Patricia Peard formed the Women's Committee in autumn 1977. Their concerns ranged from gymnasium renovations to the appointment of women to important administrative positions. Some problems were solved expeditiously—as in 1978–1979, when Kathy Nekton became the first faculty member to become pregnant, prompting the school to formulate its first maternity policy. For the most part, however, the committee was unable to accomplish much because it lacked a spokesperson. Principal Kurtz by his own admission was sympathetic rather than supportive, preferring to focus his attention on other priorities.[47]

Still, a small core of women did not abandon ship. They had good reasons for staying—the extremely able students, excellent facilities, and close collegial relationships. Some had made a life for themselves there, marrying or settling down with another member of the Exeter community. Some stayed because they wanted to change the place, and they were able to obtain the support of some of their male colleagues. "Our advances came from some really committed people," Beck observed. "I also have to say that the Exeter community has an intellectual integrity. When we were able, finally, to articulate something that resonated intellectually, people got committed. That was often at odds with the culture and their upbringing. But that intellectual integrity was a real resource for us as we tried to move the school."[48]

It would take the intervention of an outside benefactor to make a difference. In the autumn of 1979, William L. Dunfey, father of a recent alumna, anonymously gave Exeter, Dartmouth, and the University of New Hampshire, challenge grants of $30,000 "to address the problems of hiring and keeping first-rate women . . . and to improve the role of women on the faculty." Exeter was to receive the money in three $10,000 allotments over the next three years. From this grant came a new group—the Committee to Enhance the Status of Women—that would permanently change the position of women at the Academy. In the words of one of its founders, Anja S. Greer, "This was the turning-point for women at Exeter."[49]

Meeting for the first time in the autumn of 1980, the members of the CESW outlined their objectives, which included hiring a human-relations consultant, funding conferences, establishing a child care facility, and raising general awareness. But the first step was to obtain support from the administration. Approaching Principal Kurtz, they told him what was on their minds. "They complained about the arrogance of men and their inability to understand women, and how hard women work, and how much they give emotionally," Kurtz recalled. "It was a real eye-opener. It took me a long time to realize I had to be a champion of women. They had to beat me up, those women, and they did, almost literally," Kurtz recalled. "I took an oath and said I would support women, and I tried to put them in positions of influence, which is what they needed. They needed power and authority, not just verbal recognition."[50] He appointed Beck assistant to the principal in 1979, and she and Associate Dean Susan Herney joined the principal's staff. (Beck would eventually become vice principal, and Herney dean of students.)

The next step was to educate the men and women of the Academy. The CESW arranged for Edith W. Seashore, an expert on integrating women into male institutions, to make a series of visits to the campus. During 1981–1982, Seashore met with administrators, faculty, and staff and conducted a number of workshops. Her presence opened up discussion of issues often difficult to discuss in traditional male institutions. According to Peter Greer, Seashore "gave an illuminating workshop in which she talked about vertical versus horizontal structuring of institutions, and how Exeter was a vertical, hierarchical one." "She helped us understand that men and women listen differently," Susan Herney recalled, "and that numbers make a big difference." Armed with Seashore's insight, the CESW could now develop strategies for moving from discussion toward real change.

Of equal educational value were the conferences the CESW sponsored. The Conference for Women Educators in Independent Schools in 1983 was the first national conference of its kind, with an impressive list of speakers: Gloria Steinem, cofounder and editor of *Ms.* magazine and chairperson of the Women's Action Alliance, and one of the cofounders of *New York* magazine; Carol Gilligan, associate professor of psychology at the Harvard Graduate School of Education and recent author of *In a Different Voice*; and Pauli Murray, the cofounder of N.O.W. and the first black woman ordained Episcopal priest. Workshops covered a number of different subjects, including leadership techniques, personal financial planning, and gender issues in the classroom. The conference was an unqualified success. Beck recalled, "It was very emotional and teary, and almost to our surprise — since we saw this as an academic kind of endeavor — it had almost a spiritual aspect to it. I can still a remember a woman coming down the aisle after the presentation with tears pouring down her face saying, 'I never knew what it felt like to be included.'" The success of the conference prompted the leaders of the National Association of Independent Schools to host their own conference on the subject in 1984, and the following year the CESW sponsored a version for students, entitled "Women in the Workplace." The committee also provided funding for women faculty and staff to attend professional conferences.

In addition, the CESW directed its attention to matters of daily concern to girls and women of the Academy — improvement of the athletic facilities, campus safety, and the curriculum. Some of the committee's accomplishments were as symbolic as they were practical, such as the sauna in the women's locker room, with the words "One small step" on a plaque above the door. "This was an important matter for symbolic reasons," Peter Greer observed. "The locker room is the quintessential male retreat, where the power-brokering goes on. Putting a plaque there really meant something."

By far the least tractable problem on the agenda of the CESW was the school's failure to appoint and retain sufficient numbers of women faculty. When woman candidates visited the Academy, members of the committee would meet with them in an effort to point out the positive aspects of a boarding school career. But so often the women who came to campus did not wind up getting the job. The departments, which had the sole say in the selection process, professed they wished to choose "the best candidate." In a department of older men, that often meant selecting a man over a woman. The CESW urged the administration to implement an Affirmative Action policy, with the goal of making the number of women faculty proportionate to the number of girls (in 1980, girls approached 40 percent, but women only 18). In the Composition of the School Report of autumn 1983, dean of admissions John D. Herney even suggested that the Academy increase the number of girls only if more female faculty were hired.[51] Early the following year, dean of faculty John B. Heath issued an Affirmative Action statement: in recognition of the need to hire more women, the Academy's goal is that "two-thirds of all faculty hired will be women until the proportion of women to men approximates the percentage of girls to boys in the student body." Thanks to Heath's arm-twisting, the number of full-time women faculty hired rose substantially, from an average of four per year in the period 1975–1983 to ten per year in 1984–1989.

The second part of the problem, the school's poor retention rate, was somewhat more difficult to solve, since many women continued to find the workload — especially the coaching component — far too oppressive. Realizing that the triple threat was no longer a viable system of allocating responsibilities, Kurtz called on the faculty to come up with a new one. The Committee on Life and Responsibility, chaired by Andrew W. Hertig and Jacquelyn Thomas, developed a system that took into account the talents and interests of individual instructors. Those who did not wish to coach a varsity sport could choose from a number of alternatives. Some opted for committee work, while others preferred an extracurricular activity like supervising the student radio station.

By the mid-1980s, the position of women at Exeter had improved considerably. The number of women faculty stood at 35 percent, and the school had a female vice principal and dean of students. Certain important problems remained, however. When the external evaluation committee filed its report in 1985, it noted that few women held significant leadership roles, subtle biases against hiring older women and faculty spouses persisted, and support services such as day care were sorely lacking. The CESW, however, had had little success in addressing these problems. Only two women held department chairs—Kathy Nekton (Physical Education) and Jacquelyn Thomas (Academy librarian)—and since few women had the requisite seniority, there was not much the committee could do to advance their careers. The same held true of hirings, since departments still preferred male or younger female candidates to older women or spouses. Led by Thomas, the CESW submitted a report to the administration on the need for a day-care center; no action was taken, however, because child care was already available at a center the Academy subsidized.[52] The women at the Academy had reached an impasse.

And then things suddenly changed for the better, as they had with the Dunfey bequest several years earlier. In 1987, Exeter selected its first woman principal, Kendra Stearns O'Donnell. Her gender was a minor factor in the selection, but her presence on campus proved more than a symbol of change. One of her first acts, for example, was to fund the day-care center.

During her tenure, the trustees, administration, and faculty collaborated to boost the position of women on campus. Progress toward balancing the composition of the student body and faculty by gender accelerated, with both approaching fifty-fifty. Departments began hiring older women and faculty spouses. Women occupied a growing number of department chairs and key administrative positions. The role of faculty spouses in residential life was clarified and spouses were recognized for performing certain duties.

O'Donnell's actions did not go uncriticized. Some members of the faculty believed that she could have done still more for women by making it a priority coequal with her commitment to multiculturalism. It also took several years for male students to warm to her. "Boys would confront her in Assembly meetings, and she did not know how to respond," Anja Greer recalled. "Often boys' and girls' opinions were divided, with the boys criticizing her and the girls defending her." O'Donnell acknowledged this problem as a transitional phenomenon and noted that it all but disappeared once students accustomed to a male authority figure had graduated and moved on. Regardless of these criticisms, O'Donnell's appointment made things better for women at the Academy—so much so that the Committee to Enhance the Status of Women decided to disband in 1992. It had accomplished many of its goals in its twelve-year tenure. Women faculty no longer needed a special committee on their behalf. They were now an integral part of the Academy.

COEDUCATION AND THE COMMUNITY

The challenges of becoming a coeducational institution grew easier as the number of girls and women at Exeter achieved critical mass in the 1980s.

Along the way, the Academy slowly shed the view that girls and women must adapt to it and began to learn instead how to adapt to them.

In the era before coeducation, Exeter was known far and wide for its tough, disciplined atmosphere, and those who had made it through saw no reason to change it. Still, some alumni and parents wondered whether the cost was too high. Under Kurtz the Academy certainly warmed up, but he acknowledged that credit for this change was owed elsewhere. "It was the coming of women that warmed this place up," he said.[53]

The warming of the school was apparent in a number of ways. Students became more aware of gender issues, thanks to the visits of various feminists to campus and the addition of a number of courses on women's studies to the curriculum. The English Department offered courses on "Feminine and Minority Voices," "Great Women Writers," and "Voices and Visions." History courses cover subjects such as "Women and the Family," "Toward the Year 2000: Trends in Contemporary Political and Social Change," "Toward Equality: Women in Modern Western Society."

Many long-time members of the community noted that the classroom experience also changed for the better. "Class is a more pleasant place than when I was a student, as is the school as a whole," observed Peter Greer '58. "Boys have become accustomed to girls' being their intellectual equals, and teachers have become accustomed to a different sort of pedagogy." Some teachers — in particular those of the older generation — had different perspectives. Donald C. Cole, an *emeritus* history instructor who came to the Academy in 1947, began with a different perspective and then changed his opinion. "I always wanted Exeter to be as strong an intellectual school as possible, and I thought coeducation would not encourage that." He added, "But as I went through the sixties, I began to realize the school might profit academically by getting good girl students. I'm convinced that if we hadn't gone coed, we would have become a much weaker school."[54]

And yet many would argue that it need not come down to a choice between intellectual and social activity. Convinced that a humane environment was not incompatible with a highly rigorous academic program, Dean of Students Herney focused the school's attention in the late 1980s on adolescent development. In addition to a full-scale counseling service for students, she set up workshops for faculty on dormitory proctoring, which encouraged men as well as women to be nurturing. Thomas observed, "Susan really implemented very much more of a residential curriculum. Here was the first woman dean who really saw the importance of dormitory life and health services."

The Academy also came to terms with the related issue of adolescent sexuality. During the debates of the 1960s, the school had not anticipated this would be a problem. George W. Goethals, Senior Lecturer in Psychology at Harvard, had spoken of the "weenie roast syndrome," that people of the opposite sex congregated in the same place will act as siblings and not have sex. That, however, turned out not to be the case. The school reacted sharply, forbidding students to visit members of the opposite sex in their rooms. Not so easily deterred, they found other places to meet. James A. Bullock '72 told of liaisons behind the tennis court. "That was the only really private moment you could have," he said.[55] Sex education was virtually nonexistent. According to a woman who was a student in the early 1970s, "The sex education talk we received in our dormitory the first year basically boiled down to this quote, that the best form of birth control is a cold shower. Not before intercourse and not after intercourse, but instead of intercourse. To a sixteen-year-old who may be getting sexually involved and is very confused, that is not really very helpful. . . . There weren't people that you felt comfortable enough to talk to about your problems."[56]

The Academy's attitude toward student sexuality became more lenient as increasing numbers of college graduates from the 1960s joined the faculty. In the mid-1970s, the faculty voted to allow visitations on Saturday nights, but still strongly discouraged sexual activity. They revised the E-Book to say that students were to conduct visits "with the door open," and that the faculty "disapproves of sexual intimacy between students." Unauthorized visits were considered a major offense and could result in the student's expulsion. At the urging of the Student Council, the faculty gradually increased the number of visitations allowed each week. Students are now permitted to visit one another every night. The "open door" regulation remains on the books, but unauthorized visits no longer constitute grounds for expulsion. Acknowledging the need to educate students on sexual matters, the school's health services now provide counseling and support services on issues ranging from birth control to sexually transmitted diseases, and the school offers a health and human development course to assist students in their decision making on health and life issues,

Exeter has become a school that attends to the whole student without sacrificing the academic standards that made it famous. As one observer — a Harvard professor — put it, "This place hangs in a beautiful equilibrium. The intellectual training is still good, but it is now a better place for young people to grow up."[57]

MILESTONE

In 1995 the Academy marked its twenty-fifth anniversary of coeducation. The year-long celebration began in September with a gala weekend that included a ceremonial Assembly honoring the school's first women graduates, faculty, and trustees, as well as panel discussions on a variety of coeducational and gender-related topics. Former principal Kurtz reminisced about the early days of coeducation, while Pulitzer-Prize winner Doris Kearns Goodwin spoke on the marriage of Franklin and Eleanor Roosevelt. To cap off the weekend, the school hosted a formal dinner and an old-fashioned ball, with carriage rides and dance cards. Among the other events celebrating the anniversary that year were various assembly programs, Academy Library and Lamont Gallery exhibits, and "Fireside Chats" with alumni/ae about coeducation.

Another important event symbolized the magnitude of the changes since 1970. In days of yore, the lintel—the stone above the door—of the Academy Building was engraved with the Latin words, *Huc venite pueri ut viri sitis*: "Come here boys so that you may become men." The phrase captured the ethos of an all-male school, and it did not escape the notice of the girl students who entered the building in the 1970s. In the early years before the school began to accommodate to girl students, some even joked that the saying should be modified to read, "Come here boys and girls so that you may become men."

By the early 1990s, the inscription seemed clearly out of place. During an alumni/-ae gathering in 1993, John "Tex" McCrary '28 noticed the lintel and, translating it for some girls standing nearby, asked them what they thought about it. They didn't like it. The encounter lingered with McCrary, and at a subsequent alumni/ae gathering, he proposed to the administration that the inscription be revised at his expense to read, "Boys and girls come here in the pursuit of excellence," with versions translated into a hundred different languages posted on the inside of the Academy Building.

McCrary's proposal coincided with the beginning of plans to celebrate the twenty-fifth anniversary of coeducation. "The Coeducation Celebration Committee considered the idea, and many of us liked it," recalled a member, Susan Herney. "Although there were some pockets of support, the committee decided not to do anything about it because it would be too political and would distract them from the general aims of the celebration." The trustees also were divided on the issue. "Some thought the lintel was historical and should be left as is," Herney explained, "while others thought it was a symbol of the old Exeter and should be changed." (The proposal for one hundred translations was apparently quickly discarded.) Eventually, the trustees voted in favor of a new inscription and referred it to the committee to work out the details. The committee consulted with architects, while the Classics Department formulated a Latin phrase for a new inscription.

In October 1995, as part of the anniversary celebrations, the trustees approved a plan to marry Exeter's old and new traditions. They voted enthusiastically to install a new lintel above the old one and declared it would be their gift to the school. Completed later that year, the façade is a blending of the old and the new: the original inscription, with the dates "1781" and "1970" bracketing it, and directly above it, the newly carved words *Hic quaerite pueri puellaeque virtutem et scientiam* ("Here, boys and girls, seek goodness and knowledge"), a lasting monument to the coming of coeducation at Exeter.

So the quiet revolution, facilitated by Harkness discussion, has run its course. Today, the gender balance among students and faculty remains approximately equal. Female students have been chosen as editor of *The Exonian* and occupy leadership positions in many student organizations and activities. Meanwhile, many trustees, including a recent vice chair, are female, while women have served as principal, dean of the faculty (twice), dean of students, and as heads of the Library and many departments, dormitories, and administrative offices. No longer are opportunities at Exeter exclusively available to boys or men. The Academy has become a thoroughly coeducational institution, completing a chapter in its history.

Strengthening the Foundation

Strolling through the campus of Phillips Exeter Academy, even the most casual observer is likely to conclude that this is an impressive and well-maintained institution. The conclusion would be accurate: the Academy offers unusually rich opportunities to its students and also is presently one of the wealthiest private schools in the United States. Whatever the standard of measurement — the size of the endowment, the value of the physical plant, or the number of students who receive scholarships — Exeter's resources are the envy of nearly all independent schools and many private colleges.

Few people may know, however, that the Academy's robust financial health is of relatively recent origin. After the original Phillips bequest ran out in the nineteenth century, Exeter endured occasional stretches of financial difficulty. In the twentieth century, it weathered financial crises in the 1930s and 1970s that threatened its long-term ability to uphold traditions of excellence while fulfilling its mission to be a "public free school" open to "youth from every quarter." Following the events of the 1970s and a Harkness-style examination of its financial troubles, the Academy pursued a new approach to managing its finances to ensure stability in a wide range of economic conditions. It no longer relied so heavily on tuition to pay the bills and rebuilt a healthy endowment. It adopted modern, sophisticated tools of financial management and expanded its professional staff in finance, accounting, and development. Armed with strong programs for securing the future of the endowment, managing the budget, and conducting successful fundraising drives, the Academy remains dedicated to supporting the highest caliber curricular and extracurricular programs while ensuring the school's accessibility to students from a wide range of economic backgrounds.

CHALLENGES OF DEPRESSION AND WAR

When founding the Academy, John Phillips considered not only the kind of education it would provide but also how it would cover its costs. His bequest of $60,000 — Exeter's original endowment — funded operations without need of additional revenues (other than the nominal tuition fee of

$2 established in 1802) until the mid-nineteenth century, when the school built its first dormitory.[1] During the late nineteenth and early twentieth centuries, several principals made it a priority to solicit large gifts to increase the Academy's endowment and scale of operations, with Harlan Page Amen and Lewis Perry proving particularly adept at fundraising. During the 1920s, the endowment reached nearly $1 million, a total that made the Academy one of the best endowed private schools in the country. Exeter's operating budget, however, remained heavily dependent on tuition revenues, which fluctuated with enrollments. If, on occasion, enrollments were low and the school found itself in the red, it made up the difference with funds from the endowment and the annual Christmas Fund, established in 1922 to encourage voluntary donations from the alumni.[2] If the school found itself in need of a building, perhaps one of its patrons or graduates would provide the funds. In 1928, Exeter enjoyed a particularly bountiful year: bequests came to nearly $2.3 million, including more than $500,000 from Colonel Thompson '90 for a science building, administration building, and baseball cage, over $320,000 from Edward Harkness, and several bequests ranging between $10,000 and $50,000.[3] The following year, the endowment surged in value to a little over $3 million.[4] With such reserves waiting to be tapped, almost anything the Academy sought to do seemed within its power.

The "Flat Rate" Tuition

And then in the early 1930s, just after the Harkness Gift, everything changed. As an unsettled market gave way to full-fledged economic depression, many private schools shifted into a survival mode of overcrowded classrooms, part-time schedules, and extended holidays and vacations. While its endowment enabled the Academy to avoid extreme measures, it did not remain unscathed. By 1932, the endowment had lost nearly half its value, limiting funds for scholarships, student loans, salaries, and maintenance of the physical plant.[5]

In this respect, the Harkness Gift, which the donor guaranteed at the valuation of $5.8 million, could not have been timed more fortuitously. In September 1931, the Academy received the first installment, securities valued at $1,268,000, to support the salaries and board of new teachers, as well as construction of new buildings and maintenance of older ones. Over the course of the next four years, Harkness would pay off the rest of his pledge in monthly installments ranging from $2,000 to $660,000. The sum total came to $2.4 million in cash, $1.3 million in bonds, and $2.1 million in stock, which consisted of 168,400 shares in Socony Vacuum Corporation.[6]

But the Academy was not in the clear by any means. It still had to cover its operating expenses with income from tuition and the endowment, and as the decade progressed this became increasingly difficult. In 1931–1932, enrollments dropped from the customary 700 to 650 — with income from tuition falling more than $50,000 — while income from investments continued to decline, resulting in a deficit of more than $27,000 for the year.[7] To raise cash quickly, the following year Exeter sold a large number of stocks in its portfolio — an action that, thanks to the depressed value of securities, contributed to a downward spiral.[8] At the same time, the school employed a time-honored strategy for raising revenues: find applicants from well-to-do families and admit as many as possible. In early 1933, Lewis Perry issued an invitation to "applicants of good calibre who can pay their way."[9] The response was immediate. The following autumn, the Academy's enrollment numbered 714 students, the second largest in its history to date. The number, however, was not indicative of a sustained return to capacity, since many of the new admits were seniors whose families could afford to send their sons for only one year.[10]

Clearly, the trustees decided, more drastic action was in order, and in late 1933 they voted to revamp the tuition structure completely. As noted in chapter 5, the Academy had recently used a sliding scale of fees for room and board tied to the quality of room and board provided, while charging a standard tuition for all boys. In the early 1930s, the total charge for room, board, and tuition ranged from $762 to $1,112, with an average of $1,012.40.[11] Because of the need to fund an increasing share of expenses with, ideally, something to spare for added needs, through tuition, the Academy instituted an increase: beginning in 1934–1935, all students would pay a flat rate of $1,050. In addition to raising more revenue, administrators expected the new "Flat Rate Tuition" to simplify accounting and eliminate the problem of renting the higher priced rooms, which had become increasingly difficult to fill as the Depression wore on. The new policy coincided with a recent initiative reinforced by the Harkness Plan to standardize living and dining accommodations. Previously, student quarters had ranged from small attic rooms to lavish corner suites. Despite the logic of the flat-rate scheme and the hopes of its advocates, however, there was one major drawback: the scheme would make Exeter unaffordable for students of middle-class families.[12] There seemed to be no other way out. It was a difficult compromise necessitated by difficult circumstances.

As it turned out, the "flat rate" tuition did little to improve the Academy's financial health. Although prices had generally dropped during the Depression, the school had to contend with some underestimated expenses, the worst, ironically, resulting from the Harkness Plan, which had necessitated renovation of much of the physical plant to conform with the quality of the new construction.[13] In the excitement of launching the new educational enterprise, the faculty introduced many new courses without considering the cost to the school. In 1934–1935, administrative and general expenses ran almost $20,000 over budget.[14] It seems likely that the school diverted some of the $300,000 Harkness teaching endowment fund to cover its deficit. When Harkness's associate Malcolm Aldrich asked for an account of where the fund was being spent, Academy Treasurer Corning Benton admitted in embarrassment that the "bookkeeping was completely lost sight of."[15]

According to Benton, the Academy's financial situation was not truly precarious. Exeter, he noted, did not need to tighten its belt as much as it needed to avoid loosening it any further:

> Some people like to put the benefits derived from education above the terms of money. I, myself, am sordid enough to maintain that all Exeter is obligated to furnish to its patrons is their money's worth . . . successful preparation for college, the Exonian opportunity for self (largely) development of character and responsibility, plenty of good food, respectable conditions under which to work and sleep, the opportunity for physical exercise and athletic competition under good supervision, and good medical care. If we keep adding additional benefits for students, we should either ask them to pay more for them, or we should wait till we can support such benefits out of endowment received specifically for that purpose. As it is, I believe that Exeter's students are getting far more for their money than the students of any other school I know of.[16]

Under Benton's guidance, the Academy shelved expansion efforts and focused on the maintenance of the physical plant, to be funded primarily by tuition revenues. More ambitious projects—that is, those costing more than $10,000—were to be paid for over several years or funded by money raised for that purpose. As such measures took hold and general economic conditions improved, Benton in 1935 could claim "the worst days of the depression are over."[17] The next two years witnessed remodeling of the gymnasium, the installation of a biology laboratory in the Thompson Science Building, and the renovation of Gilman House, a colonial heirloom older than the Academy itself. To increase the financial security of its employees, the school adopted a group life insurance plan for faculty members, administrative staff, and maintenance employees and a retirement plan for faculty.[18]

Benton's optimism proved short-lived. In 1938, a national recession again hit hard at the Academy, reducing the yield on investments just as operating expenses reached their highest point in the decade. The gap between tuition fees and the cost of educating each student widened as donations and returns from investments continued to decline. There was a pervasive feeling among alumni that Exeter had been living above its means since the Harkness bequest and should return to its "traditions of thrift and homeliness."[19] The Academy had no choice but to slash its budget across the board, even scaling back publication of the *Bulletin*:

The necessity for economy has required such compression in this issue [October 1938] that much material prepared could not be printed. Indulgence is asked of all persons concerned. A later number will seek to make amends, although this will probably not appear before July, 1939. The miraculous good fortune which helped the Academy through the "depression" and again through the "recession" has not reappeared this year. And the "after-loss" of the depression has affected the Academy as it has individuals.[20]

Drastic cuts, however, could do only so much. "The time had come," Benton wrote in 1939, "for as many people as possible to know the details of Academy financial problems, and help share the burden of solving them."[21] At the behest of the trustees, the *Bulletin* published a short report on the cost of educating boys.[22] That effort, however, produced little response: in 1939–1940, a whopping 72 percent of the school's revenues came from tuition and fees, with 26 percent coming from endowment income and just 0.8 percent from current gifts.[23] Confronting the problem head-on, in early 1941 Academy officials sent alumni and friends a pamphlet defining Exeter's position in the educational world and explaining the financial difficulties it faced in the near future. Because of income taxes and heavy inheritance taxes, it said,

the Academy can no longer depend upon the occasional and large gifts of individual benefactors. It must turn to its many friends and alumni for their more modest support. . . . If you cherish the hope that Exeter's future may be something like its past and present, if you desire it to remain a democratic school with low costs and many scholarships available, if you wish it to continue to attract needy boys of character, if you want it to retain its unique quality and not become just another good preparatory school, it must attract the generous support of all its alumni and friends to an even greater extent than now. Only with that support can Exeter's future be secure, its vitality as keen a quarter of a century hence.[24]

That year the Christmas Fund raised over $14,000, nearly $2,000 more than the year before, but it was not enough to make a significant difference. As the rest of the country enjoyed the prosperity induced by entry into the war, Exeter struggled with the rising costs of food, fuel, and other commodities, and higher wages for maintenance employees.[25] Keeping a tight watch on the budget, the school observed various measures of economy that ranged from cutting back on care of the grounds to having students clean their own rooms.[26] The departure of many faculty for the armed services saved money as well. During this period, the physical plant saw few additions — a new Grill, installed in the basement of Alumni Hall, and the Academy Laundry, which proved considerably cheaper than the commercial equivalent.[27] Despite these efforts, the school was very much in the red in 1943–1944 and 1944–1945, and no easy solutions were in sight.[28]

Recovery

The expenses of wartime showed no signs of abating after VJ Day. There would be many new demands on the Academy's wallet — higher salaries for faculty returning from service, higher wages for a growing staff, maintenance and renovation projects deferred during the war — demands that would bring the cost of educating each student up to $1,800. To bridge the deepening chasm between revenues and expenses, in June 1945 the trustees voted to raise tuition from the "flat rate" of $1,050 set in 1934 by $200, with the change to take effect for the 1946–1947 academic year.[29]

Although the tuition hike was a step in the right direction, the Academy still had much to do to achieve solvency. Wishing to balance the budget without sacrificing Principal Saltonstall's new National School campaign, in the summer of 1946 the trustees laid the groundwork for a major fundraising drive. The Phillips Exeter Fund would eliminate the ongoing deficit, increase the scholarship fund, and make possible some general repairs as well as the construction of a service building.[30] With a target of $5 million to be raised in two years, the campaign was by far the most ambitious in Exeter's history, surpassing Lewis Perry's less structured initiative nearly forty years earlier to solicit gifts totaling $2 million (and realizing only $600,000).[31] Leery of this experience, trustee and campaign chair Joseph T. Walker, Jr., '14 set up a volunteer operation that appointed more than thirty-five regional chairmen from the alumni, scheduled luncheons and dinners in major cities, and mailed to all alumni a pamphlet *These Are the Figures*, a detailed explanation of the Academy's finances illustrated with charts and diagrams. The Academy, the mailing urged, required the support of its alumni and friends "to assure that the Exeter of tomorrow will be of as great usefulness to the nation as the Exeter of today and yesterday."[32]

The Phillips Exeter Fund drive started out in high gear, with a gift from Thomas W. Lamont for $500,000, a sum designated as the Lewis Perry Fund, followed by other gifts totaling $163,800, including $2,000 contributed by the Christian Fraternity. The campaign quickly lost steam, however, as other gifts failed to pour in. While fundraisers intensified their efforts, money at the Academy continued to be extremely tight. In 1948, the school borrowed $100,000 to offset a deficit.[33] The trustees investigated the possibility of raising tuition again but decided to postpone such a step until the conclusion of the campaign. Meanwhile, they urged, it was essential to economize as much as possible. Responding enthusiastically to the challenge, students, faculty, and administrators devised various cost-cutting measures, including the reduction of the daily allowance of milk per individual from five half-pints to four to save $14,000 on the annual food bill—one of many efforts to save money while showing potential donors that their gifts would not be misspent.[34]

In the end, the Phillips Exeter Fund surpassed its goal, totaling $5.7 million in June 1948. This success was deceptive, however, since a major share of the funds came from two wealthy alumni, Lamont and Dr. Arthur W. Elting '90, each of whom had died during the year. Each left in his will a bequest of $2 million to Exeter.[35] Both gifts were counted toward the capital campaign, although Elting's had not been so directed. Of the $5.7 million ultimately realized, then, $4.5 million came from two donors, with the remainder subscribed by nearly 5,000 parents, alumni, and friends of the school. Fewer alumni (only 31 percent) participated in the campaign than in the annual Christmas fund, and had not the Elting gift been credited in its entirety, the fund drive would have missed its goal by more than 25 percent.[36]

Although the new endowment income helped Exeter to end five consecutive years of annual deficits from 1943–1944 to 1947–1948 (amounting to nearly $324,000), it was insufficient to meet rising operating costs.[37] Believing they had no choice, the trustees voted a tuition increase from $1,250 to $1,400, to go into effect in 1949–1950. Meanwhile, the first *Bulletin* of 1950 optimistically proclaimed the beginning of a new era:

It is no exaggeration to say that the completion of the Fund dispelled all the gloom which hung over the Academy and shook off all encumbrances which had dragged on it for several years. . . . The Phillips Exeter Fund promises financial security to the Academy for years to come, and there can be little doubt that the value of the institution in service to the country will continue to grow for as long as this security is maintained.[38]

Behind the scenes, the trustees were less sanguine. They commissioned a comprehensive study of the school's operations by the prominent management consulting firm Cresap, McCormick and Paget. The consultants concluded that Exeter's endowment was "adequate to maintain its outstanding position and leadership in the school field so long as activities continue about as now and no adverse circumstances are faced that do not face other schools." Nonetheless, they recommended that Academy officials should update their financial projections every year and pursue a long-term financial policy to prepare the school for any major contingencies in the future and, in so doing, set an example for other independent schools to follow.[39]

The Anniversary Teaching Fund Campaign

In the years that followed, Academy officials considered a number of the consultants' proposals for establishing long-term financial health, including decreasing tuition (in the hope that this would encourage more and greater gifts) and increasing plant and permanent funds.[40] The demands of managing the annual operating budget, however, diverted attention from long-term financial planning. Rising expenditures for scholarships and faculty compensation were particular concerns. Between 1948–1949 and 1952–1953, the number of participants in the "National School" program grew by 78 percent, and while gifts designated for scholarships more than tripled, reaching nearly $98,000, they were not enough to cover funding demands.[41] Meanwhile, the introduction of the TIAA Retirement Plan in the early 1950s resulted in an increase in the cost of leaves and pensions for faculty — an expense anticipated to be larger than normal for the next several decades because of future retirement obligations.[42]

The trustees agreed that the Academy had to take in more revenues to pay its bills but not about how to do it. Some favored the old standby, a tuition increase, arguing that while the annual charge had seen a 33⅓ percent rise since 1946, it still lagged well below the rise in the cost of living in the same period. Furthermore, Exeter's tuition of $1,400 was significantly lower than that of most comparable boarding schools. Those who had witnessed the effects of the Depression — among them admissions director Pike Rounds — countered that an increase in tuition would exclude boys from middle-income families, thereby changing the character of the school.[43] Some even advocated lowering the annual charge while having wealthier families make up the difference with gifts.[44] Ultimately, the proponents of a hike prevailed. The trustees voted an increase of $100 effective as of 1953–1954 and gave Saltonstall the task of explaining the school's financial operations in his annual letter to parents that fall.[45]

Recognizing that even increased tuition revenues would not cover the bills, the Academy refocused attention on fundraising — an endeavor aided by growing national interest in supporting educational institutions. With General Electric leading the way, in 1954 major corporations established the practice of matching contributions their employees gave to their alma maters. Contributions to Exeter's Christmas Fund and other gifts rose immediately, enabling the school to give more generous scholarships and cover other operating expenses. In this period the Academy also embarked on two major building projects, the conversion of Alumni Hall into the Lamont Art Gallery and the construction of an outdoor hockey rink.[46]

For all its progress, however, the Academy still lagged behind in one important area — faculty salaries, which, because of inflation, had lost much of their purchasing power during the war. In the late 1940s Exeter had raised them to be comparable to prewar levels but, like other schools and colleges, had not made them commensurate with the rise in the cost of living after the war. Principal William G. Saltonstall believed that the Academy was already setting an example as a national school for its students and that it was now time to do this for its faculty as well. He called for a capital campaign to establish a new endowment for teachers' salaries:

> It will do more to strengthen the school at this juncture than anything else I know. It will encourage Exeter alumni to enter the teaching profession. It will set an example desperately needed in a period of serious national teacher shortage. And, most important of all, it will encourage and strengthen the men who are currently carrying out the purposes set by John Phillips 175 years ago.[47]

In 1955, the Academy launched the Anniversary Teaching Fund Campaign, with a $2 million target and a two-year time frame.[48] Despite its modest goals, the drive, like the Phillips Exeter Fund campaign several years earlier, struggled to penetrate the alumni base: although it surpassed its goal, reaching $2.1 million in 1957, once again nearly half of the funds raised came from two sources, the bequests of Elizabeth H. Smith and Howard C. Sherwood '89.[49] The problem could be downplayed, however, because other money-raising initiatives proved successful. Apart from the Anniversary Fund, gifts to the endowment during the 1950s came to over $5 million; aided by a generally strong market, the endowment surpassed $43 million in 1960–1961 (an increase of 106 percent in ten years). Thanks to the efforts of the burgeoning Alumni Association, in the course of the decade the annual Christmas Fund grew exponentially, topping $121,000 in 1960–1961 (an increase of 190 percent), while other current gifts totaled more than $91,000 (an increase of 24 percent).[50] Although the cost of educating each student rose nearly 50 percent between 1950 and 1960, current gifts and income generated by the endowment enabled Exeter to operate with only a 29 percent increase in tuition (from $1,400 to $1,800) and a 5 percent increase in enrollment (40 students, for a total of 787)[51] while undertaking additions to the physical plant, including the Exeter Bookstore and the Lewis Perry Music Building.[52]

With the Academy functioning so well, the trustees' thoughts turned to another difficult challenge, the long-deferred maintenance and expansion of the physical plant. The Davis Library was built in 1912 to house a collection of some 18,000 books; by 1963 the size of its collection had tripled, and new curricular needs, such as the Advanced Placement Program, had consumed every last inch of space. So, too, the Thompson Gymnasium: built in 1918 for a school of under 600 boys and a program of five interscholastic sports, it was woefully inadequate for enrollments that had grown by nearly a third and an athletic program that had nearly tripled in size. Residential space was also inadequate, especially since the trustees had authorized another increase in enrollments. To accommodate as many as 860 students, Exeter would need to build two new dormitories while renovating two older ones. Thanks to a generous gift from Neil A. McConnell '47 in honor of his father, construction had already begun on McConnell Hall, the first new dormitory since the Harkness Plan.[53]

To pay for all this, Saltonstall said, the Academy would have to launch another capital campaign to raise as much as $14 million. The figure, twice the amount recently raised during an ambitious campaign at Andover, struck the trustees as excessively high.[54] While some concurred on the need for a new campaign, they advocated one on a smaller scale. "Exeter needed a new swimming pool," Hugh Calkins later recalled, "but it could live without a separate pool for diving."[55]

As it turned out, the next capital campaign did not begin for a few more years. Following Saltonstall's retirement in 1963, the trustees authorized the establishment of a new committee of the faculty, the Academy Planning Committee, to consider Exeter's long-term needs. The committee proposed a program of expansion that included the construction of a new library, new athletic facilities, a centralized dining hall, and a theater-auditorium building.[56] In the fall of 1964, as progress on these projects began, new Principal Richard W. Day arrived on campus and called a temporary halt. A few months later, he proposed a greatly expanded program involving construction of a bigger library, a comprehensive athletic complex, two dormitories, dining facilities, and an auditorium and theater, as well as major renovation of six of the older dormitories. Thinking big, Day persuaded the trustees to engage renowned architects Kallman McKinnell and Knowles for the gymnasium complex and Louis I. Kahn for the library and adjacent dining hall. Appropriately situated in the center of the campus (on the site of the old Principal's House, One Abbot Place), the library — the biggest secondary school library in the world — would be "the intellectual center of the community" while symbolizing the academic excellence synonymous with the Academy.[57]

The Long Step Forward

To pay for these ambitious plans, Day believed, the Academy needed an equally ambitious capital campaign. While the basics of the program were still in the formative stages, the Academy received word of a $7.3 million bequest of philanthropist Edward C. Simmons, a long-time supporter of Exeter's scholarship students through the Harwood Foundation. Of the total amount, Simmons's will stipulated that $5 million would be used to fund scholarships, with use of the remainder unrestricted. Enlarging the scope of the campaign, the trustees set a goal well beyond the $14 million Saltonstall had sought a few years earlier: $21 million, the largest amount sought by an independent school to that date. The new campaign was christened "The Long Step Forward" — a phrase reflecting Day's belief in the importance and impact of the quest. Ironically, in all the excitement of planning the campaign, no one seemed to heed the warnings of Booz Allen and Hamilton, another consulting firm recently brought in to assess the Academy's organization and management. These consultants were highly critical of the school's lack of financial planning and cost consciousness — problems that would become all too evident in the coming years.[58]

The Long Step Forward was made public on Alumni Day in June 1966, when trustee vice president Philip C. Beals '38 announced the three-year campaign to raise $13 million for the building program and $8 million for scholarship funds and salary endowment. By then, the campaign had a $9 million head start, thanks to the Simmons bequest and other advance gifts (including $500,000 from the estate of the recently deceased Thomas S. Lamont, who had been the drive's honorary chairman, and $600,000 from Chairman of Major Gifts James A. Fisher '38 and his family's trust).[59] Despite this auspicious beginning, however, the drive stalled almost immediately. Reluctant to lend their support, many alumni appeared to believe that Exeter was already the richest school in the country, with unlimited funds at its disposal. The first year of the campaign ended disastrously, with additional proceeds totaling only $1.4 million, most of which consisted of a few large gifts.

Although the funding for the building program had not yet materialized, construction began in the summer of 1966 as planned. By September the renovations of Webster Hall and the administrative offices in Jeremiah Smith Hall were complete. The following year would see the expansion of the dining facilities in Merrill and Langdell and the beginning of construction of the Gymnasium, the largest and costliest of the program objectives, with construction of the Main Street dormitories starting shortly thereafter.[60]

It was a tight schedule, allowing little room for responding to national economic trends. In the two years since the trustee decision in favor of a $21 million drive and a three-year construction schedule, inflation, as measured by the Consumer Price Index, had risen approximately 6 percent and had begun to affect construction costs as well as normal operating expenses. The future of the Long Step Forward, and the Academy's general financial health, looked less than rosy. Convinced that the time for major revision of financial policies had arrived, in the fall of 1966 the trustees took the first step, raising tuition from $2,100 to $2,500, effective in 1967–1968. Eager to cash in on the current bull market, they also made a major change in the Academy's investment and spending policies, adopting a strategy used by Yale and other colleges with great success. Whereas in the past the amount of allowable spending was limited to the yield on investments, the "total return" concept said that a prudent portion of the appreciation of unrestricted endowment funds could be added to traditional yield, thus giving the endowment manager more freedom in investing the funds for maximum growth.[61] Accordingly, the trustees instructed the Academy's investment management, Morgan Guaranty Trust Company, to increase the endowment invested in common stocks to 75 percent of the portfolio.[62] At their meeting the following autumn, the trustees made an important change in the Academy's spending policy, approving the use of endowment funds consisting of unrestricted bequests (now labeled "Funds Functioning as Endowment") toward operating expenses, debt service, and plant maintenance.[63] In addition, they revised the goals of the Long Step Forward, raising the objective to $25.4 million (with the increase devoted solely to the building program), and extending the completion date by a year to June 1970.[64] Wishing also to accelerate annual giving, the board voted to change the name of "The Christmas Fund" to "The Exeter Alumni Fund," which together with The Exeter Parents Fund would henceforth be the backbone of the Annual Giving Program.[65] Though made in the space of one short year, the decisions to change policies for managing the endowment would have enormous consequences for Exeter's finances for many years to come.

Even with such boosts the Long Step Forward had trouble accelerating its pace. As inflation worsened and some construction management problems came to light, the building program sank deeper and deeper in debt—and controversy. The new gymnasium, which in the final phase of construction needed an additional 247.5 tons of reinforcing steel and added $900,000 to the budget, raised particular concern.[66] Another controversial expense was the makeover and expansion of Gilman House to become the principal's residence, a project that soon ran over budget (see chapter 2). To pay for these and other expenses associated with the building program, Exeter went into debt.

In the summer of 1969, with less than a year left, the fund drive was still about $10 million shy of its goal. Deciding that drastic action was necessary once again, the trustees made changes in the campaign leadership and launched the last and most intensive phase of the campaign, the face-to-face solicitation of all alumni. In addition, they gave the Annual Giving fund drive a mandate to increase totals and levels of participation.[67] But success was more easily planned than achieved. During the latter half of 1969, a drop of 17 percent in the Dow Jones Industrial Average put off potential donors and ate away at the existing endowment, while costs continued to exceed expectations.[68]

As the June 1970 deadline neared and the goal remained distant, the trustees extended the campaign to the end of December thinking "it was wiser to stick our necks out, borrow, build, and hope the drive would succeed or go over." Although support picked up, bringing the total number of pledges to over 7,000, almost twice the number obtained during the Phillips Exeter Fund campaign—the results remained disappointing. Even with contributions of over $3 million from former and current trustees and an additional $2 million

from the Simmons estate, the campaign ended $300,000 short of its goal —
which would take another six months to reach.[69]

In 1971, the last of the construction was completed. The Academy was duly
proud of its new facilities, an athletic complex considered state-of-the-art and
a library praised by architects worldwide. The building program had indeed
prepared the Academy for its long step forward into its third century. But it
had also left behind a debt of nearly $7 million that would take nearly two
decades to repay.

Crisis

The period following the Long Step Forward was one of high expectations, as the Academy welcomed girls and women into the community. The
financial picture was also cause for optimism, as the steep inflation of the late
1960s began easing up. To be on the safe side, however, the trustees voted on
a tuition increase to go into effect in 1971–1972, the third in as many years. To
keep the Academy affordable for students of middle-income families, they
decided against any additional increases until 1974–1975 — although opponents pointed out that this policy could have grave consequences. In June 1972,
for the first time in ten years, the Academy was able to balance the books —
exclusive of interest charges on the $7 million debt, that is.[70]

Meanwhile, under the "total return" policy the endowment recorded annual
returns averaging 10.1 percent. Sold on the concept, the trustees in January
1972 decided to transfer more than 20 percent of Exeter's endowment managed by Morgan Guaranty — $15 million — into a mutual fund that empha-
sized high-growth equities. To increase fundraising revenues and reduce the
need to withdraw capital from the endowment, the board also decided that
henceforth Annual Giving should generate enough money to cover 10 percent
of the operating budget.[71]

Ironically, although the Academy's financial condition appeared to be
healthy, the school was anything but prepared for what was to follow. The following year the Dow dropped over 200 points (nearly 20 percent) and inflation rose nearly 9 percent, the greatest increase since World War II, while the
outbreak of the October War in the Middle East and the ensuing curtailment
of oil from OPEC sparked an energy crisis of major proportions. As gas lines
and fuel shortages became a common occurrence, the Academy returned
to daylight saving time for the winter and implemented a number of other
energy-conserving measures.

By the time Principal Stephen G. Kurtz arrived at the Academy in the summer of 1974, the country was grappling with the worst inflationary recession it had seen in decades. That year the stock market plummeted almost 31 percent, causing the Academy's equities-heavy portfolio to drop precipitously. By the end of the 1973–1974 decline, the $15 million invested in the mutual fund had dwindled to just $7 million. Abandoning ship, the trustees cashed in the shares of New Horizons and invested the money with David L. Babson and Company, another firm that emphasized growth stocks. At this time, the Academy's equity holdings were reduced from 80 to 68 percent of the portfolio, and bonds increased from 5 to 25 percent.[72] As continuing inflation — now in the double digits — caused the costs of fuel oil, electricity, and food to skyrocket, the trustees raised tuition a whopping $500 and sent Kurtz on the road to raise money and consciousness among Exeter alumni/ae — a difficult task in a difficult economy.

During the next few years the Dow remained in the doldrums, and the national outlook along with it. In 1978, the vast majority of stocks were selling at lower prices than ten years earlier — and when inflation was taken into account, the typical stock had lost about half of its purchasing power. The Academy's portfolio fared even worse: between June 1969 and June 1978, it performed below the market average and significantly below the average of 19 comparable college and university endowments.

Meanwhile, Exeter's spending rate — defined as "that percentage of the total endowment, whether produced through yield or gain, that might be spent annually on operations or capital improvement" — became a source of concern. The accepted guideline was 5 percent but the Academy routinely exceeded it between 1969 and 1978 to cover expenses primarily associated with the physical plant. Given the depressed values of the stock market, some trustees grew worried. As John R. Chase '46, partner and director of the Harvard Management Company, the investment managers of Harvard's endowment, put it, the Academy "at present is in effect liquidating itself."[73]

In June 1978, the investment committee of the board of trustees held a remarkable session in New York City, with Principal Kurtz and trustee president Charlie Toll '34 as well as Hunter Lewis, a consultant with Cambridge Associates, also present. The agenda was the Academy's investment policy and the meeting proved in essence a kind of Harkness Table on the question, "If you were put in our shoes as trustees tomorrow, what would you do?" The outcome of a wide-ranging discussion was a determination to reexamine the Academy's investment policy and also its spending rate.[74] At subsequent trustee meetings, the trustees vowed to bring the Academy into the black by the time of the bicentennial and voted to implement important new spending, investment, and tuition policies. Led by investment professionals and business leaders such as Chase, Dick Tucker '58, Jim Ottaway '55, and Dick Ramsden '55, they voted that "by the end of the fiscal year in June 1981, all withdrawals from endowment principal for operating expenses must cease." To prevent inflation from further eroding the purchasing power of the endowment, the board established two goals: first, that total investment returns maintain the real purchasing power of endowment assets; and second, that the assets should be structured in such a way that interest and dividend income cover the annual spending rate.

To provide for current income needs, the trustees reduced the equities in the portfolio from 70 to 54 percent and increased the bond allocation from 28 to 40 percent.[75] After a thorough study of bond managers, they selected State Street Research and Management Company, which had a long association with Harvard and was currently managing fixed income for Dartmouth. The trustees then turned their attention to equities. After reviewing the performance of various equity managers with the help of Cambridge Associates, Inc., a consulting firm specializing in financial and organizational planning for colleges, universities, and museums, the trustees transferred the Academy's equities to two firms with superior investment performance records and different investment strategies: John W. Bristol Co. and EMW Counsellors. The trustees decided to involve State Street Research in the management of equities as well as bonds to provide flexibility to reorient assets as market changes and income requirements necessitated.[76] In addition, the board voted to impose regular tuition increases for the next few years.[77]

To replenish the endowment in time for the bicentennial, the Academy in 1978 launched a three-year $22.6 million capital campaign, the Third Century Fund.[78] It had never been easy to raise money in a capital campaign, and the recurrence of double-digit inflation certainly did not make things any easier this time around. "We never thought we could raise the money," former trustee James H. Ottaway '55 recalled. "It was the only campaign I've ever worked on where we actually stayed on the schedule the professional fund raisers laid out. That was quite a performance.[79] Thanks to numerous contributions by small donors—an exception being gifts totaling over $1 million from three members of the Love family—the campaign surpassed its goal. In the end, however, it had little impact on Exeter's long-term financial health. "We raised $25 million [over three years] and the incredible thing is the money was going in the front door, and it was going out the back door even faster," said Ramsden.[80]

Determined to keep the increase in costs below the rate of inflation, the Academy implemented drastic spending cuts in most areas, including a temporary suspension of mortgage payments. Among the initiatives undertaken in this period was a comprehensive program of energy conservation to cut consumption and develop multiple fuel capacity.[81] The only significant increase in the budget was an 8 percent raise for faculty, clerical, dining hall and maintenance staff, and a 7.5 percent raise for administrators, the first substantive salary increases in years — an attempt to restore the purchasing power of salaries eroded by years of high inflation.[82]

The investment and fiscal policies implemented in the late 1970s did help put the Academy back on firmer footing, although the decision to convert more stocks to bonds was ill-timed, coming just as stocks began recovering and bonds began producing heavy losses. Meanwhile, despite concerted effort to cut expenses and increase tuition, withdrawals from the endowment remained well above the desired 5 percent. Even the attempt to raise salaries proved unsatisfactory. "As Chairman of the Budget and Finance Committee, I spent one long session explaining to the faculty why salaries weren't going up as fast as inflation, which was running up thirteen percent," Ottaway recalled. "It was hard on the faculty, and we were not happy that we couldn't do better."[83] The only area that saw real improvement in this period was Alumni/ae Giving. Thanks to the concerted efforts of the local branch organizations and Kurtz, who scoured the country relentlessly in the search of new donors, Alumni/ae Giving reached the $1 million mark in 1980.[84]

By the end of the decade, the value of the endowment stood at $46 million, its purchasing power cut in half. While it is true that the 1970s were a very bad period in the securities market, it is also true Exeter's wounds were partly self-inflicted, especially in terms of asset allocation as well as in the decisions to tap the endowment to cover rising costs while holding tuition increases below the rate of inflation.

RESTORING THE BALANCE

The Academy embarked on the new decade of the 1980s while continuing to face older questions — how to keep the endowment on a stable course of growth amidst fluctuations in the economy while ensuring that the budget had enough funding for institutional priorities.

The school continued to benefit from the leadership of two trustees, John Chase and Dick Ramsden, a Wall Street veteran who went on to found and direct the Consortium on Finance in Higher Education and later served as vice president for administration and finance at Brown. Together these men brought considerable professional expertise in the financial side of higher education. Guided by Chase and Ramsden, the board developed new strategies for maintaining the endowment's purchasing power and balancing the budget.

The first step was to address the problem of bonds in the endowment portfolio. The trustees approved decreasing the proportion of funds invested in bonds from 47 to 34 percent, while raising the proportion of short-term notes from 4 to 11 percent. At the same time, the trustees retained Cambridge Associates to monitor the performance of these investments on an ongoing basis.[85]

Meanwhile, the Budget and Finance Committee developed a budget that cut funding in some areas while raising wages and salaries to stay ahead of anticipated inflation and increasing allocations for major renovations to forestall further deterioration of plant assets. Although the stabilization of fuel oil prices, regular tuition increases, and successful Annual Giving campaigns were a big help in the struggle to balance the budget, spending of endowment principal to meet operational and capital needs continued for several years.[86] Throughout these years, Chase recalled, "The trustees continually pushed, pushed, pushed for this institution to understand its true cost of operations. It took us time to get all these costs up on the table and out in the open."[87]

Realizing that something more had to be done, in 1984 the trustees formed a Long-Range Planning Committee to study the Academy's financial problems from a variety of perspectives — endowment, spending, tuition, and fundraising. Its findings were hardly surprising: the Academy needed to limit its endowment spending still further and increase its revenues through better endowment management, continued tuition hikes, and intensified development efforts. In response, the board adopted a spending policy that called an immediate halt to the expenditure of endowment principal and limited the spending of endowment income in a given fiscal year to no more than 5 percent of the average of the market value of the endowment over the past 3½ years.[88] To build greater resiliency into the budget process and protect the endowment from unexpected operating needs, the trustees established reserve funds for specific purposes — the Annual Fund to cover potential shortfalls in Annual Giving campaigns, and an Energy Reserve to cover possible increases in fuel or electricity costs. Recognizing that capital campaigns were a costly way to raise money, the trustees called upon the Development Office to devise new fund raising methods.[89]

The appointment of Joseph E. (Jef) Fellows '62 as Academy treasurer in 1986 and Kendra S. O'Donnell as principal the following summer greatly facilitated the implementation of these policies. Professionally trained in financial management and accounting as well as education and personally knowledgeable about the school, Fellows ably filled a role that had grown far beyond traditional accounting and bookkeeping functions into a responsibility equivalent to that of a chief financial officer in a business corporation. "Jef is analytically precise, careful in projections, and insistent on knowing all effects of any proposed action," observed trustee Robert N. Shapiro '68. "At the same time, he is open in his communications and always willing to explain and bring constituencies into a process and a decision."[90] Having spent a decade in foundation work, O'Donnell would prove invaluable to Academy development efforts. "She knew this world inside and out from her time at Rockefeller Brothers," Shapiro said. "That experience proved absolutely essential to our fund raising campaigns."[91]

Fine Tuning

A market crash in October 1987 and its aftermath soon put the new policies to the test — which Exeter passed. Between 1987 and 1991, the endowment performed in the top tier of educational institutions, with returns averaging 7.6 percent, and the Academy managed to keep spending for operations below 5 percent of the value of the endowment. In 1991, the value of the endowment reached a new high of approximately $165 million, more than triple its value in 1982. Adjusted for inflation, however, it was still only $54.5 million in 1974 dollars, less than its value in the early 1970s.[92]

Compelled by these statistics, in the fall of 1992, the trustees made further adjustments to the Academy's endowment spending policy. Aiming to protect the true purchasing power of the endowment over time, keep spending increases regular, and enhance the growth of the endowment principal in a fluctuating market, the board voted to increase endowment income budgeted for operations by the rate of inflation for colleges and schools (CPI plus 2 percent) for the period 1993–1994 through 1998–1999. After the trustees reassessed the situation, the school would, for the years that followed, apply the "Yale Formula," a spending pattern based on the prior year's spending, inflation, and the current market value of the endowment — but within certain limits, since extreme fluctuations in the market could result in excessive spending on operations or a scarcity of funds.[93] The trustees also made further adjustments to the portfolio, adding foreign equities and bonds to guard against market volatility, while seeking total returns of 10 percent annually. In 1993, the State of New Hampshire acted as a conduit for a loan to Exeter of $10 million in the form of revenue bonds, which earned a triple A rating—a sure sign of the school's fundamental financial strength.[94]

Meanwhile, the school renewed its commitment to solving the problem of deferred maintenance. "The question was how to deal with this problem while at the same time maintaining a conservative financial approach," trustee president Ricardo A. Mestres '51 explained.[95] The trustees had taken an important step in 1986, when they decided to transfer $4 million from the endowment for plant renewal (roof repairs and other major improvements).[96] In the late 1980s, the board set a new guideline to increase the percentage of the budget allotted for capital renewal at an average rate between 10 and 14 percent annually until it reached 2 percent—later close to 2.5 percent—of the replacement value of the physical plant. By 1997, the capital budget had reached $2.8 million, or 1.35 percent of the replacement value of the $200-million physical plant.[97]

The Academy also developed a more professional approach to the way it took care of the physical plant. Under the guidance of Don J. Briselden, the buildings and grounds crew became a professional management organization—aptly renamed the Facilities Management Department—responsible for capital renewal, day-to-day maintenance, and the safety and security of the campus. "In the past, the buildings and grounds people operated in a reactive mode, fixing problems when they arose," Briselden explained. "Under O'Donnell, the department became a proactive organization and maintenance of the plant became a carefully planned process."[98]

On another front, development officials devised various fundraising strategies to support the Academy's new priorities. Searching for alternatives to the capital campaign, in the late 1980s they implemented a reunion gifts program that focused on bringing in million and multimillion dollar gifts from individual donors—a total of twenty-three gifts of $1 million or more during O'Donnell's decade-long tenure.[99] In the early 1990s, they implemented targeted funding for specific projects, the first instance being the $10 million faculty compensation initiative.[100] The success of this campaign, made possible by thirteen individuals and a few reunion classes, enabled the Academy to raise the average salary nearly $10,000 between 1989 and 1994. Other targeted initiatives funded the first major building projects undertaken since the Long Step Forward: the outdoor track (1985), the Grainger Observatory (1989), and the William G. Saltonstall Boathouse (1990), funded by the Coors family and several other individuals. In the 1990s, similar mini-campaigns made possible the computerization of the Library's catalog system (funded by the Friends of the Library) and the construction of the new Forrestal-Bowld Music Center (1995), funded by the late Michael V. Forrestal '45 and by William F. Bowld, Jr., '43. Development officials also started a major gifts program that resulted in gifts of over $1 million each. The regular Annual Giving Fund campaign enjoyed great success in this period as well, breaking the $3 million mark in 1990 and the $4 million mark in 1996, both record amounts for annual giving among independent schools. All told, the Development Office, aided by countless volunteers, raised nearly $200 million in gifts between 1980 and 2000.[101]

Meanwhile, the continuation of tuition increases above the rate of inflation between 1987 and 1991 enabled the Academy to use these extra funds for, among other purposes, increasing the average financial aid package from $7,083 to $9,909. At the same time, the number of students receiving aid (including faculty and staff children) increased from 26.1 to 27.5 percent, and the portion of the scholarship budget awarded to needy students rose from approximately 32 to 42 percent — a reflection of the school's renewed commitment to serving "youth from every quarter."[102]

Rapidly rising tuition posed challenges to many parents, however. A task force appointed by trustee president Mestres '51 and headed by Rick Smith '66 to study the affordability of an Exeter education reported that, although the Academy's tuition increases were in line with increases at independent schools and colleges nationwide during the 1980s, the formulas most schools, including Exeter, used for determining financial aid eligibility were out of date a decade later. Upper-middle-income families, that is, families earning $60,000 to $120,000 annually, earned too much to qualify for financial aid under the old rules but too little to afford ever-rising tuition fees, and each successive increase would make the Academy that much less affordable. If Exeter continued on this track, the report concluded, students of middle-income families would stop applying altogether, and the quality of the overall applicant pool would soon deteriorate.[103]

The trustees devised a three-point plan in the mid-1990s to make the Academy more affordable to students of middle-income families. They produced a budget that kept operating costs down and lowered tuition increases to a level more closely matching inflation. At the same time, they developed

a new way of calculating financial aid eligibility that required smaller contributions from a family's discretionary income and therefore encouraged
middle-income kids to apply while maintaining the Academy's commitment
to lower-income families. Third, they called for a scholarship initiative to target middle-income families.

Thanks to a healthy endowment, an energetic Development Office, and
sheer frugality, these initiatives proved relatively straightforward. In the mid-
1990s, Exeter's budget grew an average of 4 percent annually, just above the
rate of inflation. Tuition remained consistently among the lowest of the leading residential schools. A targeted fundraising initiative for scholarships
proved successful and in 1995, the number of Exonians receiving financial
aid reached an all-time high of 32 percent, including fifty students of middle-
income families who would not have been eligible in the past.[104]

The Academy's financial performance and its financial discipline remained
strong under Principal Tingley, who arrived in 1997. Fellows continued as
treasurer though his title had become Chief Financial Officer in recognition
of the increased importance of the position. The trustees, meanwhile, continued to monitor closely the performance of the endowment as well as the
growth of the operating budget. And the Development Office continued to
bolster annual giving, reunion gifts, and targeted initiatives. As the Academy
Master Planning process kicked in, the community worked together to identify long-term priorities and projects to keep Exeter at the forefront of independent education well into the twenty-first century.

EYES ON THE FUTURE

More than 75 years later, the Academy is a considerably larger and more
complex institution than it was on the eve of the Harkness bequest. The number of faculty and staff has risen from approximately 75 to nearly 350, while
the campus has grown from nearly 50 buildings to more than 125. Exeter is
also considerably more expensive to run and maintain. Between 1929–1930
and 2006–2007, the operating budget soared from $877,000 to $78.7 million
and the endowment from approximately $1 million to an impressive $806
million — fourth after the endowments of The Kamehameha Schools-Bishop
Estate, Andover, and St. Paul's.[105] Tuition reached $34,500 for boarding stu-
dents and $26,600 for day students in 2006–2007, with 39 percent of students
receiving some financial aid and an average financial aid grant of $28,300.

The vital statistics have changed enormously, as has the school's approach
to financial issues, which is not simply "outsourced" to investment profes-

sionals but the subject of close day-to-day management in the office of the chief financial officer as well as to periodic Harkness-style examination and review by the trustees. Having learned to balance short-term and long-term needs, Exeter now possesses sophisticated ability to manage the endowment, contain operating costs, and increase revenues in a wide range of economic conditions. Innovations such as the regular renovation program and ongoing fundraising initiatives have contributed to robust financial health but not precluded the occasional need for a major capital campaign to give the Academy a vital boost forward. In 2004, Principal Tingley announced The Exeter Initiatives, a five-year campaign to raise $305 million "to renew and retain our talented teachers; to ensure that no qualified student is turned away from the Academy based on a lack of family resources; and to make certain that our facilities support all the needs of our residential school community, where teaching occurs in 'every quarter' of this campus."[106]

The Exeter Initiatives were well planned and structured before they were made public, and by the time of the announcement, $143 million, nearly half of the total sought, had already been donated or pledged. Through its early years, the campaign was humming smoothly as the Academy reached out to alumni and potential donors via a series of coordinated events and print and electronic communications. By the end of 2006, Exeter had received nearly $260 million in gifts and pledges, including the largest single donation ever to an independent school for faculty and staff development. An anonymous donor contributed $25 million to endow four distinguished professorships, six teaching chairs, and three instructorships as well as to support professional development. Other gifts also made themselves apparent across a range of projects and programs. Renovations to Love Gymnasium, for example, included the Fisher Squash Center, which replaced six outmoded courts with ten new ones built to international specifications, and an enlarged, state-of-the-art swimming pool and training facility. Chuck Harris '69, chair of the Exeter Initiatives campaign, contributed funds for the Harris Family Children's Center, an expansion and renovation of the day-care center opened in 1988. In keeping with Academy traditions, the facility includes two mini-Harkness Tables a part of a learning environment. Bestselling author Dan Brown '82, whose thriller *The Da Vinci Code* (2003) proved a worldwide publishing phenomenon, and siblings Valerie '85 and Gregory '93, donated $2.2 million for a fund named in honor of their father, longtime math professor Richard G. Brown, to provide computers and related technology to students receiving financial aid.

And the gifts continued to pour in. In October 2007, the Exeter Initiatives exceeded its target two years early, surpassing $307 million in donations. By then, the Academy's endowment had soared past $1 billion in value. The happy union of financial well-being and educational excellence reached during the late twentieth century thus continues in the twenty-first. By all appearances, the Academy has the financial and operating management systems in place to tackle whatever challenges come its way.

Life after Exeter

John Phillips envisioned Exeter as something more than a school where students would learn English and Latin grammar, writing, arithmetic, and other sciences. He believed that mastery of those subjects was important and would be useful in later life, but he also wanted the Academy to teach "the great end and real business of living."[1] He did not clarify or elaborate on this phrase, although clues to his meaning appear elsewhere in the Deed of Gift. He wanted students to marry knowledge with goodness so that they could lead worthy lives, serving God and helping their neighbors.

Like other significant parts of the Deed of Gift, the eighteenth-century language resonated through the years and remains potent today, despite the sharp differences in context between Phillips's time and our own. In the Academy's early years, few graduates continued their formal education, and those who did were most likely to attend Harvard or Yale in preparation for becoming clergy, teachers, or lawyers. In the early twenty-first century, virtually all Exonians go on to a diverse array of colleges and universities, and after that many attend graduate school in preparation for careers in business, law, journalism, academics and teaching, medicine, and other professions and pursuits. Wherever they choose to go, and whatever they choose to do, however, the Academy — as it has throughout its history — expects them to lead worthy lives, uniting knowledge and goodness.

How modern graduates have gone about "the great end and real business of living" is a complicated subject that varies with each individual. Yet there are clear patterns in the choices they have made about colleges and careers, as well as in the Academy's efforts to support those choices and strengthen bonds with its graduates. These patterns reflect the magnitude of changes at Exeter after the Harkness Gift as well as larger trends in American society after 1930.

CHOOSING A COLLEGE

Although Exeter settled in the 1880s on an identity as a college preparatory school (as opposed to a more general secondary or terminal-degree school), it did little thereafter for decades to guide or influence students' choices about which colleges to apply to and attend. Most graduates attended a handful of Ivy League colleges and went on to positions of leadership in the professions and community life, especially in New England and the Mid-Atlantic states. In 1930, for example, nearly two-thirds of the Academy's graduating class of 250 attended Harvard, Yale, or Princeton, and the top five choices (adding Dartmouth and MIT into the mix) accounted for more than 80 percent of matriculants. The Academy offered no formal college counseling although individual faculty, if consulted, advised students about where to apply. It was a short list. At the time, Exeter and a handful of peer institutions such as Phillips Academy in Andover, Milton Academy, St. Paul's, Choate, and Law-renceville Academy were considered feeder schools to the Ivy League. By today's standards, the relationship between the feeder schools and the institutions they fed was incestuous, with interlocking networks among trustees, faculty, administrators, and alumni.

During the middle third of the twentieth century, however, the tight relationships between Exeter and other feeder schools and the top Ivy League colleges and universities began to change. Three closely related factors brought about this outcome: (1) changes in American society, especially demographic change, advances in transportation and communications, and expanded funding of higher education; (2) changes in the admissions policies of the top Ivy League colleges and universities; and, (3) in Exeter's case, changes involving admissions policy, educational philosophy, and provision of counseling services. Together, these factors combined to produce a different pattern for choosing colleges, one in which Exeter seniors selected among a much greater variety of institutions around the United States with considerable support and encouragement from the Academy's Office of College Counseling.

Changing Contexts

In the early twentieth century, the requirements for matriculation at even the most prestigious colleges and universities were modest. The first requirement was an acceptable academic record, grades, and evaluations that showed at least average mastery of scholastic disciplines. Another requirement adopted after the establishment of the College Entrance Examination Board (CEEB) in 1900, an association of a few dozen prominent private schools and colleges — including Exeter and Harvard — was an acceptable score on the "college boards," essay examinations on various subjects that CEEB oversaw.[2] Only students who had received passing grades in their coursework were eligible to take the boards, and many came to believe the chief purpose of their secondary school studies was to prepare them for these exams. Theoretically, such criteria were meant to be screening devices for colleges, who relied on them in choosing whom to admit. Beyond the grades and the board scores, however, entry to even the best colleges was hardly competitive. Before World War II, for example, Harvard admitted more than two out of every three applicants. In a typical year, more than half of each entering class came from nearby independent schools, with Exeter, Andover, Milton Academy, and St. Paul's accounting for a third of these students.[3] Meanwhile, Exeter routinely sent at least three-quarters of every graduating class to the Ivy League.

Significant changes in American society and education soon altered this picture. The years between 1915 and 1925 witnessed an explosive growth in the number of public high schools nationwide and hence also in the number of college-bound students. This trend prompted CEEB in 1926 to adopt a new college entrance exam, the multiple-choice Scholastic Aptitude Test (SAT), and, a few years later, Achievement Tests, multiple-choice exams in a variety of subjects. The SAT eventually replaced the written college boards.[4] The increase in high school graduates began to have an impact on the colleges themselves in the late 1920s, as the demand for places began to exceed the supply. In 1927, the *Bulletin of the Phillips Exeter Academy* wrote that "so called 'selective' admissions has been made possible or necessary by the fact that for many colleges the number of applicants now exceeds the number admitted." Colleges began looking for students who were "well-rounded," and extracurricular activities became important determinants in the admission process. This change introduced an element of uncertainty into the application process and induced students to apply to several, perhaps many, colleges.[5]

Although these trends did not much affect Exeter initially, they gathered force in the following decade. James B. Conant, Harvard's president between 1933 and 1953, set an example for many top-rank colleges and universities by seeking to raise intellectual standards and using the admissions process and heightened emphasis on the SAT as one means to achieve this goal. Whereas Harvard had drawn its student body primarily from the Northeast and relied heavily on feeder schools, it sought after 1933 to make admission to the College more broadly based and meritocratic. Conant wanted admissions to be fiercely competitive, and he sought to open up the college to students from diverse geographical and socioeconomic backgrounds.[6] These objectives, however, were only partly realized in the 1930s. With the Great Depression restricting the number of students who could afford to attend Harvard, the number of public school matriculants grew only slightly, although there was a noticeable shift away from private schools in the Northeast.[7] Exeter was not immune: between 1934 and 1940, the number of Academy graduates matriculating at Harvard declined by approximately 25 percent, from 95 to 71.

Aware of these trends, Principal Lewis Perry recognized the need for an institutional response. In 1936, he appointed English master Myron Williams as director of studies, a part-time position with responsibilities including advising students on preparing for and applying to college. Williams encouraged students to consider a broader range of options, and between 1930 and 1940, the number of colleges Exonians attended climbed from eighteen to twenty-nine.

The college choices of Exeter seniors expanded again following World War II, when American higher education experienced another great burst of growth. Between 1947 and 1957, college enrollments soared by one-half, to about 3 million students.[8] Once again, Harvard led its peer institutions in fashioning a response. A new dean of admissions, Wilbur Bender, could at last implement Conant's vision. Harvard would become a university for the nation, drawing its students from all over the country. (This movement coincided almost exactly with Bill Saltonstall's drive to make Exeter a "national high school" for similar reasons: belief in meritocracy and the feasibility of appealing to a national market in which travel by car, train, and airplane and universal telephone service diminished the effects of distance.) At a Harvard reunion symposium in 1955, it was reported that the average Harvard student, compared with his counterpart of 1930, was less likely to come from New England and from an East Coast boarding school; he had less money and was more dependent on scholarship aid; and he worked harder and was more likely to graduate with honors. By 1960, the proportion of freshmen from secondary schools outside the Northeast had doubled, reaching 56 percent.[9]

As a result of these changes at Harvard and similar trends elsewhere in higher education, Exeter witnessed a gradual decline in the number of its students matriculating at a narrow range of Ivy League schools. On the other hand, Exeter benefited from a countervailing trend: the rise of many other private colleges and state universities to greater excellence. As a result, Exonians could choose from a rich variety of institutions around the country that offered an outstanding liberal arts education. In growing numbers, Exeter graduates matriculated at institutions such as Stanford, University of Chicago, Vanderbilt, University of California at Berkeley, and University of Wisconsin. At the same time, more Exonians also matriculated at smaller colleges in the Northeast such as Amherst, Williams, Swarthmore, Haverford, Colby, and Bates. Still, in the 1950s, Exeter students by and large chose the college, rather than the other way around. The experience of James H. Ottaway, Jr., '55, a former trustee, proved typical. "I said to my roommate junior year, 'Where are we going to go to college? We have to declare something to the college admissions office next Tuesday,'" Ottaway recalled. His roommate said, "'Well, let's not go to Harvard, everybody's going to Harvard. It's too much like Exeter. We've already been here. We don't want to go to Princeton. That's too much like another prep school, so we'll go to Yale.' We made this choice without knowing a whole lot about Yale. So we applied to Yale, and got in, that was that. I didn't take any grand tour of New England looking at other colleges."[10]

Most of Ottaway's classmates fared just as well: 86 percent of graduates in the class of 1955 were admitted to their first choice among colleges.[11] But increasing numbers were pursuing institutions beyond the traditional range of options. In 1955, Academy students matriculated at forty-seven colleges and universities, nearly triple the number in 1930.

Baby Boomers Apply to College

The growing egalitarianism of American society of the 1960s and 1970s became manifest in a growing number of colleges and universities that promoted socioeconomic diversity in their academic programs and admissions policies. The case of Yale is fairly typical of this period: long known as an elite WASPish institution, it embraced a new philosophy under President Kingman Brewster, Jr. (1963–1977). As Richard Shaw, Yale's dean of admissions and financial aid, explained, "Brewster moved the institution from a more historic system, in which many schools were feeders to the system, to one in which geographical and socioeconomic diversity was important."[12] Although many traditional feeder schools like Exeter were also drawing students from diverse geographical and socioeconomic backgrounds, many colleges, especially in the Ivy League, were no longer willing to have their admissions work done by the feeder schools. As admissions officers at Yale and elsewhere focused on recruiting students on academic merit, they reaped the benefit of much improved public education programs, supported by post-Sputnik government funding.

The passage of Baby Boomers through college age spurred more changes in college admissions patterns. Colleges and universities committed to racial diversity and affirmative action programs. They stepped up their recruiting efforts and further expanded their outreach to applicants from nontraditional sources. As a result, the traditional competitive advantage of private school graduates at Ivy League institutions continued to erode. In 1955, nearly 60 percent of the freshman class at Yale came from private schools; by 1982, that share had dropped to 40 percent.[13]

At first, Exeter and a handful of peer institutions successfully resisted this trend, although with increasing effort and struggle. During this period, the number of Exonians matriculating at top Ivy League colleges remained fairly consistent, with an average of seventy to seventy-five matriculants per year, nearly a third of the senior class. The Academy's success was due principally to two factors. The advent of coeducation in 1970 produced some very strong female graduates who went on to the Ivy League institutions in proportionately greater numbers than their male counterparts. Second, the Academy completely revamped its approach to college admissions and developed a two-pronged strategy to expand the range of colleges that Exeter students should consider while strengthening existing relationships with the Ivy League institutions.

Beginning in the summer of 1975, Thomas C. Hayden, director of college counseling between 1974 and 1989, drove around different parts of the country—the Midwest one year, the South the next—making official visits and establishing contacts with admissions officers that developed into a network of personal relationships. "These trips took me to over a hundred colleges in the United States," Hayden recalled, "and gave me the background I needed to conduct a wide conversation with parents and students."[14] At the same time, Hayden took a more structured approach with traditional East Coast favorites. By restricting the number of applications to six per student—two "reaches," two "middles," and two "safeties"—and allowing a maximum of two Ivy applications, he limited the amount of competition among Exonians. He also performed important services for the college admissions offices by prescreening the Exeter applicants and by basically guaranteeing a certain yield to those other schools worried about losing acceptances to the most desirable rivals. Both prongs of the strategy proved highly successful. Exeter enjoyed a cordial and candid relationship with admissions officers on the East Coast and courted good relationships with other leading colleges and universities around the country.

Meanwhile, the perceived gap in quality between the top Ivy League institutions and other colleges and universities began to narrow. In 1983, *U.S. News and World Report* began publishing its annual rankings of the best colleges and universities. Although the methodology behind the rankings was hotly contested (and remains controversial), most readers concentrated on the results. Harvard, Yale, and Princeton invariably ranked in the top ten but other institutions in the Ivy League and elsewhere occasionally bumped them from the uppermost slots. Brown University, University of Pennsylvania, and Stanford enjoyed enviable status as "hot" choices. Duke, Emory, Georgetown, and Boston University emerged as highly regarded and competitive private universities, and the list of outstanding state universities included Virginia, Illinois, Michigan, and North Carolina, among others. During the 1970s and 1980s, Exonians were to be found in numbers at all of these institutions. In 1990, Exeter graduates matriculated at seventy-nine colleges and universities.

College Admissions since 1990

Recent years have brought still more challenges and opportunities for Exonians, as admission to the top-ranked colleges and universities became still more competitive. The 1990s witnessed a sharp rise in the number of eighteen-year-olds in the United States — an "echo baby boom," as some called it, that persists into the early twenty-first century. A growing industry of test-prep services helped more secondary school students — including growing numbers schooled at home — to perform well on the SATs. Thus encouraged, many of these students applied to top colleges and universities. Meanwhile, the top colleges could cast farther afield to find applicants. The rising value of endowments enabled many institutions to offset soaring costs of tuition, room, and board with generous financial aid packages. The Internet and declining transportation costs facilitated reaching more, and more diverse, markets. Many elite institutions made determined efforts to contact secondary schools that historically had sent few applicants their way.

Hundreds of colleges adopted the so-called "Common Application," a web site–generated form that eliminates the need to complete a different application for each institution and makes it easier to apply to multiple colleges.[15] Increasing numbers of colleges introduced or further developed programs to enable students to apply and learn of their admissions status much earlier than the customary month of April. These so-called "early programs" — Early Decision and Early Action — are generally believed to enhance a student's chances for admission, and understandably, proved extremely popular, with more than four hundred institutions eventually participating.[16]

Exeter's College Counseling Office responded to these trends and pressures in true Harkness fashion. The six full-time counselors and three support staff worked with students to help them manage the college selection process—to gain the skills needed to choose the right colleges for their needs and to present themselves persuasively in the admissions process. "We are no different from teachers in the classroom or residential faculty in the dormitories," explained Mark Davis, who directed the office between 1998 and 2002. "We try to engage students and encourage them to take control of the process. We provide a supportive and structured environment in which they can explore their interests, their strengths and weaknesses, their goals, and the college options that fit them best. We encourage them to ask the right questions, an essential step in gaining control of a complex process."[17]

This approach proved effective. The absolute number of Exeter students admitted to the most competitive colleges and universities remained high, and on a percentage basis the Academy ranks with the most successful of its peer institutions. Noted Davis, "The admit rate from Exeter is still high compared with other schools. Students from Exeter do very well."[18] Meanwhile, in an average year, Exeter students applied to more than two hundred colleges and universities in the United States and abroad. In 2005, Exonians were registered at 112 of them.

Looking ahead, officials in the Academy's College Counseling Office see no signs that recent trends and patterns in college admissions will change in material ways. The number of eighteen-year-olds will continue to rise nationwide, and competition for admission to the best schools will grow keener. At the same time, these officials believe that the Harkness approach to college counseling, with its emphasis on satisfying the individual needs of each student, will stand Exonians in good stead, whatever challenges and changes the outside world may bring. "Our goal," said Davis, "is for Exeter students to have a good college experience wherever they go."[19]

LIVES AFTER EXETER: COLLEGES AND CAREERS

Once graduates left Exeter, they generally fared well in college and in later life—as might be predicted, given their family backgrounds and high intelligence, aptitudes, and achievements, as well as the rigorous, intensive education they received. Exeter provided excellent preparation for college, both in building a strong foundation of academic skills and knowledge and in readying students to keep learning at a fast rate. Grateful for the boost, most Exonians performed well in college, excelling in the disciplines they chose to pursue, and most, starting in the 1950s, sustained the momentum through graduate programs. The knowledge, values, skills, and love of learning imparted at Exeter also served its graduates well in their chosen careers. Most Exonians went on to positions of distinction in business, the professions, academic life, literature, the arts, and public service. A significant number of graduates credit the Academy with a disproportionate role in their successes.

At College

For virtually all Exonians, life after Exeter began approximately four months after graduation, at college. Although it is hazardous to generalize too broadly about their experiences in college, evidence such as their later reflections and the comments of college teachers suggests some common patterns. First, the Academy's emphasis on developing critical skills in thinking, reading, and writing and its grounding in the liberal arts disciplines enabled most graduates to manage the transition to college with relative ease. Exeter equipped its graduates with advantages that could be sustained—if the students chose to do so. Second, for many Exonians, college proved anticlimactic—less challenging and exciting than their Academy years. Finally, many Exonians found it difficult to replicate the Academy's intellectual and social environment, which they came to miss as their college years wore on.

Several of these patterns are apparent in the comments of an eminent Ivy League historian who has taught many Exonians over the years at several different institutions (and who prefers to remain anonymous). "As freshmen," he observed of graduates of the Academy and of a small number of similar schools, "they often prove vastly superior to their peers in analytical skills and writing talents. They also tend to be extremely self-confident and well prepared." After the first year of college, however, the professor saw those students diverging into three categories. "Some—probably the biggest group—maintained this lead throughout college. Another sizable group fell back into the pack by sophomore year as strong students from other schools caught up. Finally, a smaller but noteworthy group seemed never to engage in the college experience. They got by on what they learned at school, but they didn't really advance in college."

A sampling of Exonians' reflections on their college experiences preserved in several published collections, reunion books, and a sampling of oral history interviews tends to corroborate the professor's analysis.[20]

From the class of 1955: "In general, one encounters excellence very few times in one's lifetime. Exeter for me was one of those encounters. I was educated at Exeter and then went to Yale."

From the class of 1971: "Exeter provided me with unparalleled professional training — I have never been as intellectually challenged since, either at Cornell as an undergrad or at Stanford, where I got my Ph.D."

From the class of 1977: "The freshman seminar at Harvard did not have the same dynamic quality as the Harkness Table. [At Exeter] you feel as though you're exploring with a guide as opposed to college, where someone is feeding you information."

From the class of 1983: "I found academics initially very easy at Harvard and was able to cruise through my first year. The playing field evened out later."

From the class of 1992: "The Harkness System made education exciting and personal. What I missed the most while in college [at Northwestern] was the deep relationship I had with my teachers, who took a real interest in my life."

From the class of 1993: "I expected [Wellesely College] would be intellectually similar to Exeter, that when I walked into a classroom it would have the same kind of dynamics, the give-and-take among students. But the students responded to the professor and not each other: a confrontation would shut down the discussion."

From the class of 1996: "At Brown I felt distanced from the process of learning. People didn't talk to each other, they talked to the section leader. We didn't read each other's papers. It was not as immediate or exciting as Exeter."

Some Exonians fell into the history professor's third category of disengagement during college. For these students, college classes did not seem particularly challenging or stimulating, but rather a decline from the high standard set by discussions around the Harkness Table. Things that were novel for public school graduates — living away from home, meeting students from distant places and unfamiliar cultures, encountering a diverse curriculum with many options and possibilities for specialization, an excellent library, and vast athletic facilities — seemed old hat to some Exonians. For others, the relatively unstructured life in college proved disorienting after the rigors of the Academy. One member of the class of 1966 (under condition of anonymity) recalled his college experience at Harvard as "a waste. I had my adolescent rebellion in college. I didn't have time for it at Exeter. I should have taken time off in college, but because of the Vietnam War, I couldn't."

By the time this young man encountered college, a cognate experience had already acquired a label: "the Exeter Syndrome." In 1957, three years after graduating from Exeter, Christopher Jencks (subsequently an eminent sociologist) coined the term in the *Harvard Crimson* to describe a malaise of arrogance and dissatisfaction that led some Exonians to do badly in their course work and, in some cases, to drop out altogether. "The Exonian is not impressed by anything or anybody," he wrote. "He exudes sophistication from the moment that he enters his freshman dorm. He is, after all, better than his fellows, for he has been to Exeter."[21] Not all disengaged students acted out of a sense of superiority, however. Some were simply burned out and could not avail themselves of the resources at their disposal. "Some students could not recapture the intensity they had known at Exeter, and did not exploit college for what it could give them," explained David A. Bell '79 and Harvard '83.[22]

Some Exonians recaptured the Academy's intensity in their new academic environs, even if it meant resorting to extraordinary measures. "I went to Harvard with a network of classmates, and we met after class as a Harkness Table," recalled Peter E. Durham '85 and Harvard '89, software design engineer for Microsoft at MSNBC and donor of the Academy's state-of-the-art computing laboratory. "We knew how effective a learning mechanism it was to sit around and discuss things, and we all missed it."[23]

Careers

Another, perhaps more revealing, way to assess the impact of an Exeter education lies in examining the later careers of Exonians, as well as in assessing their later feelings about their secondary education. The career choices of Exeter graduates indicate a wide range of interests fostered by the broad education delivered by the Academy. Whatever their college experience, most graduates went on to professional lives that by most standards represent notable success, and an impressive number attained remarkable distinction. With Exonians occupying positions at or near the top of virtually all major professions, the Academy evidently fulfilled its mission to provide leadership to society. As the published recollections, reunion books, and interviews bear witness, many Exonians credit their schooling with reinforcing strong foundations and providing a boost toward lifelong success.[24]

During the period after 1930, Exeter graduates chose a variety of professions and careers, with relatively little change through the decades. Statistics compiled by the Office of Alumni/ae Affairs and Development reveal that the biggest number of graduates—between 28 and 40 percent of each class between 1930 and 2000—pursued careers in "business," but this broad category embraces activity ranging from shopkeeping, to entrepreneurial ventures, to employment in major corporations and professional service firms, to management positions in nonprofit organizations. The financial services industry—commercial, merchant, and investment banks, investment companies, and venture capital funds—and management consulting firms claimed a large share of Academy graduates in "business." Relatively few went on to work for major corporations, although several who followed that path rose to the very top. A significant number held senior positions in foundations and other nonprofits.

The legal profession consistently accounted for the second-largest number of Exeter graduates, about 10 percent of each class. Most of these lawyers worked in private practice but a handful, joined by a smaller group of Exonians from different backgrounds, pursued careers in public service. In the second half of the twentieth century, the Academy produced several governors, congressional representatives, and U.S. senators, as well as larger contingents of officials in state and local governments. The Academy's leaders were pleased by this record although some—Saltonstall, for instance—wished for more. The preference for careers in the private sector represented for him "the outstanding weakness" of Exeter.[25]

Medicine has been another popular career, especially in the 1960s and 1970s, as was true nationwide during an era of seemingly unlimited funding; after this, it declined in popularity among male and female graduates alike. Far fewer pursued careers in science or engineering, only 4 to 7 percent of the classes surveyed—a fact that some leaders of the school regarded as a major disappointment but also one they expected to change in light of the boost to the sciences symbolized by the Phelps Science Center, as well as the continuing growth of knowledge-based industries. In the 1980s and 1990s, a rising percentage of graduates answered the call of the information industry and careers in the converging worlds of computers, software, communications, and media.

Not surprisingly, Exonians are well represented in the various branches of higher education, in senior administrative as well as teaching positions. Several graduates became college presidents, while many became leading scholars in virtually every academic discipline.

Perhaps most impressive is the list of Exonians who have become accomplished writers—as the collection of books housed on the top floor of the Class of 1945 Library and the space devoted to book and poetry reviews in each issue of the *Bulletin* attest. Many Exonian authors credit the Academy for fostering love of writing and teaching how to write. The school's emphasis on written and verbal communication may explain why a large number of graduates — approximately 10 to 12 percent — have gone into publishing and journalism and have held prominent positions on newspapers, radio, and television throughout the country and world. By contrast, only 5 or 6 percent of each class on the average have elected to pursue careers in nonliterary arts.

The reflections and reminiscences of Exeter alumni/ae in different occupations reveal the ways in which their time at the Academy — whether a year or the full four years — contributed to their choice of career and subsequent success.

Jonathan R. Ross '71, architect: "Exeter provided me with my first formal training in architecture. The different classes I took — the studios in tenth and eleventh grade and the senior year independent project — gave me the chance to test my interest and assess my ability. I then entered Cornell's architecture program, which is notoriously brutal, and it was a breeze."[26]

Michael J. Lynch '72, television sportscaster: "The wheels of my mind had not been oiled before Exeter. I became more inquisitive because of the Harkness Table, where you confront dilemmas face-to-face. Thanks to a course on Oral Interpretation, I became confident and came to relish public speaking. These skills have proved invaluable to my work in communications."[27]

Julian Liau '88, financial services: "Thanks to Exeter's small classes, I always felt comfortable speaking up when I was in meetings with my superiors."[28]

Peter Durham, '85, software engineer: "The skills I use at Microsoft, problem-solving and learning how to learn, have their roots at Exeter. We work in small product teams with the expectation that you get a bunch of bright people together and they go off and solve problems, figuring out what we need to do as a group from the bottom up rather than with a mandate from the top."[29]

Paris R. von Lockette '60, consultant: "When I worked in government, people were amazed that I could write so well and so quickly. I then set up my own business and people with Ph.D.'s working for me, and I found I was correcting a lot of their work."[30]

James Fitzgerald '76, software engineer: "The focus on critical thinking, being able to think for yourself, and some feeling for the gray areas of life — these have stood me in good stead. These analytic skills are important in my business, in which I am constantly performing consultative functions with different businesses and must be sensitive to what makes them tick."[31]

Sometimes the academic experience helped students determine what they would *not* pursue as a career, as in the case of Somers Randolph '74, who went on to become a sculptor. "I didn't like anything they were teaching," he recalled. "I would be up all night working on a piece, then go into history class the next day unprepared, saying, 'You should see what I made last night!'"[32]

Whatever the career path, Elizabeth Trupin Campbell '74, a physician, sums up the impact of Exeter well. What has lingered with her over the years, she wrote, was "the Exeter educational philosophy that says you must go out and fulfill your unique identity. . . . Being gifted creates obligations, which means that you owe the world your best effort at the work you love."[33]

This philosophy may well explain why the Academy reserves its highest accolade for those who have dedicated their life to service. Concerned to promote the fundamental purpose of the Academy, in 1965 the trustees and Executive Committee of the General Alumni/ae Association established the John Phillips Award, to honor living graduates who dedicated themselves to "a life that contributes to the welfare of community, country, and humanity, exemplifying in high degree nobility of character and usefulness to mankind."[34] The recipients have come from many different fields of endeavor, including foreign service, politics, business, philanthropy, academia, civil rights, and medicine.

Recipients include individuals important in the history of the Academy itself, such as Bill Saltonstall '24, Francis Plimpton '17, Jim Ottaway '55, and Hugh Calkins '41, among their other notable achievements, but also a wide range of people who have made exceptional contributions to society (a complete list through 2006 is appended to this chapter):

> Burke Marshall '40, who as Assistant Attorney General in charge of the Civil Rights Division during the Kennedy administration advanced the civil rights cause;
>
> Robert A. Fortuine '52, a physician who as a member of the U.S. Public Health Service worked continuously with Eskimo and Indian books and wrote many books about the Arctic;
>
> John C. Dancy '07, Director of the Detroit Urban League;
>
> John C. Leslie '22, Senior Vice President of Pan Am after nearly 43 years with the company;
>
> Alfred L Atherton, Jr., '40, Ambassador to Egypt and then Director General of the U.S. Foreign Service;
>
> Hodding Carter III '53, political commentator, author, newspaper editor, television documentary producer, and political activist;
>
> Joshua L. Miner III '39, founding president and chair of the board of trustees of Outward Bound USA and dean of admissions at Andover;

Peter B. Bensinger '54, chairman of the Youth Commission, head of the Department of Corrections and, under President Ford, head of the National Drug Enforcement Agency; Episcopal minister and peace activist;

Cornelius D. Hastie '48, Director of the St. James Episcopal Church and Educational Center, and the founder of the Episcopal Society for Cultural-Racial Unity;

Charles C. Krulak '60, Marine commandant of the U.S. Marine Corps and head of the Marine Corps Combat Development Command, recipient of a Silver Star, Purple Heart, and two Bronze Stars in Vietnam;

Arthur M. Schlesinger, Jr., '33, noted historian, advisor to President John F. Kennedy, and prolific author;

Thayer "Ted" Scudder '48, professor of anthropology, *emeritus*, at California Institute of Technology, an expert on low-income human communities and community-based natural resource management;

Dr. Ira D. Helfand '67, a full-time emergency room physician in Northampton, Massachusetts, and a founding member of Physicians for Social Responsibility and International Physicians for the Prevention of Nuclear War; and

Dr. Daniel E. Koshland, Jr., '37, professor of biochemistry and molecular biology *emeritus* at the University of California, Berkeley, and longtime editor of *Science*, the preeminent journal of general science in the United States.

FROM A SCHOOL TO A COMMUNITY:
THE ACADEMY AND ITS ALUMNI/AE

A major theme in the Academy's history in the twentieth century and beyond is its successful efforts to form lasting relationships with its graduates. Exeter pursued this goal for a variety of motives but not least because it sought ways to honor and channel the generally warm feelings alumni/ae have toward the institution. Over time, the "old boy network" typical of Exeter and other leading private schools evolved into something much broader and more open and sustaining: an extended community of alumni/ae seeking to renew and preserve personal and social connections while also contributing to the Academy's financial, academic, and institutional welfare.

The roots of alumni/ae involvement at Exeter trace to a small number of clubs founded in the nineteenth century to enable graduates living in a particular city or region to maintain contact. In the early twentieth century, under principals Amen and Perry, these clubs evolved into a more cohesive Alumni Association, and Perry particularly recognized the potential of alumni as an important source of support as the Academy sought to bolster its financial condition and lessen its dependence on tuition to cover operating expenses. Perry and his successor, William Saltonstall, also tapped alumni for volunteer support in admissions, scholarships, and advising and mentoring students and graduates. As the number of graduates swelled and regional clubs and associations proliferated, the Alumni Association became a significant everyday factor in the life and affairs of the Academy.

The first formal groups of alumni were the New York Alumni Association, founded in 1883, and the New England Association, established three years later. Although other and similar groups sprouted in other areas of the United States, the New York and New England associations remained by far the biggest and most active. The primary purpose of the associations was social. As described by Robert C. Wiggin, the original secretary to the New England Association, "It is the purpose of the Association to hold an annual reunion . . . and to afford to every past member of the Academy an opportunity to note its progress, and to recall the many pleasant friendships and days of his school life." Membership dues were $2 per year and helped underwrite the group's expenses and also afforded in 1887 a $100 gift to the Academy—the first trickle of what was to become a mighty stream.

In 1904, Principal Amen commissioned Professor James A. Tufts '74 to publish the Academy's first Alumni Directory, an impressive and authoritative piece of research that listed graduates between 1783 and 1903. During the next dozen years, Tufts kept alumni records and visited alumni as an official representative of the Academy. The *Phillips Exeter Bulletin* was founded in 1905 "as a means of bringing the alumni into closer touch with the school and with one another."

The next principal, Lewis Perry, made alumni affairs one of his top priorities. The year after his arrival, he created the position of Alumni Register, to which he appointed William E. Soule '06, who had published the Class Report of '06 and had tutored at the Academy. Aided by an Elliott addressing machine and a Smith Premier double-keyboard typewriter, Soule compiled address records at an oak roll-top desk. During World War I, he divided his time between divinity school and the Alumni Office, where he published a list of Exeter men in the service. In 1919, Soule used his own funds to purchase a multigraph machine to make multiple copies of the fliers to be mailed out to alumni.

In the belief that the alumni were an integral part of the Academy community, Perry created a special day in the school calendar for them. Previously, graduates returned for reunions on Class Day, one of the days set aside for commencement activities, when faculty and underclassman had departed for the summer vacation and only seniors remained on campus. Starting in 1920, Perry organized Alumni Day as an occasion before the commencement festivities, when faculty and students were still on campus and could take part. The reunion events took place at Wentworth-by-the-Sea, a nearby resort. Although Perry welcomed all graduates back to the Academy, the occasion soon took on special emphasis for milestone reunions such as the tenth and twenty-fifth. Assisted by the alumni secretary, Perry continued to plan and direct Alumni Day throughout his tenure.

In 1922, Perry himself began to take an active role in alumni affairs, the first principal to see the potential of the alumni as a source of continuing funds. That year he wrote to alumni at Christmas, asking for a voluntary donation. The Christmas letter was so successful—nearly 5 percent of the alumni subscribed a total of $5,281—that Perry had it repeated the following year and it soon became institutionalized. Perry also encouraged leading alumni to form a central organization, the General Alumni Association, with its own Constitution and By-Laws, in 1924. The regional associations, directed by local officers, continued to conduct annual events, while the General Alumni Association took on large-scale efforts, such as the Christmas appeal. Class agents were appointed for all classes since 1875 to solicit donations to the Christmas Fund, later renamed Annual Giving.[35] The number of participating alumni soon reached 11 to 12 percent, with contributions surpassing $20,000 in 1928–1929.

Perry soon recognized the need to appoint a full-time, paid administrator to take charge of alumni affairs. In November 1929, in anticipation of the Academy's upcoming 150th anniversary celebration, Perry appointed Gertrude E. Starks as alumni secretary. Her major assignment was to produce another alumni directory and keep it updated. Her responsibilities quickly expanded, as did her office, which soon outgrew the original location, a small room in the Davis Library, and was relocated to Jeremiah Smith Hall, where it occupied three rooms and some storage space. By 1932, there was too much work for one person to handle. Eben Wallace, assistant treasurer of the Academy, was appointed business manager of the association and took over the management of the Christmas Fund. Other functions of the office included the addressing and mailing of the *Phillips Exeter Bulletin* and organizing reunions each year. Miss Starks also assisted in the publication of the *Bulletin*, for a time serving as coeditor with Myron R. Williams.

Perry's interest in alumni affairs, of course, extended into his personal life. He maintained close friendships with a number of prominent Exonians who gave generously to the school, including, interestingly, several graduates from the turbulent and troubled era of the late nineteenth century: George A. Plimpton '73, Thomas W. Lamont and Jeremiah Smith, Jr., both of the class of '88, James N. Hill '89, and William Boyce Thompson '90.

Saltonstall also believed that the Alumni Association could do much more for the Academy than provide annual dinners and gifts. It represented a national network that could prove useful for fundraising (especially urgent in view of the deficits of the years 1942–1944) and for the National High School campaign. Accordingly, Saltonstall sought to establish a closer relationship between the Academy and the twenty-seven branch associations existing all over the country. Most of the associations were accustomed to sponsoring a single event each year, a dinner with the principal or visiting faculty member. There were a few exceptions, such as the Southern California Association, which was active in identifying and screening candidates for the scholarship program launched by Hammy Bissell '29, and the New England Association, which established a scholarship fund in 1945. Saltonstall's aim was to expand participation from what was often a single individual to a group of men in each community who could perform many services on the Academy's behalf: answering factual questions about the school, assisting in scholarship and admissions work, meeting with boys after they were accepted, planning alumni functions, providing guidance on legal and financial matters, establishing and maintaining contact with local feeder schools, aiding in public relations (press and radio), and helping to recruit faculty. In short, Saltonstall encouraged the Association to represent the Academy effectively all over the country.[36]

While Bissell was on the road in search of scholarship boys, alumni participation in Academy affairs grew nationwide. Financial contributions, one indication of loyalty to the school, rose from nearly $40,000 (approximately 25 percent participation) in 1945–1946 to nearly $120,000 (47 percent participation) in 1960–1961. The number of members rose as well, prompting the Academy in 1955 to create the Alumni Council, an elective body that would conduct the business of the Association.

Although the alumni had played a central role in fundraising for years, the offices of alumni affairs and development had existed as separate entities from the inception of the Association. Following the advice of management consultants Booz Allen and Hamilton, in the mid-1960s the Academy combined these operations to form the Office of Alumni Affairs and Development, with different branches handling alumni affairs, publications, and annual giving. It was hoped that the professionalization of operations would prepare the school for the upcoming Long Step Forward, its largest fundraising drive to date. (See Chapter 7.)

After the Long Step Forward, the Academy continued to court its graduates — efforts driven in large part by a trustee mandate in 1972 to raise the Annual Fund to cover 10 percent of the Academy's operating budget. In 1974, the Alumni/ae Association made major changes in the format of reunions, that all-important occasion when graduates renewed ties with the Academy. In place of the traditional general reunion at Wentworth-by-the-Sea, the school would hold separate reunions for major classes (fifth year, tenth year, and so on) on the Exeter campus on different weekends in the spring and fall. "This format was unique to Exeter," director of alumni affairs and development James M. Theisen explained. "It enabled alumni/ae to come back to the school while it is in session, sit in on classes, and renew ties with their old teachers. At the same time, it enabled the Academy to build on its connection with the alumni/ae body."[37] The new format proved highly successful: in just one year, the number of donors rose nearly 16 percent and contributions rose nearly $26,000. Although the years that followed found the Academy, like the rest of the country, embroiled in a relentless recession, support of Annual Giving grew steadily — the bright lining in what otherwise was a very dark cloud.[38]

As Exeter welcomed increasing numbers of alumni/ae back into the fold, increasing numbers became actively involved in their alma mater's affairs. The raising of Academy consciousness of the needs of African-American students in the mid-1980s dovetailed with a marked rise in the number of African-American graduates in the Alumni/ae Association. In 1988, they formed the Subcommittee on Excellence through Diversity, and in 1990 it became a standing committee, the Advisory Committee on Diversity — a reaffirmation of the Academy's commitment to Phillips's ideals. Under the auspices of this committee, alumni/ae of color aided in recruiting minority students and faculty and participated in a mentoring program for minority students in their home cities. "This was a real milestone for Exeter," director of alumni/ae affairs Harold Brown, Jr., '74 explained. "It was the first time that an alumni/ae committee had direct access to what was going on on campus."[39] In 1995, the committee was subsumed under the General Alumni/ae Association — the final step in the diversification of the alumni/ae body.

By the early 2000s, the General Alumni/ae Association had become a sophisticated organization run by professional managers. The alumni/ae, who presently number well over 18,000, are active participants in Academy affairs. They elect the General Alumni/ae Association board of directors, three of whom sit on the board of trustees. Standing alumni/ae committees deal with a variety of Academy concerns: student relations, fundraising, communications, and alumni relations. "The Alumni/ae Association," Theisen observed, "plays a critical role in the life of the Academy."[40]

REFLECTIONS AND REMINISCENCES: EXONIANS LOOK BACK

The expanding and successful role of the Alumni/ae Association and the high level of financial support contributed by graduates, of course, directly reflects their overwhelmingly positive feelings about the school. For many graduates, the value of an Exeter education lies not in career success, but in the footing it provides for confronting the vagaries of life in general — "the great end and real business of living." Although every graduate takes a unique, personal view of his or her time at the Academy, one theme in particular recurs often in interviews with graduates and in the pages of reunion yearbooks: by fostering personal growth, Exeter provided education for life. The words of graduates themselves say it best:

"I was a scared boy when I arrived at Exeter," recalled Ned Hallowell '68, "and although I'm not bold enough to say I became a man while there, I left the place armed with knowledge and dreams that I draw upon every hour of every day. The teachers gave me the knowledge and drew out and nourished the dreams, and they sent me off brave enough to be myself."[41] Peter Barton Hutt '52 wrote, "I shall forever be grateful to Exeter for taking a chance on an unprepared and unimpressive young boy and providing an extraordinary foundation that has opened up endless opportunities."[42] Paris R. von Lockette '60 said, "Exeter gives you the latitude to be whatever you want to be."[43]

According to Treadwell "Ted" Ruml II '70, "My four years at the Academy were remarkably stimulating intellectually; and though I seldom seemed able to shine in my classes, the extracurricular reading and thinking that the ambiance of the Academy promoted have proved a resource to me ever since. Exeter was a kind of laboratory for trying out ideas and ways of expressing them, and if the results sounded like 'ineffable twaddle and unmitigated bleat' to some, the exercise was, I think, salubrious to all."[44]

"My two years at Exeter were the jumping-off point for entering into adulthood," Melissa C. Orlov '77 observed. "That time gave me the freedom to think and the ability to articulate thoughts, and those strengths are what I based my career on and what I do outside of work."[45] Broadcaster Mike Lynch had a similar experience. "Exeter gave me what I needed academically, socially, and athletically," he said. "If I hadn't spent that time there, my life would probably receive a grade of 'Incomplete.'"[46]

"At Exeter I clearly determined what was most important to me and what kind of person I wanted to be," said Daniel Pinkert '92. "For that reason, it was the most formative experience in my life."[47]

These views were not limited to the best-performing students, as a dropout from the class of 1957 makes clear:

> Having failed at almost everything I undertook at Exeter (writing, editing, sports, grades), I learned that I would have to work passionately and single-mindedly to fulfill my very high ambitions; I learned that a tenacious commitment to my own values is far more important than adherence to institutional prescriptions or pursuit of grades. My almost total failure at Exeter is largely responsible for the fact that I have since excelled all my classmates in my field.[48]

Many graduates recorded mixed feelings about their time at the Academy that were probably rooted in the difficult transition of adolescence as well as in being away from home and family. Commented Somers Randolph '74, "Exeter provided a tempering of the personal steel. I must have been numb to get through it."[49]

Views such as these naturally concerned leaders of the Academy and the Alumni/ae Association, which mounted a concerted effort to overcome memories of unhappy experiences. "The classes most difficult for us are those of the late 1960s and early 1970s, the period of Vietnam and the King and Kennedy assassinations," Theisen observed. "These alums have a lot of negative feelings about institutions and are reluctant to come back to Exeter. But as they've gotten older, they've started to let go of some of those feelings. People go to reunions and end up closer to the institution as they see it's become a more caring and humane place than it was."[50]

Eager to expand the number of graduates participating in alumni/ae events while remaining sensitive to the different constituencies, in the early 1990s the Office of Alumni Affairs tried to create venues appropriate for each group. "Our goal was to get 25 percent of the alumni/ae to attend an event in the course of a year," Theisen explained, "but not the same people at each event."[51] This effort has proved successful, with increasing numbers of graduates from the 1970s and 1980s taking part in alumni affairs, and a dramatic rise in the number of younger women in leadership positions.

Not surprisingly, alumnae from these years praise the Academy in much the same way as their male peers. Jen Hill '82 recalled, "At Exeter . . . I heard Arthur Miller and Carlos Fuentes discuss writing and literature in the same assembly hall where I saw *Star Trek* and watched my first movies with sub-titles. I made the friends whom I still telephone late at night and see when I travel to strange cities. I 'achieved my potential' and left to attend the kind of university Exeter is supposed to prepare you for, one that I couldn't have imagined going to a few years earlier. . . ."[52]

David Firestone '70 echoes the thoughts of many Exeter graduates, male and female:

> The sheer number of memories I have from my three years at Exeter always amazes me; and how friendships, activities, studies, phases of development were so weighty and important at that time. Also, however tough life at Exeter sometimes was, I am very proud of my Exeter education and Exeter people because of Exeter's high standards—the tremendous respect for intellect and now almost outmoded insistence on integrity which I believe I found there. I have never again been in any situation where these values have been matched.[53]

In sum, Exeter alumni/ae have proved very supportive of the Academy— "way above the norm for independent schools," Theisen noted. "Over 50 per-cent have given financial contributions for many years, and 75 to 80 percent have given at least once."[54] The Alumni/ae Association relies on support from Exonians like the member of the class of '53 who once wrote: "We all owe the school more than we can give back."[55] That gratitude, translated into finan-cial contributions and volunteer work, proved important to Exeter's success in recent decades and will remain so well into the future.

JOHN PHILLIPS AWARD RECIPIENTS

1965	Burke Marshall '40	1985	Robert H. Bates '29
1966	James F. Oates, Jr., '17	1987	Corliss Lamont '20
1967	John C. Dancy '07	1988	Calvin H. Plimpton '35
1968	Lloyd L. Duxbury, Jr., '41	1989	Richard W. Murphy '47
1969	William G. Saltonstall '24	1990	Peter B. Bensinger '54
1970	Francis T. P. Plimpton '17	1991	Hodding Carter III '53
1971	Robert A. Fortuine '52	1992	Joshua L. Miner III '39
1972	John C. Leslie '22	1994	Donald A. Hall, Jr., '47
1973	David C. Sperling '51	1995	James H. Ottaway, Jr., '55
1974	Joseph R. Burchenal '30	1996	Cornelius D. Hastie '48
1975	Charles E. Wyzanski, Jr., '23	1997	Charles C. Krulak '60
1976	Ward B. Chamberlin, Jr., '39	1998	Elkan R. Blout '35
1977	John Cowles, Jr., '47	1999	Arthur M. Schlesinger, Jr., '33
1978	John W. Nason '22	2000	Hugh Calkins '41
1979	John D. Rockefeller IV '54	2001	Patrick J. Lydon, Jr., '68
1980	Edwin H. Mosler '36	2002	John Russell Twiss, Jr., '56
1981	Forrest C. Eggleston '38	2003	Dr. Ira D. Helfand '67
1982	James P. Morton '47	2004	Randolph Barker '48
1983	John K. Fairbank '25	2005	Thayer "Ted" Scudder '48
1984	Alfred L. Atherton, Jr., '40	2006	Dr. Daniel E. Koshland '37

Epilogue

I n 1930, when Edward S. Harkness bestowed the breathtaking sum of $5.8 million upon Exeter for "something that is revolutionary in Secondary School education," he obviously intended to shake things up. He aimed at a pedagogical revolution, and he hit the mark at the Academy. The revolution inspired by the gift, however, extended far beyond the classroom, and it continues to play out more than seventy-five years later.

Inside the classroom, of course, the impact of the Harkness Gift is most evident in both the physical arrangement of instructor and students around the oval table and the exchanges of ideas and questions, with everyone participating and the instructor tending to facilitate rather than dominate the discussion. This method of teaching and learning has proved extremely powerful and is central to the warm memories and gratitude graduates bear toward the Academy. The Harkness Table equipped them to ask important questions, present themselves clearly, and listen respectfully to other points of view. The pedagogy does not so much teach content, though much content is considered and absorbed, as inculcate and reinforce an approach to continuous, lifelong learning and problem solving.

The classroom, of course, could not contain this revolution, which over the decades spilled over into the life of the school in unanticipated and profound ways. When it came time to reconsider the curriculum, or the meaning and role of residential life, or membership in the community (through admissions and faculty recruiting), or the impacts of governance, technology, or growth, or in a host of other institutional factors, Exeter found itself falling back on the method that works so well in the classroom: identify the issue, study it, examine it from different angles and perspectives, consider alternatives and contrasting points of view inside and outside, talk about it, then decide, then act. The method proved perfectly complementary to the eighteenth-century values and aspirations of the Academy, as well as to the New England traditions of town meetings and congregational self-determination, and it obviously continues to work well for the school in the twenty-first century.

At the end of a book like this, it is fair to ask how Exeter might have evolved without the Harkness Gift. Clearly there are many excellent, well endowed independent schools that never subscribed to a single, dominant pedagogy that is embedded in an institutional identity or brand.[1] These schools have also negotiated successfully the same major challenges posed to Exeter—changing requirements of colleges, evolving expectations of parents, the rising cost and complexity of operations, the coming of coeducation, the challenges of increasing diversity, the impact of new information technology, and so on. There seems little doubt that Exeter, which was one of the top independent schools in the country in 1930, could have remained in step with most of its peers and sustained its excellence into the twenty-first century without the wholesale commitment to Harkness teaching.

When the question of what Exeter would be like without the Harkness Gift is posed to Exonians, however, it is greeted with incredulity, as though both unfathomable and unhappy to imagine. "Exeter would still be a great school with a great faculty," says Julie Ann Dunfey '76, a former trustee vice president. "But I wonder whether we would have learned to listen and respect as much, whether we would have done as well as we've done."[2] Veteran history teacher Jack Herney, a former dean of the faculty, goes farther. The Harkness Table "gives us a sense of common purpose that transcends disciplinary boundaries. The faculty is in this all together. Look how the Science Department embraced the method, how central it is to the design of the Phelps Science Center. We're all interested in the same thing—what's on the student's mind is what matters."[3]

"Harkness gives us our fundamental identity," adds Herney. "I suppose Harkness is partly a marketing tool for us," Dunfey admits, "but only in the best possible sense. It's not an empty claim. There really is something powerful there at the heart of our brand."

She continues: "The Harkness method has given us a trusted process that we've used to deal with difficult issues. It works and we know it. We trust it. We don't and can't avoid controversy and we certainly have dissenters, but they also trust the process and feel they've been heard. Problems don't fester or lead to bigger problems."[4] Ricardo A. Mestres, Jr., '51, president of the board of trustees between 1993 and 1999, points out that the full impact of the Harkness Gift took a while to permeate the Academy. "It had a huge effect on teaching, residential life, and the administration before it fully affected governance. It really reached the board of trustees in the 1970s and 1980s, when first we had to respond to the decline of the endowment and then later as we figured out a new approach to managing the operating budget and then ultimately in governing ourselves." Before then, there had been "inner and outer circles" of trustees, with the inners tending to be close confidantes of the principal and taking responsibility for most of the work. "That began to change before I became president but Tucker Anderson '59, who served with me as vice president, and I worked with the board to institutionalize the change. The board operated like a Harkness Table, with everyone involved. The committees of the board functioned in the same way. All members became equal, with equal responsibility and obligation to participate. Anything could be discussed and nothing was undiscussable. Don't get me wrong—we were highly organized, delegated appropriately to the committees, and used our time together efficiently. But the approach was pure Harkness. That's how we met the major challenges facing Exeter when I was on the board and it's how the Academy still operates."[5]

The first decade of the Tingley tenure illustrates the point. The selection of the principal resulted from a Harkness process that included all segments of the community and made a strong favorable impression on the successful candidate. Although he had spent his career in progressive independent schools, "this certainly was different than what I had seen before," Tingley recalls. "It was not unusual to find a school so committed to high standards but it was to find one so committed to reaching high standards in a particular way. And it was not just in teaching. Everyone listened. Everyone expected to be heard. The interactions between the trustees and the administration, and between the administration and the faculty, were qualitatively different— more open, more direct, less political or based on private agendas."[6] At Exeter, notes Herney, "the role of the principal is less critical to making decisions or moving forward than the role of headmaster at many schools. Here leadership is by persuasion. This is a faculty-run institution, a democracy with a small 'd.' Ty understood this right away and, to his great credit, embraced the Harkness Table."[7]

The Harkness Table informed every significant initiative of the Academy under Tingley, most visibly the Academy Master Plan. "The best plans result from thorough analysis and are well considered," Tingley notes. "The Harkness approach guarantees this will happen. It does take a long time here to plan, but the investment is well worth it." As an example, he points out that when he arrived he knew that improving faculty compensation and expanding financial aid would be priorities. There was also discussion of numerous other projects ranging from redesigning the dining halls, to renovating the infirmary, to renovating dormitories, to remodeling the campus. With support and encouragement from the trustees, Tingley and representatives of the administration and faculty drafted a white paper on major initiatives that circulated widely in the community and was distributed to alumni around the country. More than six hundred alumni weighed in with comments at gatherings or submitted via mail, fax, or email. A consensus emerged around reordered priorities. The infirmary renovation morphed into a new project to build a health and wellness center, a change that reflected a new understanding of the role of health and safety on campus. Meanwhile other projects, like the dining hall redesign, were postponed.

Harkness principles informed the ambitious and far-reaching Academy Master Plan to ensure that Exeter retains the finest faculty and students and provides the finest facilities, all to ensure the best possible learning environment. The principal defined the broad objectives of the master plan, then unleashed a Harkness process to develop the specifics and guide decisions about what and what not to do. Once again in Academy history, some Harkness-informed changes proved profound—the Phelps Science Center, the Phelps Academy Center, the renovation of six dormitories to lower the student-faculty ratio—while others are more subtle—the greening of the campus, increased training for dorm faculty, the decision to allow same-sex couples to serve as dorm parents, a financial aid initiative that replaces loans with grants. All these changes are significant, however, because they were first considered and widely discussed before they proceeded.

So, too, the process can result in changes contemplated but not made—a reaffirmation of the basic structure and content of the curriculum in the early 2000s, for example. The curriculum review process included a sustained discussion of a community service requirement that garnered significant support, though it was not ultimately adopted. Nonetheless, Tingley and other Academy leaders observed growing interest in volunteer service. "We've talked a lot about *non sibi*—not for oneself—the notion that our responsibility extends to helping others less fortunate than ourselves—and it has taken root. We had students volunteer for tsunami relief in 2004 and sent many to the Gulf Coast after Hurricane Katrina in 2005. Alumni groups also began organizing trips related to community service. As we talk more about these things, and do them and learn from them, the community becomes more committed to them. The next time we do a curriculum review, don't be surprised if we have a service learning requirement. It would be consistent with the Deed of Gift, which urges us to unite knowledge with goodness. If we do it, it will be after a Harkness-style inquiry."

Harkness principles and process prepared the ground for the Exeter

Initiatives, the major capital campaign that will help the Academy rise to the challenges of sustaining excellence in the twenty-first century. Discussions among the trustees, administration, and faculty, with alumni and potential donors, and with other constituents of the community enabled widespread agreement about the purpose and goals of the campaign. When it was announced formally in 2004, the campaign already had high momentum, with pledges totaling nearly half of the stated goal of $305 million within five years. The campaign proceeded extraordinarily well and exceeded its goal after just three years. This result had an immediate significant impact. In October 2007, the trustees confirmed that the funds raised enable the Academy to address concerns about affordability and offer a free Exeter education to admitted students from families whose annual income is $75,000 or less. This step, combined with generous aid for middle-income families and a needs-blind admissions policy, means that students from 95 percent of families in the United States could be eligible for financial aid.

An expanding endowment will also support faculty recruitment and development. "When I began my career in the 1960s," Tingley points out, "teaching in an independent school was an attractive option for English majors and other liberal arts grads. Today, these young people have many more options, to go into consulting or into knowledge-based companies in industries like software and web services. It's now harder for schools like Exeter to compete."[8] The package Exeter can offer entering teachers — exciting work, outstanding students, extraordinary facilities, a good salary with the prospect of tenure and an endowed position, attractive housing, and other benefits — makes the Academy much more competitive. Its leaders are more confident that the process of replacing the generation of Baby Boomers, who themselves replaced the Harkness generation, will yield a faculty stronger than ever.

Looking out still farther, the Academy remains fully committed to Harkness principles in addressing its long-term opportunities and challenges. "After World War II Bill Saltonstall fixed a goal for Exeter to become a national high school. We've achieved that," says Tingley. "Now we're talking about what it will mean to educate the leaders of the evolving global economy. We already have a significant number of students who come from outside the United States. We may want to grow that percentage. Should we do it, it will be because we follow Harkness principles to decide it is the right course to take."[9]

Tingley's embrace and use of Harkness principles helped to ease his transition into the Academy in the late 1990s and to account for the significant achievements made since then. This attitude helped to reassure and win over the community. "The measure of good leaders is that they leave their institutions in a stronger place than when they found it," says Herney. "Ty will do this, and so will his successors. We'll have a bigger endowment, a better administrative and operational environment, and broader consensus about the direction of the school moving forward." As a result of Harkness principles, "we make good decisions. As long as we adhere to the principles and the process, Exeter will do just fine."[10]

After listening to such views, to the trustees, administrators, teachers, and alumni/ae of the Academy, all of whom sing the same song, one comes to appreciate the incredulity that greeted the question of what Exeter would have become without Harkness. The gift stimulated a new way of teaching and learning. The Harkness Table became the distinctive and indispensable part of the Academy's image and brand. And the gift gave the Academy a way of dealing with tough challenges — the Harkness method became the process by which the institution decides what to do and how to do it. The method is the vehicle for adapting to changing times and circumstances.

What would Phillips Exeter Academy be without the Harkness Table? An excellent school, no doubt, but not as good, not as distinctive, not as cohesive, not the school that it has become nor the school that it will be.

Notes

Items consulted in the archive of Phillips Exeter Academy are referenced by the series in which they are housed. These include trustee records, including minutes of meetings and correspondence; the papers of successive principals (Perry, Saltonstall, Day, etc.); records and papers of administrative offices, such as admissions, alumni/ae affairs, or development; and faculty records, including minutes of meetings and committee reports.

The Bulletin of the Phillips Exeter Academy, a magazine for alumni, first appeared in March 1905 and has been published continuously since then under different names and with varying frequency. Today it is known as *The Exeter Bulletin* and is published four times per year. All references below are simply to *Bulletin*.

NOTES TO AUTHORS' PREFACE (PAGES VII–XI)

1   Tyler C. Tingley, "Message from the Principal," www.exeter.edu (1999–2000).
2   The best account of Exeter's early history is Laurence M. Crosbie, *The Phillips Exeter Academy: A History* (Norwood, Mass.: The Plimpton Press, 1924). For Andover, see Frederick S. Allis, Jr., *Youth from Every Quarter: A Bicentennial History of Phillips Academy, Andover* (Hanover, N.H.: University Press of New England, 1979).
3   Myron R. Williams, *The Story of Phillips Exeter* (Exeter: Phillips Exeter Academy, 1957).

NOTES TO PROLOGUE: SOMETHING REVOLUTIONARY (PAGES 1–7)

1   James W. Wooster, Jr., *Edward Stephen Harkness, 1874–1940* (n.p., privately printed, 1949), pp. 110–111. Harkness's letter to Perry on March 31 is quoted verbatim in this source. Malcolm Aldrich's notes of the conversation are dated April 9. Copy in William Saltonstall Papers, PEA Archive.
2   Perry to the Trustees, October 11, 1929, Saltonstall Papers; cf. Myron R. Williams, *The Story of Phillips Exeter* (Exeter: Phillips Exeter Academy, 1957), p. 115.
3   Wooster, *Harkness*, p. 3.
4   Ibid., p. 77.
5   Richard F. Niebling, "Edward S. Harkness, 1874–1940," *Bulletin* (Fall 1982), pp. 6–8.
6   Williams, *Story of Phillips Exeter*, p. 114
7   William G. Saltonstall, *Lewis Perry of Exeter: A Gentle Memoir* (New York: Atheneum, 1980), pp. 60–61.

8   L. Perry, Letter to E. S. Harkness, October 2, 1929, Saltonstall Papers.

9   Williams, *Story of Phillips Exeter*, p. 115; G. B. Rogers, "A Brief Study of English Public Schools," *Bulletin* (April 1930), pp. 6–21.

10   "The Gift of Mr. Edward S. Harkness to the Academy," *Bulletin* (January 1931), p. 5; George B. Rogers, Three Series of Developments for the Academy, April 7, 1930, pp. 2–3, Saltonstall Papers.

11   Rogers, Three Series of Developments, p. 1.

12   Wooster, *Harkness*, p. 111.

13   Malcom Aldrich, "Memorandum of Conversation April 9th New York: M. A., E.S.H., L. P., and J. S. Jr.," April 9, 1930, Saltonstall Papers.

14   Perry, undated notes, Saltonstall Papers.

15   Perry, undated notes, Saltonstall Papers.

16   The letter is reprinted in Wooster, *Harkness*, pp. 114–115.

17   Perry, Letter to E. S. Harkness, October 30, 1930, pp. 1–6, Saltonstall Papers. It was hoped that the declining costs of labor and materials would make it possible to return some of the gift, and in fact this turned out to be the case. Without reducing salaries, the Academy eventually returned nearly $60,000 to Harkness.

18   Harkness, Letter to L. Perry, November 6, 1930, in Wooster, *Harkness*, pp. 118–119. See also, "Newspaper and Other Comments on Mr. Harkness's Gift to Exeter," *Bulletin* (January 1931), pp. 9–14.

19   Lawrenceville, Andover, Taft, Deerfield, and the Hill School received gifts ranging from one quarter of a million to a million dollars. Although Harkness gave St. Paul's a number of gifts in the course of his lifetime, the largest single gift was $1.5 million. See August Heckscher, *St. Paul's: The Life of a New England School* (New York: Scribner's, 1980), p. 295. Only two schools on this list adopted seminar-style teaching during this period. The English department at Andover created conference rooms and hired five new instructors. Lawrenceville was the only other school besides Exeter to revamp its entire system. Harkness money funded a new administration building, conference rooms, and the hiring of additional teachers. "Mr. Harkness's Gifts to Lawrenceville and Andover," *Bulletin* (July 1936), p. 4.

NOTES TO CHAPTER 1: BEFORE THE HARKNESS GIFT (PAGES 8–33)

1   Quotation from the Deed of Gift, May 17, 1781. This document is reprinted in several locations, most conveniently (and slightly abridged) as appendix A of Myron R. Williams, *The Story of Phillips Exeter* (Exeter: Phillips Exeter Academy, 1957), pp. 187–193.

2   On Wednesdays and Saturdays, classes ended at mid-day.

3   The major sources for this account of the Academy's history before 1930 are (1) Joseph G. Hoyt, "The Phillips Family and the Phillips Exeter Academy," in Hoyt, *Miscellaneous Writings: Addresses, Lectures, and Reviews* (Boston: Crosby and Nichols, 1863), pp. 228–255. This essay originally appeared in the July 1858 issue of *North American Review*. Hoyt came to Exeter as an instructor in 1840 and

the next year became professor of mathematics and natural philosophy. He left in 1859 to become chancellor of Washington University in St. Louis. (2) Charles H. Bell, *Phillips Exeter Academy in New Hampshire: A Historical Sketch* (Exeter: William B. Morrill, 1883). A trustee of the Academy between 1879 and 1893 (and president in the last year), Bell was also governor of New Hampshire from 1881 to 1883. He produced his history of the Academy for its centennial anniversary. (3) Frank H. Cunningham, *Familiar Sketches of the Phillips Exeter Academy* (Boston: James R. Osgood and Co., 1883). Also published for the centennial year, this topical volume was produced by a recent graduate and president of the Christian Fraternity; (4) Laurence M. Crosbie, *The Phillips Exeter Academy: A History* (Norwood, Mass.: The Plimpton Press, 1924). Crosbie taught English at the Academy between 1903 and 1945 and produced the most comprehensive and authoritative history of the Academy through the early 1920s. (5) Williams, *Story of Phillips Exeter*. Another long-time English instructor, Williams taught at the Academy between 1918 and 1957. Williams relied heavily on previous printed sources. Many parts of his book appeared earlier as articles in the Exeter *Bulletin*. Finally, (6), James McLachlan, *American Boarding Schools: A Historical Study* (New York: Charles Scribner's Sons, 1970), esp. chapters VII and VIII. Based on a Columbia University Ph.D. dissertation, this volume provides an excellent overview of the development of independent schools in the United States through the close of the nineteenth century.

4   Charles H. Bell, *History of the Town of Exeter, New Hampshire* (Boston: J. E. Farwell, 1888), p. 90.

5   Edward S. Chase, Jr., "Exeter, New Hampshire, 1638–1887," in Nancy Carnegie Merrill and the History Committee, *Exeter, New Hampshire, 1888–1988* (Exeter: Exeter Historical Society, 1988), p. xxv.

6   Bell, *History of the Town of Exeter*, pp. 285–286.

7   Bernard Bailyn, *Education in the Forming of American Society* (Chapel Hill, North Carolina: University of North Carolina Press, 1960), p. 9; see also, Lawrence A. Cremin, *American Education: The Colonial Experience, 1607–1783* (New York: Harper and Row, 1970), *passim*.

8   Frederick S. Allis, Jr., *Youth from Every Quarter: A Bicentennial History of Phillips Academy, Andover* (Hanover, N.H.: University Press of New England, 1979), p. 40.

9   Theodore R. Sizer, ed., *The Age of the Academies* (New York: Teachers College, Columbia University, 1964), pp. 1–2 and 12–22.

10 For Phillips's life, see Clifford K. Shipton, *Sibley's Harvard Graduates*, vol. IX (Cambridge: Harvard University Press, 1956), pp. 560–570; and Hoyt, "The Phillips Family," pp. 237–240.

11 Williams, *Story of Phillips Exeter*, p. 11.

12 Hoyt, "The Phillips Family," p. 238.

13 Allis, *Youth from Every Quarter*, chapters 3 and 5.

14 Several aspects of Phillips's final years and the disposition of his estate bear further consideration. To begin with, it is universally accepted that he was a faithful steward and shrewd investor. However, if he inherited all or most of Sarah Gilman

Phillips's estate of £75,000 (worth about $300,000 at eighteenth-century exchange rates), his final estate of about $100,000 represents a significant loss of value, even after accounting for all of his known bequests.

Two other interesting sidelights: First, when Phillips died in 1795, he left two-thirds of his estate to the Academy and one-third to Phillips Academy in Andover. He also left $1,000 and a modest annuity to his widow, Elizabeth. She believed these terms unfair, however, and persuaded the trustees of both institutions to improve the terms.

Second, before his death, Phillips freed his last remaining slave, an African named Corydon, who had long served as a handyman. After Elizabeth Phillips's death in 1797, Corydon inherited the Phillips home on Water Street in Exeter. There he lived until his death in 1818 at an age beyond 100, supported from the endowments of both academies.

15 Bell, *Phillips Exeter Academy*, p. 22.

16 Crosbie, *Phillips Exeter Academy*, pp. 49–50.

17 Ibid.

18 Hoyt, "The Phillips Family," p. 244.

19 Ibid., pp. 244–252.

20 Samuel Tenney, "A Topographical Description of Exeter, New Hampshire," in *Collections of the Massachusetts Historical Society for the year MDCCXCV* (Boston: Samuel Hall, 1795), pp. 87–98; Williams, *Story of Phillips Exeter*, p. 28; Hoyt, "The Phillips Family," pp. 241–242 and 245.

21 Cunningham, *Familiar Sketches*, pp. 78–79 and 194; Hoyt, "The Phillips Family," p. 242. For Phillips and the idea of a seminary in the Deed of Gift, see Williams, *Story of Phillips Exeter*, pp. 191–192; for the seminary at Phillips Academy, see Allis, *Youth from Every Quarter*, pp. 119–122.

22 Williams, *Story of Phillips Exeter*, pp. 35 and 38. Exeter students who graduated at other colleges included Bowdoin (73), Yale (25), Brown (18), Amherst (5), Union (3), and Williams, University of Vermont, Wesleyan, and West Point (1 each).

23 Cunningham, *Familiar Sketches*, pp. 299–300.

24 Williams, *Story of Phillips Exeter*, p. 40.

25 Ibid., pp. 46–47.

26 Crosbie, *Phillips Exeter Academy*, p. 99.

27 Trustee Minutes, August 1, 1848.

28 Crosbie, *Phillips Exeter Academy*, p. 98.

29 Crosbie, *Phillips Exeter Academy*, pp. 95–96; Cunningham, *Familiar Sketches*, pp. 116–117.

30 Trustee Minutes, March 24, 1857; Hoyt, "The Phillips Family," p. 253; Bell, *Phillips Exeter Academy*, p. 46.

31 Trustee Minutes, July 13, 1858; Crosbie, *Phillips Exeter Academy*, pp. 96–97.

32 Crosbie, *Phillips Exeter Academy*, p. 98; Williams, *Story of Phillips Exeter*, p. 209.

33 Bell, *Phillips Exeter Academy*, p. 38.

34 Cunningham, *Familiar Sketches*, p. 149. See also, John S. Goff, *Robert Todd Lincoln:*

A Man in His Own Right (Norman: University of Oklahoma Press, 1969), pp. 25–33. For the Academy's widening geographical coverage, see Williams, *Story of Phillips Exeter*, p. 46.

35 Williams, *Story of Phillips Exeter*, pp. 49–50; Crosbie, *Phillips Exeter Academy*, pp. 284–287. For Kingman, see Cunningham, *Familiar Sketches*, pp. 203–211.

36 Cunningham, *Familiar Sketches*, pp. 113, 115.

37 Cunningham, *Familiar Sketches*, p. 116. On the Exeter societies, see ibid., pp. 248–271. In 1883, there were four more societies: the G. L. Soule Society (another literary and debating group); the Boat Club, the Athletic Association, and Pi Kappa Delta, a secret fraternity.

38 Robert L. Wiebe, *The Search for Order, 1877–1920* (New York: Hill and Wang, 1967).

39 McLachlan, *American Boarding Schools*, pp. 192–194. See also Sizer, *The Age of the Academies*, pp. 40–46, and Lawrence A. Cremin, *American Education: The Metropolitian Experience: 1876–1980* (New York: Harper and Row, 1988), pp. 544–547.

40 Donald Fleming, "Eliot's New Broom," in Bernard Bailyn et al., *Glimpses of the Harvard Past* (Cambridge, Mass.: Harvard University Press, 1986), pp. 63–76; McLachlan, *American Boarding Schools*, pp. 189–190; Cremin, *American Education: The Metropolitan Experience*, pp. 555–565.

41 Crosbie, *Phillips Exeter Academy*, pp. 121–122.

42 McLachlan, *American Boarding Schools*, pp. 341–342, n. 14; Crosbie, *Phillips Exeter Academy*, p. 123.

43 McLachlan, *American Boarding Schools*, pp. 228–229; Williams, *Story of Phillips Exeter*, p. 59

44 Bell, *Phillips Exeter Academy*, p. 46. McLachlan put it a slightly different way. see *American Boarding Schools*, p. 229.

45 Crosbie, *Phillips Exeter Academy*, p. 129.

46 For Scott's tenure, see: Crosbie, *Phillips Exeter Academy*, pp. 134–143; Williams, *Story of Phillips Exeter*, pp. 66–69; and McLachlan, *American Boarding Schools*, pp. 224–225.

47 Scott was often seen about town astride a white horse. Crosbie, *Phillips Exeter Academy*, p. 136.

48 Bell, *History of the Town of Exeter*, pp. 240–242; Chase, "Exeter, New Hampshire," p. xxix; McLachlan, *American Boarding Schools*, p. 225.

49 We have not calculated the number of day students living at home, but given the geographical distribution of this class, which included many out-of-staters, it seems clear that well over a hundred students boarded with private families in Exeter.

50 The confusion pertains to whether the first two preceptors (Benjamin Thurston and William Woodbridge) are accounted as principals. Woodbridge usually appears in official lists but Thurston does not. For Fish's administration, see Crosbie, *Phillips Exeter Academy*, pp. 144–154 (with the quotation on p. 145); Williams, *Story of Phillips Exeter*, pp. 70–73; and McLachlan, *American Boarding Schools*, pp. 229–237.

51 Crosbie, *Phillips Exeter Academy*, p. 149.

52 Amen's career is covered in Crosbie, *Phillips Exeter Academy*, pp. 155–186; Williams, *Story of Phillips Exeter*, pp. 1–5 and 74–95; and McLachlan, *American Boarding Schools*, pp. 237–241

53 Quoted in Crosbie, *Phillips Exeter Academy*, p. 160.

54 Ibid., p. 162.

55 By his own estimate, Amen asked four hundred boys to withdraw during his first eight years at Exeter. In one year alone, he dismissed one hundred. "That heroic measure," wrote Crosbie, "inspired confidence among the alumni and parents that the school was at last to be made a safe place for boys." Crosbie went on to marvel that Amen "had the faculty of dismissing a boy and still keeping his friendship." *Phillips Exeter Academy*, p. 165. See also McLachlan, *American Boarding Schools*, p. 238.

56 Crosbie, *Phillips Exeter Academy*, p. 173.

57 McLachlan, *American Boarding Schools*, p. 240; Crosbie, *Phillips Exeter Academy*, pp. 168–174.

58 On Perry's administration, see Crosbie, *Phillips Exeter Academy*, pp. 187–194 (through about 1922); Williams, *Story of Phillips Exeter*, pp. 96–135; and William G. Saltonstall, *Lewis Perry of Exeter: A Gentle Memoir* (New York: Atheneum, 1980).

59 Saltonstall, *Lewis Perry*, pp. 39–46.

60 Perry's schedule is described in Saltonstall, *Lewis Perry*, p. 44; for his faculty associates, see Williams, *Story of Phillips Exeter*, pp. 111 and 166–175.

NOTES TO CHAPTER 2: GOVERNING A FACULTY-RUN SCHOOL (PAGES 34–75)

1 *Phillips Exeter* (Exeter, n.d. [1934?]), p. 9. This pamphlet was produced to describe and promote the school following the Harkness Gift.

2 Henry Phillips Jr., "News of the School," *Bulletin* (1946), p. 9. Among the wartime casualties was Navy seaman Thomas W. Lamont II '42, the trustee president's grandson.

3 Thomas W. Lamont was succeeded as president of the trustees by his son Thomas S. Lamont '16, who had followed his father not only to Exeter but also to Harvard and to J. P. Morgan and Co. The younger Lamont also served eleven years as president of the trustees but did not frequent the school as much as his father. No subsequent trustee president served longer than seven years.

4 In 1905, Amen also hired George W. Hilliard as Exeter's first full-time purchasing agent and superintendent of grounds and buildings. Myron R. Williams, *The Story of Phillips Exeter* (Exeter: Phillips Exeter Academy, 1957), p. 81.

5 Benton and Kerr served well into the Saltonstall administration. Following a brief interim replacement for Ford, who retired in 1932, Ezra Pike Rounds became director of admissions, a position he held for thirty-two years. In 1936, Rogers was succeeded as director of studies by Myron R. Williams, who remained in the office for the next twenty years.

6   Faculty Minutes, September 17, 1928, and September 19, 1939.

7   Paul Sadler, Jr., "Foreword" to "Men and Women of Exeter, 1931–1981," *Bulletin* (April 1981), p. 7.

8   Sadler, "Foreword," p. 7.

9   "Alumni Advisory Committee," *Bulletin* (April 1935), p. 33.

10 Trustee Minutes, May 31, 1940.

11 The elder Plimpton, a Harvard Law graduate and for many years president of the publishing house Ginn and Co., was a generous patron of Exeter, donating the Plimpton Playing Fields, a 400-acre tract in Exeter, and financing the purchase of Phillips Church. Francis Plimpton was a name partner in the prominent Wall Street law firm Debevoise, Stevenson, Plimpton, and Page. He served as a trustee of Exeter from 1935 to 1965, including a term as president between 1956 and 1962. Francis's son George Plimpton '44 was the well-known writer. Yet another prominent Plimpton, Francis's younger brother Calvin, later served as an Exeter trustee between 1965 and 1976, including a term as president, 1973–1975. Trained as a physician, Calvin H. Plimpton also occupied a prominent place in higher education; he was president of Amherst College from 1960 to 1971. "Calvin H. Plimpton '35," *Bulletin* (October 1970), p. 26, reprinted from *The Hampshire Gazette*, Northampton, Mass., 1970.

12 Lucien Price, "Perry of Exeter," *Atlantic Monthly* (June 1946), pp. 69–74. The quotation is on p. 70.

13 William G. Saltonstall, *Lewis Perry of Exeter: A Gentle Memoir* (New York: Atheneum, 1980), p. xix.

14 Dudley W. Orr interview, February 10, 1993: "There wasn't too much thrashing around looking for other candidates. . . . [The trustees] sort of relaxed and said, 'well, good old Bill. That would be fine.' That's how Bill became [principal]."

15 Henry F. "Ted" Bedford interview, February 28, 1994.

16 "The Graduate," *Harvard Alumni Bulletin*, April 5, 1952.

17 Corning Benton, "Increase in Tuition," *Bulletin* (Autumn 1945), pp. 7–8.

18 Trustee Minutes, June 1 and November 7, 1945.

19 Cresap, McCormick, and Paget, Survey of Phillips Exeter Academy, Exeter New Hampshire, August 1950, Section I, Reports to Trustees.

20 Ibid., Section III, p. 7.

21 James W. Griswold interview, July 22, 1991.

22 Phillips E. Wilson, "Exeter Program for Adult Education," *Bulletin* (Winter 1948), pp. 7–8.

23 Members of the Task Group included Rev. A. Graham Baldwin, Phillips Academy, Andover; Dean Wilbur J. Bender of Harvard; Henry Chauncey, president of the Educational Testing Service; Charles W. Cole, president of Amherst College; Harold B. Gross '26, president of the Exeter Alumni Association; Millicent C. McIntosh, president of Barnard College; Henry A. Murray, professor of clinical psychology at Harvard; Lester W. Nelson, principal of Scarsdale High School in New York; Leo Perlis, an officer of the Congress of Industrial Organizations (CIO);

William M. Stucky '35, executive editor of the Lexington (Kentucky) *Herald-Leader*;
Charles E. Wyzanski, Jr., '23, a federal judge and Exeter trustee; and Edward Yeo-
mans, director of the Shady Hill School in Cambridge, Massachusetts. The sessions
were chaired by Saltonstall. See Paul E. Everett, "The Exeter Study," *Bulletin* (February 1952), pp. 5–7.

24 Members of the faculty committee included Robert H. Bates (English); Richard
F. Brinckerhoff (Science); Robert M. Galt (Latin); Robert W. Kesler (German);
Arthur A. Landers (Music); Ransom Van B. Lynch (Mathematics); Theodore R.
Seabrooke, Jr. (Physical Education); Phillips E. Wilson (History); and Paul E. Ever-
ett (French), chair.

25 *Report to the Principal by the Exeter Study Committee* [hereafter *The Exeter Study*
(1953) (Exeter: Phillips Exeter Academy, 1953).

26 *The Exeter Study* (1953), p. 79.

27 *The Exeter Study* (1953), p. 91.

28 Henry F. Bedford interview, February 28, 1994.

29 Donald C. Dunbar interview, August 16, 1991.

30 The group included not only Mayo-Smith but also Jack Heath, Richard Brinckerhoff, Richard Niebling, Frank Broderick, William J. Schwartz, and Dr. James Heyl,
the school physician, among others.

31 Report to the Faculty on the Work of the Research Planning Committee, March 21,
1961, Faculty Committee Records.

32 R. Mayo-Smith, Letter to W. G. Saltonstall, January 3, 1961; id., A Proposal to
Encourage the Development of Ideas [n.p., n.d.], Saltonstall Papers.

33 W. G. Saltonstall, Letter to R. Mayo-Smith, February 8, 1961, Saltonstall Papers.

34 "Gillespie Gets New Assistant-to-Principal Post; Cole, Galt to Head History, Latin
Departments; Next Summer Session Co-ed; Irving to be New Head," *The Exonian*,
April 19, 1961, pp. 1–2. The talks were subsequently published by the staff of *The
Exonian* in *Exeter-Andover Tradition*, the official program of Exeter Alumni Day
in June 1961.

35 For the trustees' comments on Exeter in the late 1950s and early 1960s, see Thomas
S. Lamont's papers, especially in folders labeled "Exeter-9 Memoranda and Reports
on Educational Problems at Exeter," and "Exeter-26 Trustee Matters." Both folders
are included among the Lamont papers in PEA Archive.

36 Orr, Letter to Saltonstall, April 9, 1962, Lamont Papers.

37 William J. Cox, "News of Exeter," *Bulletin* (Spring 1963), pp. 1–2.

38 The committee consisted of F. William Andres '25, a Boston lawyer; J. Warren Olmsted '34, a Boston banker, and Dr. Rustin McIntosh '10, a New York physician.

39 Richard F. Niebling interview, July 24, 1991.

40 Richard Ward Day, *A New England Schoolmaster: The Life of Henry Franklin Cutler*
(Bristol, Connecticut: Hildreth Press, 1950).

41 William J. Cox, "News of Exeter," *Bulletin* (Summer 1963), pp. 3–5.

42 Report to the Principal and Trustees of the Phillips Exeter Academy from the
Academy Planning Committee, February 1965, p. 2, Faculty Committee Reports.

43 Dunbar interview, August 16, 1991.

44 "The Long Step Forward," *Bulletin* (August 1966), pp. 4–8.

45 Booz Allen and Hamilton, Organization and Administration of the Phillips Exeter Academy, Exeter, New Hampshire, October 28, 1965, pp. 8–9, Reports to Trustees.

46 Booz, Allen and Hamilton, Organization and Administration, p. 9–17.

47 Ibid., pp. 61 and 76.

48 During 1969–1970, Robert F. Brownell, Jr., served as acting dean of students.

49 Herrick H. Macomber interview, October 2, 1991.

50 Dunbar interview, August 16, 1991.

51 The change was embodied in Resolutions of Trustees Governing Faculty Retirement, May 21, 1965.

52 Booz, Allen and Hamilton, Organization and Administration, pp. 35–58.

53 James A. Newman interview, December 10, 1992; Orr interview, February 10, 1993. Orr also disagreed with the goals of the Long Step Forward and was angered by Day's decision to dismiss contractors already selected (Orr, Letter to J. W. Olmsted, September 29, 1965). In a letter about Day's decision to fire the original contractors for the library, Orr quoted the charter, "The principal instructor may not sit in the determining matters wherein he is particularly interested." (Orr, Letter to R. W. Day, September 28, 1964), Day Papers.

54 William M. Andres interview, September 17, 1991.

55 Robert N. Shapiro, "Every Relationship is an Opportunity to Teach," in *Transitions: Exeter Remembered, 1961–1987* (Exeter: Phillips Exeter Academy, 1990), pp. 39–45.

56 The Student Council recommendations to Day in 1964 are printed in *Bulletin* (Summer 1964), pp. 3–4.

57 Evan Douthit '72, "The Dunbar Shuffle," *The Exonian*, January 20, 1971, p. 2.

58 William A. Hunter IV interview, March 9, 1997; Edward S. Gleason interview, February 10, 1997.

59 Calvin H. Plimpton interview, October 31, 1992; Newman interview, December 10, 1992; James H. Ottaway, Jr., interview, August 30, 1991.

60 E. Arthur Gilcreast, First Meeting of the Agenda Committee: Summary of Proceedings, February 18, 1973, Day Papers.

61 Trustee Minutes, May 19, 1973.

62 Dunbar interview, August 16, 1991. For an appreciative portrait of Day, see a brief memoir by Edward S. Gleason, the Academy minister during much of Day's tenure, *Bulletin* (Spring 2003), p. 88.

63 "Search for 11th Principal Continues," *Exeter Today* (January 1974), p. 1.

64 "Stephen G. Kurtz, Hamilton Dean, Elected Exeter's New Principal," *Exeter Today* (April 1974), p. 1; Stephen G. Kurtz interview, August 7, 1991.

65 Charles M. Swift interview, July 24, 1991.

66 Ottaway interview, August 30, 1991.

67 Plimpton interview, October 31, 1992; Newman interview, December 10, 1992.

68 The inner circle often met for long discussions after hours at the Exeter Inn when the trustees were on campus. See Chauncey Loomis interview, August 17, 1991.

69 "Academy Administration Reorganized: Cole and Thomas named to Top Dean's Positions," *Exeter Today* (April 1975), p. 1. Later, other historians joined the top group, including Stephen C. Smith as dean of the faculty and Ted Bedford as vice principal.

70 "An Interview with Stephen G. Kurtz, the Eleventh Principal," *Bulletin* (October 1974), p. 6.

71 Kurtz, "Reflections in My Senior Year," *Bulletin* (February 1978), pp. 7–9; Kurtz interview, August 7, 1991.

72 Kurtz, Memo to the Trustees of Phillips Exeter Academy, November 7, 1975, pp. 2 and 6, Kurtz Papers.

73 Kurtz interview, August 7, 1991.

74 David E. Thomas interview, February 28, 1994; Lynda Beck interview, March 2, 1995; Kurtz interview, August 7, 1991.

75 André J. Vernet, Report of the Ad Hoc Committee on Discipline (2), April 24, 1978, pp. 9–10, appendix D, Faculty Committee Records.

76 Faculty Minutes, March 12, 1988, p. 4.

77 Richard L. Tucker, Memo on Endowment Issues and Actions, prepared for the review of the Faculty Agenda Committee on December 6, 1979, p. 3.

78 Report of the Committee on Institutional Priorities, September 1979, especially pp. 1–2 and 5–6. The committee included Lynda K. Beck, William E. Campbell, Donald B. Cole, E. Arthur Gilcreast, Colin F. N. Irving, and Kurtz, Faculty Committee Records.

79 Frederick R. Mayer interview, February 20, 1992.

80 Report of the Ad Hoc Committee on Dormitory Staffing, April 11, 1980, pp. 3–4, 7–8, Faculty Committee Recrds.

81 The committee included trustees John R. Chase, Robert D. Storey, and Richard L. Tucker and faculty members Lynda K. Beck and C. Robert Clements.

82 Report of the Ad Hoc Committee on Faculty Salaries and Benefits ("The Storey Committee") to the Trustees, November 11, 1982, esp. pp. 4–8; S. G. Kurtz, Policy for Faculty Occupancy of Academy-Owned On-Campus Housing without Students, May 17, 1983, Kurtz Papers.

83 Kurtz interview, August 7, 1991; Theodore Sizer interview, December 5, 1996.

84 Kurtz interview, August 7, 1991; Mayer interview, February 20, 1992.

85 Chauncey C. Loomis, "The Search Process," *Bulletin* (Winter 1987), p. 5; id., Memo to authors, December 14, 1997.

86 "Kendra Stearns O'Donnell Appointed Principal," *Bulletin* (Winter 1987), pp. 4–5.

87 Donald J. Briselden interview, January 29, 1997.

88 Kendra S. O'Donnell, Looking to 2000: A Management Plan for the Nineties (October 1992); Kendra S. O'Donnell interview, February 10, 1993.

89 Kendra S. O'Donnell interview, September 1991; "Stepping Back," [an interview with Kendra Stearns O'Donnell], *Bulletin* (Summer 1997), p. 7.

90 The summary document is: M. Diamonti and E. Hallowell, The Exeter Study: A Report on Student Life at Exeter, undated and unpublished [1993?].

91　O'Donnell interviews, August 8, 1991, and September 1991.

92　O'Donnell, "Boarding Schools: Educating the Whole Child," in Pearl Rock Kane, ed., *Independent Schools, Independent Thinkers* (San Francisco: Jossey-Bass, 1991), pp. 42–56.

93　O'Donnell interviews, February 10, 1993, and May 23, 1995.

94　O'Donnell interview, February 10, 1993; John R. Chase interview, August 11, 1993; Robert N. Shapiro conversation with authors, October 30, 1997.

95　O'Donnell interviews, February 10, 1993, and May 23, 1995.

96　O'Donnell interview, May 23, 1995; Shapiro conversation with authors, October 30, 1997.

97　Katherine K. Towler, "Facing the Future Together," *Bulletin* (Fall 1994), p. 8; O'Donnell interview, May 23, 1995; Ricardo A. Mestres, Jr., interview, May 5, 1994; Shapiro comment to authors, October 30, 1997.

98　Tyler C. Tingley interview, December 5, 1997.

99　Ibid.

100　"A Matter of Principals," *Bulletin* (Spring 2005), p. 92.

101　Tingley interview, December 5, 1997.

102　Tingley interview, July 17, 2003.

103　Tyler C. Tingley, An Academic and Academy Life Master Plan Process (Draft), presented to the faculty, January 14, 1998, copy in Faculty Minutes, May 13, 1998.

104　Master Planning Steering Committee, Memorandum to the Faculty, March 11, 1999, Revised Working Draft.

105　Michael Van Valkenburgh Associates, Inc., Phillips Exeter Academy: Design Principles for Renewal of the Phillips Exeter Academy Landscape, November 15, 2000.

NOTES TO CHAPTER 3: ENLARGING THE MINDS
(PAGES 76–110)

1　In September 2002, Rex McGuinn, a popular teacher widely admired for his passion and skills, died suddenly and prematurely at age fifty-one.

2　Donald B. Cole and Robert H. Cornell, eds., *Respecting the Pupil*, 3rd ed. (Exeter: Phillips Exeter Academy, 1987), pp. 3–4.

3　Lawrence M. Crosbie, *The Phillips Exeter Academy: A History* (Norwood, Mass.: The Plimpton Press, 1924), pp. 178–179.

4　Myron R. Williams, "Small Classes and Large," *Phillips Exeter Academy Bulletin* [hereafter cited as *Bulletin*] (April 1949), p. 6.

5　Frank W. Cushwa and C. E. Atwood, "Editorial Notes," *Bulletin* (January 1932), p. 5.

6　Charles M. Swift interview, July 24, 1991.

7　Richard F. Niebling interview, July 24, 1991.

8　Myron R. Williams, "The Curriculum and the War," *Bulletin* (Spring 1945), p. 2.

9　Niebling interview, July 24, 1991.

10　Report of the Harkness Committee, The Phillips Exeter Academy, undated, Saltonstall Papers.

11 Frank W. Cushwa and Myron R. Williams, "What Exeter Now Offers," *Bulletin* (March 1933), p. 8.

12 Henry S. Couse, Letter to Lewis Perry, November 10, 1931, Perry Papers.

13 Arthur M. Schlesinger, Jr., "Exeter, 1931–1933: In the Eye of the Hurricane," in *Exeter Remembered* (Exeter: Phillips Exeter Academy, 1965), p. 106.

14 Frank W. Cushwa and Myron R. Williams, "Development of the Harkness Plan," *Bulletin* (January 1934), p. 6.

15 Richard F. Niebling, "Edward S. Harkness, 1874–1940," *Bulletin* (Fall 1982), p. 9; Chauncey C. Loomis interview, August 17, 1991.

16 Alan H. Vrooman interview, August 6, 1991.

17 Niebling interview, July 24, 1991.

18 Jackson B. Adkins interview, July 2, 1991.

19 Niebling, "Edward S. Harkness, 1874–1940," p. 8; A New Curriculum at Exeter, Faculty Committee, June 1985, p. 17.

20 Herrick M. Macomber interview, October 2, 1991.

21 For the origins and impact of this study, see chapter 4.

22 Mayo-Smith later became headmaster at Roxbury Latin School in Boston.

23 John Mayher, "The Teaching of History at Exeter," *Bulletin* (April 1960), p. 4.

24 N. Chung Otterson interview, February 1, 1996; Margaret McGuinn, "Finding a Voice," *Bulletin* (Spring 1993), p. 9.

25 Loomis interview, August 17, 1991.

26 Ibid.

27 Phyllis Edgerly Ring, "At Exeter, Students Aren't the Only Ones Who Learn," *Bulletin* (Summer 1994), pp. 6–9.

28 Vrooman interview, August 6, 1991.

29 Charles M. Swift interview, July 24, 1991.

30 Stephen C. Smith interview, March 1, 1998.

31 John B. Heath, "The Harkness System," *Bulletin* (October/November 1983), pp. 56–58.

32 As the 1953 *Exeter Study* put it, "Before the Harkness Plan we accepted change reluctantly, driven to it by circumstance. But now the Harkness Gift has made it possible for us more than most schools to accept the ideal of change as a desirable principle rather than an expensive hardship. With it has come the responsibility to examine continually new ways and means to adapt our purposes to a continually changing world." *Report to the Principal by the Exeter Study Committee* (Exeter: Phillips Exeter Academy, 1953) [hereafter *The Exeter Study* (1953)].

33 Theodore R. Sizer, "The Academies: An Interpretation," in Sizer, *The Age of the Academies* (New York: Teachers College, Columbia University, 1964), pp. 9–10.

34 Donald Ogden Stewart, "Genesis to Exodus," in *Exeter Remembered*, p. 11.

35 Smith interview, March 1, 1998.

36 John C. Hogg, "Science at Exeter," *Bulletin* (July 1958), pp. 15–22.

37 Committee on Aims and Practices, Remarks Relating to a New Curriculum, 1936. Perry Papers.

38 Frederick S. Allis, Jr., *Youth from Every Quarter: A Bicentennial History of Phillips Academy, Andover* (Hanover, N.H.: University Press of New England, 1979), pp. 460–462.

39 Hogg, "Science at Exeter," p. 20.

40 Vrooman interview, August 6, 1991.

41 Myron R. Williams, Chairman's Summary of Progress, Committee on Aims and Practices, February 11, 1941, p. 2, Perry Papers.

42 Myron R. Williams, "The Anticipatory Program," *Bulletin* (February 1943), pp. 4–5.

43 Myron R. Williams, "The Curriculum and the War," *Bulletin* (Spring 1945), pp. 2–5.

44 Nicole M. J. David, "Welcome to the Company of Educated Men and Women: Curriculum Reform at Harvard College, 1942–1982," Harvard undergraduate thesis, March 1989, p. 69.

45 George Willis et al., eds., *The American Curriculum: A Documentary History* (Westport, Conn.: Greenwood Press, 1993), p. 286.

46 Mayher, "The Teaching of History at Exeter," p. 8.

47 Richard M. Freeland, *Academia's Golden Age: Universities in Massachusetts 1945–1970* (New York: Oxford University Press, 1992), pp. 77–80; Morton Keller and Phyllis Keller, *Making Harvard Modern: The Rise of America's University* (New York: Oxford University Press, 2001), pp. 42–46.

48 Philip E. Hulburd, "Mathematics," *Bulletin* (December 1955), pp. 47–48.

49 The Red Book recommended that Latin be taught in the seventh and eighth grades: *General Education in a Free Society* (Cambridge, Mass.: Harvard University Press, 1945), p. 126.

50 William G. Saltonstall, Memorandum to the Trustees, December 11, 1946.

51 Myron R. Williams, "Revision of the Curriculum," *Bulletin* (January 1947), p. 6.

52 John Cowles, Jr., "An Open Letter to the Trustees," *The Exonian*, January 18, 1947, pp. 1, 4.

53 Robin M. Galt, "Latin," *Bulletin* (December 1963), p. 2. Some believe that the enrollments remained strong in part because admissions director Pike Rounds encouraged newly admitted boys to take Latin.

54 Philip E. Hulburd, "The Mathematics Program — An Evolutionary Change," *Bulletin* (February 1959), pp. 2–4.

55 John C. Hogg, "Science," The Report of the Principal to the Trustees and Ten-Year Reports of the Department Chairman, *Bulletin* (December 1955), p. 61.

56 Henry Phillips, Jr., "News of the School," *Bulletin* (April 1949), p. 9.

57 Henry W. Bragdon, "The Advanced Placement Program 1954–1959," *Bulletin* (July 1959), pp. 2–5; *General Education in School and College: A Common Report by Members of the Faculties of Andover, Exeter, Lawrenceville, Harvard, Yale, and Princeton* (Cambridge, Mass.: Harvard University Press, 1952), *passim*; Allis, *Youth from Every Quarter*, pp. 552–553.

58 Glen A. Krause, "The Art Department," *Bulletin* (Spring 1963), pp. 7–8.

59   *The Exeter Study* (1953), pp. 29–43, 55–62.

60   John C. Hogg, "Science in the Curriculum," *Bulletin* (July 1958), p. 8.

61   William R. Jones, "The Modern Language Program," *Bulletin* (Autumn 1962), p. 7. Two years later, the departments of Latin and Greek merged to create the Department of Classical Languages.

62   The review also increased the course load for 3- and 4-year seniors and created the program of Supplementary Study to enrich advanced, senior-level courses. W. J. Cox, "News of the School: The Curriculum," *Bulletin* (Winter 1962), pp. 7–8.

63   Niebling, "Edward S. Harkness, 1874–1940," p. 8.

64   Donald C. Cole interview, July 22, 1991.

65   Stephen C. Smith interview, May 10, 1996.

66   Richard F. Niebling, "Independent Study Program," *Bulletin* (October 1969), pp. 34–35. For discussion of the curricular approaches to diversity, see chapter 6.

67   *Catalogue Issue of the Phillips Exeter Bulletin* (Exeter: Phillips Exeter Academy, 1969), p. 47.

68   Report of the Long-Range Planning Committee to the Trustees of the Phillips Exeter Academy, Faculty Minutes, May 1970, pp. 20–22.

69   Henry F. Bedford, "Is Content Where the Action Is?" Remarks to the Faculty, September 12, 1970, Day Papers.

70   Christopher M. Brookfield, Report of the Curriculum Committee, September 15, 1972, p. 1, Day Papers.

71   Faculty of Arts and Sciences, *Report on the Core Curriculum* (Harvard University, 1978); Daniel Tanner and Laurel N. Tanner, *Curriculum Development: Theory into Practice*, 2nd ed. (New York: Macmillan, 1980), p. 510.

72   E. Arthur Gilcreast, "A New Curriculum at Exeter, Question Mark," *Bulletin* (Winter 1985), p. 5

73   Ibid., p. 4.

74   E. Arthur Gilcreast interview, May 21, 1996.

75   Gilcreast, "A New Curriculum at Exeter," p. 5.

76   Ibid., p. 3.

77   Gilcreast interview, May 21, 1996.

78   Gilcreast, "A New Curriculum at Exeter," pp. 6–11.

79   Ibid., p. 7.

80   Ibid., pp. 11–13.

81   Gilcreast interview, May 21, 1996.

82   Some of these forecasts and their obvious limitations are discussed in John Seely Brown and Paul Duguid, *The Social Life of Information* (Boston: Harvard Business School Press, 2000), chapter 8.

83   Tyler C. Tingley interview, December 5, 1997.

84   Phillips Exeter Academy, Voice and Computing Handbook, 1999–2000, pp. 6–8.

85   Susan Keeble, Background Information, Academic Technology Use, March 2000.

86   Tingley interview, December 5, 1997.

87   Susan Keeble interview, March 30, 2000.

88 Ibid.

89 Katherine K. Towler, "Science Teaching Harkness Style," *Bulletin* (Fall 1997), p. 12–15; see also chapter 3 above.

90 Scott Saltman interview, March 23, 2000.

91 Quoted from www.exeter.edu/scibuilding_new/mission.html.

92 Quoted from www.exeter.edu/scibuilding_new/sciprogram.html.

93 www.exeter.edu/scibuilding_new/view6.html.

94 Katherine K. Towler, "Architecture 101," *Bulletin* (Spring 1998).

95 Phillips Exeter Academy, "The Architecture of Teaching Science," video, June 17, 1999.

96 Towler, "Architecture 101."

97 John J. Hughes III, "Phelps Science Center Under Way," *Exonian*, October 8, 1999, pp. 1 and 4.

98 "METIC: Mid-Term *Effort* to Improve Classes," Faculty Minutes, September 17, 1997, pp. 1–2.

99 This account draws heavily on Susannah Clark, "Teaching and Learning at Exeter: The Next Curriculum," *Bulletin* (Winter 2003), pp. 17–21 and 29.

100 Tyler C. Tingley interview, July 24, 2006.

101 John D. Herney interview, May 8, 2006.

102 Quotations in this and the following paragraphs are drawn from Chauncey C. Loomis '48, "The Harkness Table Revisited," *Bulletin* (Spring 1995), pp. 11–13.

NOTES TO CHAPTER 4: FORMING THE MORALS (PAGES 111–148)

1   All quotations from the Deed of Gift have been drawn from appendix A in Myron R. Williams, *The Story of Phillips Exeter*, (Exeter: Phillips Exeter Academy, 1957), pp. 187–193.

2   Laurence M. Crosbie, *The Phillips Exeter Academy: A History* (Norwood, Mass.: The Plimpton Press, 1924), pp. 49–50.

3   Rev. George W. Barber, quoted in "The Fiftieth Anniversary of the Christian Fraternity," *Bulletin* (September 1906), p. 15.

4   Arthur G. Leacock, "The Christian Fraternity," *Bulletin* (March 1905), p. 19.

5   Arthur G. Leacock, "The Christian Fraternity Semi-Centennial," *Bulletin* (December 1905), pp. 17–19.

6   Frederick J. Libby, "Morals and Religion at Exeter," *Life at Phillips Exeter* (Exeter: Phillips Exeter Academy, October 1913), p. 21.

7   *Catalogue of the Phillips Exeter Academy 1937–1938*, p. 72.

8   Crosbie, *Phillips Exeter Academy*, pp. 203–251.

9   E-Books of 1904/5–1918/19.

10 E-Book of 1911–1912, p. 9.

11 Crosbie, *Phillips Exeter Academy*, pp. 324–338.

12 Libby, "Morals and Religion," p. 19. At this time, as subsequently, the term *in loco parentis* was used at the Academy in a casual sense rather than in its strict legal sense, which connotes responsibility in place of parents. Exeter has pointedly

refused to make such a claim: parents sign permission slips and otherwise have the final say on matters concerning their children. This chapter, like the rest of the book, uses the term in its casual sense only.

13   George B. Rogers, Letter to Parents, 1905, quoted in Myron R. Williams, *The Story of Phillips Exeter Academy* (Exeter: Phillips Exeter Academy, 1957), p. 90.

14   S. Perry Chadwick, Letter to L. Perry, December 3, 1918, pp. 1–2, Perry Papers.

15   Ibid., p. 2.

16   Lucien Price, "Perry of Exeter," *Atlantic Monthly* (June 1946), p. 72.

17   Corliss Lamont interview, April 24, 1992.

18   George B. Rogers, Letter to L. Perry, April 6, 1918. Perry Papers.

19   W. Ernest Gillespie, Letter to Parents, October 7, 1963, Day Papers.

20   Faculty Minutes, April 22, 1987, p. 4.

21   E-Book for 1927–1928, pp. 20–22.

22   C. Lamont interview, April 24, 1992.

23   Myron R. Williams, "News of the School," *Bulletin* (January 1935), p. 17.

24   George E. Bennett, "Dormitories for Young Boys, *Bulletin* (April 1935), pp. 17–18.

25   "The Harkness Gift to Phillips Exeter Academy," *Bulletin* (April 1932), p. 9.

26   "The Gift of Mr. Edward S. Harkness to the Academy," *Bulletin* (January 1931), p. 8.

27   Herrick M. Macomber interview, October 2, 1991.

28   Henry F. Bedford, Jr., interview, February 28, 1994.

29   Rosemary Coffin interview, August 14, 1991.

30   George Plimpton, "How Failing at Exeter Made a Success of George Plimpton," *Bulletin* (Spring 2002), pp. 15–19 and 82; Ransom V. Lynch interview, June 3, 1997.

31   *Catalogue of the Phillips Exeter Academy 1937–1938*, p. 71.

32   "The Wise and the Foolish," *Bulletin* (January 1934), p. 8.

33   Nathan C. Shiverick, "'Each on his own anvil,'" in *Exeter Remembered* (Exeter: Phillips Exeter Academy, 1965), p. 105.

34   Lynch interview, June 2, 1997.

35   Perry, Letter to G. Marshall, November 27, 1944; G. Marshall, Letter to L. Perry, December 7, 1944; Perry, Letter to Marshall, October 20, 1945; Marshall, Letter to Perry, October 25, 1945, Perry Papers.

36   T. B. Thomas, "Labor Enters the Curriculum," *Bulletin* (April 1943), pp. 7–9.

37   See Diane Ravitch, *The Troubled Crusade: American Education 1945–1980* (New York: Basic Books, 1983), pp. 81–113.

38   William T. Loomis interview, March 6, 1997.

39   William G. Saltonstall, "Letter to Parents," September 8, 1949, reprinted in *Bulletin* (October 1949), p. 2.

40   William G. Saltonstall, The Faculty Advisor at Exeter, September 1949, pp. 2–3, Saltonstall Papers.

41   Donald B. Cole interview, February 12, 1997.

42   W. T. Loomis interview, March 6, 1997.

43   E. M. Swift, "Sports in a School Curriculum," Pearl Rock Kane, ed., *Independent*

Schools, Independent Thinkers (San Francisco: Jossey-Bass Publishers, 1992), pp. 179–189.

44 *Report to the Principal by the Exeter Study Committee* (Exeter: Phillips Exeter Academy, 1953), p. 14.

45 William G. Saltonstall, "Conviction," *Bulletin* (July 1950), p. 4.

46 William G. Saltonstall, Report of the Principal to the Trustees 1953–1954 (1954), p. 8.

47 George E. Beilby, Jr., "Religion — and the School Community," *Bulletin* (July 1955), p. 6.

48 "An Experiment," *The Exonian*, April 14, 1956, p. 2.

49 Warren T. Vaughan, Jr., Report to the Faculty Concerning Activities of the Psychiatric Program, October 15, 1951, p. 1, Saltonstall Papers.

50 Robin M. Galt, Senior Counseling, April 1956, pp. 1–2.

51 Dr. James Heyl interview, June 4, 1997.

52 Richmond Mayo-Smith, Jr., Counselling Committee Report 1959–1961, September 4, 1961, p. 1, Faculty Committee Records.

53 R. Mayo-Smith, Jr., Report to the Principal of the Research Planning Committee, December 1960, pp. 1–2, 23–26.

54 The Latin is translated, "Come here, boys, so that you may become men."

55 W. T. Loomis interview, March 6, 1997.

56 Robert N. Cunningham, "The Dean's Office," *Bulletin* (December 1955), pp. 7–8.

57 "Dean Cunningham Resigns; Kesler Named as Successor," *The Exonian*, April 11, 1956, p. 1; Donald C. Dunbar interview, June 2, 1997.

58 Loomis interview, March 6, 1997.

59 Edward S. Gleason interview, February 10, 1997.

60 John Phillips Committee Interim Report, November 1962.

61 Donald B. Cole interview, July 22, 1991.

62 William R. Jones and David E. Thomas, Memorandum to the Faculty, November 3, 1964, pp. 5–6.

63 C. Arthur Compton, Letter to W. E. Gillespie, October 22, 1963, Day Papers.

64 Ibid. Setting a goal "of creating greater responsibility for a student in the governing of himself, the following year the Student Council had its most successful year to date, establishing a church cut system, and a Student Judicial Committee that would take part in the disciplinary system. J. G. Miller, Memorandum to R. W. Day, June 1, 1965[?], pp. 1–2, Day Papers.

65 "SC Judiciary Committee to Continue; Group Will Advise in Student Cases," *The Exonian*, October 9, 1969.

66 Report to the Principal and Trustees of the Phillips Exeter Academy from the Academy Planning Committee, February 1965, p. 3.

67 Ibid., pp. 8–10, 16.

68 Colin F. N. Irving, Memorandum to R. W. Day, February 22, 1965, Day Papers.

69 Robert H. Thompson interviews, January 13 and June 3, 1997.

70 Warren Grad and Lee Barton, Student Council Religion Committee Report, December 14, 1961, Saltonstall Papers.

71 Report of the Student Council Religion Committee, May 1966, Day Papers.

72 Henry F. Bedford, Jr., Memorandum to R. W. Day, June 9, 1966, Day Papers.

73 See Frederick S. Allis, Jr. *Youth from Every Quarter: A Bicentennial History of Phillips Academy, Andover* (Hanover, N.H.: University Press of New England, 1979), pp. 648–654.

74 Gleason interview, February 10, 1997.

75 David E. Thomas, Report of the Religion Committee to the Principal and Trustees, May 1968, p. 3.

76 Trustee Minutes, May 31, 1968, p. 1.

77 Faculty Minutes, June 4, 1969, p. 1. After the decision was made to admit girls, officials changed the planned size of the Assembly Hall to accommodate 1,200.

78 Report of the Religion Committee, February 1969, pp. 1–2, Faculty Committee Records; *Catalogue of the Phillips Exeter Academy 1968–1969*, pp. 66–67.

79 Gleason interview, February 10, 1997.

80 Daniel W. P. Morrissey interview, January 18, 1996; Charles H. Toll, Jr., Letter to R. W. Day, December 22, 1969.

81 Kathleen J. Birney, Robin J. Kemper, Laura A. B. Nelson, and Douglas G. Rogers, *Book of Meditations: Readings from Phillips Exeter Academy 1983–1994* (Exeter: Phillips Exeter Academy, 1995), p. vi.

82 Report of the Ad Hoc Committee on Student Health Services to the Trustees, May 1976, p. 10.

83 Approximately 90 percent of the student body responded. Results of Questionnaire on Drug Use, June 1968, p. 2, Day Papers.

84 Faculty Minutes, March 4, 1969, p. 2.

85 Gleason interview, February 10, 1997.

86 William R. Jones, Report of the Sub-Committee on Student-Faculty Communication, November 26, 1968, pp. 1–6, Day Papers.

87 Ibid., pp. 5–7.

88 *The Pean of 1970*, p. 141.

89 Exeter Tomorrow: Report of the Long-Range Planning Committee to the Trustees of Phillips Exeter Academy, May 1970, p. 8.

90 C. Arthur Compton, *The Hoffman Proposal*, May 1971.

91 Dr. James Heyl interview, August 1, 1991.

92 James Heyl, On a Drug Education Program, in the Faculty Minutes, January 22, 1973, pp. 3–4.

93 Donald C. Dunbar interview, June 2, 1997.

94 Heyl, Memorandum to R. W. Day, January 20, 1971.

95 Allis, *Youth from Every Quarter*, p. 657.

96 Leslie Ann Pederson, Interim Report of the Special Committee on Shared Responsibility, Spring 1972, p. 1, Faculty Committee Records.

97 Ransom V. Lynch, Memorandum to R. W. Day, April 16, 1971, Day Papers.

98 Thomas C. Hayden, A Social Center at Exeter, February 1971, Day Papers.

99 Susan Jorgensen [Herney], Memorandum to Day, Kesler, Bedford, Irving, Dunbar, and Holbrook, September 26, 1972, Day Papers.

100 Susan Herney interview, March 23, 1995.

101 W. Ernest Gillespie, Commencement Speech, June 11, 1967.

102 See, for example, *The Pean of 1973*, p. 89.

103 James H. Ottaway, "A Former Trustee Remembers Steve and Jeanne Kurtz," *Bulletin* (Spring 1987), p. 6.

104 Ibid., p. 4.

105 Stephen G. Kurtz, Address to the Assembly, September 29, 1995.

106 Ibid.

107 John B. Heath, Student Life Committee 1976 Report to the Principal, August 25, 1976, p. 1.

108 "Moral Education," *Newsweek* (March 1, 1976), p. 74.

109 P. J. Culver, Report of the Ad Hoc Committee on Health Services to the Trustees of the Phillips Exeter Academy, May 16, 1976; Heath, Student Life Committee Report, pp. 2–5.

110 Joseph E. Fellows and Jill Nooney, Counseling at Exeter, Spring 1980, p. 1, Kurtz Papers.

111 Ibid., pp. 2–3.

112 New England Association of Schools and Colleges, Inc., *The Evaluation Report for Phillips Exeter Academy* (Exeter: Phillips Exeter Academy, 1976), p. 1.

113 Theodore R. Sizer, "Moral Education: Provocations for an Institute," in Charles L. Terry, ed., *Knowledge Without Goodness Is Dangerous: Moral Education in Boarding Schools* (Exeter: Phillips Exeter Academy, 1981), p. 5.

114 Stephen G. Kurtz, "The Bicentennial: One Man's View," *Bulletin* (July 1979), p. 5. For a thoughtful discussion of the subject, see Harvard V. Knowles and David R. Weber, "The Residential School as a Moral Environment," *Bulletin* (November 1978), pp. 15–18, reprinted in Terry, *Knowledge Without Goodness*, pp. 79–87.

115 Kurtz, Memorandum to Richard Hoffman, May 11, 1976, Kurtz Papers; Kurtz, Memorandum to the Ad Hoc Committee on the Academy Discipline System, January 12, 1977, Kurtz Papers; Faculty Minutes, November 7, 1980. For a detailed discussion of the events leading to this reform, see chapter 7.

116 Faculty Minutes, January 19, 1982.

117 Faculty Minutes, March 12, 1988, p. 4.

118 Susan Herney interview, March 23, 1995.

119 New England Association of Schools and Colleges, Inc., *The Evaluation Report for Phillips Exeter Academy* (Exeter: Phillips Exeter Academy, 1986), p. 5.

120 Kathleen J. Brownback interview, February 11, 1997.

121 Ethan S. Shapiro interview, February 18, 1997.

122 David McIlhiney, Report to the Faculty from the Ad Hoc Committee on Counseling, September 20, 1983, p. 2, Faculty Committee Records.

123 Ibid.

124   John W. G. Tuthill, Annual Report to the Principal, Student Health Services, July 1984, pp. 1–2, Kurtz Papers.

125   Susan J. Herney, "Educating the Whole Student: A Dean's View," *Bulletin* (Winter 1991), pp. 11–12.

126   Susan Herney interview, March 23, 1995.

127   Anja S. Greer, Draft of the Report of the Ad Hoc Committee on Academic Counseling and Support Services, July 17, 1986, pp. 2, 9, Kurtz Papers.

128   Anja S. Greer, Scott Balcomb, Memorandum to Stephen G. Kurtz, December 15, 1983, pp. 1–2.

129   E. Arthur Gilcreast, "A New Curriculum at Exeter, Question Mark," *Bulletin* (Winter 1985), p. 5.

130   New England Association of Schools and Colleges, Inc., *The Evaluation Report for Phillips Exeter Academy* (Exeter: Phillips Exeter Academy, 1986), p. 5.

131   Kendra S. O'Donnell, "Boarding Schools: Educating the Whole Child," in Pearl Rock Kane, ed., *Independent Schools, Independent Thinkers* (San Francisco: Jossey-Bass, 1991), p. 56.

132   "From Dress Code to Dorm Life, the Other Curriculum Project Is Examining the Issues," *Bulletin* (Spring 1990), p. 21.

133   Report of the Ad Hoc Committee on Discipline, Faculty Minutes, May 23, 1990, pp. 1–3.

134   Faculty Minutes, May 15, 1991, pp. 2–3. In 1996, the Dean's Office put an associate dean in charge of discipline.

135   O'Donnell, Letter to the Faculty, Summer 1990.

136   *Academy Mission Statement*, 1991.

137   Michael Diamonti and Edward Hallowell, The Exeter Study: A Report on Student Life at Exeter, undated and unpublished [1993?].

138   Gregory M. Burdwood, "Helping Students Cope with Increased Pressures," *Bulletin* (Winter 1991), pp. 13–14.

139   Faculty Minutes, February 5, 1992, pp. 2–3.

140   Admissions Statement, Faculty Minutes, October 14, 1992.

141   Kendra O'Donnell interview, August 7, 1991.

142   Faculty Concerns Expressed in Group Meetings with Residential Life Committee Members, October 1993–November 1993, pp. 2–5.

143   Residential Life Statement, Faculty Minutes, Addenda, 1, May 18, 1994.

144   Faculty Minutes, October 6, 1993.

145   "New Dean of Students on Campus," *Parents Newsletter*, October 1996, p. 2.

146   Faculty Minutes, June 3, 1995, p. 5.

147   Faculty Minutes, September 20, 1995, p. 3.

148   Alessandra Phillips, "Hazing Addressed in All-School Meeting," *The Exonian*, April 29, 1989, p. 1.

149   Kendra O'Donnell interview, February 10, 1993.

150   Rev. Thompson interviews, January 13 and June 3, 1997.

151   Faculty Minutes, April 9, 1997, p. 1.

152 Ethan Shapiro interview, March 5, 1998.

153 Katherine K. Towler, "Learning Goodness: Knowledge and Goodness at Exeter Today," *Bulletin*, Special Edition, 2004, pp. 36–44. Quotation on p. 40.

154 Quoted in Laura Chisholm, "Harkness Outside the Classroom: The Elizabeth and Stanford N. Phelps '52 Academy Center," *Bulletin* (Fall 2006), p. 42.

NOTES TO CHAPTER 5: THE COMPOSITION OF
THE COMMUNITY (PAGES 149–181)

1 John Price Jones, Report on the Scholarship Situation, May 1938, p. 6, Perry Papers.

2 Lewis Perry, "From the Principal," *Bulletin* (March 1933), p. 3.

3 Hamilton H. Bissell, The Work of the Admissions Office, [1946?], p. 4, Saltonstall Papers.

4 Report on Charges to Students, Phillips Exeter Academy Treasurer's Office, October 1932, p. 1.

5 Jones, Report on the Scholarship Situation, pp. 7–9.

6 Ibid., pp. 11–12.

7 Corning Benton, Report to the Board of Trustees, 1940, p. 1. The same held true of Andover, St. Paul's, and Lawrenceville. Report of the Foundation Grant Committee to the Trustees, June 1938, p. 19.

8 Brochure on Regional Grants, January 1940.

9 Perry, Letter to Parents, September 1941, pp. 1–4, Perry Papers.

10 Joseph T. Walker, Jr., Letter to L. Perry, June 16, 1943, p. 1, Perry Papers.

11 By 1943–1944, the number of scholarship boys had dropped to 114 (15 percent of the student body), a decline from 154 (approximately 21 percent) two years earlier and the lowest number since the introduction of grants in 1933–1934. Statistics and Proposals Submitted for Study to the Special Committee on the Awarding of Scholarships and Foundation Grants, April 30, 1944, p. 2, Faculty Committee Records.

12 Hamilton H. Bissell, Catalogue Supplement on Scholarships at Exeter, 1960–1961.

13 Hamilton H. Bissell, Statement on Scholarships at Exeter, 1946; Report of the Special Committee on the Awarding of Scholarships and Foundation Grants, February 1945, p. 34, Faculty Committee Records.

14 Quoted by Myron R. Williams, "Editor's Column," *Bulletin* (Summer 1946), p. 4.

15 Katherine K. Towler, "Spreading the News," *Bulletin* (Summer 1995), p. 8.

16 Hamilton H. Bissell, Report to the Trustees, June 1, 1946, pp. 1–2.

17 C. K. Jefferson, "Radio Interview with Mr. Bissell," *Bulletin* (May 1953), p. 10.

18 In 1960, 60 of the 171 boys attending Exeter on scholarship were newspaper boys from 20 different papers throughout the country (Towler, "Spreading the News," p. 10). The Academy still uses the program today, though it is limited to one newspaper, the *Charleston Post and Courier*.

19 Hamilton H. Bissell, Letter to J. P. Jones, October 10, 1947, Saltonstall Papers.

20 Robert Storey interview, July 26, 1991; William I. Witkin, Address to the Assembly, June 1995.

21 *Exeter Daily Bulletin*, September 19, 1961.

22 William G. Saltonstall, *Lewis Perry of Exeter: A Gentle Memoir* (New York: Atheneum, 1980), pp. 77–78.

23 William G. Saltonstall, Letter to Thomas S. Lamont, July 2, 1946, Saltonstall Papers.

24 Id., "Academy Policies in Regard to (I) Admission and (II) Distribution of Boys in Dormitories," June 4, 1949, p. 1, Saltonstall Papers.

25 P. Richards Mahoney interview, October 19, 1995.

26 Statement by Charles M. Rice, director of admissions and scholarships, May 15, 1967, Day Papers. Exeter student records begin in 1851, but many believe that blacks were enrolled in the school as early as 1790.

27 Donald C. Dunbar, "Special Urban Program Means *SPUR*," *Bulletin* (August 1966), pp. 12–15.

28 Mahoney interview, October 19, 1995.

29 In the early 1970s, federal support began drying up and ABC was forced to confine its activities to identifying talented minority kids; it was then up to the individual schools to provide the financial aid. ABC continues to be an important source of minority students for the Academy today.

30 Robert F. Brownell, Comments on the Role of Intellect in Selection of Candidates for the Phillips Exeter Academy and the Relationship This Has Had on the National Role of Exeter, March 21, 1968.

31 Richard W. Day, Report to the Trustees of Phillips Exeter Academy, June 1966.

32 Statistics provided by the Dean of Students Office.

33 Joe Smith, quoted in "The Struggle to Retain 'Blackness' at Exeter," *The Exonian Supplement*, May 22, 1968.

34 Theophus Smith, "Smith's Chapel Speech: 'I Am a Black First,'" *The Exonian*, May 22, 1968, p. 7.

35 James A. Snead, Letter to R. W. Day, October 18, 1971, pp. 2–3, Day Papers.

36 Theophus Smith, "Versions of Exeter in Rilke's Verse," in *Transitions: Exeter Remembered 1961–1987* (Exeter: Phillips Exeter Academy, 1990), p. 57.

37 James A. Snead, "The Afro-Set Five," in *Transitions*, p. 69.

38 James A. Snead, Address to the Assembly, February 1, 1985.

39 R. M. Galt, Memorandum to R. W. Day and R. W. Kesler, April 18, 1968, Day Papers.

40 Harold H. Brown, Jr., interview, October 17, 1995.

41 Dolores T. Kendrick interview, June 16, 1993.

42 Snead, Letter to Day, op. cit.

43 George E. Beilby, Jr., "Religion — and the School Community," *Bulletin* (July 1955), p. 7. After describing the various types of service available to students, Beilby concludes: "An opportunity is thus available to all boys to make their acquaintance

with the three great traditions of Western religion: Judaism, Catholicism, and Protestantism" — a statement of diversity in the mid-1950s. (At this time, the number of Asian students on campus was negligible.)

44 H. U. Ribalow, "A Jewish Boy at Exeter," *The Chicago Jewish Forum* 26 (Winter 1967–1968), pp. 111–112.

45 Lincoln Caplan interview, October 25, 1995.

46 Ibid.

47 Judd Levingston, "Shabbat," *Transitions*, pp. 169–172.

48 Daniel J. M. Morrissey interview, January 18, 1996.

49 John D. Herney, Report to the Faculty, Phillips Exeter Academy, October 18, 1983, p. 4.

50 John D. Herney, Composition of the School Report of the Admissions Committee, October 1983.

51 Robert H. Thompson interview, October 17, 1995.

52 John D. Herney interview, October 19, 1995.

53 Mahoney interview, October 19, 1995.

54 Kendra Stearns O'Donnell, "On Becoming a More Diverse Institution," *Bulletin* (Spring 1991), p. 13.

55 Kendrick interview, June 16, 1993.

56 Subcommittee of Excellence through Diversity, Mission Statement, August 1988.

57 Minutes of the Directors' Meeting of the General Alumni/ae Association, September 22, 1990.

58 Multicultural Assessment Plan Visiting Team Report for Phillips Exeter Academy, National Association of Independent Schools, May 21–24, 1989, p. 7.

59 Ibid., pp. 5–22.

60 Nadine Abraham-Thompson interview, October 17, 1995.

61 Kelly Dermody, "My Closet at Lamont," in *Transitions*, pp. 171–173

62 Christine Robinson interview, November 3, 1995.

63 Susan J. Herney interview, December 10, 1995.

64 E-Book for 1992–1993, p. 45.++

65 E. Howard, "KKK Activity Shocks Exeter Community," *The Exonian*, October 7, 1989, pp. 1, 9; id., "Town of Exeter Declares Opposition to KKK," *The Exonian*, October 14, 1989, p. 1; L. Johnston, "KKK Rally Makes History," *The Exonian*, December 2, 1989, p. 7; Allesandra Phillips and Liz Witham, "KKK Activity Causes Alarm," *The Exonian*, October 6, 1990, pp. 1, 6.

66 Kerry Landreth, "Martin Luther King Day To Be Recognized," *The Exonian*, December 9, 1989, p. 1.

67 Abraham-Thompson interview, October 17, 1995.

68 Randolph Carter interview, January 30, 1996.

69 Faculty Minutes, November 5, 1997, p. 1.

70 Harold Brown interview, January 8, 1998.

71 Faculty Minutes, November 5, 1997, p. 1.

NOTES TO CHAPTER 6: COEDUCATION: THE QUIET
REVOLUTION (PAGES 182–206)

1   Kendra Stearns O'Donnell, "20 Years of Coeducation," *Bulletin* (Fall 1990), p. 16.

2   *Report to the Principal by the Exeter Study Committee* (Exeter: Phillips Exeter Academy, 1953), p. 106.

3   Donald B. Cole and Susan W. Cole interview, August 28, 1995.

4   Colin F. N. Irving interview, July 29, 1991.

5   Trustee Subcommittee on Faculty Matters, The Size and Composition of Exeter Over the Next Quarter Century, September 8, 1961, pp. 3, 7, Saltonstall Papers.

6   Irving, Memorandum to William G. Saltonstall, July 6, 1961, Saltonstall Papers.

7   Minutes of the Initial Meeting of the Summer School Committee, September 14, 1961, Saltonstall Papers.

8   Irving interview, July 29, 1991.

9   The Committee on Possible Coeducation at Exeter, Report to the Trustees, October 23, 1962.

10 The Academy Planning Committee, Report to the Principal and Trustees, Phillips Exeter Academy, February 1965, pp. 25–27, Day Papers.

11 For discussion of the Long Step Forward, see chapter 7.

12 Irving interview, July 29, 1991.

13 Bruce K. Eckland, "Student, Faculty, and Alumni Opinion: Some Findings from the 1967–1968 Alumni Research Study," *Bulletin* (May 1969), pp. 20–24.

14 Colin F. N. Irving, Report to the Trustees, August 1968.

15 Janet Lever and Pepper Schwartz, *Women at Yale: Liberating a College Campus* (Indianapolis: Bobbs-Merrill, Inc., 1971), pp. 28–42.

16 Report of the Coordinate School Philosophy Committee, January 1969, Day Papers.

17 Trustee Minutes, May 29, 1969.

18 Trustee Minutes, February 28, 1969; S. P. Castle, "The Decision," *Bulletin* (Fall 1990), p. 19.

19 The boarding girls who were admitted at this time were in grades 10 through 12. By a trustee vote in November 1975, ninth-grade boarding girls were admitted in September 1977.

20 Trustee Minutes, January 13, 1970, p. 3.

21 Irving, Report to the Trustees on Financial Aspects of a Coordinate Girls' School, August 9, 1968.

22 Boston Women's Focus Group, December 2, 1992.

23 The diploma that year read: "In Recognition of His Having Completed Well and Faithfully the Required Course of Study. In Testimony Whereof We Have Fixed Our Signatures And the Seal of the Academy This Fifth Day of June 1971." Soon after Commencement, the school issued another set of certificates, with the pronouns emended, to its female graduates (R. Armstrong, Memorandum to Barry, June 10, 1971).

24 Ellen A. Fowler interview, September 29, 1995.

25 Ibid.

26 Kathy N. Nekton interview, August 31, 1995.

27 Thirty percent of the boys who graduated in the first three coeducational classes matriculated to Harvard, Yale, Princeton, or Brown, whereas approximately 34 percent of the girls went on to these universities.

28 Richard W. Day, "Report of the Principal to the Trustees for the Year 1970–1971," reprinted in the *Bulletin* (May 1972), p. 6.

29 J. Hall, in "Women at Exeter: Looking Backward, Looking Forward," Panel Discussion, Phillips Exeter Academy, May 15, 1981.

30 S. Kimberly Welch interview, September 29, 1995.

31 Hall, "Women at Exeter."

32 Joyce Maynard, "An 18-Year Old Looks Back on Life," *New York Times Magazine*, April 23, 1972, p. 84.

33 Joan Barrett Wickersham, in "Women at Exeter."

34 Peter C. Greer interview, August 24, 1995.

35 Jacquelyn H. Thomas interview, July 31, 1995.

36 Carol France interview, September 29, 1995.

37 Janet Kehl interview, September 29, 1995.

38 France interview, September 29, 1995.

39 Susan J. Herney interview, August 15, 1995.

40 Barbara Eggers, interviews of Susan Wilson and Helen Stuckey, July 31, 1987; Connie Brown, *In a Man's World: Faculty Wives and Daughters at Phillips Exeter Academy 1781–1981* (Lincoln, Nebr.: Universe, Inc., 2003), passim; Katherine K. Towler, "Women at Exeter Before Coeducation," *Bulletin* (Winter 1996), pp. 7–10.

41 Jane Scarborough, in "What Did You Choose to Do with Your Life or What Did It Choose to Do with You?" Coeducation Celebration, September 30, 1995.

42 Jacquelyn H. Thomas, in "What Did You Choose to Do with Your Life?"

43 Anja S. Greer interview, August 24, 1995.

44 Thomas interview, July 31, 1995.

45 Ibid.

46 Irving's recommendations included: a Trustee statement of the intent to operate as an Equal Opportunity Employer; a "thorough study of the status of women at the Academy *conducted by female employees*, recruiting of new women and promotion and retraining of existing women employees; and a significant increase in the number of women in policy-making positions.

47 Steven G. Kurtz, Address to the Assembly in Honor of the Twenty-fifth Anniversary Celebration of Coeducation, September 29, 1995.

48 Lynda Beck interview, March 2, 1995.

49 Dunfey continued to provide financial support of the CESW until its disbanding in 1992.

50 Steven G. Kurtz interview, August 7, 1991.

51 John D. Herney, Composition of the School Report, Autumn 1983, pp. 5–6, Kurtz Papers.

52 The Newmarket/Exeter Child Care Center had serviced the town since the mid-1970s. See Nancy Carnegie Merrill and the History Committee, *Exeter, New Hampshire, 1888–1988* (Exeter: Exeter Historical Society, 1988), p. 395.

53 Kurtz interview, August 7, 1991.

54 Donald Cole interview, August 28, 1995.

55 James A. Bullock, "The Wonder Years," Panel, Coeducation Celebration, September 30, 1995, videotape 58 in PEA Archive.

56 "Women at Exeter: Looking Backward, Looking Forward," Panel Discussion, May 15, 1981.

57 Quoted by Kurtz in his Address to the Assembly, September 29, 1995.

NOTES TO CHAPTER 7: STRENGTHENING THE FOUNDATION (PAGES 207–231)

1   Laurence M. Crosbie, *Phillips Exeter Academy: A History* (Norwood, Mass.: The Plimpton Press, 1924), pp. 95–96.

2   William J. Cox, "The Spirit of the Christmas Fund," *Bulletin* (February 1949), p. 4.

3   Corning Benton, Report of the Treasurer to the Trustees, Phillips Exeter Academy for the Year Ending August 31, 1923; id. Report of the Treasurer to the Trustees, Phillips Exeter Academy for the Year Ending August 31, 1924, 1926, 1927, and 1928.

4   Benton, Report of the Treasurer to the Trustees, Phillips Exeter Academy for the Year Ending August 31, 1929, p. 24.

5   Frank W. Cushwa and Myron R. Williams, "Mid-Summer Letter to the Alumni," *Bulletin* (August 1934), p. 1.

6   Richard F. Niebling, "Edward S. Harkness, 1874–1940," *Bulletin* (Fall 1982), p. 9.

7   Corning Benton, Report of the Treasurer for the Year Ended August 31, 1932, p. 10.

8   Benton, Report of the Treasurer for the Year Ended August 31, 1933, p. 11.

9   Lewis Perry, *Bulletin* (March 1933), p. 3.

10 Cushwa and Williams, "Mid-Summer Letter to the Alumni," p. 2.

11 Benton, Report on Charges to Students, Phillips Exeter Academy Treasurer's Office, October 1932, p. 1.

12 Benton, Report on Charges to Students, pp. 1–46; see chapter 6.

13 Benton, Report of the Treasurer for 1933–1934, p. 11.

14 Ibid., p. 10. Benton later acknowledged that funds Harkness had designated for teachers' fellowship were not used for that purpose until after World War II. See Niebling, "Edward S. Harkness," p. 8.

15 Benton, Letter to M. P. Aldrich, June 11, 1935, p. 1.

16 Benton, Letter to D. Leighton, December 12, 1935, p. 6.

17 Benton, Report of the Treasurer for 1935–1936, p. 6.

18 Benton, "Social Security Plans for the Academy," *Bulletin* (January 1938), p. 17.

19 Benton, Report of the Treasurer for the Year Ended August 31, 1939, p. 16.

20 Myron R. Williams, "Editorials," *Bulletin* (October 1938), p. 6.

21 Benton, Report of the Treasurer for 1938–1939, p. 17.

22 "Phillips Exeter," *Bulletin* (March 1939), pp. 45, 47.

23 Cresap, McCormick and Paget, "Survey of Phillips Exeter Academy," August 1950, p. II-3, Saltonstall Papers.

24 Williams, "Editorials," *Bulletin* (April 1941), p. 3.

25 Benton, Report of the Treasurer for 1941–1942, p. 18; Cresap, McCormick and Paget, p. II-6.

26 Williams, "Editor's Column," *Bulletin* (Summer 1948), p. 2.

27 Williams, "News of the School," *Bulletin* (April 1941), p. 19.

28 Williams, "Editor's Column," *Bulletin* (Summer 1948), p. 1

29 Williams, "Editor's Column," *Bulletin* (Autumn 1945), pp. 1–2.

30 Williams, "Editor's Column," *Bulletin* (Summer 1948), p. 1.

31 Myron R. Williams, *The Story of Phillips Exeter Academy* (Exeter: Phillips Exeter Academy, 1957), pp. 109–110.

32 Corning Benton, These Are the Figures, March 1947, p. 12.

33 Benton, Letter to the Trustees, November 12, 1948.

34 Williams, "Editor's Column," *Bulletin* (Winter 1948), p. 1.

35 Williams, "Editor's Column," *Bulletin* (Winter 1947), p. 1; id., "The Phillips Exeter Campaign for Five Million Dollars Opened on April 3," *Bulletin* (Spring 1947), p. 3.

36 Williams, "Editor's Column," *Bulletin* (Summer 1948), p. 1.

37 Cresap, McCormick and Paget, pp. I-10, II-6, 7.

38 Williams, "Editor's Column," *Bulletin* (February 1950), p. 2.

39 Cresap, McCormick and Paget, pp. II-19–20.

40 See, for example, *Report to the Principal by the Exeter Study Committee* (Exeter: Phillips Exeter Academy, 1953), pp. 139–140.

41 James G. Griswold, Tuition Increase? Points for Consideration, November 1952, p. 2; "Report on the Finances of the Academy," *Bulletin* (December 1953), p. 16.

42 Ibid., p. 4.

43 Ibid., p. 6.

44 *Report to the Principal by the Exeter Study Committee*, pp. 139–140.

45 Trustees Minutes, March 6, 1953, p. 7.

46 Williams, *Story of Phillips Exeter*, p. 149; Griswold, The Report of the Treasurer for the Year 1953–54, p. 1.

47 W. G. Saltonstall, "The Report of the Principal to the Trustees, November 11, 1955," reprinted in *Bulletin* (December 1955), p. 6.

48 William J. Cox, "Editor's Column," *Bulletin* (November 1957), p. 4.

49 Paul Sadler, Jr., "Campaign Solicitation Ends as Tabulation Continues," *Bulletin* (February 1971), p. 9.

50 The increase in tuition and enrollments generated a 35 percent increase in tuition revenues, well below the rate of inflation (James W. Griswold, "Excerpts from the Treasurer's Report, 1960–61," *Bulletin* (February 1962), p. 8; id., Report of the Treasurer to the Trustees, October 1, 1962, p. 2).

51 James G. Griswold, Report of the Treasurer to the Trustees, October 2, 1961, p. 1.

52 William J. Cox, "News of the School," *Bulletin* (January 1958), p. 9.

53 William J. Cox, "News of Exeter," *Bulletin* (Summer 1962), p. 15.

54 Frederick S. Allis, Jr., *Youth from Every Quarter: A Bicentennial History of Phillips Academy, Andover* (Hanover, N.H.: University Press of New England, 1979), pp. 583–587.

55 Hugh Calkins interview, September 24, 1991.

56 Other APC proposals included a need-blind admissions policy, expansion of the scholarship program, and a tuition reduction to make Exeter accessible to families of modest income. Curiously enough, there was no mention of how the school would pay for it all. C. Arthur Compton, An Interim Report to the Trustees and Faculty of a Program for Phillips Exeter Academy, January 1965, p. 31.

57 Paul Sadler, Jr., "The Long Step Forward," *Bulletin* (August 1966), pp. 5–6.

58 Booz Allen and Hamilton, Report on the Phillips Exeter Academy, August 1965.

59 Paul Sadler, Jr., "What the Alumni Want to Know Now: The Answers to Some Basic Questions," *Bulletin* (Winter 1968), p. 8.

60 "The Long Step Forward: A Report of Progress and Promise," unpaginated addendum to *Bulletin* (April 1967).

61 Colin F. N. Irving, A Report on Resources Development, December 29, 1970, p. 2.

62 Irving, Report to the Trustees, October 1, 1968, p. 1.

63 Ibid.

64 Sadler, "What the Alumni Want to Know Now," p. 6.

65 The Exeter Parents Fund had its origins in Christmas Fund lists in the 1930s; it was then formalized in a Committee of Parents formed in 1963 to conduct the Christmas Fund appeal to parents of present and former students. Cox, "The 41st Annual Christmas Fund," *Bulletin* (Winter 1963), p. 11.

66 Minutes of the Trustee Buildings and Grounds Committee, February 11, 1969.

67 Marts and Lundy, The Long Step Forward: Phase II, August 1969, Records of the Long Step Forward.

68 Colin F. N. Irving, Report of the Treasurer for 1969–1970, October 1, 1970, p. 1.

69 Paul Sadler, Jr., "Campaign Solicitation Ends as Tabulation Continues," *Bulletin* (February 1971), p. 11.

70 Colin F. N. Irving, Report of the Treasurer for the Year 1971–1972, October 1, 1972, p. 1.

71 Thanks to rapidly rising inflation and a rapidly declining economy, Annual Giving would not generate 10 percent of budget until 1977. Richard L. Tucker, "Exeter's Endowment — Issues and Actions," *Letters from Exeter* (Exeter, N.H.: Phillips Exeter Academy, December 1979), p. 5.

72 Richard J. Ramsden, The Financing of Exeter, September 21, 1984.

73 Board of Trustees, Investment Committee Meeting, June 13, 1978; Ramsden, Summary of Investment Meeting, June 13, 1978, pp. 1–11. In the late 1960s, Stanford, Harvard, and a number of other private universities had concluded that endowment income used for operating purposes should not exceed 5 percent of market value. This policy was based on the assumption that total return (income plus

appreciation) would cover operating expenses and inflation. Ramsden and Irving, The Financing of Exeter, September 21, 1984, p. 3, n. 1; Ramsden interview, July 28, 1992.

74   Investment Committee meeting, June 13, 1978.

75   Ramsden and Irving, The Financing of Exeter, September 21, 1984, Exhibit VI.

76   Irving, Report of the Treasurer to the Trustees for the year ending June 30, 1981, p. 1.

77   Ramsden and Irving, The Financing of Exeter, p. 14.

78   Kurtz, Report of the Principal to the Trustees for the School Year 1977–1978, September 1978, p. 1.

79   James Ottaway interview, August 30, 1991.

80   Richard J. Ramsden interview, July 28, 1992.

81   Irving, "Two Decades of Energy Problems," *Letters from Exeter*, February 1981, p. 4.

82   Stephen G. Kurtz, "Message from the Principal," *Bulletin* (September/October 1980), p. 50.

83   Ottaway interview, October 30, 1991.

84   James M. Theisen, "The Exeter Annual Giving Fund," *Bulletin* (June/July 1980), p. 3.

85   Colin F. N. Irving, Report of the Treasurer to the Trustees, June 1982, p. 1.

86   Stephen G. Kurtz, "Message from the Principal," *Bulletin* (Fall 1983), p. 74.

87   John Chase interview, September 16, 1991.

88   The formula excluded "life income funds and any funds where income must by deed of gift be added back to principal for a period of time." Ramsden, Draft of Memorandum to the Trustees, January 3, 1992.

89   Ramsden and Irving, The Financing of Exeter, pp. 1–15.

90   Robert N. Shapiro interview, November 26, 1997.

91   Shapiro interview, October 30, 1997.

92   Ramsden, Draft of Memorandum to the Trustees, January 3, 1992, pp. 1–3.

93   Endowment Spending Policy, n.d.

94   New Hampshire Higher Educational and Health Facilities Authority, *Official Statement Relating to $10,000,000 New Hampshire Higher Educational and Health Facilities Authority Revenue Bonds, Phillips Exeter Academy Issue, Series 1991*, pp. 1, A-21.

95   Ricardo A. Mestres interview, May 5, 1994.

96   Ramsden, Draft of Memorandum to the Trustees, p. 1.

97   New Hampshire Higher Educational and Health Facilities Authority, *Official Statement*, p. A-20.

98   Donald Briselden interview, January 29, 1997.

99   Katherine K. Towler, "Fund Raising," *Bulletin* (Summer 1997), p. 14

100 David W. Johnson, "A Conversation about the Academy's Finances," *Bulletin* (Fall 1991), pp. 20–21.

101 Towler, "Fund Raising," *Bulletin* (Summer 1997), pp. 14–15.

102   Ramsden, Financial Aid at Exeter: An Assessment, May 3, 1991, pp. 4–10.

103   Statistics for the 1990s have been provided by the Academy Treasurer's Office.

104   Towler, "Fund Raising."

105   The endowment of The Kamehameha Schools–Bishop Estate, located in Hawaii and serving only children of native Hawaiian descent, was $11 billion. Value of Exeter endowment as of June 30, 2006. http://www.exeter.edu/documents/ facts2_2007.pdf, accessed March 2007.

106   *Bulletin*, Special Edition 2004, p. 3. http://www.exeter.edu/ei/, accessed March 2007. As of December 31, 2006, more than $259 million had been pledged.

NOTES TO CHAPTER 8: LIFE AFTER EXETER (PAGES 231–253)

1   Deed of Gift, May 17, 1781, second paragraph.

2   Nicholas Lemann, *The Big Test: The Secret History of the American Meritocracy* (New York: Farrar, Straus, and Giroux, 1999), pp. 26–27. Lemann portrayed CEEB as "a tweedy, clubby association of a few dozen private schools and colleges that had been founded in 1900 to perfect the close fit between New England boarding schools and Ivy League colleges. The boarding schools wanted a uniform admissions test that all the colleges would accept, and the colleges wanted to impose some curricular order on the schools so their subjects would arrive reliably prepared."

3   Morton Keller and Phyllis Keller, *Making Harvard Modern: The Rise of America's University* (New York: Oxford University Press, 2001), pp. 33–34.

4   John A. Valentine, *The College Board and the School Curriculum: A History of the College Board's Influence on the Substance and Standards of American Education, 1900–1980* (Princeton: The College Board, 1987), pp. 31–45; Lemann, *The Big Test*, pp. 32–33 and 38–41.

5   "Selective Admission for Colleges," *Bulletin* (April 1927), pp. 3–4.

6   See Jerome Karabel, *The Chosen: The Hidden History of Admission and Exclusion at Harvard, Yale, and Princeton* (Boston: Houghton-Mifflin, 2005), chapters 5 and 6. Karabel points out a contradiction between Conant's rhetoric and the reality of Harvard's admissions process, which continued to favor applicants from privileged backgrounds and to limit the number of Jewish matriculants. Nonetheless, Conant had an immense effect on democratizing college admissions across the country. See also James G. Hershberg, *James B. Conant: Harvard to Hiroshima and the Making of the Nuclear Age* (New York: Knopf, 1993), pp. 80–83.

7   Richard M. Freeland, *Academia's Golden Age: Universities in Massachusetts, 1945–1970* (New York: Oxford University Press, 1992), pp. 54–56, 128–129

8   Frank H. Bowles, *Admission to College: A Perspective for the 1960's* (Princeton, N.J.: College Entrance Examination Board, 1960), p. 7.

9   William J. Cox, "Selective Admissions," *Bulletin* (July 1955), p. 4; Karabel, *The Chosen*, pp. 181–184 and chapter 9, again noting a contradiction between official Harvard rhetoric and actual admissions results; and Freeland, *Academia's Golden Age*, p. 158.

10   James H. Ottaway, Jr., interview, August 30, 1991.

11 Myron R. Williams, "College Admission," *Bulletin* (December 1955), p. 13.

12 Richard H. Shaw interview, August 9, 1996.

13 George Wilson Pierson, *A Yale Book of Numbers: Historical Statistics of the College and University, 1701–1976* (New Haven: Yale University Press, 1983), p. 96; Karabel, *The Chosen*, chapter 11; Peter W. Cookson, Jr., and Carol Hodges Persell, *Preparing for Power* (New York: Basic Books, 1985), p. 171.

14 Thomas C. Hayden interview, July 18, 1996.

15 Information provided by the Common Application Web site, http://www.common app.org.

16 Both Early Decision and Early Action programs require that applications be submitted in the fall (between October 15 and November 15) and notify applicants of their status in December. Early Decision is a binding agreement: students can apply to only one college and, if accepted, are legally bound to go; if deferred, they are considered with the regular applicant pool and notified in April. Early Action, by contrast, is a nonbinding agreement that allows students to apply to other colleges simultaneously. See http://www.collegeboard.com/student/apply/the-application/104.html. A handful of colleges and universities, including Harvard, have dropped the programs, believing them to be biased toward students from sophisticated backgrounds and affluent private and public schools.

17 Mark C. Davis interview, April 3, 2000; "Applying the Harkness Teaching Model to the College Process," *Parents Newsletter* (October 1999), pp. 1–2.

18 Davis interview, April 3, 2000.

19 Ibid.

20 The following summaries and analysis are drawn from interviews or based on published and printed sources, including two books of reminiscences by Exeter graduates — Henry Darcy Curwen, ed., *Exeter Remembered* (Exeter: Phillips Exeter Academy, 1965) and Barbara Eggers, et al., *Transitions: Exeter Remembered, 1961–1987* (Exeter: Phillips Exeter Academy, 1990) — and a sampling of 25th, 40th, and 50th anniversary reunion books.

21 Christopher Jencks, "The Exeter Man: Rebel Without a Cause," *The Harvard Crimson*, November 9, 1957, pp. 9–12.

22 David A. Bell interview, December 14, 1998,

23 Peter E. Durham interview, December 16, 1998.

24 This discussion is based on statistics for the classes of 1936, 1946, 1956, 1966, 1976, and 1986. The average response rate was 80 to 85 percent, with the exception of the class of '36, which was 71 percent. Statistics provided by the Office of Alumni/ae Affairs and Development.

25 Saltonstall was reacting to a census published in 1959 that revealed that an average of 21 percent of the graduates from the classes of 1930–1939 held public office, in contrast with 10 percent of the classes that graduated in the 1940s. Exonians were found in the legislative bodies of twelve states, but only one alumnus was a member of Congress. William J. Cox, "The Alumni Census," *Bulletin* (February 1959), pp. 20–21.

26 Jonathan R. Ross interview, February 4, 1999.

27 Michael J. Lynch interview, December 21, 1998.

28 Julian H-C. Liau interview, January 12, 1999.

29 Durham interview, December 16, 1998.

30 Paris R. von Lockette interview, December 28, 1998.

31 James J. Fitzgerald interview, December 22, 1998.

32 Somers Randolph interview, November 10, 1998.

33 Elizabeth T. Campbell, in *Class of '74 25th Reunion Yearbook*, pp. 9–10.

34 John Phillips Award Guidelines, n.d.

35 William J. Cox, "The Spirit of the Christmas Fund," *Bulletin* (February 1949), p. 4.

36 Harvey C. Emery, Memorandum to Alumni Association Presidents, February 24, 1949, pp. 1–4; id., "Toward a New Alumni Association," *Bulletin* (April 1949), p. 4.

37 James M. Theisen comment to authors, January 9, 1998.

38 Annual Participation Report from 1922 to 1984, p. 2, n.d.

39 Harold Brown, Jr., comment to authors, January 9, 1998.

40 James M. Theisen interview, June 10, 1996.

41 Edward Hallowell, "Firsts," in *Transitions*, p. 37.

42 Peter Barton Hutt, in *Class of '52 Fortieth Reunion Yearbook*, p. 44.

43 Von Lockette interview, December 28, 1998.

44 Theodore Ruml II, in *Class of '70 Twenty-fifth Reunion Yearbook* (Exeter: Phillips Exeter Academy, 1995), p. 50.

45 Melissa C. Orlov interview, November 10, 1998.

46 Lynch interview, December 21, 1998.

47 Daniel C. Pinkert interview, November 10, 1998.

48 Bruce K. Eckland, "The Spirit of Exeter" (Exeter: Phillips Exeter Academy, March 1971), p. 13.

49 Randolph interview, November 10, 1998. This is a common theme among boarding school graduates. See A. H. Glass, "Emerging into the Outside World," in Louis M. Crosier, ed., *Casualties of Privilege: Essays on Prep Schools' Hidden Culture* (Washington, D.C. 1991), pp. 143–146.

50 Theisen interview, June 10, 1996.

51 Ibid.

52 Jen Hill, "Fields of Possibility," in *Transitions*, p. 157.

53 David Firestone, *Class of '70 Twenty-fifth Reunion Yearbook*, p. 25.

54 Theisen interview, June 10, 1996.

55 *Class of '53 Fortieth Reunion Yearbook* (Exeter: Phillips Exeter Academy, 1993), unpaginated.

NOTES TO EPILOGUE (PAGES 254–259)

1 The other exemplar of using a distinctive pedagogy at the core of institutional identity is Harvard Business School, which relies exclusively on case method teaching. Not coincidentally, Harvard Business School is also a leader in its domain.

2 Julie Ann Dunfey interview, April 28, 2006.

3   John D. Herney interview, May 8, 2006.
4   Dunfey interview, April 28, 2006.
5   Ricardo A. Mestres, Jr., interview, May 22, 2006.
6   Tyler C. Tingley interview, July 24, 2006.
7   Herney interview, May 8, 2006.
8   Tingley interview, July 24, 2006.
9   Ibid.
10 Herney interview, May 8, 2006.

Index

Figure numbers refer to photographs located in the insert following page 178.

Illustration Credits

1. PEA Archive.
2. PEA Archive.
3. PEA Communications Office. Eastern Topographics.
4. PEA Archive.
5. PEA Archive.
6. PEA Archive.
7. PEA Archive.
8. PEA Archive.
9. PEA Archive.
10. PEA Archive.
11. PEA Archive.
12. PEA Archive.
13. PEA Archive.
14. PEA Communications Office. Zig Wronsky '08.
15. PEA Archive.
16. PEA Archive.
17. PEA Archive.
18. *Look* magazine photograph, October 13, 1947, courtesy of PEA Archive.
19. PEA Archive.
20. PEA Archive.
21. PEA Archive. Robert Gambee '60.
22. PEA Archive. Peter Leslie '54.
23. PEA Archive.
24. PEA Archive.
25. *Look* magazine photograph, October 13, 1947, courtesy of PEA Archive.
26. PEA Communications Office. Nicole Pellaton.
27. PEA Archive.
28. PEA Archive. *Exonian.*
29. PEA Communications Office. Brian F. Crowley.
30. PEA Communications Office. Brian F. Crowley.
31. PEA Communications Office. Barbara Hobson.
32. PEA Communications Office. Peter Randall.
33. PEA Archive.
34. PEA Archive. Robert Gambee '60.
35. PEA Archive.
36. PEA Communications Office. Art Durity.
37. PEA Communications Office. Brian F. Crowley.

38. PEA Communications Office. Art Durity.
39. PEA Communications Office. Zig Wronsky '08.
40. PEA Communications Office. Zig Wronsky '08.
41. PEA Communications Office. Pat Hurley.
42. PEA Communications Office. *PEAN*.
43. PEA Communications Office. Tara Misenheimer.
44. PEA Communications Office. Art Durity.
45. PEA Communications Office. Bill Truslow.
46. PEA Communications Office. Brian F. Crowley.
47. PEA Communications Office. Brian F. Crowley.
48. PEA Communications Office. Brian F. Crowley.
49. PEA Communications Office. Dan Courter.
50. PEA Communications Office. Art Durity.
51. PEA Communications Office. Beth Brosnan.
52. PEA Communications Office. Brian F. Crowley.
53. PEA Communications Office. Brian F. Crowley.
54. PEA Communications Office. Art Durity.
55. PEA Communications Office. Brian F. Crowley.
56. PEA Communications Office. Nate Shepard '08.
57. PEA Communications Office. Brian F. Crowley.
58. PEA Communications Office. Richard Howard.
59. PEA Communications Office. Dan Courter.
60. PEA Communications Office. Brian F. Crowley.
61. PEA Communications Office. Brian F. Crowley.